The **Territories** of the **People's Republic of China**

The **Territories** of the **People's Republic of China**

FIRST EDITION

Europa Publications
Taylor & Francis Group

LONDON AND NEW YORK

First Edition 2002

© Europa Publications Limited 2002
11 New Fetter Lane, London EC4P 4EE, United Kingdom
(A member of the Taylor & Francis Group)

ISBN   1-85743-149-9

Editors: Tara Boland-Crewe, David Lea
Surveys: Gareth Wyn Jones for Globeworm Ltd
Cartographer: Eugene Fleury

Chronology data manipulation and database design: Bibliocraft Ltd

Typeset by Bibliocraft Ltd, Dundee
Printed and bound by TJ International Ltd, Trecerus Industrial Estate, Padstow, Cornwall

Foreword

The Territories of The People's Republic of China is the third in Europa's *Territories* series, following the established title on the Russian Federation, and the publication earlier this year of a volume concerning India. The world's most populous nation differs from the two previous subject countries in that it is a unitary state, while the others are governed on a federal system. This, however, does not disguise the economic, geographic, social and cultural diversity to be found among the provinces, autonomous regions and municipalities of China. It is an insight into this diversity that Europa hopes to provide with this title.

The book is divided into three parts. Part One contains two essays concerning regionalism within China, one from an economic standpoint, one from a political/administrative angle. A Chronology of the country, some key statistics, and a description and directory of the national government are also provided. In Part Two, each of the 22 provinces, five autonomous regions, four special municipalities, as well as the two Special Administrative Regions (the recently reincorporated territories of Hong Kong and Macao), is covered by a survey of its geography, history and economy, together with a map and a directory of principal officials. Part Three gives the reader a list of alternative names and an explanation of the macro-regions often cited by the country's government and others.

At a time when commercial and technological advances, allied with political change in the country itself, are gradually ending China's isolation and expanding the country's role in international affairs and trade, this book is intended to assist in the understanding of the emerging power's internal political and economic structure.

November 2002

Acknowledgements

The editors gratefully acknowledge the interest, co-operation and advice of all who have contributed to this volume. In particular we would like to thank the contributors of the two introductory articles (see below), Eugene Fleury for the maps used, and Gareth Wyn Jones for the surveys. We are also extremely grateful to the National Bureau of Statistics of China, whose publication *China Statistical Yearbook 2001* provided many of the statistics and economic data used herein.

The Contributors

Chun Lin is Lecturer in Comparative Politics at the London School of Economics and Political Science.

Hans Hendrischke is Associate Professor in the Department of Chinese Studies at the University of New South Wales.

Contents

PART ONE

Introduction

Economic Regionalism in the People's Republic of China
HANS HENDRISCHKE   3

Governing China: Unity, Control, Decentralization and Global Integration
CHUN LIN   13

Chronology of the People's Republic of China   23

Statistics   62

The Government of the People's Republic of China   65

PART TWO

Surveys

Provinces

Anhui	75	Jiangsu	149
Fujian	82	Jiangxi	157
Gansu	88	Jilin	162
Guangdong	95	Liaoning	167
Guizhou	104	Qinghai	174
Hainan	109	Shaanxi	180
Hebei	117	Shandong	185
Heilongjiang	124	Shanxi	192
Henan	131	Sichuan	197
Hubei	138	Yunnan	204
Hunan	144	Zhejiang	210

Autonomous Regions

Guangxi	215	Xinjiang	231
Nei Mongol	220	Xizang (Tibet)	238
Ningxia	226		

Special Municipalities

Beijing	244	Shanghai	252
Chongqing	248	Tianjin	256

Special Administrative Regions

Hong Kong   259   Macao   264

PART THREE
Indexes

Index of Alternative Names   271   Appendix: Taiwan   275
Index of Areas   273

Abbreviations

AD	*Anno Domini*
AH	*Anno Hegirae* (Islamic year)
BC	before Christ
C	Celcius
c.	*circa*
cu	cubic
Dr	Doctor
EC	European Communities
EEC	European Economic Community
EU	European Union
etc.	et cetera
F	Fahrenheit
GDP	Gross Domestic Product
Gen.	General
ha	hectare(s)
kg	kilogram(s)
km	kilometre(s)
kWh	Kilowatt hours
m	metre(s)
m.	million
mm	millimetre(s)
MW	Megawatt(s)
n. a.	not available
Prof.	Professor
tel.	telephone
UN	United Nations
US	United States
USA	United States of America
USSR	Union of Soviet Socialist Republics

PART ONE
Introduction

Economic Regionalism in the People's Republic of China

Hans Hendrischke

China, with its vast size and enormous diversity, has a long tradition of various forms of regionalism based on subnational and transnational differences, loyalties, and commitments. Over long periods of its history, including the first half of the 20th century, China has been divided and not under a unified government. The People's Republic of China built a strong central state that unified the country politically, economically, and socially and put an end to regionalist tendencies. Yet, since the beginning of economic reforms in the early 1980s, the central government itself has imposed economic devolution on occasionally reluctant provinces and encouraged local self-interest and autonomy. Provinces and subordinate cities in particular have gained considerable autonomy in pursuing their own economic interests and are expanding their economic links across internal and external borders. Regional differences in living standards and economic opportunities between the developed coastal region and the inland and western parts of the country have become so strong that Chinese policy advisers have declared them a threat to national unity. The strength of centrifugal tendencies seems credible, as there is no constitutional structure to give regions a formal voice in central state affairs. However, it is partially counterbalanced by informal consultation and negotiating mechanisms and the general strengthening of state capacity in recent years. Economic regionalism in its various forms of regional cross-border links, regional economic integration, and regional enterprise developments has created opportunities that benefit both central government and the various units of local administration. Nevertheless, the central government is facing the prospect of political instability and social unrest if it is not successful in solving the two major regional issues of reducing the economic gap between the country's West and East and of instituting a new market-based social-security system in conjunction with local governments. This latter task depends crucially on local enterprises and their contribution to tax revenue.

REGIONAL DIVISIONS

In Chinese common usage, the country is divided along natural topographic divisions into eight major regions: north-east China (the Manchurian plains), north China (the North-China plain), central China (the middle and lower Yangzi valley and its tributaries), south China (the southern mountain ranges and the Pearl River valley), south-west China (the Sichuan basin and the south-east karst plateau), inner Mongolia, north-west China (the Loess plateau) and Qinghai-Tibet.

Geographers divide China into various natural regions or biomes. A broad climatic and geological division differentiates the three large-scale natural regions of eastern monsoon China, north-western arid China, and the

Qinghai-Tibet plateau. These can be further subdivided into seven intermediate regions and 33 smaller regions. Another division is based on topographic characteristics of drainage basins or watersheds. The three major rivers-the Huang He (Yellow River) in northern China, the Chang Jiang (Yangzi River) in the centre and the Zhu Jiang (Pearl River) in the south-form the largest of these systems. In the 1960s the US scholar William Skinner proposed a division of China into nine macroeconomic regions on the basis of market structures and the intensity of economic exchange. The nine macro-regions were defined as Manchuria, North China, Northwest China, Lower Yangzi, Middle Yangzi, Upper Yangzi, Southeast Coast, Lingnan, and the Yunnan-Guizhou Plateau. The identification of these macro-regions of concentrated economic exchange—and of other regions excluded from this exchange—strongly influenced the social and economic understanding of traditional China, as it illustrated the relative independence of social and economic exchange from political borders. However, natural regions and the macro-regions, which largely coincided with major drainage basins, could not account for long-distance trade and economic exchange under the increasingly industrialized and internationalized economy of 20th century China.

New economic regions emerged under the impact of China's early industrialization when Shanghai and other treaty ports became the centres of China industrialized economy. In Manchuria, China's first heavy industrial basis was built up under Japanese occupation, when Japanese industry made use of the coal and iron ore deposits in the region. China's industrial infrastructure developed along the coast and along its north-south railway network. When the Chinese Communist Party (CCP) came to power in 1949, the country's industrial infrastructure was concentrated along the coast in Shanghai, Tianjin, Guangzhou and in Manchuria.

REGIONALISM IN CHINA'S HISTORY

China has a long history of political, economic, and cultural regionalism. Social and cultural regionalism in China can be dated back as far as historical records go, and even further, through archaeological finds that prove the diverse local origins of Chinese culture and civilization. The imperial account of a unified and unitary China is more a political and historiographic construct than an adequate description of a unitary state that existed only during some relatively brief periods in Chinese history. The ideology of the unified Chinese state emerged from a period of prolonged warfare for hegemony among competing states. Archaeological finds in the late 20th century indicate that the eventual unification of China under the short-lived Qin dynasty at the beginning of the second century BC was less a restitution of an earlier historical unity, but rather the submission of originally independent local cultures under one dominant state. The subsequent Han, one of China's great dynasties, created its own imperial myth of an originally existing Chinese unitary state, as it went on to expand Chinese territory and perfected imperial rule over the regions. This origin of the Chinese state out of a diversity of local states meant that China's rulers were, from the beginning of the imperial period, confronted with a problem in conducting local government. In order to guarantee the stability of the state, they had to rely on their officials to secure revenue from the regions on the one hand, while providing incentives for autonomous local economic development on the other.

The Qin and Han dynasties introduced the county (*xian*) as the most durable institution of local government. Counties were the seats of local magistrates and thus the lowest echelon of local government to which the reach of the central government extended. Between the central government and the counties there were additional layers of local administrations, although these mutated over time. Under the Han, the empire was subdivided into approximately 1,000 counties. As the territory that could be administered by a Chinese government expanded and was secured over ensuing dynasties, the number of counties gradually increased to around 2,000. The county magistrate system that developed after the Han defined the structure of local administration until the end of Imperial China. It secured control of the central government over the county magistrates in two ways. One was the requirement that local magistrates pass an imperial examination in order to qualify for the position. Linked to this was the power of the central government to regularly change county officials. The other mechanism of central control was the rule of avoidance, which stipulated that no official be allowed to serve in his own locality. This proved to be a barrier against regionalism. This structure also proved durable enough to enable foreign dynasties, like the Yuan (Mongols) in the 13th and 14th centuries and the Qing (Manchus) from the mid-17th to the early 20th century to establish their rule over the country. Provinces came into being as a unit of administration during the Yuan dynasty, when they facilitated military and administrative control; they were not intended as economic units. Characteristic of this structure was the division between the official government sphere and the local social and economic sphere, which remained largely outside government control. Local government officials were generally agents of the central government, and were expected to co-operate with local élites to secure tax revenue. In return for this tax revenue (and a measure of ideological support), these local economic and social élites enjoyed considerable independence, although there was no prospect of their participation in government through a formal federalist structure. Political regionalism only occurred when the central government was too weak to control the regions, and even then the actual power of regional governors was often not made explicit. Chinese reformers in the late 19th century identified this structure as one of the reasons for China's economic weakness and turned to Western ideas of federalism. In their view, economic, educational, military and other reforms could only be realized within a formal political structure of regionalism and with the assent and participation of élite groups within these regions.

The collapse of imperial rule in China occasioned a gradual fragmentation of the country, culminating in a period of intense regionalism under the warlords during the first half of the 20th century. Some of the warlords, such as Yan Xishan in Shanxi, were, in fact, regional reformers who used their military power to institute economic and industrial reforms that the central government had not been able to pursue. The central government under the Nationalist Party (Guomindang) in the 1930s was never able to establish effective central control over the whole country and remained a competing regime for warlords and, later, the Japanese occupation forces and the CCP. However, during these years the foundations were laid for greater central control, with the expansion of the reach of the state into society through state-organized popular education, propaganda and the beginnings of modern mass media.

The CCP pursued a strong centralist agenda during the first years of the People's Republic of China to consolidate its military control and then its political and economic rule over the country. By placing reliable cadres in county-level positions and through continuous political campaigns, the Communist government dominated local economies and society to an unprecedented extent. During the initial years of Communist rule, local government above the county level was based in six Greater Administrative Areas. Once military and political control over the country had been secured by 1954, government functions for supra-provincial regions were only retained for the military and on an *ad hoc* basis for other purposes, and provinces became the principal unit of local administration.

ECONOMIC REGIONALISM DURING THE MAO PERIOD

China's planned economy during the first three decades of the People's Republic was characterized by the development agenda of the central state, which was intent on building a heavy-industry infrastructure and creating new industrial centres in the country's interior. This shift of economic activity and investment away from the coast (and, in particular, away from the 'treaty ports') occurred in several stages and with different regional focal points. During the period of Sino-Soviet friendship and co-operation under the First Five Year Plan (1953–57), many thousands of Soviet advisers helped China build 156 major industrial complexes in heavy industry, chemicals, mining and other sectors. These projects, though thinly spread and concentrated in relatively few areas, were designed to form the backbone of China's industrial structure. They were positioned to take advantage of mineral deposits and energy resources and, unlike projects in later periods, were linked to existing population centres and/or transport infrastructure. The developed coastal cities were the biggest losers in this programme, as they received no major investment projects and only limited funds for reconstruction (although their living standards remained far higher than those of the interior).

During the economic programme known as the Great Leap Forward (1958–61), China distanced itself from the Soviet development model by promoting local economic initiative and decentralization down to the county level. The programme, the ensuing years of catastrophic famine and the subsequent period of economic readjustment until 1965 did not bring a change in regional industrial policies. State investment in industrial projects in the interior provinces continued at previous or even higher levels of around 60% of the national total.

From the early 1960s, after the Sino-Soviet split had ended the co-operation between the two countries, China's regional economic policies were increasingly influenced by strategic and military concerns. Ideological radicalization instilled the fear in Mao Zedong and other Chinese leaders that the country's industrial basis was threatened by attacks from both the Soviet Union and the USA. The resulting Third Front Policy shifted industrial investment into defence-related and strategically important industries in inaccessible locations in western and central provinces. One of China's largest automobile plants was located in a mountainous region of Hubei province, several hours' journey from the nearest major highway. In two waves, from 1964–66 and 1969–72 over one-half of state investment was channelled to Third Front projects, which were concentrated in the six provinces of Sichuan, Gansu, Hubei, Shaanxi, Henan and Guizhou.

In hindsight, Chinese economists are generally critical of the development strategy of forced industrialization and regional redistribution. Even if the Third Front projects are discounted, as they were not aimed at economic efficiency and less than half of them proved economically viable in the market environment of the reform period, in the overall account the regional policies of the Mao period did more harm to the coastal economy than they brought benefit to the inland provinces. In other words, a more balanced economic strategy would have avoided the relative de-industrialization that occurred in the established urban centres. A gradual change away from these policies began in 1972, but at the beginning of the reform period the inland provinces still felt disadvantaged. As the economies of the interior fell further behind those of the coastal provinces, a number of inland provinces formed a loose alliance to pressurize the government into providing them with more assistance.

REGIONAL DISPARITIES DURING ECONOMIC REFORM

The major redirection of investment flows and economic activity came after 1979 in response to international (and later national) market forces. Once China opened its door to foreign investment, the obvious advantages of the coastal provinces in terms of infrastructure, human resources, management know-how, and access to markets meant they, in particular their major cities, once again became magnets for foreign and domestic investment. As the central government gradually withdrew its administrative interference in economic activities and concentrated on macroeconomic control, it lost the ability to direct the regional distribution of enterprise activity. National tax reform in the mid 1990s increased tax revenues for local governments, but at the same time overburdened them with social responsibilities, and thus decreased funds available for transfers to poorer areas. Instead, the government resorted to propaganda and persuasion and finally to a specifically targeted spending programme to alleviate the problems of the provinces worst affected by the interior–coast divide.

The policy of opening the country's economy to foreign investment started from the four Special Economic Zones (SEZs—Shenzhen, Zhuhai, Shantou and Xiamen), which were established close to Hong Kong in 1979. These zones, modelled on the East Asian and South-East Asian export-processing zones, provided easy access and various infrastructure and financial incentives for foreign investors. The success of these four SEZs in attracting mainly overseas capital led to an extension of the programme in 1984, when 14 cities along the coast, from Beihai in Guangxi on the Gulf of Tongking to Dalian, on the peninsula delineating the Bo Hai from the Yellow Sea in Liaoning, were given Open City status, enabling them to attract and absorb foreign invest-ment. The provinces which benefited most from these policies were those with traditional links to overseas Chinese communities, such as Guangdong and Fujian, those which could exploit links with neighbouring countries and economies, such as Fujian with Taiwan or Shandong with the Republic of

Korea (South Korea), and those which provided infrastructure and access to the domestic market, such as Shanghai with the adjacent provinces of Zhejiang and Jiangsu, and Tianjin in the north. During the 1980s these coastal provinces developed considerably faster than inland provinces.

The central government's initial response to the emerging disparities was to rely on an expected 'trickle-down' effect to reduce inequality gradually, as investors and enterprises would move westwards in search of lower-cost labour and better access to raw materials. By the end of the 1980s it became clear that this 'trickle-down' effect had not materialized and that, to the contrary, regional disparities were still widening. As development policies became an instrument used in the attraction of foreign investment, the inland provinces frequently complained that they lacked 'special policies' (that is, the right to grant tax derogations and other financial incentives to foreign investors). The central government instead emphasized Greater Development Regions (GDRs) as a means of overcoming disparities in wealth and development between provinces. These GDRs combined coastal provinces and poor inland provinces and were meant to be coordinating institutions channelling investment flows and technologies from the richer provinces to the poorer. In practice, they had very little internal cohesion (such as a Greater South-West Region that included Sichuan, Yunnan, Guizhou, Guangxi and Xizang—Tibet) and relied on the voluntary efforts of the provincial leaders to create technological and investment partnerships and enterprise co-operation. At a time when even local state-owned enterprises were increasingly exposed to market forces, the GDRs produced impressive bureaucratic procedures but little actual progress. Their limited success convinced the central government of the need for more decisive action to equalize the imbalances between rich and poor areas.

One attempt to give some inland provinces an equivalent of 'special policies' was made in the early 1990s, when border trade was allowed to flourish. This was the time after the collapse of the Soviet Union, when China suddenly became a dominant economic power in Russian Siberia, Central Asia and along its southwestern borders with Burma and Viet Nam. In the liberal economic climate which prevailed after Deng Xiaoping's Southern Tour in early 1992, provinces were allowed to develop border trade as a development option that, in the opinion of one leading government economist, was equivalent to the coastal trade conducted in the SEZs. Border crossings and trading posts sprang up in Heilongjiang, Jilin, Xinjiang, Yunnan, and Guangxi and produced local 'boom' economies. However, this boom did not last long, as it coincided with a severe loss of central state revenue in the mid 1990s. In 1996 the central Ministry of Foreign Trade and Economic Co-operation issued new border-trade regulations that imposed severe restrictions on the type of companies entitled to conduct border trade and on their activities—the move curtailed smuggling of consumer goods (particularly cars) and other commodities and brought long-distance trade back under central control and, therefore, back into the taxation regime.

Poverty in China occurs along the urban–rural divide even in wealthy provinces, but the regional divide is more pronounced—for example, in the 1990s over 80% of China's over 300 officially poor counties were located in the West. National minorities inhabited nearly one-half of them. The central government eventually took the advice that the only way to counteract this was to target development incentives at the poorest western provinces. The most prominent supporter of this plan was the Beijing-based economist Hu An'gang, who had warned that China's economic disparities were comparable to those of Yugoslavia before its final fragmentation in the early 1990s. Support for the West was the core policy of the 10th Five Year Plan for the years 2001–05. It was originally targeted at ten units (the special municipality of Chongqing, the provinces of Gansu, Guizhou, Qinghai, Shaanxi, Sichuan and Yunnan, and the autonomous regions of Ningxia, Xinjiang and Xizang—Tibet), to which were later added the province of Guangxi and the Nei Mongol autonomous region. The 'Great Opening of the West' addressed primarily those areas where widespread poverty among large minority populations and limited integration in the national economy was most likely to create popular resentment and pose risks of political instability. The strategy combined the economic equalization agenda with strategic and environmental considerations. The equalization strand focuses on the creation of opportunities and is predominantly realized through funding of education, training and business-support programs, representing a shift away from direct subsidies. The strategic agenda is manifest in a programme of infrastructural improvements, including communications and transport projects, a closer integration of western energy resources with the Chinese economy through petroleum and gas pipelines and electricity transmission, as well as military infrastructure. Environmental concerns are addressed in irrigation, afforestation, and other programmes, which, if successful, would also reduce pollution and ameliorate the chronic water shortage in the north of the country. The policy is funded through government bonds and part of the deficit spending by the central government, and enterprises from all over China are encouraged to participate in the major infrastructure projects. This reflects the insight that the government has limited means to its avail and that a long-term improvement of regional inequalities will depend on the integration of the western and central provinces into the domestic market.

CHINA'S NEW ECONOMIC REGIONALISM

As private economic activity expanded parallel to reduced administrative interference, new forms of regionalism emerged. They were linked to the separation of government functions between central and local authorities and had both local and translocal dimensions. One landmark in this separation was the reform of the taxation system in the mid-1990s, which gave local governments greater economic autonomy. Other, less obvious, signs of economic regionalism were the autonomy that local governments acquired in promoting the growth of local private enterprise, the development of horizontal links across provincial borders, and stronger economic integration between regions across national or jurisdictional borders.

A cornerstone for China's new market-based economic regionalism was laid with the tax reform in 1994 and subsequent changes to the tax administration. These reforms instituted a tax-sharing system and two separate tax bureaucracies, which divided revenue between central and provincial governments. As part of these reforms, the 31 provinces, autonomous regions and special municipalities ('top-level' administrative units) gained substantial autonomy in structuring both their own expenditure and those of the 331 prefectures, 2,109 counties and 44,471 townships. Under China's Budget Law, government units at each level have an independent budget and are linked in a nested hierarchy. Each sub-ordinate unit is only accountable to the level directly above, which has the right to specify revenue-sharing and expenditure assignments. This limited fiscal autonomy at each level is counterbalanced by the reliance on extra-budgetary revenues, for which there is no accountability to upper levels. Consequently, richer provinces are able to benefit more from this system than poorer ones. In 2002, a World Bank report concluded that 'although China has a unitary system of government, the inter-governmental fiscal arrangements give it a strong federalist character'.

Another claim of informal federalism is made by institutional economists, who argue that the devolution policy (by which the central and provincial governments delegated the administrative and financial responsibility over state-owned enterprises to lower levels of government), combined with increasingly onerous budget constraints imposed by the taxation reform, forced local governments to pursue their own privatization policies. This is corroborated by research on the regional emergence of private enterprises, which shows surprising local variance in the way provincial and sub-provincial authorities assign and protect property rights and create institutional support for private or mixed state-private enterprises. The resulting differences in enterprise culture and operational environment are reflected in the higher shares of private enterprise in economic activity in economically advanced provinces such as Guangdong, Zhejiang and Jiangsu. As these enterprises expand, regional economic integration is occurring within provincial borders, where enterprises find a consistent and reliable institutional environment.

The extent of these disparities can be seen by comparing the figures for gross domestic product (GDP) per head and for foreign direct investment in a number of the 'top-level' units. In 2000, for example, the wealthiest units in terms of GDP per head were three of the special municipalities: the figure was 34,457 yuan per head in Shanghai, 22,460 yuan in Beijing and 17,993 yuan in Tianjin. With GDP per head of 13,461 yuan, Zhejiang was the wealthiest of the provinces by this measure, followed by Guangdong (12,885 yuan), with Fujian, Jiangsu and Liaoning all having figures in excess of 11,000 yuan per head. It is worth noting that all of these units, with the exception of that around the national capital, are coastal. In contrast, Guizhou's GDP per head was just 2,662 yuan in the same year, while six other provinces (none of which have a coastline) and three of the five autonomous regions (including the coastal Guangxi) have corresponding figures of less than 5,000 yuan.

With regard to foreign direct investment a similar picture emerges. The most attractive unit by far to foreign investors is Guangdong, whose advantages include several of the SEZs, proximity to the commercial centres of Shanghai, Hong Kong and Macao (the last two, being, Special Administrative Regions, are not included in these calculations), good infrastructure and a history of commercial activity. Foreign direct investment in Guangdong in 2000 totalled US \$11,281m., compared with \$6,426m. for the next most attractive unit, Jiangsu. In all, nine units (the eight referred to above as having relatively high figures for GDP per head, with the addition of another coastal province, Shandong), received more than \$1,000m.-worth of foreign direct investment in 2000. This contrasts even more starkly with Qinghai province, and the autonomous region of Xizang—Tibet, neither of which received any official foreign direct investment in that year. Four other units—the provinces of Gansu and Guizhou and the Ningxia and Xinjiang autonomous regions, all in the interior—attracted less than $100m.

Thus, it can be seen that the disparities in wealth and living standards between the units of the People's Republic remain stark, and that the coastal–interior cleavage remains serious. Moreover, the figures for foreign investment suggest that these gaps are more likely to widen than narrow in the coming years, despite government efforts to accelerate the development of the interior.

In spite of official promotion of 'development corridors', 'river deltas' and other regional conglomerations, it would be premature to speak of the emergence of supra- or inter-provincial economic regions. The principal reason for this is that considerable local protectionism—a remnant of the planned economy and its emphasis on local autarky—persists, mainly at provincial and county level. Under reform policies, this served to safeguard local markets and the interests of local producers. These persisting irrational market restrictions were one of the items addressed during the negotiations for China's accession to the World Trade Organization (WTO)—the central government eventually committing itself to the creation of nationally unified markets. Local protectionism is not only manifest in product markets and services but also in the weakness (or, in some cases, total absence) of national legislation protecting property rights. This limits the expansion of private enterprises, including those with foreign investment, across provincial borders and remains one of the obstacles for the formation of larger market-based economic regions. Even in relatively integrated areas such as the lower Yangzi valley or around Beijing, there are no general common markets for products and services across provincial borders.

The most advanced form of economic regionalism is found in the south, with the trade and investment links between Hong Kong, Shenzhen and parts of Guangdong Province, and further afield, Taiwan and Fujian Province. While the concept of a 'Greater China' has strong political overtones, linked to the integration of Hong Kong into the People's Republic and in relation to Taiwan, it has resulted in a highly integrated and dynamic region. Meanwhile, strong trade and investment links and international integration with Japan and, particularly, South Korea, are also emerging in the north of the country.

PROSPECTS IN ECONOMIC REGIONALISM

Economic regionalism has a variety of different meanings and implications within the People's Republic, and includes centralizing and centrifugal aspects. Traditionally, it refers to the effects of the central government's regional development policies. 'New Regionalism', an international trend towards non-state vertical integration, will be enhanced in China by the country's WTO membership (thereby strengthening economic institutions), and the concomitant reduction of local protectionism. Economic regionalism at provincial and sub-provincial level has led to federalist traits that give local governments substantial autonomy in revenue-raising and responsibilities for economic and social policies. However, these aspects of federalism evident in the economic sphere have not led to open political regionalism, at least, not beyond various informal groups of units pursuing their interests through bargaining with the central government. Officially, China remains a strong unitary state and pursues the traditional model of 'top-down' regionalism, and in order to reduce the severe regional economic and social disparities, the main interest of the central government is to increase revenue. For this to happen, however, the centre depends on the development of an integrated national market and, in the course of ongoing reforms (in particular those of the enterprise and financial sectors), it can only benefit from individual provinces and other primary units taking an active and autonomous role in privatization and regional integration.

Governing China: Unity, Control, Decentralization and Global Integration

CHUN LIN

The People's Republic of China, proclaimed in 1949 on the victory of the Communist revolution, had by 2001 a population of 1,265m.—constituted by the Han majority (92%) and 55 recognized minority nationalities—and a vast and unevenly developed territory. Some 2,400 km (1,500 miles) separate Beijing, the capital, close to the country's east coast, and Urumqi, the provincial capital of Xijiang autonomous region in the west, which is home to 8 m. Uygurs and other Muslim communities. The distance from Mohe, the farthest northern city, bordering Russian Siberia, to the Wuzhi Mountain area on Hainan island, where the Red Detachment of Women engaged in guerrilla warfare in the revolutionary years, is over 1,110 km greater. Moreover, these vast distances do not include the extremities of Chinese territory in the South China Sea—the most remote of the Nanshu (Spratly Islands), is over 1,000 km from Hainan. What are the institutional and organizational resources and mechanisms that have, over the past half-century, and despite many changes, sustained unity and control in a political entity of such a demographic and geographic scope? Has China's ongoing effort towards further internal decentralization on the one hand, and deeper global integration on the other, inevitably led to a steady decline in the country's order and cohesion? In any case, are the old patterns of central command and national co-ordination irreversibly obsolete in the new environment of market transition, political liberalization and increasing assertion of cultural diversity? Does the regime have a strategy for managing this contradiction between an imperative centripetal need and the growing centrifugal trends?

This essay will begin with an outline of the government structure and institutions of the People's Republic, tracing briefly their origins in the Chinese imperial tradition as well as through modern revolutionary legacies and foreign influences. It will then discuss central–local interactions and decentralization policies, both those of the Mao Zedong era and the different, globally aware methods used by the reform leaderships since 1978. The next section will be devoted to a comparative analysis of these developments and their impacts on state capacity and governability, and a conclusion will summarize the main arguments.

TRADITIONS, OLD AND NEW

The Middle Kingdom's successive dynasties, interrupted by periodic upheavals of peasant rebellions, wars and territorial splits, inherited without exception the

13

Qin-Han state system initially configured in the late 3rd century BC. The First Emperor, Qin Shi Huang, for all his despotic ruthlessness, unified the warring states (221 BC) and envisioned a political framework for his empire, then limited to the middle and lower reaches of the Huang He (Yellow River). Within merely a dozen years, he began, even if he did not complete, the ambitious projects of dividing the 'king's land under heaven' into military commanding (*jun*) and administrative (*xian*) units, imposing a universal written script (which eventually progressed into modern *hanyu*) and a unitary copper currency, and building standardized roads and vehicles (for speedy royal-military movements, after the earlier standardization of weights and measures). He also initiated numerous major construction schemes, such as the Great Wall. A meritocratic bureaucracy was consolidated during the subsequent Han dynasty (206 BC–AD 220) and refined later through a rigorous examination system. The Han system, in turn, flourished, laying not only the institutional but also the ideological foundation for China's lasting ruling order. Confucianism was declared official ideology, although Legalism (a doctrine emphasizing repression and punishment) remained highly practical, and politically detached religion-philosophies (such as Buddhism and Daoism) also survived. Even after the Qing court fell in 1911 and the empire became a nation in its self-consciousness and a republic in its international recognition, the basic state configuration was largely intact.

In other words, neither of China's 20th century revolutions, whether republican or Communist, really destroyed the tradition of its fundamental mode of governance. Despite strongly anti-traditional movements, from advocating 'science and democracy' around the 4 May uprising of 1919, to attempting radical transformations during the Mao years, contemporary Chinese politics retained many deep-rooted structural features of the imperial polity. These can be identified, to offer some particularly outstanding examples, in the excessive power of personalities, the persistence of hierarchical relations, and the functioning of informal networks while formal symbols and rituals retained significance. This lack of a clear break with the past, however, may not be purely negative if one appreciates the 'modernity' of certain elements in the pre-modern Chinese state and bureaucracy, and if, furthermore, one realizes how tradition could be reinvented in the service of modern or modernizing aims. It is likely that, taking into account weighty local histories and knowledge, even a thorough-going democratization process would not be able completely to erase such elements. The Communists, indeed, deliberately exploited some old ruling techniques. For instance, they reworked the ancient experiences of self-governing communities, making them supportive in organizing collective production and life. In a huge country like China where, as the saying goes, 'the sky is high and the emperor is far away', the quality of local leadership is of great importance. As communal autonomy retained its desirability, the middle cadres who, under Communism, replaced the gentry, continued to negotiate between directives from above and demands from their immediate constituencies, weaving a 'social intertexture' of both a pre- and post-reform body politic.

The most obvious and essential factor here is that a unified territory, a centralized authority and a sophisticated administrative apparatus, which China as an empire had achieved early, and then time and again regained and developed throughout two millennia, must be seen as a magnificent heritage for its modern nation and state-builders. This helps explain why the People's Republic, confronted with its own formidable tasks and obstacles, nevertheless escaped the kind of difficulties that trapped so many 'emerging states' with missing or weak governing institutions in the postcolonial world.

Yet this is only part of the story. The Communist trajectory itself amounted to an alternative tradition under the combined influences of indigenous aspirations, western ideologies (especially Marxism, liberalism and republicanism) and the Russian revolution. Western ideas were often transmitted and assimilated into the Chinese mind via a Russian route (although some arrived via Japan). Although Mao had resisted the impositions of the Soviet leader, Stalin, from the outset, and the Communist parties in the two countries eventually became fierce ideological opponents, the new regime in Beijing once depended on Soviet aid and copied a great deal in the 1950s from the world's supposedly first socialist state. It might be argued that the Communist monopoly of power was modified in China by the populist 'mass line', and the united front institutionalized in the Chinese People's Political Consultative Conference (constituted by the leading Chinese Communist Party—CCP—and eight small, subordinate 'democratic parties'). In essence, however, the political system of the People's Republic resembled that of its Soviet counterpart in a party-state structure. On the whole, these influences, altered over time as interpretation varied and situations demanded, must be seen as ingredients of, and hence internal to, China's modernization experience.

Particularly notable is the impact of revolutionary 'total politics' that had, unintentionally, contained some remnants of imperial despotism, while growing more powerful than the empire had ever been. As a total response to a total societal crisis, the Communist revolution was an immense undertaking in extreme conditions of war, insurgency, mobilization and underground resistance, in which organization and communication had to be kept under the secretive command of the party in association with its armed forces and base-area government. During its transformation from a local to a national force, the CCP began the process of nation- and state-building for the new China well before the founding of the People's Republic. The fact that the revolution was, by and large, indigenous in origin and independently carried out under the banner of national and social liberation partly resolves the question as to why Communism there, after a tortuous path with major legitimacy crises, could have so far avoided a collapse similar to those witnessed throughout the former Soviet bloc. The transformation in the CCP came largely from within, in defiance of the logic of totalitarianism. In addition, the CCP's close links with the military left an imprint on the country's social and even economic organization. In the end, although the dependence on 'total politics' diminished in 1980s and 1990s, it was remarkable that China's central and local governments, barely separable from the party, did not intervene but were themselves managers of the changes in the economy and the wider social framework.

PARTY AND GOVERNMENT

In spite of its massive membership (63m. by 2001) the CCP followed the Leninist organizational doctrine of 'democratic centralism' for a vanguard party. This doctrine, as stated in the party constitution, requires subordination of the individual to the organization, minority to majority, lower to higher levels, and the entire party to its central committee. Meanwhile, in theory, minority rights and dissenting voices are protected on the condition of resolutions being obeyed. The pyramid of the party hierarchy opens downward from the national congress, its central committee and politburo to provincial, municipal, county and township committees, and then reaching over 3.5m. 'grass-roots' branches in work- and residence-based units. The General Secretary is concurrently the Chairman of the Central Commission for Military Affairs. Central and provincial Commissions for Inspecting Discipline inspect party members at the same or lower levels. The Communist Youth League, along with state-sponsored 'transmission belts' of trade unions, women, and professional, business and religious groups, constituted the party core's extensive outer circle. In the mid-1990s the All China Women's Federation took a lead in claiming itself a non-governmental organization (and was recognized as such by the UN), and many other associations also became increasingly autonomous. The penetration of the CCP in the management of Chinese state and society was the single most important key to understanding unity and control in the People's Republic. For one thing, as party and government organizations operated parallel to one another at all levels, the political commissar (transformed into the party secretary in administrative and judicial offices and production and service enterprises) assumed unquestionable primacy in responsibility for final decisions. For another, the fact that the everyday Chinese vocabulary did not distinguish between notions of 'state', 'government', 'public' and 'society' only reflected real perceptions. By the same token, the retreat of the party not so much from governing bodies as from social organization in general could threaten the total collapse of a society which still structurally depended on that party's leadership and penetrating power at all levels.

The organizational principle of democratic centralism was also applied to government in the Chinese socialist republic: the constitutional mandate that 'all power belongs to the people' found an institutional expression in the people's congresses, of which the deputies were directly (at and below the county level) or indirectly (above the provincial level) elected. The National People's Congress (NPC) as the 'highest organ of state power' and its standing committee are simultaneously legislative and executive through the State Council, having also the authority to amend the Constitution, to decide on major governmental appointments, and to oversee the Supreme People's Court and the Supreme People's Procuratorate. The new Constitution of 1982 included clauses legitimizing the reforms of the post-Mao order, and the document was amended in 1988, 1993 and 1999, chiefly to accommodate the transition to a degree of participation in the international market economy, in particular to satisfy a growing private sector which demanded private property rights. The separation of powers between legislature, executive and judiciary is considered to fit only conflicting interests within a bourgeois state—there is no need of such separations when the NPC is designed to represent the people's aggregated interests. As the People's Republic is a unitary multinational state, according to the Constitution all nationalities are equal and national minorities enjoy extensive rights of autonomy (with the exception of the right to secede). Though not formally federal, the country's regional and ethnic cleavages are translated into an elaborate arrangement of administration for 22 provinces (excluding Taiwan, which is not under the People's Republic's administration, but is, nevertheless officially counted as the 23rd), four centrally administered municipalities, five minority autonomous regions and two special administrative regions (Hong Kong since 1997 and Macao since 1999).

Under Communism China developed the largest bureaucracy in world history, by virtue of its responsibility for the management of capital and society in such a huge country. The government's near-monopoly over goods and services, particularly in times of scarcity, only reinforced bureaucratic expansion, which even the fiercely anti-bureaucratic Cultural Revolution was unable to reverse. This 'bureaucratic leviathan' was described by Lieberthal as a complex 'matrix muddle' of vertical and horizontal lines of authority. As such, it also entailed fragmentation in governmental operation and policy implementation. A local electrical-supply project, for example, would be under directives from the relevant county government as well as the provincial electricity bureau; the latter, in turn, must report to both the provincial government and the central energy department. On the other hand, Lieberthal also used the term 'fragmented authoritarianism' to describe the existence of opportunities for initiatives and creative actions at ground level. While the reforms of the late 20th century further fragmented government structure and generated a grave problem of official corruption, efforts had also been made to improve efficiency and professional competence, including the restoration of civil service examinations.

FROM MAOIST DECENTRALIZATION TO FEDERALIZATION DURING THE REFORM PERIOD

As their myriad administrative institutions manifested, neither the CCP itself nor the People's Republic party-state was ever monolithic. There existed inner party factions, known in Chinese as the 'mountain-stronghold mentality', referring to regionally or personally based loyalties (especially those to the legendary Red Army commanders). Likewise, state politics was at once centralized and decentralized, by virtue of the country's vast size and diversity—the centre retained power by permitting local self-government and tolerating some local variations. Analytically, the Chinese state must be divided, so as to distinguish between its components and locations of power, in order to identify the conditions and incentives for performance at different layers and by various actors.

At one time, the CCP did indeed aspire to follow a decentralized, non-bureaucratic path of economic and social development. The Maoist critiques of the Soviet political economy focused on managerial bureaucracy and alienated labour, stressing the value of human agency and creativity from below (qualities that Stalinist modernization was held to have neglected and repressed). As a result, compared with its Soviet predecessor, central planning in China was more flexible, with a large collective sector mostly under regional planning. In addition, the state sector was less rigidly commanded by central bodies and was able to experiment with forms of economic democracy, while provincial and lower-level governments had partial independence in investment decisions and in the management of state firms. Mao famously advocated the 'walking on two legs' strategy for full participation—drawing inspiration from the centre and localities, cadres and masses, indigenous and foreign ideas, and so on. Even though mass mobilization during government campaigns revealed some inherent weaknesses in the system, from the deficiency of the legal framework to political opportunism by individuals and groups, extensive participation was evident among ordinary citizens in work units, people's communes and neighbourhood organizations. The crux of the Maoist legacy of administrative and economic decentralization lay precisely in the support given to these 'ground-level' institutions.

The Chinese attempt at an alternative to the highly centralized and statist model of socialism was, nevertheless, largely unsuccessful in the light of the country's persistent regional inequalities, its urban-rural divide and the problems of mismanagement, not to mention the famine during the disastrous Great Leap Forward (1959–61) or the chaos of the Cultural Revolution (1966–69). However, as researchers agree, many reform measures and post-reform developments would not have been possible without preparations made before 1978. The flourishing of township and village enterprises (TVEs) had an origin in communal industries. The redistribution of power with significant gains by lower level authorities was a continuation of the 'two legs' policy. When the 1982 Constitution and the 1998 organic law recognized village and neighbourhood committees as the building blocks of self-government in China, they only confirmed the renewal of a tradition. Yet the reform regimes did also foster a decentralized development regime seen, for example in the rise of 'local state corporatism', of collective management and collective financing between county- and lower-level governments and TVEs for the community-enhancing corporate good (Oi, 1995). The decentralization of the fiscal system 'more than any other factor accounts for local variation' and thus a proper understanding of post-reform changes in central-local relations requires a clear financial picture (Saich, 2001). Successive fiscal reforms spread market risks to be borne by the authorities from the provincial level downwards, but also empowered those localities where profitable enterprises were located. In poor areas without developed rural industries, conversely, local governments were often financially deprived, facing a collapse of their system of basic welfare provision, previously secured by the state treasury. This situation, frequently combined with corruption, led to arbitrary fees and overtaxation of peasant households and, in consequence, widespread unrest. The centre's inability either to halt such illegal extraction or to collect legally stipulated taxes (combined with the delay in the formal adoption and enforcement of income tax) demonstrated its own weakened financial standing, as well as the contradictions inherent in the policy. The central government's revenue steadily decreased to around 12% of gross domestic product (GDP) in most years since 1995, compared with over 38% before 1976, and this was combined with a surging budget deficit.

As regional inequalities widened and ethnic problems intensified, the central government launched a grand westward programme in 2000 (for the period 2001–05), aiming to stimulate the economies of the backward inland provinces and autonomous regions. To what degree the participation of foreign investment and entrepreneurship would be encouraged in these ethnically and militarily sensitive regions remains to be seen.

The degree of integration in the global market which China chooses to pursue is where the novelty and rationality of the country's reform strategy as a whole can be measured. It began with the coastal Special Economic Zones being granted certain legislative powers, enabling them to regulate transactions in foreign capital and trade, bypassing the centre. Since then, the country has completed a radical phase of transformation, symbolized by its entry into the World Trade Organization (WTO) in 2001, whose immediate detrimental influence on the economy (notably accelerating unemployment as domestic producers struggle to adapt to the new trade regime) could well be counter-balanced by more gradual benefits (Lardy, 2002). These changes in decentral-ization coupled with globalization critically altered central-local configuration, amounting to an institutional innovation of 'federalism, Chinese style' (Montinola, et al., 1995). This, in turn, challenged the requirement sufficient state capacity at each level of governance for stability, transition and growth. Tensions between the constant drive to decentralize and the imminent danger of losing control posed a serious political question, one which has yet to be answered.

COMPARISONS AND CONCLUSIONS

The widely held impression of post-reform contraction of the Chinese state needs some qualifications. Deng Xiaoping's restoration of order, after the anarchism of the Cultural Revolution, re-establishing the privileges positions of party bureaucrats and implementing legal reforms, might be seen as effectively recentralizing. Also, involvement of officials in business greatly inflated their power—a case of public power abused for private ends, known in China as the return of 'bureaucratic capitalism'. Moreover, in response to the chronic legitimacy problems created by mounting social problems and protests, the party was forced to reassert its dominance by returning to hand some of the already dispersed powers. All these developments point to a disjunction between the trend of decentralization and the retreat of the state. On the other hand, the impact of 'making global linkages' (*jiegui*)—economic and political liberalization, quasi-privatization and market competition-was felt everywhere. Regional autonomy was hardly unaffected by the imposing international forces. Further, sub-national regionalism and the discretion of powerful provinces over crucial decisions could undermine centrally imposed policy coherence. Gone with state paternalism were also some essential public services and the corresponding financial commitment for national and social security. Although the changing central-local relationship in China could be viewed as interdependent (Li, 1997) and the political logic of reform was shown to be conducive to bargaining and compromise for achieving reciprocal accountability (Shirk, 1993), regional autonomy and capacity is a larger issue because of the intervening external variables. It calls for debate over the costs, benefits and risks of decentralization in terms of sustainable national development.

What explains the continuing national unity and state control which has accompanied Mao's decentralization, despite recurrent political turbulence? Among many possible contributory factors the following stand out most clearly. First, the relative isolation of the People's Republic kept the country inward-looking and self-containing. Self-reliance generated, as much as demanded, devotion, discipline and solidarity. The revolutionary legitimacy of the CCP sustained sufficient support (or, at least, conformity) from the majority of the population, as though the single-minded and ruthlessly pursued national goals of socialist modernization in a hostile international environment were historically and self-evidently justified. This strong nationalism not only permitted but also nurtured a resourceful and predatory state. Such a state was necessitated by developmental priorities and redistributive tasks, a 'dictatorship over needs', as depicted by the critics of former East European state socialism (Feher, et al., 1983). Secondly, and relatedly, this state enjoyed a greater degree of autonomy in its domestic and international relations than any other post-war regime in the developing world. Enough room was, in turn, left for the flexibility needed for effective control and crisis management. The biggest difficulty facing the current reform regime is precisely that these two pivotal conditions, the nationalism and the autonomy, are both diminishing.

Next, the institutional foundation for unity and cohesion in the Mao period was sophisticated and powerful, and for the most part did not obstruct moves towards decentralization. Above all, as mentioned, the absolute leadership of the CCP ensured a unified polity with the party's formidable organizational resources. This organizational strength extended to the micro-societies of working and residential units at the grass-roots, which combined productive, welfare and ideological/educational functions, aided by a rigid registration system to limit migration. As nearly every citizen and family was part of, and hence likely to be materially and psychologically dependent on, such a unit, extraordinary control became almost 'natural' through the lowest-tier party branch. Alongside the party, the People's Liberation Army unconditionally accepted the party's leadership, effectively acting as a political force while remaining strictly professional. The commanders of the eight military regions across the country were periodically rotated to avoid the build-up of any sectarian interests and loyalty, echoing the ancient Chinese tradition preventing magistrates from serving in their own districts. These institutional guarantees, once again, are deteriorating amid the decentralizing/globalizing trend of the 2000s. The claim made by President Jiang Zemin that the CCP constituted 'three representatives' (that is to say, it represented the developed productive forces, advanced culture, and ordinary people) rang hollow to the rank and file of the party's members, as the appeal of much of the ideology that had sustained CCP rule was dwindling. Most work units survived but only with a reduced function; and decollectivization had once again rendered the bulk of rural China a 'sheet of loose sand' as put by Sun Zhongshan nearly 100 years earlier on the eve of the republican revolution. Meanwhile, as the army had involved itself in business and the suppression of strikes and demonstrations, it was losing its reputation of 'serving the people'. More alarming still was the prospect that the army could develop into a destabilizing and divisive force if the party's influence (both on it and on society) continued to decline.

Apart from nationalism and patriotism, Chinese culture inspired groups and individuals to comply while disregarding their attitudes towards the government. This was also helped by the myth of Chinese homogeneity and the fear of instability prevalent in Confucianism as well as socialism. Whether democracy, human rights, or constitutional federalism becomes the focus of China's future political reforms, the primacy of unity and stability is likely to remain a powerful consensus. Despite the profound and painful identity crisis being experienced by many in the reform years, manifesting itself in a variety of ways, from the rise of non-traditional religions to superficial Americanization, the sense of cultural belonging within China (at least within the Han groups) still seemed unlikely to be lost.

Taking into perspective these historical, institutional and cultural aspects of the dialectics between retaining central control and achieving beneficial decentralization and pluralism, the comparative disadvantages of an open, transitional system are manifest. Decentralization could endanger social cohesion in China if the party withdraws from its pre-eminence without healthy growth and empowerment of alternative organizations, such as the NPC. Market integration is not itself necessarily destabilizing, but if the government fails to curb polarization and social injustice, it may become so. Economic exploitation and insecurity can be explosive if not properly tackled in laws and policies, even though the state is no longer the sole provider of public goods. It is almost paradoxical for the Chinese Communist regime to maintain power and mandate while complying with the global impositions.

SUMMARY

The central point of this essay can perhaps be best illustrated by a practical example. Shanxi, one of China's driest provinces, has been preparing for a major water project, open to foreign investment and pending on the centre's approval, for almost a decade. However, opposition from the neighbouring provinces, through which the lower reaches of the rivers in question flow, continues to delay the beginning of work on the project. In Taiyuan, the provincial capital, competing departmental interests around the project and the conflicting concerns of the affected counties are likewise yet to be resolved. This could merely be a case of inefficiency and frustration, but it also demonstrates that, for all the country's newly flourished central-local-global interactions, China remains one chessboard. Another example would be the centrally mediated twinning of the country's most wealthy unit, the city of Shanghai, and the less-developed Yunnan, a multiethnic province in the south-west (other such pairs include Guangdong and Guangxi). Their co-operation as part of the centre's effort in overcoming regional and ethnic disparities shows that substantial vertical accountability as well as horizontal co-ordination are still in place. The political conditions for mutually beneficial relationships here are not given, but must be created. Crucial to managing these relationships is the strength of central and local states, so that vital national, societal and local interests can be protected. Moreover, though a daunting challenge, China knows that it must ally with other developing countries to participate in making and remaking the rules of globalization.

To conclude, it can be seen that strength and stability remain the key aims of the Chinese state. However, it is increasingly evident that a modern state cannot be truly strong and stable until it is not only socioeconomically and technologically developed, but also politically democratic. The central problem facing China under the CCP is that democratization must now be seen as an essential component of, and not a threat to, the unity, strength and stability which have proved so vital to the People's Republic since its foundation.

BIBLIOGRAPHY

Feher, F., Heller, A. and Markus, G. *Dictatorship Over Needs*. New York, NY, St Martin's Press, 1983.

Haggart, S. *Developing Nations and the Politics of Global Integration*. Washington, DC, Brookings Institution, 1995.

Lardy, N. *Problems on the Road to Liberalisation*, in the *Financial Times*. London, 15 March 2002.

Li, L. *Towards a Non-Zero-Sum Interactive Framework of Spatial Politics: the Case of Centre-Province in Contemporary China*, in *Political Studies*, 45:1. Oxford, Blackwell, 1997.

Lieberthal, K. *Governing China: From Revolution Through Reform*. New York, NY, WW Norton, 1995.

Mao Zedong. *A Critique of Soviet Economics*, 1959 (as reproduced, New York, NY, Monthly Review Press, 1977).

Montinola, G., Yingyi Qian and Weingast, B. *Federalism, Chinese Style: the Political Basis for Economic Success in China*, in *World Politics*, 48:1. Baltimore, MD, Johns Hopkins Univ. Press, 1995.

Oi, J. *The Role of the Local State in China's Transitional Economy*, in *China Quarterly*. Oxford Univ. Press, 1995.

Saich, T. *Governance and Politics of China*. Basingstoke, Palgrave Macmillan, 2001.

Schurmann, H. F. *Organisational principles of the Chinese Communists*, in *China Quarterly*, 2. Oxford Univ. Press, 1960.

Selden, M. *The Yenan Way in Revolutionary China*. Cambridge, MA, Harvard Univ. Press, 1971.

Shirk, S. *The Political Logic of Economic Reform in China*. Berkeley, CA, Univ. of California Press, 1993.

Shue, V. *The Reach of the State: Sketches of the Chinese Body Politic*. Palo Alto, CA, Stanford University Press, 1988.

Tsou Tang. *Interpreting the Revolution in China: Macrohistory and Micromechanisms*, as reprinted in *Modern China*, 26:2. Thousand Oaks, CA, Sage, 2000

Whyte, M. *Bureaucracy and Modernization in China: the Maoist Critique*, in *American Sociological Review*, 38. Washington, DC, American Sociological Asscn, 1973.

Chronology of
the People's Republic of China

c. **1500** BC: The Shang kingdom existed in the area of modern-day Henan province.

1100 BC–**221** BC: Period of the Zhou dynasty.

c. **800** BC: The feudal system instituted at the foundation of the Zhou dynasty disintegrated and China became a land of contending kingdoms.

479 BC: The philosopher Confucius (K'ung Fu-tzu) died.

6th–3rd centuries BC: Various schools of philosophy (Confucian, Daoist, Moist and Legalist) arose.

221 BC: The western state of Qin won the struggle between China's kingdoms; its ruler assumed the title of Huang Di ('emperor'), imposing a harsh Legalist code of laws and administration.

206 BC–AD **221**: During the rule of the Han dynasty, the new empire was expanded to include the Guangzhou (Canton) region and the feudal system was replaced by a civil service. Confucianism became the established orthodoxy.

316–589: Following the invasion of Tartar tribes, China was divided, with Tartar rulers holding the north and Chinese dynasties the south (Yangzi valley). Literature flourished and Buddhism was introduced and disseminated widely.

618: The foundation of the Tang dynasty (618–907) reunited the empire on a lasting basis. The aristocratic military class gave way to a bureaucracy recruited by public examination open to all literates.

960: T'ai-tsu, the Inspector-General of the imperial forces, carried out a *coup d'état* and founded the Song dynasty (960–1279). Whereas other dynastic founders had eliminated threatening generals, Emperor T'ai-tsu (960–976) offered them honorary titles and pensions in exchange for their positions of command, and developed a civil service system. During Song rule gunpowder was developed and maritime trade with southern and western Asia expanded.

1127: The Song lost northern China to an invasion of the Jin Tartars who established the Jin dynasty. The Song continued to rule their lands in southern China.

1211: Mongol forces under Temujin (Chinggis or Genghis Khan) began their invasion of the Jin territories.

1250: Under the leadership of Mongke and his brother Khubilai Khan (Temujin's grandsons), the Mongols began their advance into the southern territories of the Song.

1279: The Mongols achieved control of the whole of China. Mongol rule was largely exercised through foreign officials from western Asia and even Europe; the Italian Marco Polo was one such ruler.

1368: The Mongols were expelled by Chinese rebel armies. The Ming dynasty came to power and expanded the empire to include South Manzhou (modern-day Liaoning province) and Yunnan. The first Roman Catholic missionaries reached China.

16th century: The Manzu tribes (kindred of the Jin Tartars) of Manzhou (Manchuria) coalesced into a new kingdom and renounced their allegiance to the Ming. They began to encroach on the Ming territory of South Manzhou.

1557: The Portuguese were granted permission by China to establish a trading post at Macau (Macao).

April 1644: The Ming dynasty fell to an internal rebellion, which allowed the Manzhous (Manchus) to seize the imperial throne.

1773: The British became the main suppliers of opium to China.

1788–1792: Nepalese attacks on Tibet angered the Chinese authorities, who sent a large army into the territory; a guerrilla war ensued. Following the defeat of the Nepalese forces near Kathmandu, an agreement was signed with China that put Nepal in a position of vassalage to Beijing (Peking) and withdrew Nepalese trading privileges in Tibet.

March 1839: Following his appointment by the emperor to end the British importation of opium into China through Guangzhou, the Governor of Hunan province, Lin Tse-hsu, ordered the surrender and destruction of 20,000 chests of opium and demanded reassurances from merchants that they would not import opium into China in the future. The British Chief Superintendent of Trade, Captain Charles Elliot, ordered the traders to retreat to the British merchant fleet anchored off Hong Kong.

September 1839: Elliot fired at a Chinese fleet and sank several ships, thereby beginning the First Opium War.

26 January 1841: The British planted their flag on Hong Kong Island.

1842: China was defeated and the Treaty of Nanking (Nanjing), the first of the so-called 'Unequal Treaties', was signed. It established the system of Treaty Ports, concession areas, the right of extraterritorial jurisdiction, and ceded Hong Kong Island to the United Kingdom in perpetuity.

1855: Nepal made peace with Tibet.

1856: The Second Opium War began.

1858: The United Kingdom and France occupied Beijing following China's refusal to ratify the Treaty of Tientsin (Tianjin), by which foreigners would acquire the right to diplomatic representation in Beijing.

1860: The Second Opium War ended with the signing of the Convention of Peking (Beijing), by which the British acquired the Kowloon Peninsula.

1880s: France seized Indo-China and forced Beijing to renounce its suzerainty.

17 April 1895: The Sino-Japanese War (1894–95) for possession of Korea ended and the Treaty of Shimonoseki was signed; Korea's independence was recognized and China ceded the island of Taiwan (Formosa) and the Liaodong peninsula in South Manzhou—including Lushun (Port Arthur)—to the Japanese. Within a few days Japan was forced by Russia, Germany and France to waive its claim to Manzhou.

1898: Russia established control of Lushun and its hinterland.

1 July 1898: China leased the area known as the New Territories to the United Kingdom for a period of 99 years.

1900: The anti-foreigner peasant movement known as the Boxer Rebellion erupted; it was supported by the imperial court and threatened to massacre the diplomatic corps in Beijing.

14 August 1900: The Boxer Rebellion was crushed when an international expedition captured Beijing and drove the empress dowager, Ci Xi, and her court to Xian (Hsi-an or Sian).

5 September 1905: The Treaty of Portsmouth was signed, by which Russia granted Japan primacy in Korea and South Manzhou, including the Liaodong peninsula.

1908: Following the death of Ci Xi, there was no competent successor to continue the regency in the name of the infant emperor, Xuan Tong (Pu Yi), and the three-year-old was enthroned as emperor in Beijing's Forbidden City.

October 1911: Influenced by the revolutionary ideas of Dr Sun Yat-sen, a native of Guangzhou educated in Hawaii and Hong Kong and leader of the Nationalists (Guomindang), an army revolt broke out at Wuhan and led to the fall of the Qing (Manzhou) dynasty and the abolition of the monarchy.

December 1911: Dr Sun was elected as provisional President of the Republic of China.

1912: The Guomindang revolutionary league became a political party.

12 February 1912: Emperor Pu Yi abdicated; the following day Dr Sun resigned as President.

14 February 1912: Yuan Shikai, the former Commander-in-Chief of the imperial army, was elected President.

February 1913: China's first parliament (National Assembly) was elected, the Guomindang winning the majority of the seats.

10 October 1913: Yuan was officially inaugurated as President.

10 January 1914: Yuan dissolved China's first parliament and attempted to obtain support for a new dynasty, with himself as emperor.

25 December 1915: A revolt broke out against Yuan, aided by Japan, which bribed and armed Yuan's secret opponents, his own generals. Yuan later renounced his plans and died in June 1916.

1917–1927: During the 'war-lord era' a series of civil wars was fought between rival militarists, in order to gain control of revenues and of the Government in Beijing.

4 May 1919: In what later became known as the 'May Fourth Movement', students in Beijing rioted against the Government's acceptance of a secret arrangement whereby Japan was to acquire the former German-leased port of Qingdao in Shandong (Shantung).

July 1921: The Chinese Communist Party (CCP) was founded at a meeting attended by 11 members, one of whom was Mao Zedong (also known as Mao Tse-tung). The CCP and the Guomindang co-operated on the basis that members of the CCP might join the Guomindang as individuals, but there was no affiliation of the two parties.

1923: Having failed to obtain help from the Western powers to reinstate his government, Dr Sun Yat-sen turned to the USSR, which gave him arms and advisers.

February 1923: Dr Sun regained control of Guangzhou and organized a new, efficient Guomindang Government and model army.

May 1925: Following the shooting of student demonstrators in Shanghai by International Settlement police, there was an outbreak of violence nation-wide. British and Japanese trade and enterprise were boycotted and Hong Kong's labour withdrawn.

1926: War began between the Guomindang Government in Guangzhou and the southern warlords.

1927: The central Changjiang region fell to the Guomindang; their armies, commanded by Gen. Jiang Jieshi (Chiang Kai-shek), approached Shanghai early in the year. Shanghai workers, organized by the Communists, seized the Chinese-governed area of Shanghai, expelling the war-lord army. Jiang carried out a coup and massacre of the Communists and broke with the CCP, setting up a right-wing Guomindang Government at Nanjing. The former Guangzhou Government was subsequently established at Wuhan.

1928: The two Guomindang Governments coalesced at Nanjing; Jiang became President of the Republic of China.

18 September 1931: Japanese forces in South Manzhou carried out a coup against the Chinese in Shenyang (Mukden) and later took the whole of Manzhou by force.

9 March 1932: The Japanese combined Manzhou's three provinces (Liaoning, Jilin and Heilongjiang) into the puppet state of Manchukuo. Pu Yi was installed as President of Manchukuo and later as emperor (1934–45).

1935: The Communists set out on the 'Long March', with about 100,000 men and their dependants, reaching Yanan, in north Shaanxi, about one year later. During the march Mao Zedong emerged as the unquestioned leader of the CCP and became Chairman of the party.

December 1936: Jiang's army mutinied and held him prisoner until he agreed to end the civil war and accept the slogans 'Chinese do not fight Chinese' and 'unite to resist Japanese aggression'.

July 1937: The Japanese struck near Beijing and the fighting escalated into a large-scale, but as yet undeclared, war.

8 August 1945: The Soviet army invaded Manchukuo.

9 August 1945: Pu Yi was taken prisoner by the Soviets.

15 August 1945: Following Japan's defeat in the Second World War, Japanese forces surrendered. Taiwan was returned to Chinese control and became a province of the Republic of China.

27 August–10 October 1945: Talks were held in Chungking between the Chinese Communists and the USSR.

15 December 1945: US Secretary of State Gen. George C. Marshall held talks with Jiang Jieshi in an attempt to mediate between the Guomindang and the Communists.

10 January 1946: The People's Consultative Council was convened.

February 1946: Civil war broke out.

1 March 1946: T. V. Soong resigned as President of the Executive Yuan (Council of Ministers).

23 April 1946: Gen. Chang Chung was appointed to head a coalition government.

25 December 1946: The Republican Constitution was enforced.

24 May 1948: Wong Wen Hao was appointed as Prime Minister.

20 December 1948: Dr Sun Fo was appointed as Prime Minister.

20 January 1949: Li Tsung-jen succeeded Jiang Jieshi as President, following his resignation.

15 March 1949: Ho Ying-chin was appointed Prime Minister.

11 June 1949: Yen Hsi-shan was appointed Prime Minister.

21 September 1949: The Chinese People's Political Consultative Conference was convened.

1 October 1949: The People's Republic of China was proclaimed by the victorious Communists. Mao Zedong was appointed as President, Chou En-lai (Zhou Enlai) as Chairman of the State Administrative Council.

3 December 1949: Following the defeat of the Guomindang Government's forces by the Communist revolution, Jiang withdrew with his supporters from the Chinese mainland to Taiwan, where he established a Guomindang regime and imposed martial law. The regime asserted that it was the rightful Chinese Government.

February 1950: The Sino-Soviet Treaty was signed; this agreement guaranteed mutual assistance and was valid until 1980.

30 June 1950: An Agrarian Reform Law was enacted; the property of rural landlords, some foreign nationals and Guomindang members was confiscated and redistributed.

24 October 1950: The occupation of Tibet by Communist forces began.

27 October 1950: After US forces advanced beyond the 38th parallel into North Korea and towards the Yalu River, on the Chinese border, China sent 200,000 troops to assist North Korean forces.

1951: The Macau peninsula and two nearby islands became a Portuguese Overseas Province.

23 May 1951: Tibet signed an agreement to Chinese suzerainty.

6 July 1955: Details of the first Five-Year Plan were announced and a programme of collectivization of agriculture began.

26 January 1956: A 12-year agricultural plan was declared, which proposed complete collectivization by 1960.

2 May 1956: Mao Zedong inaugurated the 'Hundred Flowers' campaign, in which the Government permitted open criticism of some of its policies.

June 1957: The 'Hundred Flowers' campaign came to an end.

August 1958: The second plenum of the Eighth Central Committee adopted the 'Great Leap Forward' policy, which aimed to bring Chinese industrialization rapidly up to the level of that of the United Kingdom.

29 August 1958: The Second National People's Congress approved the policy of grouping agricultural co-operatives into large communes.

27 September 1958: China's first nuclear reactor came into operation in Beijing.

21 October 1958: A unit of Chinese troops patrolling the Indian border killed nine Indian policemen and captured a further 10 in the disputed Ladakh region.

17 March 1959: The Tibetan spiritual leader, the Dalai Lama, fled from Lhasa.

28 March 1959: The Dalai Lama crossed into India.

5 April 1959: The Panchen Lama was appointed Chairman of the Preparatory Committee for the proposed Tibetan Autonomous Region.

27 April 1959: Liu Shao-chi replaced Mao Zedong as Chairman of the People's Republic.

1960: The USSR ended its financial and technical aid to China.

3 May 1962: Pakistan and China reached a border agreement on the disputed region of Azad Kashmir.

20 October 1962: China launched a major border attack against India, which ended with a unilateral cease-fire on 21 November.

16 October 1964: The first nuclear test took place in Xinjiang (Sinkiang).

21 December 1964: The third session of the National People's Congress opened.

20 September 1965: The Tibetan Autonomous Region (Xizang) was created.

30 April 1966: The Great Proletarian Cultural Revolution was launched in a speech made by Chou En-lai.

17 June 1967: The first thermonuclear test was carried out in Xinjiang.

October 1968: Liu Shao-chi was reported to have been dismissed from party posts.

2 March 1969: An armed confrontation took place on Damansky (Chen-pao) Island on the Ussuri River—the first in a series of border clashes that took place during the year along the frontier between the USSR and China.

1–24 April 1969: The Ninth Communist Party Congress was held; Lin Piao, the Minister of Defence, was officially designated as Mao's heir in the new party constitution.

8 August 1969: China and the USSR reached an agreement at Khabarovsk during talks on the issue of navigation along border rivers.

13 August 1969: Sino-Soviet border clashes occured in the Xinjiang region.

11 September 1969: The Soviet Prime Minister, Aleksei Nikolaevich Kosygin, held talks with Chou En-lai in Beijing.

October 1969: A number of foreign detainees held during the Cultural Revolution were released.

20 October 1969: Peace negotiations over border incidents between the People's Republic of China and the Soviet Union opened in Beijing.

24 April 1970: China's first earth satellite was launched into orbit.

13 October 1970: Canada established full diplomatic relations with the People's Republic of China; relations with Taiwan (the Republic of China) were broken off.

15 July 1971: President Richard Nixon of the USA announced that he would visit the People's Republic of China in February 1972.

26 October 1971: The People's Republic of China was admitted by a convincing margin to the UN as one of the five permanent members of the Security Council, and Taiwan, which claimed to be the sole representative of China at the UN, was expelled.

15 November 1971: The People's Republic of China was formally installed as a permanent member of the UN Security Council.

30 January 1972: Chi Peng-fei was appointed as Foreign Minister in succession to the late Marshal Chen Yi.

21–28 February 1972: President Nixon visited China and attended meetings with Mao Zedong and Chou En-lai.

27 February 1972: A joint communiqué was issued by the People's Republic of China and the USA, in which it was agreed that: (a) Taiwan was the chief obstacle to normalization of Sino-American relations, that (b) the USA would withdraw militarily from Taiwan as tension in the area decreased, that (c) contact and exchanges in the fields of science, technology, culture, journalism and sport should be fostered and that (d) a US representative should be sent to Beijing to hasten the process of normalization.

13 March 1972: Full diplomatic relations were established at ambassadorial level between the United Kingdom and the People's Republic of China.

25 August 1972: The admission of Bangladesh to the UN was vetoed by China.

25–30 September 1972: Prime Minister Tanaka of Japan visited China and held meetings with Chou En-lai and Mao Zedong.

29 September 1972: A Sino-Japanese communiqué was issued that included the following chief points: (1) the establishment of peaceful relations to be incorporated into a formal treaty of friendship and peace; (2) the recognition by Japan of the Chinese People's Republic as the legitimate and sole government of China and *ipso facto* of the Chinese claim to sovereignty over Taiwan; (3) the immediate establishment of diplomatic relations at ambassadorial level; (4) the conclusion of trade and commercial agreements.

15–19 February 1973: It was announced, at the end of a visit by US Secretary of State Henry Kissinger to Beijing, that liaison offices would be set up in Beijing and Washington, DC, to facilitate the normalization of relations.

24–28 August 1973: The 10th Congress of the Chinese Communist Party in Beijing elected a new Central Committee; Lin Piao was officially denounced by name for the first time since his death in 1971.

3 September 1973: The Mongolian central newspaper accused China of having violated the Mongolian border and created tension on the borders for several years.

31 October 1973: Gough Whitlam, the Prime Minister of Australia, began a five-day tour of China.

10–11 November 1973: Henry Kissinger visited Beijing again to speed the progress of normalization of relations.

1 January 1974: Eight of China's highest-level military commanders were reported to have been reshuffled.

5 January 1974: Japan and China signed a most-favoured-nation trade agreement.

19 January 1974: China expelled five Soviet nationals, including three diplomats, for alleged spying. In retaliation, a Chinese national in the USSR was arrested and expelled.

19 January 1974: Chinese and South Vietnamese naval vessels were engaged in battle over rival claims to the Paracel Islands in the South China Sea. The Chinese were reported to have taken possession of the islands.

31 January 1974: South Viet Nam sent reinforcements to the Spratly Islands, which were also claimed by China.

20 April 1974: The People's Republic of China and Japan signed a civil aviation agreement providing for the establishment of air services between the two countries and beyond. On the same day Taiwan terminated its air links with Japan.

31 May 1974: China and Malaysia announced the establishment of diplomatic relations.

17 June 1974: China carried out its 16th nuclear test since 1964.

13–17 January 1975: The Chinese National People's Congress met in Beijing for the first time in 10 years. The Congress adopted a new, simplified constitution of 30 articles. A new State Council was approved, headed by Chou En-lai.

17 March 1975: China granted an amnesty to all Guomindang war criminals in its custody.

9 June 1975: The Philippines established diplomatic ties with the People's Republic of China, terminating all official links with Taiwan.

1 July 1975: Thailand established diplomatic ties with China.

8 January 1976: Premier Chou En-lai died.

7 February 1976: It was officially confirmed that Hua Kuo-feng, a Deputy Premier and Minister of Public Security, had been appointed acting Premier.

12 February 1976: Posters denouncing Vice-Premier Teng Hsiao-p'ing (Deng Xiaoping), who had been expected to succeed Chou En-lai, appeared in Beijing.

7 April 1976: Teng Hsiao-p'ing was dismissed from all his party and government posts. Hua Kuo-feng was confirmed by the Communist Party's Politburo as Premier and first Vice-Chairman of the Party's Central Committee.

15 April 1976: The Indian Government announced that diplomatic relations with China, which had been suspended in 1962, would be resumed.

15 June 1976: It was officially announced that Mao Zedong would no longer receive distinguished foreign visitors.

28 July 1976: A severe earthquake in Tangshan in Hebei (Hopei) province virtually destroyed the city, with enormous loss of life.

9 September 1976: Mao Zedong died.

7 October 1976: The 'Gang of Four', led by Mao Zedong's widow, Jiang Qing (Chiang Ch'ing), were arrested and charged with plotting to seize power; Hua Kuo-feng was appointed Chairman of the Communist Party in succession to Mao.

15 November 1976: An earthquake struck Tianjin (Tientsin) province.

30 November 1976: Border talks between China and the USSR were resumed in Beijing after an 18-month break.

2 December 1976: Huang Hua replaced Ch'iao Kuan-ha as Minister for Foreign Affairs.

9 January 1977: Posters appeared in Beijing calling for the reinstatement of Teng Hsiao-p'ing.

31 January 1977: An earthquake registering 6.5 on the Richter scale was reported in the north-east.

10 May 1977: Chinese radio reported that troops had been sent to Chekiang, in Fujian (Fukien) province, to quell anti-Government disorders arising from the arrest of the 'Gang of Four'.

16–21 July 1977: A meeting of the Communist Party Central Committee restored Teng Hsiao-p'ing to all his former posts and expelled the 'Gang of Four' from the party.

21 July 1977: Beijing wall posters announced that the 'Gang of Four' had been expelled from the Communist Party.

22 July 1977: The rehabilitation of Teng Hsiao-p'ing was officially announced.

12–18 August 1977: The 11th Congress of the Communist Party adopted a revised party constitution and elected a new Central Committee.

19 August 1977: The new Communist Party Central Committee elected its Politburo.

29 November 1977: The appointment of Chao Tsang-pi as Minister of Public Security was officially announced.

30 January 1978: Gen. Saifudin was deposed as head of the Xinjiang (Sinkiang) autonomous region.

3 February 1978: A five-year trade agreement was signed with the European Economic Community.

15 February 1978: Vice-Premier Teng Hsiao-p'ing was publicly cleared of responsibility for riots that had taken place in Beijing in April 1976.

16 February 1978: China and Japan signed an eight-year trade agreement.

26 February–5 March 1978: The Fifth National People's Congress was held in Beijing; it ended with the re-election of Hua Kuo-feng as Premier, the adoption of a new Constitution and the announcement of a 10-year development programme.

13 June 1978: The leading intellectual and writer, Kuo Mo-jo, died.

3 July 1978: It was announced that economic and technical aid to Viet Nam was to be suspended.

11 July 1978: All economic aid to Albania was withdrawn.

12 August 1978: China and Japan signed a 10-year agreement of peace and friendship.

9 September 1978: The National Women's Congress began its first meeting for 20 years.

26 September 1978: The Government suspended peace talks with Viet Nam.

10 October 1978: The Chairman of the Beijing Revolutionary Committee, Wu De, was dismissed and replaced by Lin Hujia, Chairman of the Tianjin Revolutionary Committee.

23 October 1978: The Chairman of the Henan Revolutionary Committee, Liu Qianxun, was removed and replaced by Duan Junyi, Minister of Railways.

16 November 1978: Political leaders were freed in the Xizang Autonomous Region (Tibet); China called on all Tibetan exiles to return home.

19 November 1978: A wallposter appeared on the Democracy Wall attacking the late Chairman Mao.

22 November 1978: Vice-Premier Ji Dengkui was reported to have been dismissed from the post of First Political Commissar of the Beijing Military Region.

14 December 1978: The Chairman of the Shaanxi Revolutionary Committee, Li Ruishan, was dismissed.

22 December 1978: The Communist Party Central Committee was expanded and four leading figures were rehabilitated.

26 December 1978: Wang Renzhong was appointed as a Vice-Premier in State Council changes.

1 January 1979: The Government established full diplomatic relations with the USA. The Pinyin system for the phonetic transcription of Chinese characters into the roman alphabet was officially introduced (see note at end of Chronology).

3 January 1979: It was reported that Communist Party Vice-Chairman Wang Dongxing had been relieved of several important duties.

28–31 January 1979: Vice-Premier Deng Xiaoping made an official visit to the USA.

8 February 1979: China established diplomatic relations with Portugal; the status of Macau was to remain unchanged.

17 February 1979: Chinese troops invaded Viet Nam in protest against the Vietnamese invasion of Kampuchea (now Cambodia), the mass expulsion of ethnic Chinese and border violations.

23 February 1979: Changes were made to the membership of the State Council; the new State Agriculture Commission and the Ministry of Agricultural Machinery were also established.

5 March 1979: The withdrawal of troops from Viet Nam began; it was completed on 16 March.

3 April 1979: Minor changes were made to the State Council.

4 April 1979: China announced its intention not to renew the Sino-Soviet Treaty of Friendship (see February 1950) when it expired in 1980.

18 May 1979: China broke off peace talks with Viet Nam. They were resumed in Beijing on 29 June.

4 June 1979: A meeting of the Standing Committee of the Chinese People's Political Consultative Conference (CPPCC) opened.

6 June 1979: He Zizhen, the second wife of Mao Zedong, was rehabilitated and elected to the CPPCC.

17 June 1979: The Government announced that direct elections would be held to local people's congresses and that local revolutionary committees would be abolished.

18 June 1979: The Second Session of the Fifth National People's Congress opened.

22 June 1979: China completed the exchange of prisoners of war with Viet Nam.

29 June 1979: The Government announced a 20% rise in defence expenditure for 1979.

1 July 1979: The National People's Congress ended with the appointment of three new Vice-Premiers.

4 July 1979: A wallposter accused Chairman Hua Guifeng of allowing right-wing control of the Communist Party.

7 July 1979: China and the USA signed a trade agreement, granting each other most-favoured-nation status.

24 July 1979: China's leading newspaper, the *People's Daily*, admitted to publishing misleading reports in the past.

25 July 1979: The USSR agreed to a Chinese proposal for talks on improving relations.

22 August 1979: It was announced that the 'Gang of Four' would be tried publicly.

25 August 1979: The former Communist Party Secretary-General, Zhang Wentian, was rehabilitated.

31 August 1979: US Vice-President Walter Mondale opened the first US consulate in China for 30 years.

1 September 1979: The Chinese Chairman of the People's Government of Xizang Autonomous Region (Tibet) was replaced by a Tibetan, Tian Bao.

12 September 1979: Changes were made to the State Council; Ji Pengfei was named as a Vice-Premier, Wu Bo named as the new Minister of Finance and three new ministries were established.

28 September 1979: Peng Zhen, the once-disgraced former Chairman of the Beijing Revolutionary Committee, and Zhao Ziyang were rehabilitated and elected to the Politburo.

10 October 1979: Some 2,000 staff and students of Beijing University marched through the capital demanding the withdrawal of an army unit from university premises occupied in 1972.

12 October 1979: Chairman Hua left for a three-week visit to Western Europe.

12 November 1979: Christian church services were resumed in Shanghai after 13 years of prohibition.

21 November 1979: In the first elections since 1949, the Communist Party won 218 of 348 seats contested in Beijing District People's Congress.

5–9 January 1980: The US Defense Secretary, Harold Brown, visited China.

31 January 1980: The population passed 1,000m.

15 February 1980: The anti-Maoist *Beijing Evening News* reappeared 13 years after its suppression during the Cultural Revolution.

25 February 1980: Deng Xiaoping, the Deputy Prime Minister, stepped down as army Chief of Staff, to be replaced by Gen. Yang Dezhi, former Commander of the Kunming military region.

29 February 1980: Four political opponents of Deng Xiaoping were removed from the Politburo.

6 March 1980: China suspended peace talks with Viet Nam, which had been frozen since December 1979.

16 April 1980: Two new Deputy Premiers were appointed: Zhao Ziyang and Wan Li.

17 April 1980: China was admitted to the International Monetary Fund (IMF); Li Baohua was appointed as China's IMF Governor.

3 May 1980: President Zia of Pakistan arrived for an official visit.

19 May 1980: China successfully fired an inter-continental-range missile for the first time.

23 June 1980: China opened Tibet's borders to trade with neighbouring countries.

31 July 1980: The Chinese authorities cut short a visit to Tibet by a delegation from the Dalai Lama after a demonstration of popular support for the exiled spiritual leader.

25 August 1980: The Petroleum Minister, Song Zhenming, resigned after his ministry was accused of covering-up an oil rig disaster in November 1979, in which 72 people had died.

1 September 1980: A budgetary deficit of approximately US$12,000m. was announced for 1979.

3 September 1980: Zhao Ziyang was announced as the successor to Hua Guofeng as Prime Minister; five Vice-Premiers resigned on age grounds.

4 September 1980: Three British warships arrived in Shanghai on the first visit to China by the Royal Navy for 30 years.

9 September 1980: The fourth anniversary of Mao Zedong's death was officially ignored.

10 September 1980: Gen. Zhang Aiping, Yang Jingren and Huang Hua were appointed Vice-Premiers.

9 October 1980: The Government warned the USA against *rapprochement* with Taiwan.

19 October 1980: President Giscard d'Estaing of France became the first western head of state to visit Tibet (Xizang) for 30 years.

22 October 1980: The Government announced that it was to buy a record 6m.–8m. tons of US wheat and maize worth US$1,000m. for each of the next four years.

29 October 1980: A total of 11 people were killed and over 70 were injured when a bomb exploded at Beijing's main railway station.

20 November 1980: The trial of the 'Gang of Four' began.

12 December 1980: Jiang Qing, the widow of Mao Zedong, was dragged from court after abusing prosecution witnesses and the bench at her trial.

22 December 1980: An unprecedented attack on the late Mao Zedong in the *People's Daily* accused him of personally launching and directing the Cultural Revolution.

23 December 1980: The Vice-Minister of Foreign Affairs, Zhang Wenjin, said China would attend any international conference on Kampuchea without the precondition of Vietnamese withdrawal from the country.

25 January 1981: At the end of the trial of the 'Gang of Four', a two-year suspended death sentence was passed on Jiang Qing and Zhang Chunqiao, Wang Hongwen was sentenced to life imprisonment, Yao Wenyuan was sentenced to 20 years' imprisonment and six others were given prison sentences of between 15 and 18 years.

1 February 1981: Following talks with Prime Minister Prem Tinsulanond of Thailand, the Government announced that it was to end material support for Communist insurgents in South-East Asia.

10 February 1981: The Government announced the development of a high-flux atomic reactor for research purposes.

26 February 1981: China asked for the recall of the Dutch ambassador from Beijing because of the Netherlands' refusal to halt the sale of two nuclear submarines to Taiwan.

6 March 1981: The State Council (Cabinet) was reorganized.

8 April 1981: The Government offered to hold unconditional talks with India towards the restoration of good relations.

21 May 1981: Fighting occurred on the southern border with Laos.

29 May 1981: Song Qingling, the widow of Sun Yat-sen and sister of Madame Jiang Jieshi (Chiang Kai-shek), died.

8 June 1981: Monsignor Dominic Tang was appointed Archbishop of Canton by Pope John Paul II.

14 June 1981: US Secretary of State Alexander Haig began an official visit.

18 June 1981: The US Government confirmed that two US-equipped stations in north-western China were monitoring Soviet missile tests.

23 June 1981: Dominic Tang was rejected by Chinese Catholics.

28 June 1981: India and China agreed to negotiate a settlement of their long-standing border dispute.

29 June 1981: Hu Yaobang replaced Hua Guofeng as Communist Party Chairman.

31 July 1981: Yang Shangkun was appointed as Secretary-General of the Communist Party Military Commission.

12 August 1981: A Taiwanese air force officer, Maj. Huang Zhicheng, who had defected to the People's Republic on 11 August, was given a reward worth US $400,000 by the People's Liberation Army (PLA).

11 September 1981: A cabinet reorganization was announced; Li Qiang resigned as Minister of Foreign Trade.

30 September 1981: In an interview with the Xinhua news agency, Marshal Ye Jianying, Chairman of the Standing Committee of the National People's Congress, made further overtures to Taiwan on the subject of ultimate political union with the mainland.

10 October 1981: On the anniversary of the 1911 revolution, Hu Yaobang, Communist Party Chairman, invited President Chiang Ching-kuo and Prime Minister Sun Yun-suan of Taiwan to visit the mainland, irrespective of their views on holding reunification talks.

14 October 1981: Diplomatic sources in Beijing said that 100 men had died when their submarine exploded during ballistic missile tests in September.

15 October 1981: It was revealed by diplomatic sources that China had launched its second nuclear-powered submarine in May.

14 November 1981: The Government agreed to pay its contribution of US $59m., which had been outstanding for 10 years, to the UN budget.

26 November 1981: The Government formally postponed the scheduled revision of the Constitution.

10 December 1981: An Indian delegation began talks in Beijing intended to improve relations between the two countries; they were the first such discussions since the border war of 1962.

8 March 1982: Four Government ministers were dismissed; Chen Muhua was appointed to head the new Ministry of Foreign Trade and Economic Relations, Liu Yi was made Minister of Commerce, and Qin Zhongha became Minister of the Chemical Industry.

29 May 1982: The State Economic Commission, an organ of the State Council, was inaugurated.

26 August 1982: The Government announced its intention to open a consulate in London, and the United Kingdom its intention to open one in Shanghai, 16 years after the previous office had been sacked by Red Guards.

1 September 1982: The post of Communist Party Chairman was abolished on the opening day of the 12th Party Congress. The existing Chairman, Hu Yaobang, was expected to become Party General Secretary, and the older Vice-Chairmen to join a newly-created Advisory Commission.

12 September 1982: It was announced that the population numbered 1,008m., according to the results of a census carried out in July.

12 September 1982: Hua Guofeng and Marshal Lin Bocheng were dismissed from the Party Politburo; Deng Xiaoping did not step down as expected; Hu Yaobang was elected Party General Secretary.

13 September 1982: Deng Xiaoping was confirmed as Chairman of the Advisory Commission.

22 September 1982: The British Prime Minister, Margaret Thatcher, arrived on an official visit to discuss the future of Hong Kong with Chinese leaders.

4 October 1982: Leonid Ilyichov, a Soviet deputy foreign minister, arrived to resume the Sino-Soviet dialogue that had been broken off by China after the Soviet invasion of Afghanistan.

14 October 1982: China became the fifth country able to launch ballistic missiles from submarines after the successful launch of an intermediate-range weapon.

4 November 1982: The trials of the followers of the 'Gang of Four' began in Beijing.

10 November 1982: The United Kingdom became the first Western country to sell arms to China, signing a deal worth £100m. for a package including missiles, radar and electronic equipment, and the refit of destroyers.

19 November 1982: Wu Xueqian replaced Huang Hua as foreign minister; Gen. Zhang Aiping replaced Gen. Biao as Minister of Defence.

3 December 1982: Zhang Wenjin, Vice-Minister of Foreign Affairs, was appointed as ambassador to the USA.

4 December 1982: A new Constitution, the fourth since 1949, was announced.

13 December 1982: The Government published a five-year economic plan for the first time in 25 years.

17 January 1983: Wang Zhong, former Communist Party Secretary and district head of Haifeng county, Guangdong, was executed for fraud involving 58,000 yuan.

25 January 1983: Death sentences on Jiang Qing and Zhang Chunqiao, members of the 'Gang of Four', were commuted to life imprisonment.

25 February 1983: Marshal Ye Jianying, aged 85, announced his retirement as Chairman of the Standing Committee of the National People's Congress.

7 April 1983: China cancelled all sports and cultural exchanges with the USA for 1983 over its granting of political asylum to the tennis player, Hu Na.

25 April 1983: Huang Zhizhen was elected Governor of Hubei province.

2 May 1983: Gu Xiulian was appointed Governor of Jiangsu province.

10 May 1983: British Petroleum (BP) became the first foreign oil company to be awarded a Chinese offshore drilling licence.

6 June 1983: China finally took up its place in the International Labour Organization (ILO), 13 years after the ILO offered the People's Republic membership instead of Taiwan.

6 June 1983: The Government announced the creation of the Ministry of State Security to combat espionage.

18 June 1983: Li Xiannian was chosen as the first President since the 1960s; Ulanhu was made Vice-President and Deng Xiaoping elected Chairman of the newly-created Central Military Commission.

11 July 1983: Sir Edward Youde, the Governor of Hong Kong, arrived for talks over the future of the territory.

25 July 1983: A second round of talks with the United Kingdom on the issue of Hong Kong began.

17 August 1983: The former foreign minister, Ji Pengfei, was named head of the Hong Kong and Macau Affairs Office, which was handling negotiations with the United Kingdom over the future of Hong Kong.

1984: Discussions began between Bhutan and the People's Republic of China regarding the formal demarcation of Bhutan's northern border.

September 1984: British and Chinese representatives met in Beijing and initialled the Sino-British Joint Declaration on the future of Hong Kong following its return to China in mid-1997. The territory was to become a 'special administrative region' (SAR) of the People's Republic. China guaranteed the continuation of Hong Kong's capitalist economy and way of life for 50 years after 1997 and the retention of its identity as a free port and its separate customs territory.

October 1984: Leaders of the People's Republic urged Taiwan to accept proposals for reunification on the basis of 'one country—two systems'. The Taiwan Government insisted that it would not negotiate with Beijing until the mainland regime renounced Communism.

December 1984: Following its approval by the National People's Congress and the British Parliament, the Sino-British Joint Declaration was signed in Beijing by the British and Chinese Prime Ministers.

May 1985: The British and Chinese Governments exchanged documents ratifying the Sino-British Joint Declaration.

June 1985: A 58-member Basic Law Drafting Committee (BLDC) was formed in Beijing with the aim of drawing up a new Basic Law (Constitution) for Hong Kong, in accordance with article 31 of the Chinese Constitution, which provides for special administrative regions within the People's Republic.

July 1985: The first meeting was held of the Joint Liaison Group (JLG), established to monitor the provisions of the Sino-British Joint Declaration.

January 1986: An 'anti-corruption' campaign was launched to investigate reports that many officials had exploited the programme of economic reform (introduced in 1978) for their own gain.

May 1986: Following the diversion of a Taiwanese cargo aircraft to the People's Republic by a pilot wishing to defect, negotiations were held in Hong Kong between the airlines of the two countries, leading to the return of the aircraft to Taiwan. The discussions represented the first ever direct contact between the two countries.

June 1986: China and Portugal opened formal negotiations for the return of the Portuguese overseas territory of Macau to full Chinese sovereignty.

September 1986: China and Pakistan signed an agreement on co-operation in the peaceful use of nuclear energy.

September 1986: The sixth plenary session of the 12th CCP Central Committee adopted a detailed resolution on the guiding principles for building a 'socialist society', which redefined the general ideology of the CCP, to provide a theoretical basis for the programme of modernization and the 'open door' policy of economic reform.

16 January 1987: It was announced that Hu Yaobang had resigned as CCP General Secretary, having been accused of 'mistakes on major issues of political principles'; Prime Minister Zhao Ziyang became acting General Secretary.

13 April 1987: Following the conclusion of the fourth round of negotiations, a joint declaration was formally signed in Beijing by the Portuguese and Chinese Governments, by which Macau was to become an SAR of the People's Republic on 20 December 1999.

25 October 1987: The 13th National Congress of the CCP opened; Deng Xiaoping retired from the Central Committee, but amendments to the Constitution of the CCP permitted him to retain the positions of Chairman of the State and of the CCP Central Military Commissions.

November 1987: Li Peng replaced Zhao as Acting Premier of the State Council.

March 1988: At the first session of the Seventh National People's Congress (NPC), Li Peng was confirmed as Premier and Yang Shangkun, a member of the CCP Politburo, was elected President.

April 1988: The first draft of the Basic Law for Hong Kong was published, and a Basic Law Consultative Committee (BLCC) was established in Hong Kong to collect public comments on its provisions, over a five-month period.

August 1988: The Chinese Government announced the establishment of a Macau Basic Law Drafting Committee to draft a law determining the territory's future constitutional status within the People's Republic.

December 1988: During Rajiv Gandhi's visit to China (the first such visit by an Indian Prime Minister for 34 years), the two countries agreed to establish a joint working group to negotiate on the issue of their long-standing Himalayan border dispute.

January 1989: It was announced that Portuguese passports were to be issued to about 100,000 ethnic Chinese inhabitants born in Macau before October 1981; these Macau residents were to be granted the full rights of a citizen of the European Community (EC, now European Union—EU).

February 1989: A second draft of the Basic Law for Hong Kong was approved by China's National People's Congress, which ignored all five options previously proposed for the election of a chief executive.

15 April 1989: Hu Yaobang died and the most serious student demonstrations ever seen in the People's Republic of China broke out, in which students criticized alleged corruption and nepotism within the Government. Negotiations between government officials and the students' leaders failed and workers from various professions joined the demonstrations in Tiananmen Square, Beijing.

May 1989: At a summit meeting held in Beijing, Deng Xiaoping and the Soviet President, Mikhail Gorbachev, formally restored normal state and party relations between their countries.

mid-May 1989: Some 3,000 students began a hunger strike in Tiananmen Square, with protesters demanding the resignation of both Deng Xiaoping and Li Peng. The students ended their hunger strike at the request of Zhao Ziyang, who was generally regarded as being sympathetic to the students' demands.

20 May 1989: A state of martial law was declared in Beijing and some 300,000 troops assembled.

30 May 1989: Demonstrators erected a 30-m high replica of the US Statue of Liberty (called the Goddess of Democracy) in Tiananmen Square.

4 June 1989: Troops of the People's Liberation Army (PLA) attacked pro-democracy protesters in and around Tiananmen Square, killing an unspecified number of people. The Government rejected television evidence and eye-witness accounts estimating the total dead at between 1,000 and 5,000, and claimed that a counter-revolutionary rebellion had been taking place. Japan criticized the Chinese Government's suppression of the pro-democracy movement and subsequently suspended (until late 1990) a five-year aid programme to China.

23–24 June 1989: A plenary session of the CCP's Central Committee dismissed Zhao from all his party posts. He was replaced as General Secretary of the CCP by Jiang Zemin, the Secretary of the Shanghai municipal party committee. Zhao was accused of participating in a conspiracy to overthrow the CCP and was placed under house arrest.

November 1989: Li Peng visited Pakistan and announced that China would provide Pakistan with a 300,000 kW nuclear power station.

9–10 December 1989: The US National Security Adviser visited Beijing.

26 December 1989: Yao Yilin was removed from the post of Minister in Charge of the State Planning Commission and was replaced by Zou Jiahua.

11 January 1990: Martial law was lifted in Beijing.

18 January 1990: It was announced that 573 prisoners, detained following the pro-democracy demonstrations of 1989, had been released.

13–16 February 1990: A meeting of the Basic Law Drafting Committee approved the final draft of the Basic Law, whereby Hong Kong was to be ruled as a Special Autonomous Region from 1997.

21 March 1990: Deng Xiaoping resigned from his last official post, that of Chairman of the State Central Military Commission.

4 April 1990: The National People's Congress approved the Basic Law for Hong Kong.

5–6 April 1990: A Muslim uprising in Xinjiang was suppressed by troops.

23 April 1990: Li Peng commenced an official visit to the USSR, the first by a Chinese Premier for 26 years.

1 May 1990: Martial law was lifted in Lhasa, Xizang (Tibet).

10 May 1990: It was announced that a further 211 political prisoners had been released; 431 remained in custody.

31 May 1990: Following the resignation of Doje Cering, Gyaincain Norbu became Chairman of the Xizang (Tibet) Autonomous Region.

25 June 1990: The leading dissident, Fang Lizhi, and his wife were permitted to leave the country for the United Kingdom.

25–27 July 1990: Francis Maude, Minister of State at the British Foreign and Commonwealth Office, visited Beijing for talks on the future of Hong Kong.

8 August 1990: Diplomatic relations between China and Indonesia were formally restored.

3–4 September 1990: A secret meeting of senior government and party leaders from China and Viet Nam took place.

7 September 1990: Li Peng, Premier of the State Council, resigned from the post of Minister in Charge of the State Commission for Restructuring the Economy.

3 October 1990: Diplomatic relations were established with Singapore.

30 November 1990: In Washington the Chinese Minister of Foreign Affairs and US President George Bush met for discussions.

28 December 1990: The Ministers of Public Security and of Foreign Economic Relations and Trade were replaced.

5 January 1991: The trials of those arrested after the pro-democracy protests of June 1989 began.

21 January 1991: The Governor of Hong Kong began a visit to Beijing.

3 March 1991: It was reported that the Ministers of Communications and of Construction had been dismissed.

25 March 1991: The fourth session of the Seventh National People's Congress opened.

8 April 1991: Government changes included the appointment of two new Vice-Premiers.

14 May 1991: Jiang Qing, leader of the 'Gang of Four' and widow of Mao Zedong, committed suicide.

15 May 1991: Jiang Zemin began a visit to the USSR, the first by a CCP General Secretary since 1957.

1 July 1991: A large rally to commemorate the 70th anniversary of the founding of the CCP took place in Beijing.

9 September 1991: The Vietnamese Minister of Foreign Affairs began a visit to Beijing, in preparation for the restoration of normal relations.

10 November 1991: Talks in Beijing resulted in the restoration of normal relations between China and Vietnam.

17 November 1991: A visit by the US Secretary of State, James Baker, ended with an agreement on arms control and trade.

25 November 1991: The eighth plenary session of the 13th Central Committee of the CCP commenced in Beijing.

16 December 1991: Li Peng ended a visit to Delhi, India, the first by a Chinese Premier for 31 years.

16 December 1991: The Association for Relations across the Taiwan Straits (ARATS) was founded.

11 January 1992: The President of China began a visit to Malaysia, the first by a head of state of the People's Republic.

13 January 1992: A delegation from the Hong Kong and Macau Affairs Office of the People's Republic of China concluded a visit to Hong Kong.

20 March 1992: Following the opening of the fifth plenary session of the Seventh National People's Congress, Premier Li Peng affirmed China's commitment to reform, while emphasizing the need for stability; on the same day a pro-independence demonstration in the Tibetan capital, Lhasa, was reported to have been violently dispersed by the security forces.

6 April 1992: Jiang Zemin began a visit to Japan, the first by the General Secretary of the CCP for nine years.

20 May 1992: A report issued by Amnesty International was critical of the Chinese authorities' violations of the human rights of monks and nuns in Tibet.

7 June 1992: Lord Wilson, the outgoing Governor of Hong Kong, began a six-day visit to China.

29 June 1992: Discussions began in Indonesia on the sovereignty of the disputed Spratly Islands, situated in the South China Sea and claimed by Brunei, the People's Republic of China, Taiwan, Malaysia, the Philippines and Viet Nam.

24 August 1992: China and the Republic of Korea established full diplomatic relations.

4 September 1992: Government changes included the replacement of the Minister of Finance, Wang Bingqian, by Liu Zhongli, following the former's resignation.

27 September 1992: President Roh began an official visit to the People's Republic of China, the first by a South Korean leader.

18 October 1992: A new 319-member Central Committee of the CCP was elected, prior to the closure of the Party's 14th National Congress.

19 October 1992: The first plenary session of the incoming Central Committee was held, at which a new Politburo, Secretariat and other bodies of the CCP were chosen; Jiang Zemin retained the post of General Secretary of the Central Committee.

22 October 1992: During his first visit to Beijing, the Governor of Hong Kong, Chris Patten, met the Chinese Minister of Foreign Affairs for discussions.

23 October 1992: Emperor Akihito began a six-day visit to China, the first ever Japanese imperial visit to the People's Republic.

30 November 1992: Premier Li Peng began a five-day visit to Hanoi, the first by a Chinese head of government for 21 years.

12 March 1993: Vice-President Wang Zhen died.

27 March 1993: During the first session of the Eighth National People's Congress, Jiang Zemin was elected as the country's President, replacing Yang Shangkun.

29 March 1993: Following Premier Li Peng's reappointment on the previous day, an extensive reorganization of the State Council was announced.

22 April 1993: China and the United Kingdom resumed negotiations on the future of Hong Kong, thus ending an impasse of several months.

27 April 1993: Historic talks between senior officials of the People's Republic of China and Taiwan commenced in Singapore.

24 May 1993: As many as 3,000 Tibetans were reported to have demonstrated in Lhasa against Chinese rule.

7 September 1993: The Chinese Premier and his Indian counterpart signed an agreement to reduce the numbers of troops along their common frontier and to resolve their border dispute by peaceful means.

10 March 1994: The second session of the Eighth National People's Congress opened in Beijing.

19 March 1994: The Japanese Prime Minister began a three-day visit to China.

31 March 1994: A total of 24 Taiwanese tourists were among those murdered on board a pleasure boat in Zhejiang Province, leading to a sharp deterioration in relations with Taiwan.

29 April 1994: During an official visit by Premier Li Peng to Mongolia, a new Sino-Mongolian treaty of friendship and co-operation was signed.

3 August 1994: Tang Shubei, the Vice-Chairman and Secretary-General of ARATS, arrived in Taipei for discussions; he was the most senior Chinese Communist official ever to visit Taiwan.

31 August 1994: China's intention to disband all of Hong Kong's recently-elected bodies in 1997 was confirmed at a meeting of the Standing Committee of the National People's Congress in Beijing.

31 August 1994: During the second visit by the Governor of Macau, Rocha Vieira, to China, the Chinese Minister of Foreign Affairs declared Sino-Portuguese relations to be sound.

2 September 1994: President Jiang Zemin began a visit to Russia, the first by a Chinese head of state since 1957.

14 September 1994: The Dalai Lama, the spiritual leader of Tibet, admitted that his attempts to negotiate with China on the question of greater autonomy had failed, and that his strategy was to be reviewed.

25–28 September 1994: At the fourth plenary session of the 14th Central Committee of the CCP, Huang Ju, the Mayor of Shanghai, was elected a member of the Politburo. Wu Bangguo and Jiang Chunyun, both members of the Politburo, joined the Secretariat of the CCP Central Committee.

5 October 1994: The Governor of Hong Kong, Chris Patten, offered to co-operate fully with China during the 1,000 remaining days of British sovereignty.

4 November 1994: China and the United Kingdom signed an accord relating to the overall financing arrangements for Hong Kong's new airport.

14 November 1994: Relations were strained when, in an apparent accident during a training exercise, Taiwanese anti-aircraft shells landed on a mainland Chinese village.

20 November 1994: As part of an official tour, which also incorporated Singapore, Malaysia and Indonesia, President Jiang Zemin began an historic four-day visit to Viet Nam.

10 December 1994: The Director of the Chinese mainland Hong Kong and Macau Affairs Office formally confirmed that Hong Kong's Legislative Council would be disbanded in 1997.

16 December 1994: Nine political activists, including a university lecturer, received prison sentences of up to 20 years for 'counter-revolutionary activity'.

19 January 1995: During a visit to Portugal, Vice-Premier Zhu Rongji confirmed that China would not impose the death penalty in Macau after the transfer of sovereignty in 1999.

30 January 1995: President Jiang Zemin announced an 'eight-point' policy for Taiwan.

9 February 1995: China announced that it was to play an active part in Hong Kong's forthcoming municipal elections.

17 March 1995: At the third plenary session of the Eighth National People's Congress, the appointment of Wu Bangguo and of Jiang Chunyun as Vice-Premiers of the State Council was approved.

22 March 1995: Discussions between China and the Philippines on the two countries' territorial dispute relating to the Spratly Islands ended in Beijing without agreement.

4 April 1995: Following allegations of corruption, Wang Baosen, deputy mayor of Beijing, committed suicide.

8 April 1995: President Lee of Taiwan announced a 'six-point' programme for cross-Straits relations.

10 April 1995: Chen Yun, revolutionary veteran and conservative reformer, died.

27 April 1995: Chen Xitong, Secretary of the Beijing Municipality Committee of the CCP and Politburo member, was arrested on suspicion of corruption.

14 May 1995: The Dalai Lama's nomination of the 11th incarnation of the Panchen Lama (second in the spiritual hierarchy of Tibetan buddhism) was condemned by the Chinese authorities.

22 May 1995: In protest at a recent nuclear test by China, the Japanese Government announced a reduction in grant aid.

26 May 1995: During a visit to Macau, the Director of the Chinese mainland Hong Kong and Macau Affairs Office proposed the swift establishment of a preparatory working committee to facilitate the transfer of sovereignty.

9 June 1995: China and the United Kingdom reached agreement on the establishment, in 1997, of the Hong Kong Court of Final Appeal.

16 June 1995: The postponement of a second session of negotiations at senior level between China and Taiwan was announced in Beijing.

30 June 1995: China and the United Kingdom signed an agreement detailing the financial arrangements for Hong Kong's new airport.

4 July 1995: Anson Chan, the Chief Secretary of Hong Kong, confirmed that she had held clandestine meetings with Chinese officials during a three-day visit to Beijing.

18 July 1995: China announced that it was to conduct a series of missile tests off the northern coast of Taiwan, arousing much anxiety on the island.

4 August 1995: The Dalai Lama began a visit to Mongolia.

11 August 1995: On the second day of consultations, China and the Philippines issued a statement declaring their intention to resolve peacefully their claims to the disputed Spratly Islands.

24 August 1995: Following his arrest in June, (Harry) Wu Hongda, a Chinese-born US citizen and political activist, was found guilty of espionage, sentenced to 15 years' imprisonment and immediately expelled from China.

28 September 1995: Chen Xitong was expelled from the Politburo and from the Central Committee of the CCP. Gen. Zhang Wannian and Gen. Chi Haotian were appointed as Vice-Chairmen of the CCP Central Military Commission.

3 October 1995: An improvement in Sino-British relations with regard to Hong Kong was confirmed by the visit of Qian Qichen, the Chinese Minister of Foreign Affairs, to London, where he had discussions with the British Prime Minister and Foreign Secretary.

16 October 1995: President Jiang Zemin's offer to visit Taiwan in person was cautiously received on the island.

24 October 1995: Meeting in New York, Jiang Zemin and US President Bill Clinton agreed to resume dialogue on various issues, the USA reaffirming its commitment to a 'one China' policy.

5 November 1995: The Chinese Government rejected a request by the UN Commission on Human Rights that from mid-1997 it file reports on the situation in Hong Kong.

13 November 1995: President Jiang Zemin arrived in Seoul, on the first ever visit to South Korea by a head of state of the People's Republic of China. The two Governments were united in their criticism of Japan's failure to offer a full apology for its war record.

26 November 1995: Do Muoi, General Secretary of the Communist Party of Viet Nam, began a visit to Beijing, where he had discussions with his Chinese counterpart.

8 December 1995: While attending celebrations to inaugurate Macau's new airport, President Soares of Portugal held discussions with the Chinese Vice-President, Rong Yiren.

8 December 1995: The Chinese Government's choice of Panchen Lama was enthroned in a ceremony in Lhasa. The whereabouts of the Dalai Lama's choice for the position remained unknown.

13 December 1995: The dissident leader, Wei Jingsheng, received a 14-year prison sentence upon conviction of conspiring to overthrow the Government.

26 January 1996: The 150-member Preparatory Committee of the Hong Kong SAR was formally inaugurated in Beijing. The new body was to appoint a 400-member Selection Committee responsible for the choice of Hong Kong's future Chief Executive.

2 February 1996: Li Peiyao, a Vice-Chairman of the Standing Committee of the National People's Congress, was murdered.

5 March 1996: The fourth session of the Eighth National People's Congress opened in Beijing; at the meeting the Ninth Five-Year Plan (1996–2000) was endorsed.

8 March 1996: As Taiwan's first direct presidential election approached, the People's Republic of China began missile tests in the Taiwan Strait.

24 March 1996: The Preparatory Committee in Beijing approved a resolution to appoint a provisional body to replace Hong Kong's Legislative Council, upon the transfer of sovereignty in mid-1997.

11–19 April 1996: A rare visit to Hong Kong by Lu Ping, the Chinese Director of the Hong Kong and Macau Affairs Office, was disrupted by pro-democracy demonstrators.

15 April 1996: The Government initiated a new campaign, 'Strike Hard', against crime.

23 April 1996: For the sixth consecutive year China survived a motion of censure at the UN Commission on Human Rights in Geneva.

24 April 1996: President Boris Yeltsin of Russia began an official visit to China for discussions with President Jiang Zemin.

26 April 1996: China, Russia, Kazakhstan, Kyrgyzstan and Tajikistan signed a treaty aimed at reducing border tension.

29 April 1996: The Straits Exchange Foundation (SEF—f. 1991) in Taipei urged the resumption of discussions with Beijing's ARATS.

18 May 1996: Following a number of violent incidents in the Autonomous Region of Xinjiang Uygur, the authorities began a campaign of action against Muslim separatists.

27 May 1996: Bao Tong, the most senior Communist Party official to be imprisoned after the Tiananmen Square massacre of 1989, was released at the end of a seven-year prison sentence and placed under house arrest.

5 July 1996: Ouyang De, a former Vice-Chairman of Guangdong Provincial People's Congress (who had been dismissed from the Communist Party in April), was sentenced to 15 years' imprisonment upon conviction on bribery charges.

13 July 1996: The right-wing Japan Youth Federation erected a lighthouse on one of the Diaoyu/Senkaku Islands—uninhabited islets situated in the East China Sea—leading to protests from the People's Republic of China and Taiwan, which also laid claim to the territory.

26 September 1996: China and the United Kingdom finally reached agreement on arrangements for the ceremony to mark the transfer of Hong Kong's sovereignty on 30 June 1997.

5 October 1996: In Beijing details were confirmed of the procedures for the establishment of the Provisional Legislative Council of the Hong Kong SAR after the transfer of sovereignty.

6 October 1996: Yao Wenyuan, a member of the 'Gang of Four', was released from prison at the end of his 20-year sentence.

29 October 1996: The Mayor of Beijing, Li Qiyan, resigned, owing to his implication in a corruption scandal in 1995.

30 October 1996: Wang Dan, a leading dissident, was sentenced to 11 years' imprisonment upon conviction of conspiring to subvert the Government.

15 November 1996: Wang Dan lost an appeal against his prison sentence.

28 November 1996: President Jiang Zemin began a four-day visit to India, the first by a Chinese head of state.

25 December 1996: A powerful bomb was detonated outside a government office in Lhasa, Tibet.

26 December 1996: Premier Li Peng began a visit to Russia.

22 January 1997: Shipping representatives of the two sides reached a preliminary agreement on the establishment of direct shipping links between mainland China and Taiwan.

12 February 1997: Hwang Jang Yop, a senior North Korean official, defected to the Republic of Korea, taking temporary refuge in the South Korean Embassy in Beijing.

19 February 1997: Deng Xiaoping, the country's 'paramount' leader, died at the age of 92.

23 February 1997: The Standing Committee of the National People's Congress in Beijing voted to repeal or amend various laws regarding civil liberties in Hong Kong.

25 February 1997: Following serious rioting in the region by Muslim separatists earlier in the month, three bombs planted on buses in Urumqi, Xinjiang Uygur, killed nine people and injured more than 70.

7 March 1997: A bomb explosion on a Beijing bus injured 11 people; responsibility was claimed by Xinjiang Uygur separatists.

10 March 1997: Citing political repression, an unemployed journalist hijacked a Taiwanese aircraft on a domestic flight and forced it to travel to Xiamen, in the Chinese mainland's Fujian province.

22 March 1997: The Dalai Lama began a six-day visit to Taiwan, provoking outrage in Beijing.

19 April 1997: The first commercial mainland Chinese ship to sail directly to Taiwan for 48 years arrived at the port of Kaohsiung.

22 April 1997: President Jiang Zemin began a five-day visit to Russia.

24 April 1997: In Moscow the Presidents of China, Russia and three central Asian republics signed an agreement to limit troop levels in their respective border zones.

25 April 1997: Following the execution of three Muslim separatists on the previous day, police opened fire on protesters in Xinjiang, killing two.

30 April 1997: It was reported that Bao Tong, a senior aide of Zhao Ziyang, the disgraced former General Secretary of the CCP, had been released from detention.

30 April 1997: The Philippine Government issued a formal protest over the entry of Chinese warships into waters near the disputed Spratly Islands.

6 May 1997: Four people, including an opposition member of the Japanese House of Representatives, landed on the largest of the disputed Diaoyu/Senkaku Islands and raised the Japanese flag. The Chinese Ministry of Foreign Affairs issued a severe condemnation and the Taiwanese Ministry of Foreign Affairs expressed grave concern, while the Government of Japan distanced itself from the action.

30 June 1997: After more than 150 years of British colonial rule, at midnight Hong Kong reverted to Chinese sovereignty.

1 July 1997: In the early hours of the morning more than 4,000 troops of the Chinese People's Liberation Army crossed the border into Hong Kong. Later in the day Hong Kong's Chief Executive, Tung Chee-hwa, was sworn in, as were the members of the Provisional Legislative Council.

4 August 1997: The Deputy Secretary-General of ARATS arrived in Taipei to attend a seminar.

4–5 August 1997: The 10th round of border talks between India and China was held in New Delhi.

5–7 August 1997: Preliminary discussions between representatives from North and South Korea, China and the USA, on the agenda for the full quadripartite negotiations on a Korean peace settlement, were held in New York.

6 September 1997: Chen Xitong, the disgraced former Secretary of the Beijing Municipality Committee, was expelled from the CCP.

19 September 1997: At the First Plenum of the 15th Central Committee of the CCP, a new Politburo was elected.

13 October 1997: The official mainland Chinese news agency announced that the Government was prepared to hold cross-Straits talks with Taiwan.

26 October 1997: President Jiang Zemin embarked upon a visit to the USA, the first by a Chinese head of state for many years.

11–16 November 1997: The Chinese Premier, Li Peng, visited Japan for discussions with his Japanese counterpart.

16 November 1997: Wei Jingsheng, a leading dissident, was released from prison on medical grounds and exiled to the USA.

8 December 1997: The election of 36 deputies from Hong Kong to the Ninth National People's Congress in Beijing took place.

9–10 December 1997: Representatives from North and South Korea, China and the USA participated in the first session of full quadripartite discussions on the situation in the Korean peninsula.

20 January 1998: The People's Republic of China proposed the resumption of negotiations with Taiwan, which had been suspended since 1995.

26 January 1998: As a precondition for the resumption of cross-Straits talks, the People's Republic of China conceded that Taiwan was not obliged to recognize the Government of the mainland as the central government.

8 February 1998: Wang Bingzhang, a prominent exiled dissident who had re-entered China in an attempt to establish a political organization, was expelled.

11–17 February 1998: The Prime Minister of Pakistan paid an official visit to China.

24 February 1998: ARATS dispatched a letter to its Taiwanese counterpart, the SEF, proposing the resumption of bilateral discussions.

5–19 March 1998: The first session of the Ninth National People's Congress took place in Beijing.

16 March 1998: Jiang Zemin was returned to the post of President of the People's Republic; Hu Jintao was elected Vice-President, while the outgoing Premier, Li Peng, replaced Qiao Shi as Chairman of the National People's Congress.

16–21 March 1998: The quadripartite talks on a Korean peace settlement resumed.

17 March 1998: Zhu Rongji was elected Premier by the Ninth National People's Congress, replacing Li Peng.

18 March 1998: The composition of a new State Council was approved by the National People's Congress. Changes included the appointment of Tang Jiaxuan as Minister of Foreign Affairs and Xiang Huaicheng as Minister of Finance.

17–23 April 1998: During an official visit to Macau, the Portuguese Prime Minister expressed the hope that after the transfer of sovereignty in December 1999 China would respect the territory's civil rights and liberties. He travelled on to Beijing, where he had discussions with the Chinese President and Premier.

18 April 1998: Wang Dan, the pro-democracy campaigner, was released from prison and sent into exile in the USA.

22–24 April 1998: Taiwanese negotiators visited the Chinese mainland to discuss the resumption of cross-Straits dialogue, the first such visit since 1995.

5 May 1998: The Preparatory Committee for the Establishment of the Macau SAR, which was to oversee the territory's transfer to Chinese sovereignty, was inaugurated in Beijing.

6 May 1998: The UN High Commissioner for Human Rights, Mary Robinson, began a 10-day visit to China, her itinerary incorporating two days in Tibet but no personal meetings with dissidents.

29 May 1998: The stationing of mainland Chinese troops in Macau upon its reversion to Chinese sovereignty in December 1999, was among the topics discussed at a meeting of representatives of the Chinese and Portuguese Governments.

25 June 1998: US President Bill Clinton embarked on a nine-day tour of the People's Republic and Hong Kong.

31 July 1998: Having been found guilty of charges of corruption and dereliction of duty, Chen Xitong, the former mayor of Beijing and the most senior official to date to be thus exposed, was sentenced to 16 years' imprisonment.

18 August 1998: In defiance of the government ban on direct travel between Taiwan and the mainland, a group of 18 activists set sail from the island to the south-eastern Chinese city of Xiamen. Upon their return to Taiwan they were detained and subsequently indicted.

20 August 1998: The Supreme People's Court rejected an appeal by Chen Xitong against his prison sentence.

6 October 1998: Tony Blair, the Prime Minister of the United Kingdom, began a five-day official visit to China and Hong Kong. On the same day it was announced that, from mid-October, the travel restrictions on mainland residents visiting relatives in Hong Kong were to be relaxed.

14–19 October 1998: For the first time since the suspension of cross-Straits discussions in 1995, Koo Chen-fu, Chairman of the SEF, visited the People's Republic of China, where he met with President Jiang Zemin—the highest level of bilateral contact since 1949—and had talks with his mainland counterpart and other senior officials.

16 October 1998: In Beijing the Singaporean Minister of Foreign Affairs, Prof. Shanmugam Jayakumar, had discussions with Vice-President Hu Jintao, Vice-Premier Qian Qichen and the Chinese Minister of Foreign Affairs.

19 October 1998: Phan Van Kai commenced an official five-day visit to China, the first by a Vietnamese Prime Minister since 1991.

21–24 October 1998: Further quadripartite talks were held between North and South Korea, China and the USA.

2 November 1998: Tonga withdrew its recognition from Taiwan and established diplomatic relations with the People's Republic of China.

3 November 1998: In Pyongyang (North Korea) the People's Republic of China, North Korea and Russia signed an inter-governmental agreement demarcating their common borders.

4 November 1998: Following devastating floods in July–August 1998, the Minister of Water Resources, Niu Maosheng, was dismissed; he was replaced by Wang Shucheng.

5 November 1998: The Taiwanese Government relaxed its policy on visits by officials to the People's Republic of China, those up to the rank of governor and municipal mayor henceforth being permitted to travel to the mainland for cultural and educational purposes or to attend international conferences. Regulations prohibiting civil servants from entering the People's Republic in their official capacity were abolished.

9–11 November 1998: The US Energy Secretary, Bill Richardson, paid a visit to Taiwan, where he met with President Lee Teng-hui. The visit prompted a complaint from the People's Republic of China.

11 November 1998: China lodged a strong protest with the USA, following President Bill Clinton's informal meeting with the Dalai Lama on the previous day in Washington, DC.

11–15 November 1998: President Kim Dae-Jung of South Korea paid an official visit to China.

11 November 1998: The mainland Chinese Government expressed serious concern at New Zealand's decision to accord Taiwanese government officials in Wellington similar privileges to those granted to diplomatic representatives of the People's Republic.

20 November 1998: Taiwan and the Marshall Islands established full diplomatic relations. The People's Republic of China subsequently severed its links with the Pacific nation.

22–25 November 1998: President Jiang Zemin paid a visit to Russia, where he had an informal meeting with the Russian President, Boris Yeltsin.

25–30 November 1998: President Jiang Zemin paid a state visit to Japan, the first by a Chinese head of state since the Second World War. In a joint declaration of friendship and co-operation, Japan expressed deep remorse for past aggression against China, but failed to offer a full apology for wartime atrocities.

1 December 1998: Three prominent dissidents and members of the China Democratic Party (CDP), Wang Youcai, Qin Yongmin and Xu Wenli, were detained and interrogated by the authorities. Later in the month they were convicted on charges of subversion and sentenced to prison terms of 11, 12 and 13 years respectively. Their immediate release was demanded by the EU.

8 December 1998: The People's Republic of China reasserted its indisputable sovereignty over the Spratly Islands.

8 December 1998: The Bhutanese and Chinese governments signed an interim border agreement in Beijing.

9 December 1998: The Dalai Lama announced that he had established links with the Chinese authorities and was prepared to hold discussions without preconditions.

10 December 1998: The Taliban regime in Afghanistan signed a military accord with China.

10 December 1998: President Bagabandi of Mongolia began a state visit to China.

20 December 1998: Liu Nanchan, the labour activist, was released into exile in the USA.

27 December 1998: Zhang Shanguang, who had given an interview to a radio station funded by the USA, received a 10-year prison sentence for subversion.

7 January 1999: Activists from the Tibetan Youth Congress attempted to storm the Chinese embassy in New Delhi, India.

15 January 1999: ARATS invited the Deputy Secretary-General of the SEF to visit the People's Republic in order to discuss preparations for the forthcoming visit to Taiwan of Wang Daohan, the Chairman of ARATS. The SEF subsequently replied that ARATS officials should visit Taiwan to discuss preparations.

29 January 1999: In a significant declaration, the Hong Kong Court of Final Appeal ruled that mainland-born children with at least one parent permanently resident in the territory had, without restriction, the right of abode in Hong Kong, thus overturning legislation approved by the Provisional Legislative Council. Concerns regarding the independence of the Hong Kong judiciary were subsequently raised.

30 January 1999: Lin Liyun, an adviser to ARATS, visited Taiwan for discussions with his counterparts, including Koo Cheu-fu, Chairman of the SEF.

8 February 1999: Taiwan dispatched nine convicted mainland Chinese hijackers to the island of Chinmen (Quemoy) in preparation for their repatriation. Four of them, however, were returned to Taiwan to stand trial, following an in-flight attack on a Taiwanese official.

10 February 1999: Liu Qi became Mayor of Beijing, replacing the acting incumbent, Jia Qinlin.

24 February 1999: Premier Zhu Rongji began a state visit to Russia.

26 February 1999: While not altering its judgment, the Hong Kong Court of Final Appeal clarified its ruling on the right of abode of children of immigrant parents and accepted that it could not question the authority of the Chinese National People's Congress or its Standing Committee.

28 February 1999: The US Secretary of State, Madeleine Albright, began an official visit to China.

5–15 March 1999: The second session of the Ninth National People's Congress was convened in Beijing. Tian Jiyun was appointed Secretary-General. At the final meeting amendments to the country's Constitution were approved.

6 March 1999: China warned the USA that the inclusion of Taiwan in the Theater Missile Defense System would have serious consequences for bilateral relations.

10 March 1999: On the 40th anniversary of their exile from their homeland, some 5,000 Tibetans attended a demonstration in New Delhi.

17–19 March 1999: A delegation from ARATS, led by Deputy Secretary-General Lin Yafei, travelled to Taiwan, where it was agreed that the Chairman of ARATS, Wang Daohan, would visit the island later in the year.

22–23 March 1999: Senior officials of China and the Philippines held discussions in Manila on the disputed sovereignty of the Spratly Islands.

28 March 1999: China condemned the USA's decision to sponsor a UN resolution criticizing China's record on human rights; China subsequently prevented the vote from taking place.

6–14 April 1999: Zhu Rongji paid an official visit to the USA, the first by a Chinese Premier for 15 years.

8 April 1999: President Lee Teng-hui of Taiwan reaffirmed that the Government of the People's Republic must recognize Taiwan as being of equal status, that cross-Straits negotiations should concentrate on practical issues and that reunification could take place only if the mainland were to become a democracy.

10 April 1999: With Macau's transfer to Chinese sovereignty scheduled for December, the Selection Committee, consisting entirely of Macau residents, was established in Beijing.

24–27 April 1999: Further quadripartite talks on the future of Korea, in which the USA also participated, took place in Geneva.

25 April 1999: More than 10,000 members of the Falun Gong religious cult staged a silent protest in Beijing, demanding recognition for their movement.

8 May 1999: Following the accidental bombing of the Chinese embassy in Belgrade, Yugoslavia, and the killing of four Chinese citizens during the NATO campaign against Yugoslavia, the largest mass protests since the pro-democracy demonstrations of 1989 began. The British and US embassies in Beijing came under attack. A subsequent apology for the bombing by US President Bill Clinton was rebuffed.

18 May 1999: The Legislative Council of Hong Kong voted to seek Beijing's assistance in restricting the influx of mainland immigrants to no more than 200,000.

21 May 1999: Following the bombing of the Chinese embassy in Belgrade, Yugoslavia, the People's Republic banned all US warships and military aircraft from using Hong Kong facilities. The ban remained in force until late July.

23 May 1999: A Chinese fishing boat sank following a collision with a Philippine patrol vessel near Scarborough Shoal, a disputed area 200 km west of Luzon. A similar incident occurred in July.

25 May 1999: The 700-page *Cox Report*, prepared by a select committee of the US House of Representatives and accusing China of the systematic theft of secret nuclear information from the USA, was released.

3 June 1999: The President of the Presidium of the North Korean Supreme People's Assembly began a visit to China, along with a 60-member official delegation.

4 June 1999: While the mainland Chinese authorities attempted to suppress coverage of events marking the 10th anniversary of the Tiananmen Square killings, a rally in Hong Kong to commemorate those who died in the massacre was attended by 70,000 people.

14 June 1999: Three Hong Kong students who had travelled to Beijing were refused permission to submit directly to the Standing Committee of the National People's Congress a 15,000-signature petition opposing the reinterpretation of the Basic Law of Hong Kong.

26 June 1999: The Standing Committee of the National People's Congress in Beijing delivered its reinterpretation of the Basic Law: mainland Chinese were to be entitled to the right of abode in Hong Kong if one parent was a permanent resident of the territory at the time of their birth; procedures for other applications were established.

27–29 June 1999: A delegation from the SEF visited Beijing, where a preliminary agreement was reached on a forthcoming visit to Taiwan by Wang Daohan, Chairman of ARATS.

1 July 1999: On the second anniversary of the resumption of Chinese sovereignty in Hong Kong, more than 2,000 pro-democracy demonstrators protested against the administration.

8–10 July 1999: The Japanese Prime Minister, Keizo Obuchi, paid an official visit to China.

9 July 1999: In an interview for a German radio station, President Lee Teng-hui of Taiwan declared that relations with the People's Republic were 'state-to-state'. China responded to the statement with a threat of war.

15–17 July 1999: President Jiang Zemin paid an official visit to Mongolia.

18 July 1999: Jenny Shipley, the Prime Minister of New Zealand, arrived in Beijing at the start of an official visit, during which she reaffirmed support for the 'one China' policy, Taiwan being regarded as an integral part of China.

18 July 1999: In an attempt to intimidate Taiwan, China conducted its first military exercise in the Taiwan Straits since 1996.

19 July 1999: In an altercation in the disputed Spratly Islands, Philippine warships reportedly opened fire on Chinese fishing boats, sinking one vessel. The Philippines described the incident as an 'accidental collision'.

22 July 1999: The Government banned the Falun Gong religious sect on the grounds that it constituted a 'threat to society'. Some 5,000 members were arrested for allegedly challenging the authority of the CCP. An arrest warrant for the movement's leader, Li Hongzhi, who was resident in the USA, was subsequently issued.

2 August 1999: A new ballistic missile, believed to be capable of carrying a nuclear warhead to the USA, was tested.

4 August 1999: Eight leaders of the hitherto-unknown dissident 'Anti-Corruption Army of the People, Workers and Farmers' were charged with subversion.

5–9 August 1999: A sixth round of quadripartite talks on North and South Korea was held in Geneva.

9 August 1999: China refused to grant permission for the Pope to visit Hong Kong later in the year, owing to the Holy See's close links with Taiwan.

11 August 1999: The composition of the Government of the future SAR of Macau was announced by the State Council in Beijing.

12 August 1999: As China threatened to attack in the event of a declaration of independence by Taiwan, army missile units were deployed along the mainland's 'front line' with Taiwan.

22 August 1999: ARATS suspended contacts with its Taiwanese counterpart, SEF, on the grounds that it was impossible to conduct normal exchanges following Taiwan's recent insistence on the 'two-state' theory—a reference to the island's relations with the People's Republic.

24 August 1999: In Beijing the South Korean Minister of National Defence, Cho Seung-Tae, met with his Chinese counterpart, Gen. Chi Haotian. The meeting represented the highest level of bilateral military contact since the end of the Korean War in 1953.

2 September 1999: President Jiang Zemin began an official visit to Thailand.

6–10 September 1999: President Jiang Zemin paid an official visit to Australia.

19–22 September 1999: During a session of the Central Committee of the CCP, Vice-President Hu Jintao appointed a Vice-Chairman of the Central Military Commission.

24 September 1999: Following a severe earthquake on the island, the Government of Taiwan accused the mainland of contravening humanitarian principles by obstructing international aid with its attempt to compel all offers of emergency assistance to be referred first to the Government of the People's Republic of China for approval.

1 October 1999: The People's Republic commemorated 50 years of Communist rule with mass official celebrations in Beijing.

19 October 1999: President Jiang Zemin began a 17-day official tour of six nations in the United Kingdom. His visit to London was disrupted by demonstrators protesting against China's record on human rights, particularly in relation to Tibet.

26 October 1999: President Jiang Zemin arrived in Portugal for discussions on the forthcoming reversion of Macau to Chinese sovereignty.

27 October 1999: Xie Fei, a Vice-Chairman of the Standing Committee of the National People's Congress and member of the Politburo of the Central Committee of the CCP, died.

30 October 1999: Following the recent arrest of 3,000 supporters, it was reported that more than 10,000 members of the banned Falun Gong movement had converged on Beijing to protest against the adoption of legislation outlawing the sect.

5 November 1999: The Mongolian and Chinese premiers had a meeting in Beijing on the occasion of the 50th anniversary of the establishment of diplomatic relations between the two countries.

7 November 1999: A human rights group reported that more than 500 members of the banned Falun Gong religious cult had been sent to labour camps by the Chinese authorities.

15 November 1999: Following six days of negotiations, an agreement relating to China's accession to the World Trade Organization (WTO) was signed with the USA.

30 November 1999: The Prime Minister, Zhu Rongji, began an official visit to Singapore, where he had discussions with his Singaporean counterpart, Goh Chok Tong, and President S. R. Nathan.

3 December 1999: The Hong Kong Court of Final Appeal rejected an appeal by 17 mainland Chinese immigrants regarding the right of abode under the Basic Law, as reinterpreted by the National People's Congress in Beijing, thus ruling that the Government of the People's Republic of China had the fundamental right to overrule the judgments of the highest court of the Hong Kong SAR.

16 December 1999: Following a settlement in July relating to injuries and loss of life, the USA agreed to pay China the sum of US $28m. in compensation for the damage caused to the Chinese embassy in Belgrade.

19 December 1999: At midnight, after 442 years of Portuguese rule, Macau was transferred to Chinese sovereignty in a ceremony attended by the Presidents and heads of government of Portugal and China. Edmund Ho was inaugurated as the Chief Executive of the SAR (renamed Macao).

6 January 2000: The 14th Karmapa Lama, the first to be recognized as the reincarnation of a 'living Buddha' by both Beijing and the Dalai Lama, arrived in Dharamsala, India, having defected from Tibet some days previously.

16 January 2000: In Lhasa, Tibet, Soinam Puncog, a two-year-old boy selected by the Chinese authorities but rejected by followers of the Dalai Lama, was ordained as the new Reting Lama.

2 February 2000: Amnesty International, the human rights organization, reported that in 1998 China had executed a total of 1,769 people—as many as the rest of world combined.

21 February 2000: In a policy document published in Beijing, China threatened to use military force if Taiwan continued to postpone negotiations on reunification.

1 March 2000: Zhou Yongkang was unexpectedly dismissed as Minister of Land and Resources and replaced by Tian Fengshan.

5–15 March 2000: The third session of the Ninth National People's Congress was convened in Beijing.

8 March 2000: Hu Changqing, former Vice-Governor of Jianxi province, was executed following his conviction on charges of corruption.

20 March 2000: In response to the Taiwanese President-elect's proposal for the holding of a peace 'summit' without preconditions, President Jiang Zemin restated that this could only take place following recognition by Taiwan of the 'one China' principle. On the following day the Taiwanese legislature approved a law to permit the opening of direct transport links between Taiwan's outlying islands and the People's Republic.

29–30 April 2000: Kim Jong Il, the North Korean leader, paid a secret visit to China, his first trip abroad for 17 years.

16 May 2000: President Joseph Estrada of the Philippines began an official visit to China, where a commitment to resolve all territorial disputes through peaceful means was reaffirmed.

29–31 May 2000: On his first official overseas visit for 17 years, Kim Jong Il headed a large delegation to Beijing, where he met President Jiang Zemin for discussions; few details were disclosed.

29 May 2000: President K. R. Narayanan of India embarked upon a state visit to China.

22 June 2000: During a visit to China, the US Secretary of State, Madeleine Albright, criticized the country's human rights record and urged Beijing to increase its efforts to negotiate a peaceful solution to the question of Taiwan.

29 June 2000: The People's Republic of China rejected the new Taiwanese President's offer to reopen negotiations on the basis that each side was free to interpret the 'one China' formula as it saw fit.

17–19 July 2000: During an official visit to China, President Vladimir Putin of Russia had discussions with President Jiang Zemin and other senior officials.

31 July 2000: Cheng Kejie, former Vice-Chairman of the Standing Committee of the National People's Congress, was sentenced to death for bribery. Upon his death in September, he became the most senior official to date to be executed in the People's Republic.

20 August 2000: The Nepalese Minister of Foreign Affairs began an official visit to China.

19 September 2000: The US Senate approved legislation granting China the status of Permanent Normal Trading Relations with the USA. President Clinton signed the bill in the following month.

20 September 2000: Maj.-Gen. Ji Shengde, former head of military intelligence of the PLA, was formally charged with bribery; his trial formed part of the biggest corruption case in the history of the People's Republic.

1 October 2000: On the anniversary of the foundation of the People's Republic, as many as 1,000 members of the banned Falun Gong spriritual sect were arrested during a demonstration in Tiananmen Square. On the same day the Pope provoked an angry reaction from China by canonizing 87 Chinese Catholic martyrs and 33 European missionaries who had died defending their faith.

9–11 October 2000: The 10th Five-Year Plan, approved by members at the plenary session of the Central Committee of the CCP, included pledges to 'step up the building of democratic politics' and 'expand citizens' orderly participation in politics'. The Party also announced that it would support the development of private enterprises and promote an open-style economy.

12 October 2000: Premier Zhu Rongji embarked upon an official visit to Japan.

16 October 2000: In a major defence policy document issued in Beijing, China specified that it was prepared to use force to prevent the secession of Taiwan.

18 October 2000: During a visit to South Korea by Zhu Rongji, China and Korea agreed to co-operate closely on the establishment of a peace mechanism for the Korean Peninsula, through the resumption of the quadripartite conference, incorporating the two Koreas, China and the USA.

22 October 2000: The Chinese Minister of National Defence, Gen. Chi Haotian, flew to Pyongyang, North Korea, for bilateral discussions.

25 October 2000: A leading organizer of resistance to Chinese rule in Xinjiang, imprisoned three years previously, was reported to have died of pneumonia while in custody. International groups alleged that he had been tortured and murdered.

27 October 2000: Following a two-year investigation, government auditors reported the embezzlement or serious misuse of the equivalent of more than US $11,000m. of public funds by government officials.

30 October 2000: Following strong opposition from Beijing, the Republic of Korea refused to grant a visa to the Dalai Lama, on the grounds that it would be 'inappropriate'.

4 November 2000: Negotiations were finalized for the Government to buy five *Ilyushin A-50E* early warning aircraft and two naval destroyers from Russia. The agreement was condemned by the governments of Taiwan and the USA for posing a threat to Taiwan.

early December 2000: The Government admitted that it had made contact with the Dalai Lama.

28 December 2000: Zhang Fusen, former Deputy General Secretary of the CCP, was appointed Minister of Justice. Gao Changli had been dismissed from this post in late November and was the subject of an investigation into suspected corruption.

3 January 2001: For the first time since 1949, boats were legally allowed to sail between China and the Taiwan-controlled islands of Chinmen (Quemoy) and Matsu (Mazu). This marked the beginning of negotiations to restore full direct travel and communication links between the two countries.

20–22 January 2001: UN Secretary-General Kofi Annan visited President Jiang Zemin to discuss China's role in UN peace-keeping missions and proposals to reform the UN Security Council.

26 February 2001: The Deputy Mayor of Taiwan led a delegation of city officials to Shanghai, to discuss with their Chinese counterparts issues of education, environment and urban development.

9 March 2001: A new social security system was inaugurated by the Government. The responsibility for providing pensions and unemployment benefit was transferred from state-owned enterprises to the Government. Workers were expected to make individual contributions to pension plans.

28 March 2001: The Government informed the UN that it had ratified its Human Rights Covenant on Economic and Social Rights, except for one clause concerning the right to form trade unions.

1 April 2001: Following a collision with a Chinese fighter aircraft, the pilot of which was killed, a US reconnaissance aircraft was forced to make an emergency landing on Hainan, resulting in the detention of its 24-member crew by the Chinese authorities and provoking a serious diplomatic dispute; the crew was released later in the month after the USA issued an apology (but not an admission of responsibility) for the incident.

3 April 2001: The Chinese and North and South Korean governments condemned a new Japanese school history textbook, which they claimed gave a sanitized account of Japanese militarism in South-East Asia during the Second World War.

22 April 2001: Relations with Japan were strained when Japan permitted a former Taiwanese President, Lee Teng-hui, to visit the country for health reasons. Bejing accused Lee of seeking support for Taiwanese independence.

27 April 2001: The Chinese Government accused the USA of regarding Taiwan as its own overseas protectorate, following President George W. Bush's statement that the USA would defend the island in the event of an invasion by China.

8 May 2001: President Jiang Zemin's speech at the inauguration of the Global Fortune Forum in Hong Kong was interrupted by protests from Falun Gong members and pro-democracy groups.

23 May 2001: China reacted angrily when it emerged that both the Dalai Lama and the President of Taiwan had begun visits to the USA.

1 July 2001: At a ceremony marking the 80th anniversary of the CCP, President Jiang Zemin advocated the modernization of the party, stating that entrepreneurs would be welcome as members.

16 July 2001: President Jiang Zemin signed a Treaty of Friendship and Co-operation between his country and Russia, the first such agreement since 1950.

28 July 2001: The US Secretary of State, Colin Powell, held discussions in Beijing with President Jiang Zemin. The USA had made a formal complaint the previous day over allegations that China was continuing to export military equipment to Pakistan, which China denied.

14 August 2001: Large-scale military operations were undertaken in Xinjiang and the Taiwan Straits.

19 August 2001: Lengthy prison sentences were imposed upon members of the banned Falun Gong movement.

24 October 2001: The Pope expressed an apology for the sins committed by adherents of Christianity against China, and urged the renewal of diplomatic relations between China and the Holy See.

12 December 2001: Following lengthy negotiations, China was formally admitted to membership of the World Trade Organization.

21 February 2002: US President Bush visited China for talks with President Jiang Zemin.

8 May 2002: A dispute arose after Chinese forces entered the Japanese consulate in Shenyang and forcibly ejected a group of North Korean asylum-seekers (who were later permitted to travel to South Korea).

5 June 2002: The government began an official campaign to impose stricter controls on the internet.

Note: For the purposes of this Chronology, most names referred to prior to the introduction of the Pinyin transliteration system by the People's Republic of China on 1 January 1979 have been rendered in the Wade-Giles transliteration system prevalent before that date. Some of the more important figures carry the Pinyin version in brackets after the first reference. After that date, Pinyin is generally used (the most notable exception is Mao Zedong, who is designated in Pinyin style throughout). Thus, pre-1979 references are to Teng Hsiao-p'ing, those for subsequent dates to Deng Xiaoping, etc.

Statistics

MAJOR DEMOGRAPHIC AND ECONOMIC INDICATORS

	Area ('000 sq km)	Population (millions, at 1/11/00 census)	Pop. density (per sq km)
Anhui 12	139.9	59.86	429
Fujian. 13	121.3	34.71	282
Gansu. 28	366.5	25.62	70
Guangdong. 19	197.1	86.42	438
Guizhou 24	174.0	35.25	203
Hainan 21	34.3	7.87	229
Hebei 03	202.7	67.44	333
Heilongjiang 08	463.6	36.89	80
Henan 16	167.0	92.56	554
Hubei 17	187.5	60.28	321
Hunan 18	210.5	64.40	306
Jiangsu 10	102.6	74.38	724
Jiangxi 14	164.8	41.40	251
Jilin 07	187.4	27.28	146
Liaoning. 06	151.0	42.38	281
Qinghai. 29	721.0	5.18	7
Shaanxi. 27	195.8	36.05	184
Shandong 15	153.3	90.79	592
Shanxi 04	157.1	32.97	210
Sichuan. 23	487.0	83.29	171
Yunnan 25	436.2	42.88	98
Zhejiang 11	101.8	46.77	459
Guangxi 20	220.4	44.89	204
Nei Mongol 05	1,177.5	23.76	20
Ningxia. 30	66.4	5.62	85
Xinjiang 31	1,646.9	19.25	12
Xizang 26	1,221.6	2.62	2
Beijing 01	16.8	13.82	823
Chongqing 22	82.0	30.90	377
Shanghai. 09	6.2	16.74	2,700
Tianjin 02	11.3	10.01	910
Total	9,571.3	1,265.83 (incl. 2.50m. military)	132
Hong Kong*	1.0990	6.71	6,125
Macao‡	0.0258	0.44	16,870
Taiwan	36.0	22.28	619

(also administers Jinmen and Mazu, islands formally part of Fujian province; only official People's Republic statistics shown)

* Population statistics at census of 15 March 2001; population density at mid-2001.
† Figures refer to World Bank estimates of gross national product (GNP) for 2000, measured at average 1998–2000 prices, in US dollars.
‡ Population and density statistics at census of 23 August 2001.
Source: mainly China Statistical Yearbook 2001.

Urban Pop. (as % of total)	GDP (2000) (current prices, million yuan)	GDP per head (current prices, yuan)	Inflation (2000) (CPI, gen. index, 1999 = 100)	FDI (US$m.) (foreign direct investment, 2000)
27.81	303,824	4,867	100.7	318.47
41.57	392,007	11,601	102.1	3,431.91
24.01	98,336	3,838	99.5	62.35
55.00	966,223	12,885	101.4	11,280.91
23.87	99,353	2,662	99.5	25.01
40.11	51,848	6,894	101.1	430.80
26.08	508,896	7,663	99.7	679.23
51.54	325,300	8,562	98.3	300.86
23.20	513,766	5,444	99.2	564.03
40.22	427,632	7,188	99.0	943.68
29.75	369,188	5,639	101.4	678.33
41.49	858,273	11,773	100.1	6,425.50
27.67	200,307	4,851	100.3	227.24
49.68	182,119	6,847	98.6	337.01
54.24	466,906	11,226	99.9	2,044.46
34.76	26,359	5,087	99.5	0.00
32.26	166,092	4,549	99.5	288.42
38.00	854,244	9,555	100.2	2,971.19
34.91	164,381	5,137	103.9	224.72
26.69	401,025	4,784	100.1	436.94
23.36	195,509	4,637	97.9	128.12
48.67	603,634	13,461	101.0	1,612.66
28.15	205,014	4,319	99.7	524.66
42.68	140,101	5,872	101.3	105.68
32.43	26,557	4,839	99.6	17.41
33.82	136,436	7,470	99.4	19.11
18.93	11,746	4,559	99.9	0.00
77.54	247,876	22,460	103.5	1,683.68
33.09	158,934	5,157	96.7	244.36
88.31	455,115	34,547	102.5	3,160.14
71.99	163,936	17,993	99.6	1,166.01
36.22	8,940,360	7,078	100.4	40,714.81
			(incl. $381.92m. of national govt FDI)	
n.a.	176,438†	25,950†	99.4	n.a.
n.a.	6,161†	14,200†	99.5	n.a.
n.a.	n.a.	n.a.	n.a.	n.a.

CURRENCY AND EXCHANGE RATES

Monetary units

100 fen (cents) = 10 jiao (chiao) = 1 renminbiao (People's Bank Dollar), usually called a yuan.

Sterling, Dollar and Euro equivalents (31 May 2002)

£1 sterling = 12.139 yuan;
US $1 = 8.277 yuan;
€1 = 7.769 yuan;
1,000 yuan = £82.38 = $120.82 = €128.71

Average Exchange Rate (yuan per US $)

1999 8.2783
2000 8.2785
2001 8.2771

Note: Since 1 January 1994 the official rate has been based on the prevailing rate in the interbank market for foreign exchange.

The Government of the People's Republic of China

(October 2002)

The current Constitution of the People's Republic of China was adopted by the Fifth National People's Congress on 4 December 1982. In its 138 articles the document, which was amended in 1993 and 1999, states that the People's Republic of China is a socialist state under the people's democratic dictatorship, led by the working class and based on the alliance of workers and peasants. It asserts that all power in the country belongs to the people, and that this power is exercised through the National People's Congress and the local people's congresses at different levels, and enshrines the socialist system and the principle of democratic centralism. All administrative and judicial organs are responsible to and supervised by the people's congress that created them. Legislative power is exercised by the National People's Congress, elected for a five-year term, and its Standing Committee. The head of state is a President, who is elected by the National People's Congress to a five-year term in parallel to its own, and may serve no more than two consecutive terms of office. The President is empowered to appoint the Premier, Vice-Premiers, State Councillors, Ministers and a number of other offices of state. These appointees comprise the highest executive and administrative organ of state, the State Council. The Constitution establishes a number of fundamental rights and duties of citizens.

The People's Republic of China is a unitary state, divided, for administrative purposes, into provinces, autonomous regions and municipalities directly under the central government. In addition, the State has the right to establish special administrative regions, with political systems prescribed by legislation in accordance with the prevailing circumstances in the area concerned. There are currently 22 provinces, five autonomous regions, four special municipalities and two special administrative regions (Hong Kong and Macao). In addition, the Constitution states that 'Taiwan is part of the sacred territory of the People's Republic of China'that territory is classed as a 23rd province, although it is not administered by the People's Republic. Each of the 31 basic territorial units has a people's congress and a governor (provinces), mayor (special municipalities) or chairman (autonomous regions). The autonomous regions are located where there is a large concentration of people of one or more of China's minority nationalities, and the right of these nationalities to use their own languages and preserve their own cultures is enshrined in the Constitution. The national language is Mandarin Chinese (Putonghua), although various Chinese dialects are in localized use.

The Government

HEAD OF STATE

President: JIANG ZEMIN (elected by the Eighth National People's Congress on 27 March 1993; re-elected by the Ninth National People's Congress on 16 March 1998).

Vice-President: HU JINTAO.

STATE COUNCIL

Premier: ZHU RONGJI.

Vice-Premiers: LI LANQING, QIAN QICHEN, WU BANGGUO, WEN JIABAO.

State Councillors: Gen. CHI HAOTIAN, LUO GAN, WU YI, ISMAIL AMAT, WANG ZHONGYU.

Secretary-General: WANG ZHONGYU.

Minister of Foreign Affairs: TANG JIAXUAN.

Minister of National Defence: Gen. CHI HAOTIAN.

Minister of State Economic and Trade Commission: LI RONGRONG.

Minister of State Development and Planning Commission: ZENG PEIYAN.

Minister of Education: CHEN ZHILI.

Minister of Science and Technology: XU GUANHUA.

Minister of State Commission of Science, Technology and Industry for National Defence: LIU JIBIN.

Minister of State Nationalities Affairs Commission: LI DEZHU.

Minister of Public Security: JIA CHUNWANG.

Minister of State Security: XU YONGYUE.

Minister of Civil Affairs: DOJI CERING.

Minister of Justice: ZHANG FUSEN.

Minister of Supervision: HE YONG.

Minister of Finance: XIANG HUAICHENG.

Minister of Foreign Trade and Economic Co-operation: SHI GUANGSHENG.

Minister of Agriculture: DU QINGLIN.

Minister of Water Resources: WANG SHUCHENG.

Minister of Construction: WANG GUANGTAO.

Minister of Land and Natural Resources: TIAN FENGSHAN.

Minister of Railways: FU ZHIHUAN.

Minister of Communications: HUANG ZHENDONG.

Minister of Information Industry: WU JICHUAN.

Minister of Personnel: ZHANG XUEZHONG.

Minister of Labour and Social Security: ZHANG ZUOJI.

Minister of Culture: SUN JIAZHENG.

Minister of Public Health: ZHANG WENKANG.

Minister of State Family Planning Commission: ZHANG WEIQING.

Governor of the People's Bank of China: DAI XIANGLONG.

Auditor-General of Auditing Administration: LI JINHUA.

MINISTRIES

Ministry of Agriculture: 11 Nongzhanguan Nanli, Chao Yang Qu, Beijing 100026; tel. (10) 64192293; fax (10) 64192468; e-mail webmaster@agri.gov.cn; internet www.agri.gov.cn.

Ministry of Civil Affairs: 147 Beiheyan Dajie, Dongcheng Qu, Beijing 100721; tel. (10) 65135333; fax (10) 65135332.

Ministry of Communications: 11 Jianguomennei Dajie, Dongcheng Qu. Bei-jing 100736; tel. (10) 65292114; fax (10) 65292345; internet www.moc.gov.cn.

Ministry of Construction: 9 Sanlihe Dajie, Xicheng Qu, Beijing 100835; tel. (10) 68394215; fax (10) 68393333; e-mail webmaster@mail.cin.gov.cn; internet www.cin.gov.cn.

Ministry of Culture: 10 Chaoyangmen Bei Jie, Dongcheng Qu, Beijing 100020; tel. (10) 65551432; fax (10) 65551433; e-mail webmaster@whb1.ccnt.com.cn; internet www.ccnt.com.cn.

Ministry of Education: 37 Damucang Hutong, Xicheng Qu, Beijing 100816; tel. (10) 66096114; fax (10) 66011049; e-mail webmaster@moe.edu.cn; internet www.moe.edu.cn.

Ministry of Finance: 3 Nansanxiang, Sanlihe, Xicheng Qu, Bei-jing 100820; tel. (10) 68551888; fax (10) 68533635; e-mail webmaster@mof.gov.cn; internet www.mof.gov.cn.

Ministry of Foreign Affairs: 225 Chaoyangmennei Dajie, Dongsi, Beijing 100701; tel. (10) 65961114; fax (10) 65962146; e-mail webmaster@fmprc.gov.cn; internet www.fmprc.gov.cn.

Ministry of Foreign Trade and Economic Co-operation: 2 Dongchangan Jie, Dongcheng Qu, Beijing 100731; tel. (10) 67081526; fax (10) 67081513; e-mail webmaster@moftec.gov.cn; internet www.moftec.gov.cn.

Ministry of Information Industry: 13 Xichangan Jie, Beijing 100804; tel. (10) 66014249; fax (10) 66034248; e-mail webmaster@mii.gov.cn; internet www.mii.gov.cn.

Ministry of Justice: 10 Chaoyangmennan Dajie, Chao Yang Qu, Beijing 100020; tel. (10) 65205114; fax (10) 65205316.

Ministry of Labour and Social Security: 12 Hepinglizhong Jie, Dongcheng Qu, Beijing 100716; tel. (10) 84201235; fax (10) 64218350.

Ministry of Land and Natural Resources: 3 Guanyingyuanxiqu, Xicheng Qu, Beijing 100035; tel. (10) 66127001; fax (10) 66175348; internet www.mlr.gov.cn.

Ministry of National Defence: 20 Jingshanqian Jie, Beijing 100009; tel. (10) 66730000; fax (10) 65962146.

Ministry of Personnel: 12 Hepinglizhong Jie, Dongcheng Qu, Beijing 100716; tel. (10) 84223240; fax (10) 64211417.

Ministry of Public Health: 1 Xizhinenwai Bei Lu, Xicheng Qu, Beijing 100044; tel. (10) 68792114; fax (10) 64012369; e-mail zhou@chsi.moh.gov.cn; internet www.moh.gov.cn.

Ministry of Public Security: 14 Dongchangan Jie, Dongcheng Qu, Beijing 100741; tel. (10) 65122831; fax (10) 65136577.

Ministry of Railways: 10 Fuxing Lu, Haidian Qu, Beijing 100844; tel. (10) 63244150; fax (10) 63242150; e-mail webmaster@ns.chinamor.cn.net; internet www.chinamor.cn.net.

Ministry of Science and Technology: 15B Fuxing Lu, Haidian Qu, Beijing 100862; tel. (10) 68515050; fax (10) 68515006; e-mail officemail@ mail.most.gov.cn; internet www.most.gov.cn.

Ministry of State Security: 14 Dongchangan Jie, Dongcheng Qu, Beijing 100741; tel. (10) 65244702.

Ministry of Supervision: 4 Zaojunmiao, Haidian Qu, Beijing 100081; tel. (10) 62256677; fax (10) 62254181.

Ministry of Water Resources: 2 Baiguang Lu, Ertiao, Xuanwu Qu, Beijing 100053; tel. (10) 63203069; fax (10) 63202650.

STATE COMMISSIONS

State Commission of Science, Technology and Industry for National Defence: 2a Guang'anmennan Jie, Xuanwu Qu, Beijing 100053; tel. (10) 63571397; fax (10) 63571398; internet www.costind.gov.cn.

State Development and Planning Commission: 38 Yuetannan Jie, Xicheng Qu, Beijing 100824; tel. (10) 68504409; fax (10) 68512929; e-mail news@sdpc.gov.cn; internet www.sdpc.gov.cn.

State Economic and Trade Commission: 26 Xuanwumenxi Dajie, Xuanwumen Qu, Beijing 100053; tel. (10) 63192334; fax (10) 63192348; e-mail webmaster@ setc.gov.cn; internet www.setc.gov.cn.

State Family Planning Commission: 14 Zhichun Lu, Haidian Qu, Beijing 100088; tel. (10) 62046622; fax (10) 62051865; e-mail sfpcdfa@public.bta.net.cn; internet www.sfpc.gov.cn.

State Nationalities Affairs Commission: 252 Taipingqiao Dajie, Xicheng Qu, Beijing 100800; tel. and fax (10) 66017375.

Legislature

QUANGUO RENMIN DAIBIAO DAHUI

(National People's Congress)

The National People's Congress (NPC) is the highest organ of state power, and is indirectly elected for a five-year term. The first plenary session of the Ninth NPC was convened in Beijing in March 1998, and was attended by 2,979 deputies. The first session of the Ninth National Committee of the Chinese People's Political Consultative Conference (CPPCC, Chair. LI RUIHUAN), a revolutionary united front organization led by the Communist Party, took place simultan-eously. The CPPCC holds discussions and consultations on the important affairs in the nation's political life. Members of the CPPCC National Committee or of its Standing Committee may be invited to attend the NPC or its Standing Committee as observers.

Standing Committee

In March 1998 134 members were elected to the Standing Committee, in addition to the following:

Chairman: LI PENG.

Vice-Chairmen: TIAN JIYUN, JIANG CHUNYUN, ZOU JIAHUA, PAGBALHA GELEG NAMGYAI, WANG GUANGYING, CHENG SIYUAN, BUHE, TOMUR DAWAMAT, WU JIEPING, PENG PEIYUN, HE LULI, ZHOU GUANGZHAO, CAO ZHI, DING SHISHUN, CHENG SIWEI, XU JIALU, JIANG ZHENGHUA.

Secretary-General: HE CHUNLIN.

PART TWO
Territorial Surveys

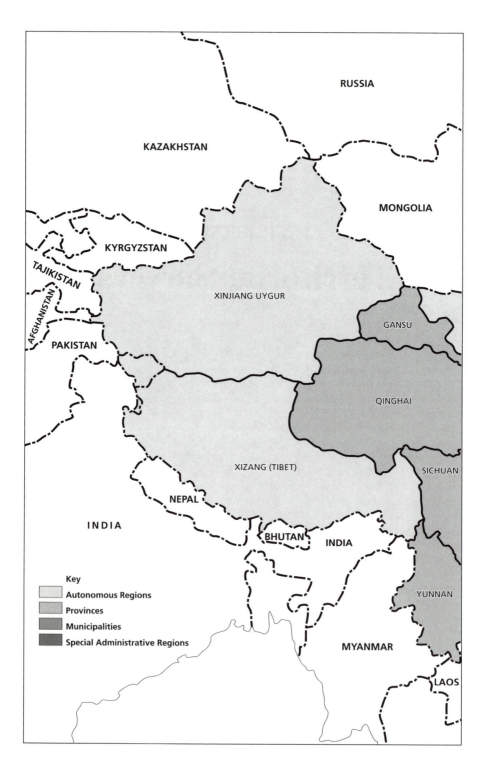

Key

Autonomous Regions

Provinces

Municipalities

Special Administrative Regions

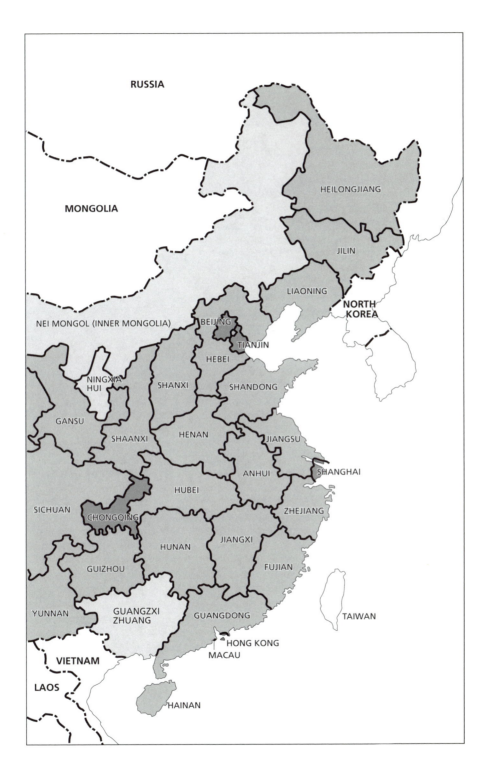

PROVINCES

Anhui

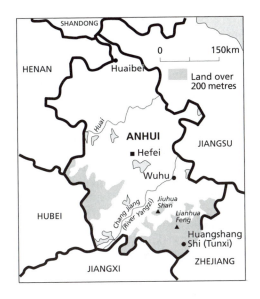

The Province of Anhui (Anhwei) lies in eastern China, inland from the neighbouring coastal provinces of Jiangsu to the east and Zhejiang to the south-east. Jiangxi is to the south, Hubei to the south-west, Henan to the north-west and there is a short border with Shandong in the north. Anhui is a central Chinese province straddling the watershed of the Huang He (Yellow River) and the Chang Jiang (River Yangzi) basins. The latter river crosses southern Anhui from the south-west in a north-easterly direction. This part of the province is known as Huizhou, and the combination of its territories and name with those of another ancient province, Anching, during the Qing dynasty, is what created modern Anhui (which means 'peaceful emblem'). Apart from some minor adjustments to the boundary with Jiangsu, its territory has remained essentially the same since imperial times. Anhui covers an area of 139,900 sq km (54,000 sq miles).

In the very south of Anhui is the Huang Shan (Yellow Mountains) range, its riven landscape famous as an ideal of beauty for over 1,000 years. Across the Chang Jiang, in the west of the province, rise the Dabie Shan. The dusty but fertile plains to the north and east of these mountains are drained by the Huai He and tributaries of the mighty Huang He (for some 700 years the Huai was itself a tributary of the Huang He, until a catastrophic flood in 1855 changed the course of the lower reaches of the temperamental Yellow River, which no longer reaches the sea through the Huai). Anhui's varied topography of lowlands, lakes and rivers, and hills and mountains reaches its highest point in the Huang Shan, at Lianfua Feng (Lotus Flower Peak—1,864 m or 6,118 feet). About 30 of the 72 peaks in the Huang Shan rise above 1,500 m. North of the Huang Shan, on the southern edge of the Chang Jiang plain, lies one of China's four Buddhist holy mountains, Jiuhua Shan (Nine Brilliant Mountains), sacred since the third century. The climate in Anhui consists of distinct seasons, characterized by the so-called 'plum rains' of late spring, sometimes followed by summer (June–August) droughts. North of the Huai it is temperate, if warm, a fairly humid, monsoon climate, very prone to spring droughts and summer flooding. Southern Anhui, along the Chang Jiang, is more subtropical and humid, although altitude tempers the climate. During 2000 the average monthly temperature in Hefei, the provincial capital, was 29.9°C (85.8°F) in the hottest month, July, and 1.5°C (34.7°F) in January, while rainfall totalled a less-than-average 901.0 mm (35.2 inches) for the year. Most of this normally falls in the late spring and through the summer (May–August).

At the census of 1 November 2000 the total population of Anhui was 59.86m., giving an average density for the province of 429 people per sq km (the sixth-most densely populated of the 22 provinces). The growth rate was rather below the national average. Most people live in towns and cities along the Huai, in the north, or on the southern banks of the Chang Jiang, and the ethnicity of the overwhelming majority of the population (99.4%, according to initial results of the national census of 2000) is Han Chinese. There is a small community of Hui (Chinese-speaking Muslims) and even fewer She (in the southern mountains). The homogeneity implied by the definition of the Han Chinese as a single ethnic group, however, is belied by the dialects of the spoken language, and Anhui is a good example of such variety. Most people in Anhui speak one or other of the Mandarin (Putonghua) Chinese dialects, but in the south-east (and in north-west Zhejiang) some still speak Huizhou Chinese. This latter was once considered part of the Lower Yangzi sub-group of Mandarin dialects, but is now itself regarded as one of the major varieties of Chinese, distinct from the Mandarin spoken to the north and the Wu to the south. There are a fair number of Huizhou dialects, reflecting the persistence of clan traditions in south-east Anhui. While linguistic variety has persisted, however, traditional religion was more severely disrupted during the 20th century, particularly in the Cultural Revolution, although practice is now more tolerated. The province is the site of one of Chinese Buddhism's four sacred mountains (the others are Putuo Shan in Zhejiang, Emei Shan in Sichuan and Wutai Shan in Shanxi), Jiuhua Shan, which once again supports temple communities and receives pilgrims. The Hui provide the basis for a small Muslim community.

In 2000 the urban population of the province comprised 27.8% of the total, indicating a more rural population than is usual in northern and eastern China. At the end of 2000 Anhui contained 17 prefectures (all cities), 61 counties (of which five were cities), and there were 45 districts under the jurisdiction of the various cities. The major cities were the capital, Hefei (with a population of 4.4m. at the end of 2000, or 1.4m. in the city itself), in the centre of the province, and Huangshan City (Huangshanshi—formerly Tungxi) in the south, Huainan and Bengbu in the north and Huaibei in the far north, and Tongling on the Chang Jiang.

History

The territory of modern Anhui was on the fringes of the Chinese heartland under the ancient Zhou dynasty. Indeed, before and during the time of the Warring States Anhui generally lay under the suzerainty of the southern state of Chu, which, though increasingly sinicized, was alien to the more conservative northern states. With the establishment of a Chinese Empire in the third century BC under the short-lived Qin dynasty, maintained by the Han, northern Anhui became part of the Han Chinese heartland and high levels of immigration as far south as the Chang Jiang (River Yangzi) confirmed this. However, the region's history was to fate it to remain on the fluctuating border between northern and southern China, particularly as the settlement of the Yangzi basin by the Han Chinese improved the south's economic ability to withstand the northern states, which were based on the developed lands along the Huang He (Yellow River).

Thus, in the immediate aftermath of the Han dynasty (the last emperor, Xiandi, abdicated in AD 220), Anhui was the scene of much military action as the successor states fought for supremacy. This struggle had begun even before the official demise of the Han, as the generals vied for territorial supremacy. The main power in the north was to be the Wei, a dynasty proclaimed in 221 by a son of the famed Cao Cao (who died in 220), a Han general. Cao Cao's battles against the emerging power of Wu, a realm based south of the Chang Jiang, involved the defence of Hefei. A lieutenant of Cao Cao, Zhang Liao, was ordered to defend the city against the numerically superior Wu forces, and his victory remains commemorated in the modern city. Wei briefly reunited the empire, only to be supplanted by the Jin dynasty, which had itself succumbed to foreign invasion and local military powers by the early fourth century. However, as was often to be the case in succeeding centuries, the Jin court clung to some power in the east and one of its generals won a famous battle near Hefei against overwhelming odds. This battle of Feishui is famous for illustrating the insight and conduct of the great Jin minister, Xie An (An Shi), as well as the use of strategy and trickery by his nephew, the commanding general, Xie Xuan. However, China was not properly reunited, and Anhui remained a contested territory, until the end of the sixth century.

Under the Tang dynasty Anhui, like the rest of China, was able to enjoy peaceful development. Thus, Jiuhua Shan became a Buddhist pilgrimage site from the eighth century, after a Korean prince and proselytizer, Jin Qiaojue (Kim Kiao Kak) established the worship of Ksitigarbha, the guardian of the earth, here. However, Anhui south of the Chang Jiang remained a remote and isolated land, particularly from the north and its conflicts. For instance, although Yixian, a town in a basin of the Huang Shan was founded in the third century BC, in AD 904 nearby Xidi was still a suitable refuge for the eldest son of the last Tang emperor (he founded the still dominant Hu clan of the town). Generally, the area was becoming more settled and was beginning to take advantage of its fertility and its position on the main trade routes across China. The initial remoteness may account for the conservatism of culture and language that already characterized those from 'Anhui' (or, at least, Huizhou, the southern part) by the beginning of the second millennium of the Christian era. The supposedly typical honesty, as well as the cleverness, of those in the region is illustrated by the story of a Song judge from this period, Lord Bao (his tomb can still be seen in a Hefei park), who was posthumously honoured for his integrity. More importantly, this reputation helped the rise of the Huizhou (or Xinan) merchants, whose commercial syndicate (originally based on the salt trade) dominated Chinese trade under the Ming and Qing dynasties. That the prosperity of Anhui should really start with the Ming is appropriate, as the father of the first Ming emperor is buried in Anhui (indeed, it was at his grave in 1368 that the Chinese phoenix was supposed to have last appeared). The wealth of the Huizhou merchants was such that many developed into precursors of modern-day industrialists, but just before the crucial stage of transition, plague effectively destroyed the region's pre-eminence during the 1800s.

With the fall of the Qing and the rise of the warlords and the Republic, Anhui also found itself once again a territory to be contested. The province also provided its name to a warlord clique that followed one of its sons, Duan Qirui, who was a minister, premier and president in the republican Government. However, he did not actually control the province. Meanwhile, Anhui's military governor, Zhu Jiabao, was late to declare independence from the Qing Empire, in the name of a still nascent 'Republic of China', in November 1911. He was briefly replaced by Sun Yuyun before the province acceded to the Central Military Government at the end of the month. There were then two brief periods of warlord 'independence', under Bo Wenwei (17 July–7 August 1913) and Ni Sichong (29 May–22 June 1917). Anhui found itself on the front line of open conflict in both the succeeding decades, in the war against Japan and then in the civil war between the Nationalists and the Communists. During the civil war northern Anhui was crucial to the Communist drive for Beijing (which fell in January 1949), while the Nationalist capital, Nanjing (now in Jiangsu—the city fell in April), was not far downriver on the Chang Jiang, just beyond Anhui's south-east (under the Republic, much of Anhui was included in Nan Zhili, the directly administered area around Nanjing). This history contributed to the brief emergence of two provinces, North Anhui and South Anhui, from the time of the Communist conquest in July 1948, but they were merged in 1952.

From the 1950s the province's main upheaval was to be the rapid industrialization of many of its cities and other experiences common to the rest of China, such as the Cultural Revolution. In the 1990s the province appeared in the news as a result of the 1993 anti-corruption campaign, the results of which were ironic given the traditional reputation of the people of Anhui. An investigation involving 10,000 inspectors eventually found over 300,000 civil servants guilty of misappropriating for personal use some US $140m. in government funds—although it was reported that most of the money was returned, many of those convicted retaining their jobs.

Economy

Anhui is an agricultural province, although many of the cities witnessed rapid development of industry in the mid-20th century and there are significant coal reserves. The regional gross domestic product (GDP) in 2000, at current prices, was 303,824m. yuan or 4,867 yuan per head (the national average was 7,078 yuan per head and, of the northern and eastern provinces, only Jiangxi was lower). In real terms, GDP had grown strongly by just over 14% annually in

1995–96 and by 12.7% in 1997, but was more in line with the national average in each of the three years thereafter, at between 8.1% and 8.5%. Infrastructure is fairly well developed (although the volume of freight traffic declined in the late 1990s), with 44,493 km of highways in the province at the end of 2000, of which 470 km were national expressway, 264 km first-class highway and 6,347 km second-class highway. At the same time there were 1,842.9 km of railway in operation. Anhui also remains an important transit route on the inland waterways system, with both the Chang Jiang (River Yangzi) and the Huai He (traditionally, a more important transport artery for the north than the Huang He—Yellow River) flowing through its territory, contributing to the 5,611 km of navigable waterways in the province. Five of China's 23 major inland ports are in the province: Wuhu, Anqing, Tongling, Chizhou and Maanshan. In 2000 Anhui produced 35,544m. kWh of electricity. Anhui's capital, Hefei, is the site of the prestigious University of Science and Technology of China, although, by contrast, the predominantly rural population has the highest rate of illiteracy in eastern China. However, between the two most recent censuses Anhui was the region in the People's Republic to record the best improvement in the literacy rate, with the proportion of illiterate or semi-literate people in the population (aged 15 years or over) at 24.4% in 1990, but only 10.1% in 2000.

The primary sector of the economy contributed a high 24.1% to provincial GDP in 2000 (and accounted for an equally high 59.8% of employed persons), mainly because Anhui's climate and soil have long made the province rich in agricultural potential. Although flood and drought have often blighted fulfilment (studies of historical records reveal 8,614 natural disasters in the period between 960 and 1949), Anhui is now one of the richest agricultural provinces in China. It boasts some well-known products such as grapes, pears and pomegranates, Huang Shan green tea and Keemum black tea, and livestock including Fuyang yellow cows, Dingyuan pigs and Luan white geese. Over two-fifths of the province's land area is cultivated (597,170 sq km in 1996), accounting for 4.6% of the nation's total, although Anhui occupies only 1.5% of the total area. The total area sown with farm crops was put at 9.0m. ha in 2000, 5.8% of the national total. Less land was given to orchards than anywhere else in central China. Rice and wheat accounted for the largest share of the sown area, followed by plants grown for their oil (rape and groundnut). The major staple crops are rice, wheat, maize, beans, sorghum and sweet potato, while cash crops included cotton, tobacco, groundnuts (peanuts), sesame, rape, tea, hemp and, of course, fruit. Other agricultural products of Anhui include tung oil, raw lacquer and silk. In 2000 the largest harvest was of rice, at 12.22m. metric tons, while all foodgrains (including other cereals, pulses and tubers) together took the yield to 24.72m. tons. The same year produced 1.57m. tons of rapeseed, 1.11m. tons of groundnuts, 1.11m. tons of fruit (mainly pears and apples) and 24,563 tons of mulberry-silkworm cocoons. In 2000 there were 5.5m. head of cattle and buffaloes, 7.9m. goats and 18.6m. pigs. Livestock products in the same year included 3.0m. tons of meat (mainly pork), 41,000 tons of cows' milk and 1.1m. tons of eggs. The province possesses significant forest reserves (there is almost as much woodland as farmland), rich as a source not only of timber but also of the herbs used in traditional Chinese medicine (the market at Bozhou, in the far north-west, is one of the most important trading centres for traditional medicine in central China). The main forest products, by volume, are tea-oil seeds, pine resin and tung-oil seeds. There is also a flourishing fishing industry. Anhui is famed for freshwater crab and silver fish, notably from Chao Hu (Lake Chao). In 2000 the total fish catch was 1.31m. tons, most of it cultured, while crabs, shrimps, prawns and shellfish contributed a further 237,900 tons. The gross output value of farming, animal husbandry, forestry and fishing in 2000 was 122,000m. yuan.

The secondary sector of the economy accounted for 42.7% of GDP and 15.8% of employed persons in 2000. This industrial sector has been helped by extractive activity based on coal and iron, with Anhui being one of the leading coal producers in eastern China. In 2000 the province produced 47m. metric tons of coal, about 5% of the national total. The coalfield lies to the north of Hainan, in northern Anhui. Exploitation of such resources lies at the heart of the province's industrial policy, which seeks to emulate the Ruhr area of Germany. Industry itself has only been developed in Anhui since the establishment of the People's Republic—between 1949 and 1980 industrial output grew by an annual average of 12.2% per year. It continued to expand at similarly high rates thereafter, but the sector remained structurally weak because of the predominance of small-scale enterprises. In 2000 there were 3,680 industrial enterprises (all state units and all non-state ones with an annual sales income in excess of 5m. yuan) recorded in the province, of which 193 were large and 436 medium-sized. The gross industrial output value of these enterprises totalled 166,144m. yuan, with just under one-half (48%) of them engaged in heavy industry. The main industrial centres are in northern Anhui and along the Chang Jiang, and, despite the heavy and large-scale industries based on local coal and iron, most industrial activity continues the tendency to be small-scale or to be based on the processing of agricultural production. Anhui is noted for several alcoholic beverages, including beer and Xiaoxian wine from the north, and for producing the 'four treasures' of traditional scholarship, notably Anhui ink sticks (also Shexian ink slabs, Xuan paper and Xuan brushes). Wuhu, on the Chang Jiang, produces wrought-iron pictures. Some major manufactures are household refrigerators, iron and steel, fertilizers and other chemicals, machine tools and some commercial motor vehicles. Construction is a powerful motivator of industrial activity and the output value of this sector was 30,282.4m. yuan in 2000 and it alone provided 6.4% of GDP in that year.

The services sector (which in 2000 provided 33.2% of GDP and 24.4% of paid employment) has a long history of strong activity in Anhui, particularly in the south, the location of the Huang Shan (effectively a tourist destination for over 1,200 years) and from where the Huizhou merchants dominated trade under the Ming and Qing dynasties. Trade and catering remains the main contributor to the services sector (10.4% of GDP), followed by transport and communications services (5.9%). Although long established, tourism is not as significant a contributor to the economy of Anhui as it is in some provinces. In 1998 the province attracted 1.8m. tourists, of which almost one-half were foreign, although this was less than the 2.9m. (over two-fifths were foreign) in the previous year. The Asian financial crisis that had begun in mid-1997 brought contraction to the industry, which saw foreign visitor numbers in 1998 still exceed the total number of tourists in 1990. Official statistics (measuring international tourism in person-times) record an increase from a total of

84,700 (24% foreign) in 1990 to 318,400 (53% foreign) in 2000. Apart from the Huang Shan, Anhui can boast the sacred heights of Jiuhua Shan, and natural attractions like protected wildlife species, such as the South China tiger, the rhesus monkey, the Chinese (or Yangzi) alligator and the Yangzi river dolphin (baiji). Historical and cultural sites are mainly to be found in southern Anhui; the town of Fenyang is famous for originating the Flower Drum Opera tradition.

The total value of commodities originating in Anhui in 2000 was US $2,119.4m., while imports to Anhui were worth $1,570.4m., both having increased significantly on the previous few years. On balance, the province's international transactions did not earn a significant proportion of the national earnings of foreign exchange. This feature of the economy is a disadvantage for the finances of government at the provincial level. In 2000 the final statement of government revenue put Anhui's contribution at 17,871.87m. yuan (of which, the operations tax raised 17.9%, agricultural taxes 16.9%, value added tax 14.7% and income tax on enterprises 13.1%). Government expenditure in the province, meanwhile, totalled 32,347.28m. yuan (16.7% of this on education, 12.7% on capital construction and 10.7% on government administration). The provincial economy also benefited from foreign direct investment of $318.47m. in 2000, although this amounted to less than 1% of the national total.

Directory

Governor: WANG JISHAN (acting); Office of the Provincial People's Government, Hefei.

Secretary of the Anhui Provincial Committee of the Chinese Communist Party: WANG TAIHUA; Office of the Secretary, CCP Secretariat, Hefei.

Chairman of the Standing Committee of the People's Congress of Anhui: MENG FULIN; Office of the Chairman, Congress Secretariat, Hefei.

Chairman of the Anhui Provincial Committee of the Chinese People's Political Consultative Conference: FANG ZHAOXIANG; Office of the Chairman, CPPCC Secretariat, Hefei.

Fujian

The Province of Fujian (Fukien or Hokkien—literally, 'happy establishment') lies on the south-eastern coast of the People's Republic of China, facing the island of Taiwan (Formosa) across the Taiwan Strait. The administration in Taiwan ('Republic of China') not only controls the territory of that island province, but also Jinmen (Chinmen or Quemoy), Mazu (Matsu) and some other smaller islands that are traditionally part of Fujian. Neighbouring provinces of the People's Republic are Guangdong to the south-west, Jiangxi inland, to the north-west, and Zhejiang to the north. Fujian has a total area of some 121,300 sq km (46,820 sq miles).

A mountainous province, Fujian's hilly terrain lies crumpled between the heights along the inland borders (the Wuyi Shan and, in the north, the Xianxia Ling) and the narrow coastal plains. The highest point is on the border with Jiangxi, at Huanggang Shan (2,157 m or 7,079 feet), in the north. Other ranges include the Daiyun, the Jiufeng, the Daimao and the Boping. The main river is the Min, for which the province was originally named from the third century BC, and it drains about one-half of Fujian. The climate is mild, subtropical and subject to the monsoons, making it relatively humid. The average annual rainfall, most of which usually falls during the spring (April) and then in the summer (June–August), in 2000 was 1,560 mm (61 inches) in Fuzhou, making the city the third wettest provincial capital in China (exceeded only by the capitals of Hainan and Guangdong). Average daily temperatures range between 5°C and 13°C (41°–55°F) in January and 25°C and 30°C (77°–86°F) in July. Elevation and distance from the coast affect weather conditions.

At the time of the national census of 1 November 2000 Fujian had a total population of 34.71m., making it one of the less populous provinces, but one with a higher-than-average population growth rate (since 1990). It is also one of the smaller provinces (only Hainan, Zhejiang and Jiangsu cover less ground), and the population density in 2000 was 282 per sq km, placing Fujian towards the middle of the ranking in this category. The province has also spawned a large overseas population claiming descent from the sea-faring Chinese of Fujian, and most of the ethnic Chinese in Taiwan make a similar claim. However, although Fujian lies in eastern China, the region with the greatest preponderance of Han Chinese (or, as is often affected in southern China, Tang Chinese), it is the province with the greatest proportion of minority ethnicities in that region—still only 1.7% in 2000. There are a few She and some Gaoshan (most of whom live on Taiwan), but perhaps of more significance are the large numbers of the Hakka (Kejia), a Han minority who fled from the north many centuries ago. The main local dialect, however, is Minnanhua ('language of south of the Min'), which is essentially the same as Taiwanese, although the official language is, of course, Mandarin Chinese. In terms of religion, traditionally Fujian is very eclectic, with Buddhism and the native religions joined by a large Muslim community centred on Quanzhou—the city was reckoned to include a population of some 100,000 Arabs under the Mongol Yuan dynasty. The island of Meizhou is revered by Taoists as the birthplace of the widely venerated sea-goddess, Mazu (known as Tin Hau in Hong Kong or Thien Hau in Viet Nam).

The urban population in 2000 was put at 41.6% of the total, although there were only two cities with populations of over 0.5m. (most had under 200,000), those being the provincial capital of Fuzhou and the separate planning city (special economic zone) of Xiamen (Amoy). Fuzhou, on the northern coast, at the mouth of the Min, had a population put at some 1.7m. at the end of 2000 (including all areas under the city administration, there was a total population of 5.9m.), while Xiamen, on the southern coast, had an urban population of 662,200 (the greater city area had a population of 1.3m.). In all there were 23 cities, of which nine were of prefectural status, as well as 46 other counties in Fujian. Other major cities include two other old coastal centres, Quanzhou to the north-east of Xiamen and Zhangzhou to the west, as well as Putian, which lies midway between Quanzhou and Fuzhou, and, inland, four cites parallel to the coast: Nanping, on the Min; then, southwards, Sanming and Yongan; and, finally, Longan.

History

Fujian became incorporated into the Chinese Empire when the Qin ended the era of the Warring States in the third century BC, although it was another century before the region was firmly under imperial control, when a Han emperor finally conquered a rival local kingdom of snake-worshipping, jungle warriors, Minyue. Another minority group of Han Chinese to leave archaeological evidence in Fujian, though at a much later period, was that of the Hakka. They built 'earth buildings' (*tulou*) in the province upon first settling here (as refugees from Henan) in about the 12th century AD. At around the same time the flourishing maritime trade of the Fujian coast had attracted large numbers of Muslim Arab settlers, whose main centre was in the great port of Quanzhou. By now Fujian had long been an integral part of China, but its history was also particularly influenced by its sea-faring and commercial traditions.

From the third century AD Fuzhou (originally known as Yecheng, the 'smelting city') became an important port, specializing in tea exports, but was soon eclipsed by Quanzhou, which, under the Song and Yuan dynasties, was one of the busiest ports in the world. It was at its height at the time of Marco Polo, the Venetian (Italian) explorer (who called the city Zaiton), in the 13th century, but went into decline with Ming restrictions on maritime commerce from the 15th century. The whole province suffered from these regulations, although the accompanying large-scale emigration created a diaspora still important today (many went to Taiwan). Fujian, therefore, seconds Guangdong as the origin of most Chinese overseas. Meanwhile, the Ming emperors had established Xiamen (also known as Amoy) as a fortified port in the 14th century, and in the 17th century the city was to become the refuge of the dynasty as they fled the Manchu (Qing) invaders. The port was one of the bases of the powerful trading and privateering Zheng family, a son of which house, Chenggong, became the most eminent loyalist general of the displaced dynasty. Zheng Chenggong is more familiarly known to history as Guoxingye (Koxinga), 'lord of the imperial surname', owing to him being granted the use of the Ming emperors' family name, Zhu, because of his loyal support after their defeat by the Manchus in 1644. When finally driven from the Fujian mainland, the pirate-general moved his base to Taiwan shortly before his death in 1662, although the Ming succession had by now petered out; Taiwan was eventually seized from the Zhengs by a Qing force in 1683. Meanwhile, Fujian was administratively united with Zhejiang in 1656, until the end of Qing power in 1911.

Another feature of Guoxinge's conquest of Taiwan was that he forcibly displaced the Dutch in the process. The Dutch and other Europeans had followed the Portuguese into the region during the 17th century, and Xiamen was a favoured site for trading bases. However, this was closed to foreigners in the 1750s and it was almost one century before Europeans forced themselves back into the Chinese market. In 1841 a British naval force of 38 ships sailed into Xiamen and forced the port to open. The 1842 Treaty of Nanjing, which ended the so-called Opium War between the United Kingdom and the Chinese Empire, therefore made Xiamen one of the first treaty ports (along with Fuzhou in Fujian and three other cities elsewhere in China). Other powers soon followed the British into China and the island of Gulang Yu, in Xiamen, became a foreign enclave.

From November 1933 until February 1934 a People's Government in Fuzhou was in revolt against the republican Government, in one of the last examples of the Communists attempting to use the urban proletariat rather than the rural peasantry to further the revolutionary cause. The Guomindang regained control, but the city was seized outright by foreigners, the Japanese, between 1941 and 1945 (the Japanese had slowly advanced into the province from Shantou, Guangdong, which they had occupied in 1938). Strife in this part of Fujian did not cease with the Second World War. Off shore are the islands of Jinmen and Xiao Jinmen, which were occupied and retained by Nationalist troops when the Communists took over most of the rest of province in October 1949. These islands, and a few others in the Strait, remain under the jurisdiction of the Taiwan-based 'Republic of China', and have been a focus of potential conflict with the People's Republic, in 1954, 1958 and 1996, for instance. Generally, however, Taiwan in the late 20th century meant more to the related people of Fujian as a source of investment. In 1979 Xiamen was among the first four special economic zones (and the only one outside Guangdong) established by the central Government. Since then it has attracted increasing amounts of Taiwanese and foreign investment, as have, more recently, Fuzhou and other parts of Fujian. It was for just this reason that the Government encouraged links between Chinese communities abroad and their ancestral homes.

Economy

The gross domestic product (GDP) of Fujian province in 2000 was 392,007m. yuan, in current prices. In real terms, this was growth (mainly led by industry) of 9.5% on the previous year—a lower rate of economic growth than the 10.0% of the previous year, the 11.4% of 1998 and the 14.5% of 1997. With GDP per head in 2000 at 11,601 yuan, Fujian was the fourth wealthiest province in the People's Republic. Much of this growth was fuelled by investment from Taiwan and elsewhere abroad, while the principal centres are the provincial capital of Fuzhou and one of the oldest special economic zones in China, Xiamen. The gross industrial output value and the total of wages paid is similar in value in both cities, as is local-government revenue and investment in fixed assets, although the capital remains ahead in population, the amount of savings deposits, and volumes of freight (especially air freight) and passenger traffic. The province has well-developed infrastructure, particularly its road network, with the total length of highways at the end of 2000 reaching 51,073 km, of which 345 km were expressways and 406 km first-class highways. At the same time Fujian also possessed 874 km of railway in operation and 3,701 km of navigable waterways. During 2000 the province had produced 40,373m. kWh of electricity and, with 48.4% of that from hydroelectric generation, Fujian was the third largest hydroelectric producer in China in 2000. Despite the above-average population growth between censuses, the educational infrastructure succeeded in lowering the illiteracy rate from 15.6% in 1990 to 7.2% in 2000.

The primary sector of the economy only contributed 16.3% of GDP in 2000, but, at the end of the year, employed 46.9% of employed persons in Fujian. The total area sown with farm crops during that year in Fujian was 2.79m. ha (1.8% of the national total). Rice alone accounted for 43.8% of this area (one-half as much again as the other grains put together), fruit orchards 20.0%, vegetables 19.3% and tubers 13.2%, while tea plantations covered a further 129,200 ha (4.6%). The major crops by harvested tonnage were rice (6.33m. metric tons), tubers (1.66m. tons) and sugarcane (0.83m. tons—making Fujian one of the main sugar producers outside the more southerly provinces). The province is China's main tea producer (125,969 tons in 2000—including the prestigious Wuyi Shan variety), and a leading fruit grower (3.56m. tons in 2000—mainly citrus and bananas, Fujian being the most northerly of the eastern provinces to grow the latter). At the end of 2000 there were 11.09m. pigs, 1.11m. cattle and buffaloes and 962,000 goats in Fujian. Most of the meat produced, therefore, is pork (1.07m. tons in 2000), while 99,000 tons of milk (mainly cows' milk), 0.41m. tons of poultry eggs and 5,000 tons of honey were also produced in that year. Fujian's wooded hillsides mean that the province is a major timber producer, although other forest products include pine resin, tea-oil seeds and tung-oil seeds. Fishing produced a total catch of 5.28m. tons in 2000, of which fish accounted for 2.17m. tons (over three-quarters from the sea), and shellfish and crustaceans 2.73m. tons. Much of the shellfish and crustacean catch is artificially cultured.

The secondary sector is the largest contributor to provincial GDP (43.7% in 2000), although it only accounts for 24.5% of employed persons. Industry alone contributed 37.5% of GDP and construction 6.2%. Extractive industry is not as important as processing, although the province possesses some mineral reserves (in 2000 some 4m. metric tons of coal were produced). In 2000 Fujian had 6,011 enumerated industrial enterprises (i.e. all those owned by the state and all others above a certain size), together achieving a gross output value of 261,612m. yuan at current prices, of which the state sector accounted for 1,367 enterprises and 32.7% of the total gross output value. Foreign funds had been received by 615 enterprises, while 2,076 received investment from Hong Kong, Macao and Taiwan. Most firms were engaged in light industry (3,656 in number, accounting for 52.2% of gross output value). Activities include agricultural processing (most notably that of sugar), textiles and paper, and specific products include beer, computers, colour television sets, glass and some chemicals and iron and steel.

The tertiary sector accounted for 40.0% of provincial GDP (mainly transport and communications—alone employing 172,000 people in 2000—and trade) and 28.6% of employed persons in 2000. That year Fujian exported commodities worth US $13,623m. (a significant increase on 1999, a year that had seen a slight decline on the previous year), against imports of $9,334m. Particularly given the importance of foreign business in Fujian, it is no surprise to find that tourism is an important activity, with international tourism contributing to the province's impressive foreign-exchange record (see below). As measured by person-times in the official Chinese statistics, international tourism increased by more than one-half between 1995 and 2000, reaching 1.61m. (30.8% foreigners) in the latter year. Foreign-exchange earnings from tourism increased steadily through the 1990s, to reach US $894m. in 2000, making Fujian the best regional earner after Beijing, Shanghai and Guangdong (undoubtedly helped by business travellers). Sights include, for example, the beauty of the Wuyi Shan scenery, the colonial legacy of Xiamen (especially Gulang Yu island) and the venerable trading past of Quanzhou.

According to the final government statement for 2000, total revenue in Fujian was 23,410.61m. yuan, of which 24.9% was provided by the operations tax, 15.1% by value added tax and 13.8% by an income tax on enterprises. Expenditure by the provincial government (final statement, 2000) was, in total, 32,418.39m. yuan, with 9.0% going on capital expenditure, 19.1% on education, 8.3% on general government administration and 6.6% on the justice system. The levels of foreign direct investment (actually used) in Fujian are quite significant, amounting to US $3,431.91m. (8.5% of the total invested in all the regions of the People's Republic) in 2000 and $4,024.03m. in the previous year.

Directory

Governor: LU ZHANGONG (acting); Office of the Provincial People's Government, Fuzhou.

Secretary of the Fujian Provincial Committee of the Chinese Communist Party: SONG DEFU; Office of the Secretary, CCP Secretariat, Fuzhou.

Chairman of the Standing Committee of the People's Congress of Fujian: YUAN QITONG; Office of the Chairman, Congress Secretariat, Fuzhou.

Chairman of the Fujian Provincial Committee of the Chinese People's Political Consultative Conference: CHEN MINGYI; Office of the Chairman, CPPCC Secretariat, Fuzhou.

Gansu

The Province of Gansu (Kansu), 'pleasant respectful', is a long province stretching north-westwards from central China to touch the northern international border of the People's Republic with Mongolia. The Chinese autonomous region of Inner Mongolia (Nei Mongol) is to the east, lying north and east of the gently arcing corridor that connects north-western Gansu and south-eastern Gansu. Also east of the corridor, but north of the main part of south-eastern Gansu is another autonomous region, Ningxia (which formed part of Gansu until 1958). Here, directly to the east, Gansu then abuts into Shaanxi, an ancient province. To the south lies Sichuan and to the west Qinghai, which Gansu curves around and ends to the north of, while west of this north-western part of Gansu is Xinjiang, also an autonomous region. Over 1,000 km (620 miles) in length, Gansu has an area of 366,500 sq km (141,470 sq miles), making it larger than all but four other provinces, as well as being larger than two of the five autonomous regions.

The geography of the province is defined by the ancient Gansu or Hexi ('west of the river') Corridor. The most populous part of Gansu lies on the middle reaches of the Huang He (Yellow River), where it descends eastwards out of the highlands and crosses the waist of the province at the start of its great loop northwards. Here on the loess plains is the heartland of Chinese civilization, while to the north-west of the Huang He begins a conduit for trade and travel to the western regions and beyond. The Corridor is strung along a series of oases, lying between the great heights of the Qilian Shan (which here edge the Tibet–Qinghai plateau) and the bleak Mongolian plateau. This is the start of the great 'Silk Road' of the past, wending its way between the inhospitable Scylla and Charybdis of the Qilian Shan and the Gobi Desert. Some 70% of the province is mountain and plateau, which has a significant effect on the weather. Gansu generally has a temperate monsoon climate, but this shifts to more continental extremes further towards the north-west, and becomes more markedly subtropical and humid in the south-eastern extremities. The Qilian highlands are cold and more humid than the remainder of the north-west. Generally, Gansu is dry (which has helped the preservation of its antiquities), with average annual rainfall ranging from only 30 mm to 869 mm (1.2–34.2 inches); Lanzhou (Lanchow), the provincial capital, received 360 mm in 2000. Most rain falls in the summer (over one-half in about June–August) and to the south of the 37th parallel (a latitude of 37°N), which crosses Gansu near the narrowest part of the province, roughly where the Great Wall first enters from the east. Average minimum and maximum temperatures in January ranged from -14°C to 3°C (6.8°–37.4°F), and in July from 11°C to 27°C (51.8°–80.6°F).

The total population of Gansu province at the national census of 1 November 2000 was 25.62m., giving it a population density of only 70 per sq km, the lowest of any province but Qinghai (and lower than two of the autonomous regions). Minority nationalities constituted 8.7% of this total, the two main officially recognized ethnic groups of the province (each with an autonomous prefecture as a centre) being Hui and Tibetan (Xizangzu). Other groups represented over large parts of China include some Mongols (Menggu), Kazakhs and Manchus (Manzu), as well as a few of the Salars of Qinghai. Groups exclusive to or mainly based in Gansu include the Baoan (Bonan) and the Yugur (each with populations of about 12,000), and the Dongxiang (about 370,000, some in Xinjiang, but most based on Linxia; the Dongxiangs speak an Altaic language—they were originally moved here from Central Asia in the 13th century) and the Tu (190,000 of them, mainly in Gansu; the Tus are noted for speaking very little Mandarin, relying on their own Mongolian or Monguor language). Most groups generally have some facility with official Northern Mandarin Chinese. The Hui people are a traditional Muslim presence in the province, while the ancient dominance of Buddhism (which arrived in China down the Silk Road and produced two of China's four largest temple groups or grottoes) is still attested to by the Tibetan Buddhists. Xiahe, south of Linxia, is an important Buddhist centre, the location of one of the six principal monasteries of the dominant Geluk pa ('Yellow Hat' sect) of lamaism. In addition, the province contains the most sacred of Taoist mountains, Kongdong Shan, which is on the border with Ningxia Hui, not far from Pingliang in south-eastern Gansu.

At the 2000 census 24.0% of the population were counted as urban. The largest city and the seat of government is Lanzhou, which sits on the Huang He and claims to be located at the geographical centre of China. The city, excluding the country districts under its administration, had a population of 1.6m. in 2000. All other cities had populations of less than 0.5m. The other main urban centres are, in the south, Tianshui (south-east of Lanzhou), Pingliang (north-east of Tianshui, beyond a narrow neck of land crossing the Liupan Shan, where Gansu widens into an enclave beyond the mountains) and Linxia (just south-west of Lanzhou); in the north, along the Corridor and the main transport routes, are strung oasis towns such as Wuwei and Zhangye, with the city of Jinchang just to the north-west of Wuwei, on the edge of the desert, and culminating in the closely grouped cities of Jiayuguan and Yumen (Laojunmiao). From the early Ming period Jiayuguan was considered the official end of the Great Wall and the last major outpost of the Empire in the west, although the Wall (and imperial authority) had earlier extended, in a haphazard fashion, further along the Silk Road, to reach Dunhuang in the far west. There are 14 urban centres with official city status in Gansu, of which five are ranked as prefectures and two at county level as minority nationality autonomous areas, according to the administrative hierarchy. In all, Gansu is divided into 14 prefectures (including the Gannan or Southern Gansu Tibetan Autonomous Prefecture, based at Xiahe, and the Hui Autonomous Prefecture of Linxia) and 76 counties (21 of which are reported to have autonomous status). In the autonomous areas the minority nationalities comprised 56% of the population in 2000.

History

Gansu is isolated and barren and has long been on the edge of central control, but it is the start of the great 'Silk Road', a corridor of oases allowing China and the lands to the west to trade in commodities, armies, and artistic, intellectual and religious ideas. The early Han first developed the region and the beginning of the Silk Road through northern Gansu, forging links even with the distant empire of Rome before the time of Christ. Widespread demographic upheavals from about the second century AD contributed to a decline in this trade, although at this time Buddhism came down the Silk Road into China. Gansu possesses a number of sites showing the development of Buddhism in China, and the movement may have benefited from the uncertainties of this time of disunity and upheaval—with the early Tang the religion became widespread throughout the Empire.

The most dramatic interruption of the trade routes came with the Toba invasions of the fourth century. The Gansu region was then dominated by several dynasties of Toba or mixed Toba-Chinese descent. Finally, one such dynasty, that of the Sui, reunited northern and southern China in the latter part of the sixth century. Two ruthless emperors effectively rebuilt the Empire and extended its frontiers, although the necessary policies contributed to the unpopularity of the dynasty. The first Sui, the Emperor Wendi, certainly succeeded in securing the north-western frontiers around Gansu, with effective military strikes and the reinforcing and extending of the Great Wall, and by marriage, taking a Xiongnu (Hiung-nu, Huns or, more loosely, any northern nomads) empress. The son of this marriage, Yangdi, later suffered a defeat in Turkestan, to the west of Gansu, and the failure on this border as well as the exactions for a war in Korea resulted in his murder and the deposition of the dynasty in 618. The great Tang dynasty continued Sui policies in the north-west, extending the Wall as far as Dunhuang, the strategic town where the Silk Road first diverged (and a pre-eminent trading post and Buddhist centre for 1,000 years from the fourth century), and stretching the Empire into the 'western regions' beyond. However, the Turkic tribes of inner Asia were still strong and, to the south, the Tibetans (Xizangzu) were a menace to Chinese hegemony. In 751 Muslim forces crushed the Chinese armies in Central Asia and in 781 the Tibetans occupied Dunhuang (holding it until 847). The main imperial challenge in the region until 840, however, was that of the Uygurs (Wei Wuer, Uyghurs or Uigurs).

The next power in this part of the north-west was the Tangut state, which came to be known as Xi Xia or Western Xia by the Chinese. The Buddhist Tanguts, a people related to the Tibetans, built a powerful polity in Gansu and Ningxia Hui in the 10th and 11th centuries, and adopted the Xia dynastic name in 1038, as part of an attempt to conquer China that was defeated in 1044. During the 11th century they participated in a three-way 'balance of power' that dominated northern China. An already weak Xi Xia was annihilated by the Mongols in 1227. It was the Mongols, reigning in China as the Yuan dynasty, who, therefore, finally reunited the Hexi Corridor and the north-west with the rest of the Empire. However, Chinese power in the 'western regions' from the late 13th century was a Mongol achievement and, four years after the Ming dynasty assumed the 'mandate of Heaven', when a fortress was built at Jiayuguan in 1372 it was considered the terminus of the Wall and the limit of empire. By then Mongol rule had added to the Muslim population that had already settled along the Silk Road with settlers from Central Asia.

Under the Manchu dynasty of the Qing, Chinese expansion into the 'new frontier' of Xinjiang resumed in the 18th century. Qinghai—apart from Xining and its environs, to the west of Lanzhou, which have been under Chinese influence for far longer—as part of the Tibetan world also fell increasingly under imperial suzerainty from the 18th century. Gansu was the base for much of this penetration into the north-west and, once Xinjiang became a province in the 1880s, it ceased to be a border territory, although for administrative purposes it had been part of Shengan (with Shaanxi and Shanxi) since 1749 (until 1912). An undeveloped area, it was also a focus of Muslim settlement, creating a religious divide that exacerbated social and economic tensions. The sinicized Hui (Huihui or Dungans) were treated with suspicion by their more orthodox Han neighbours, and serious Muslim revolts in Gansu and Shaanxi between 1862 and 1878 devastated large parts of the region. Although the Hui population was severely reduced in the suppression of the revolts, enough remained to cause further disruption on the borders of Gansu and Qinghai in 1895. Such incidents have contributed to an enduring official Chinese suspicion of Muslim separatism.

At best the whole region was only under tenuous central authority and, with the fall of the Qing in 1912, Gansu and the rest of the north-west was very much an area competed over by rival warlords. In the mid-1920s Gansu was part of the territory controlled by Feng Yuxiang, a warlord based in Shaanxi, who had kept the region largely free of strife. His rule survived until the end of the decade, by accommodation with the republican authorities, but he was defeated when he broke with the Guomindang. Gansu itself was in revolt between 1928 and 1932. The Nationalists retained influence in the area until 1937, although Gansu was never directly threatened by the Japanese advance. The province only began to be integrated properly with the rest of China after the Communist victory in 1949 (they occupied Gansu in August–September). Industrialization was helped by the expansion of the rail network, most crucially the completion of the link between Lanzhou and Urumqi (Xinjiang), much of it along the Gansu Corridor, in 1963. Between 1950 and 1954 it had been united with its neighbours under the North-West Administrative Council, while in 1958 an autonomous Hui region was formed in Ningxia and separated from Gansu province.

Economy

Gansu, despite its historic associations with the major overland trade route of Asia, and its potential mineral reserves, remains one of the poorest provinces. Consistent real economic growth of over 8% annually in the second half of the 1990s, has taken gross domestic product (GDP) in the province to 98,336m. yuan (current prices, 2000) or 3,838 yuan per head. Of all the regional economies in China, the figure for GDP per head is lower only in Guizhou, far to the south. Infrastructure is sparse for the area covered, but includes transport links important for the whole of China. At the end of 2000 the highway system totalled 39,344 km (although this included only 13 km of expressway and 75 km of first-class highway) and navigable inland waterways 1,306 km. The total length of railways in operation was 2,318 km, with the importance of Gansu coming not so much from the extent of its network as from the role of Lanzhou, in particular, as a transport hub and of the Hexi Corridor as a conduit of the great 1,892-km line to Urumqi (Xinjiang). The latter was one of the early achievements of the People's Republic and opened the province to development, encouraging the massive growth of the ancient strategic garrison city of Lanzhou. Although the hilly terrain limits transport infrastructure, it has made Gansu rich in hydroelectric potential. In 2000 40.4% of the 25,352m. kWh of electricity generated in the province was by this method. However, the illiteracy rate is the highest in the People's Republic after Xizang (Tibet) and Qinghai (14.34% in 2000), though it showed one of the best improvements since 1990. Rural illiteracy, particularly among the minority nationalities, remains the main problem.

The primary sector of the provincial economy is not a growth area and, although it only accounted for 19.7% of GDP in 2000, this is a problem for 59.7% of employed persons who work in the sector. Climate means that the main cereal crop is not rice but wheat: of the total sown area in Gansu (3.74m. ha in 2000), 74.8% is for cereals, 31.9% for wheat alone. Much of the rest is planted with corn (maize) and millet. Tubers, vegetables, soybeans, rapeseed and fruits are also important. Crop yields in 2000 included 5.71m. metric tons of cereals (2.66m. tons of wheat, 2.11m. tons of maize), 1.05m. tons of tubers and 1.22m. tons of fruits (over one-half of which are apples). Gansu is a major walnut producer (20,095 tons in 2000). Livestock numbers in 2000 amounted to 11.63m. head of sheep and goats (8.62m. sheep), 5.48m. pigs, 3.43m. cattle and buffalo, 1.25m. donkeys, 656,000 mules (more than any other region of the People's Republic), 264,000 horses and 22,000 camels. The total output in 2000 was 589,000 tons of meat (389,000 tons of which was pork), 137,000 tons of milk (mainly cows' milk), 14,145 tons of sheep wool (most of it fine and semi-fine wool), as well as 1,559 tons of goats' wool and 503 tons of cashmere, and 112,000 tons of poultry eggs. The province also produces 14,100 tons of fish (freshwater, obviously), 95% of which catch is farmed.

The secondary sector is the main contributor to the economy, providing 44.7% of GDP in 2000 (construction accounts for about one-quarter of this).

The sector only employs 13.8% of employed persons. The development of industry, which has been state-led, has recently been helped by the abundant mineral resources now being exploited—these include iron ore, nickel, cobalt, zinc, platinum, selenium and hydrocarbons (in 2000 Gansu produced 16m. metric tons of coal, almost 6m. tons of crude petroleum and 20m. cu m of natural gas). Heavy industry and the largest companies dominate the sector. In 2000 the number of industrial enterprises in Gansu was 2,851, together achieving a gross output value of 84,058m. yuan, at current prices. Heavy industry accounted for 58% of the enterprises and 84% of the gross output value. There were 85 large enterprises (62% of the total gross output value) and 110 medium-sized enterprises (6%). The state sector included 34% of the enterprises and accounted for 76% of the gross output value; collective-owned industrial enterprises accounted for a surprisingly high 47% of enterprises (though only 15% of gross output value). Beer and cigarettes are produced in quantity. There are iron, steel, glass-making, chemicals and plastics industries, and Gansu is the only producer of electronic integrated circuits in the north-west. The total output value of construction activity, a major contributor to industrial GDP, remained fairly constant through the 1990s, and was at 12,512m. yuan in 2000.

The tertiary or services sector accounted for 35.6% of GDP and 26.5% of employed persons in 2000. Wholesale and retail trade and catering services (which alone contributed 11.6% of total GDP) was worth slightly more than the next two largest contributors to GDP (transport and communications, and finance and insurance) together. The transport system, especially the railways, is also an important employer. Tourism is a vital cash contributor to a tradition-ally poor economy. Sights include sections of the Great Wall, the well preserved grottoes of Bingling Si on the Huang He or other Buddhist sites, some dating from as early as the fourth century, royal tombs, and desert scenery or other natural attractions such as the wildlife (giant pandas, golden monkeys, red deer, snow roosters and wild donkeys). International tourist visits in 2000 reached 213,100 (143,400 by foreigners). Helped by the growth in the number of visiting foreigners, foreign-exchange earnings from tourism steadily rose over the 1990s, from US $6m. in 1990 to $55m. in 2000.

Commodity trade showed a slight fall in exports in 1999, but recovered strongly in 2000, only for the value of imports to leap more dramatically: US $420.8m. was earned for exports and $270.8m. paid for imports. Foreign direct investment totalled $62.4m. in 2000. The final statement of government revenue by region in 2000, put the total for Gansu at 6,128.49m. yuan, of which 1,589.95m. yuan came from the operations tax and 1,194.71m. yuan from value added tax, but only 609.57m. yuan from enterprises' income tax (this was rather less than the national average). The expenditure total for 2000 was put at some three times the amount of revenue, 18,823.22m. yuan—14.6% went on education, 10.9% on capital construction and 10.4% on the general administration.

Directory

Governor: LU HAO; Office of the Provincial People's Government, Lanzhou.

Secretary of the Gansu Provincial Committee of the Chinese Communist Party: SONG ZHAOSU; Office of the Secretary, CCP Secretariat, Lanzhou.

Chairman of the Standing Committee of the People's Congress of Gansu: LU KEJIAN; Office of the Chairman, Congress Secretariat, Lanzhou.

Chairman of the Gansu Provincial Committee of the Chinese People's Political Consultative Conference: YANG ZHENJIE; Office of the Chairman, CPPCC Secretariat, Lanzhou.

Party Committee Secretary of the Gannan Tibetan Autonomous Prefecture: LUO XIAOHU.

Head of the Linxia Hui Autonomous Prefecture: (vacant).

Gansu Government Office: 1 Central Square, Lanzhou; tel. 8465941; internet www.gansu.gov.cn.

Guangdong

The Province of Guangdong (Kuangtung) lies in southern China, a rough crescent of territory on the south-eastern coast, centred on the fertile Zhu Jiang (Pearl River) Delta. Guangdong is sometimes conflated with the provincial capital, Guangzhou, which used to be known as Canton (this name was probably derived from the name of the province). The province is known as Yue for short, but Guangdong, meaning 'wide east', is itself a contraction of an older name. This indicated that the province was the eastern route from the core, northern Chinese lands to the broad southern territories (neighbouring Guangxi provided the western route). Although now entirely surrounded by Chinese territory, Guangdong retains institutionalized reminders of its history at the forefront of contact with foreigners—from its territory were carved the former Portuguese enclave of Macao and the former British enclave of Hong Kong. These two territories, now special administrative regions of the People's Republic of China, flank the entrances to the Zhu Jiang estuary, in the centre of the province. Other parts of its territory to be disputed with foreign nations included the South China Sea islands to the south, but these are now part of the Province of Hainan, which was finally separated from Guangdong only in 1988. Hainan, therefore, lies only some 20 km (12 miles) south of the Leizhou peninsula, which is at the western end of Guangdong and is itself the southernmost part of mainland China. To the west and north-west is the Guangxi Zhuang autonomous region, to the north Hunan, to the north-east Jiangxi and to the east, stretching north-eastwards up the coast, is Fujian. The total area of the province is 197,100 sq km (76,080 sq miles).

Guangdong lies south of the Nan Ling range, on the coast of the South China Sea, centred on the fertile Zhu Jiang Delta where the great West River (which allows communications with Guangxi Zhuang) unites with the lesser North and

East Rivers. The Zhu Jiang is China's fourth longest river, at 2,214 km, after the Chang Jiang (River Yangzi), the Huang He (Yellow River) and the Heilong Jiang (River Amur), the last forming the north-eastern border. The estuary of the Delta clefts the coast of Guangdong mid-way, its entrance flanked by the enclaves of Macao to the west and Hong Kong to the east. At the eastern end of the province the generally west-south-westerly coastline (at 3,368 km in length, the longest provincial coastline in China) ends in the Leizhou peninsula, which reaches towards Hainan. The main mountains of Guangdong are the Dayu Ling, in the north, the highest point at Shikengkong (1,902 m or 6,242 feet), on the border with Hunan. The climate is humid, somewhere between subtropical and tropical, with a monsoonal pattern of 'plum rains' in early summer (May or June) and further heavy rainfall in the late summer and early autumn (around August–September). Annual rainfall over 2000 in Guangzhou was 1,799 mm (70 inches), of China's regional capitals a total only exceeded by Haikou on the island of Hainan. Hainan is also the only province to record a higher average annual temperature. In 2000 the city of Guangzhou recorded its lowest average monthly temperature in February (14.0°C or 57.2°F) and its highest in July (28.9°C or 84.0°F)

The total population of Guangdong was 62.83m. at the census of 2000, meaning that the province recorded the largest regional increase since the previous census—37.6% between 1990 and 2000. Almost 18% of the national increase in population over this period was in Guangdong alone, much of it owing to immigration from other areas. It is the fifth-most densely populated province, with 438 persons per sq km in 2000. The population is overwhelmingly classed as ethnic Han Chinese, although the 1.4% of the total recorded as being of minority nationalities in the last census year consisted of 42 different groups. Those traditionally present in Guangdong include the Zhuang, the Miao (Hmong), the Yao, some She, Li (mainly of Hainan) and Yi (the last are believed to be the oldest ethnic group in China), and the Gin or Jing (of Guangdong and Guangxi Zhuang). Communities of the widespread Hui and Manchu (Manzu) peoples are also represented, the former being inheritors of the long tradition of Islam in the province (the first mosque in China is said to have been established in Guangzhou as early as 627—AH 5). Both these last groups speak Chinese, traditionally the official Mandarin tongue, although the predominant dialect in Guangdong is known as Cantonese, which is common among the Chinese diaspora world-wide. There are also more local dialects, such as, in the east, one known as Chaoshan (for the cities of Chaozhou and Shantou) in Mandarin or Taejiu locally. It is the language of many of the Chinese who emigrated to Thailand.

In 2000 55.0% of the population was classed as urban. Guangzhou has long been the largest city—in 2000 the urban area had a population of 4.4m. and 'greater' Guangdong 7.0m. Other major cities include Shenzhen, to the south-east of Guangzhou and on the borders with Hong Kong, the port of Shantou (Swatow) at the eastern end of the coast, Meizhou (Mexian), inland from there, and on the base of the Leizhou peninsula another port city, Zhanjiang (held by the French between 1898 and the Second World War). For administrative purposes the province is actually divided into 52 cities, of which 21 have prefecture status and the rest county status. There are 46 other counties. Three counties are minority nationality autonomous areas.

History

The region now known as Guangdong became part of China in the third century BC, existing as the Southern Yue kingdom in the Han hierarchy. It was consolidated into the Empire under the Tang (hence the Cantonese, like others in southern China, prefer to refer to the dominant ethnicity of the country as Tang Chinese rather than Han Chinese). Initially on the borders of the Chinese world, Guangdong also had a considerable amount of exposure to foreigners through trade. This was a pattern that was to continue throughout its history, starting with long-distance contacts with India and even Rome by the second century AD. The Chinese themselves ventured into such voyages from the fourth century, notably under the Tang, but this declined in the 10th century. By then Muslim (Persian and Arab) traders were firmly established as the pre-eminent traders on the South China Sea. They were strong enough to burn Guangzhou in 758, but generally operated more peacefully, establishing large communities in many of the major Chinese ports, Guangzhou among them. These communities suffered from the growing xenophobia towards the end of the Tang period, notably in the massacre of Arab traders by the followers of Huang Chao when he seized Guangzhou in 879. The shipping industry never really recovered, and nor did the dynasty—Huang Chao, who had been in revolt since 875, menaced the imperial capitals in the north until his defeat in 883, but the last Tang emperor was deposed in 907. Thereafter, in the 10th century interregnum known as the 10 Kingdoms, Guangdong and Guangxi Zhuang formed part of the so-called Southern Han realm, until reincorporated into an Empire under the Song (who survived in the south until the Mongol dynasty of the Yuan conquered them in the 13th century). From 1689, until the end of the Qing period, Guangdong was administered with Guangxi as Liangguang province (based in Guangzhou).

The next major foreign contact along the southern coast was with the Europeans, starting with the Portuguese in the 16th century. A Portuguese embassy to the emperor arrived in Guangzhou in 1517, eventually being allowed to proceed to the imperial court in Beijing in 1520. It never gained an audience with the emperor and the embassy was later permanently imprisoned in Guangzhou. However, the Portuguese proceeded to infiltrate the trade of the southern coast and effectively gained Macao (although it was not formally ceded) from 1557. The Dutch and the British soon followed, with tea soon becoming the main commodity favoured by the Europeans.

Most of this early trade was conducted through Guangzhou, but the merchants began to favour more northerly ports, nearer the main tea-producing areas. The Guangzhou commercial class were anxious to keep this trade, still profitable to China, and were influential in persuading the Qing Government to ban foreign trade in 1757, restricting it to dealings through the great merchant houses (hongs) of Guangzhou. This so-called Co Hong (being the Cantonese pronunciation of *gong hang*, 'officially authorized firms') system was unpopular with the Europeans, and the timing of its introduction was unfortunate for China. The Europeans, particularly the British, were industrializing rapidly and were becoming firmly established in other Asian countries, while the balance of trade was beginning to shift against the Chinese—owing to the import of opium on a large scale from the late 18th century China was suffering a negative balance of trade by the early 19th century. Moreover, the Qing dynasty was in decline, but also unaware of the military advantages that the Europeans now possessed.

Opium had become fundamental to British trade in China when the emperor appointed a commissioner for Guangdong with orders to eliminate the trade in illegal drugs. This official, Lin Zexu, demanded all opium stores from foreign merchants in Guangzhou. Eventually, the British envoy took responsibility for the merchants he represented and handed over 20,000 chests (the first major shipment of the drug from India by the British took place in 1773 and consisted of 1,000 chests of Bengal opium). This was promptly destroyed, in March 1839, but the Qing thereby insulted the official representative of the British Government and provided an excuse for a military reaction. Thus, the first Opium War began and Guangzhou was besieged. With the occupation of Shanghai by the British in 1842 and the threat to supplies for the imperial capital in Beijing, the Qing Government had little choice but to submit to the first of the 'unequal treaties'. The 1842 settlement opened China to foreign trade, abolishing the Co Hong, making Guangzhou one of the first 'open ports' and ceding Hong Kong island (the development of which slowly usurped much of the traditional trading wealth of Guangzhou) to the British. The Second Opium War or the Arrow War was concluded by the 1860 Treaty of Tianjin, which opened more ports to the British (such as Shantou—Swatow—although there had been foreign development of this old fishing village near Chaozhou since the 18th century) and the French. The latter had joined the conflict, which had stemmed from an incident involving a British merchant vessel, the *Arrow*, after the British seized Guangzhou in December 1857 (the city was permanently occupied by the British and French from January 1858 until October 1861). This process of forcibly opening the Chinese Empire to foreign trade also involved a larger European presence and an increasing exposure to new ideas, particularly in Guangdong. In a province already distant from the centres of imperial power and still suspicious of a Manchu dynasty, this encouraged an atmosphere that fermented the questioning of authority and even outright revolt.

By the time of the Arrow War the Qing Government was already experiencing the serious threat of the Taiping Rebellion. The peace process with the European powers, in a way, helped strengthen the authorities against the internal challenge, and enabled a beginning to the modernization of China, although increased contact with foreign ideas did not necessarily help the long-term chances of survival for the imperial system. Moreover, in order to crush the Rebellion the Qing permitted the rise of local warlords. The early activities of the Taiping Rebellion had taken place in Guangdong, and its leader, Hong Xiuquan was born in 1814 into a Hakka family in the north-west of the province, at Huaxian. He founded a socio-religious movement, which initiated its revolt in the turbulent Guangxi province in 1851. The rebellious forces moved north to take Nanjing (Jiangsu), where the Taiping, the 'Heavenly Kingdom' regime, became based. The movement was only ended in 1864, after the reform of the military forces at the command of the Qing.

The days of the final imperial dynasty were now numbered, and after the fall of the Qing Guangdong became a republican stronghold. The province continued its tradition of resistance even then, however, by participating in the unsuccessful 'Second Revolution' against Yuan Shikai in 1913. After his death Guangdong's republican credentials were affirmed by the location of the main seat of the Republic in Guangzhou from 1917. This was led by Dr Sun Yixian (Yatsen in Cantonese), as President of the Republic of China, and he is considered a founding figure of both the Communist state and the Guomindang, the Nationalists whose legacy is the continuing Taiwan-based 'Republic of China'. Sun Yixian had been born at Cuiheng, in the south-west of Guangdong, near Macao, on 12 November 1866. That county has subsequently been renamed Zhongshang in his honour—he is always known in China as Sun Zhongshang, the latter name being the Chinese rendition of the surname Nakayama, which he used in Japan when in exile. He is also called Sun Wen. His revolutionary Revive China Society had attempted an uprising in Guangzhou in 1895, but it failed and he was forced to flee abroad. In the early 1920s Sun Yixian went on to head the Guomindang in Guangdong and directed campaigns against the northern warlords, but his death on 12 March 1925 plunged the Guomindang leadership into crisis. Eventually, the military-triumphed in the person of Jiang Jieshi (Chiang Kai-shek, 1887–1975), who secured his leadership by the 1926 Guangzhou Coup. In late March he effectively became the party leader and consolidated his position by the Northern Expedition against the warlords. The Expedition set off from Guangdong in July and reached what became the new Guomindang capital of Nanjing (the seat of the National Government from 1928–1937) in March 1927. This was done with the help of the Chinese Communist Party (CCP), but this co-operation ended in April 1927 when Jiang Jieshi moved against the Communists in the Shanghai Coup. The Guangdong Communists reacted by seizing control of Guangzhou on 1 December, setting up a commune or soviet, which lasted barely two weeks before the Nationalist forces counterattacked. This marked the beginning of the change in Communist strategy, abandoning working on revolution in the cities to encourage peasant support (CCP-Guomindang co-operation resumed cautiously against the Japanese during the Second World War).

Between 1929 and 1936 Guangdong was effectively independent of Nationalist China, under its own warlord, but returned to Guomindang authority for a couple of years before the Japanese invasion. Guangdong the provincial capital fell to the invader in 1938, as did Shantou, and Hong Kong (then a British outpost) was occupied in 1941–45. When the Communists won the Civil War many Nationalists fled Guangdong to take refuge in Hong Kong and Macao, as well as on Taiwan with the 'Republic of China' Government. In the early People's Republic Guangzhou was constituted as a special municipality, but it was merged into Guangdong in 1954.

More recently, economics not politics have led the changes in Guangdong, although the tradition of exposure to foreign ideas through the medium of trade has continued. In 1979 Guangdong was only the 10th most-prosperous province in the People's Republic of China. It was in that year that the CCP authorities permitted the start of economic reform by designating four cities (Xiamen in Fujian and three places in Guangdong: Shantou in the east; the fishing village of Shenzhen, just outside Hong Kong; and the farming town of Zhuhai, near Macao) as the first special economic zones. Another reform of Deng Xiaoping at the time was the introduction of a free, private market in Guangzhou, then a radical innovation, but now a feature of many

Chinese cities. Thus, a capitalist economy was introduced into the province, which flourished as it became a hinterland for the burgeoning Hong Kong economy and, increasingly, a Western gateway to the vast economic potential of China.

Economy

Guangdong is now the richest province in the People's Republic of China, largely owing to the economic reforms of the 1980s and the region's link with the wealth of Hong Kong. In terms of the overall size of the regional economy, Guangdong has no equal, with a gross domestic product (GDP) of 966,223m. yuan in 2000. However, in per-head terms (12,885 yuan in 2000) Guangdong ranked after the cities of Shanghai, Beijing and Tianjin, and the province of Zhejiang. It still boasts among the strongest growth rates in the People's Republic, and its cities of Guangzhou and Shenzhen are among the most active economic centres in China (the gross industrial output value for each of them is just ahead of Beijing and just behind Tianjin—still well behind Shanghai). It has good infrastructure, with the greatest road length compared to area in China; although the rail and waterway networks are not as widely present, they are well used. The total length of highways at the end of 2000 was 102,604 km, of which 1,186 km were expressway and 5,391 km were first-class highway (the latter figure being more than double the next largest regional total). The length of railways in operation was only 693.8 km. Guangdong has a network of navigable inland waterways, which, in total length (13,696 km) is exceeded only by that of Jiangsu. The province also has three of China's major seaports—Guangzhou, Zhanjiang and Shantou—with the provincial capital being the third largest in the People's Republic, the volume of freight shipped there standing at 111,280 metric tons in 2000 (20,380 tons for Zhanjiang and 12,840 tons for Shantou). Over the course of the 1990s Guangzhou overtook Qinhuangdao (Hebei) and Dalian (Liaoning) in terms of tonnage handled; Shanghai remained the major port of China, while Ningbo (Zhejiang) advanced into second place. The overall value of trade in Guangdong, however, is higher. The province is also the largest regional electricity producer in China, generating 129,269m. kWh in 2000 (mostly thermally generated), almost 10% of the national total. This burgeoning economic situation has attracted much immigration, often of rural labour, but the provincial education system still managed to improve the illiteracy rate during the 1990s. Despite the massive increase in population, Guangdong has kept one of the lower rates in the country, at 3.8% in 2000.

Primary activities only contributed 10.4% to provincial GDP in 2000, the lowest percentage for any province or autonomous region (and lower than the municipality of Chongqing); a similar comparison also puts Guangdong in the same position for the percentage of employed people in the sector compared to the total (41.1%), with the addition of Zhejiang province also being lower. The value of the sector, nevertheless, remains more than the entire GDP of six other regions. The main cereal crop is rice, which in 2000 covered 47.8% of the entire area sown with farm crops (5.2m. ha), while vegetables covered 19.6% (with tubers a further 9.4%). Fruit orchards covered 1.0m. ha. The main crop yields in 2000 amounted to 14.23m. metric tons of rice (other foodgrains only amounted to a further 3.4m. tons), 12.5m. tons of sugarcane and 777,000 tons of peanuts (the main oil-producing crop). Fruit production of 6.4m. tons was exceeded only by Shandong and, barely, Hebei. The main fruit was bananas (2.4m. tons), but citrus fruits, mangoes and other tropical produce are also grown. Other tree or forest crops include rubber (Guangdong is not a major producer, although it is one of only five regional producers in China, but at 26,168 tons in 2000 it accounted for just 5.4% of the total) and pine resin (113,118 tons or 20.5% of national production in China—exceeded only by Guangxi Zhuang). Some 2.75m. cu m of timber were produced in 2000, and 30,909 tons of mulberry-silkworm cocoons. Large livestock in Guangdong at the time were almost entirely cattle and buffaloes (4.2m. head), apart from some horses. There were, however, also 20.3m. pigs. The 293,000 goats recorded in official statistics gave the province the fewest goats of any region in the People's Republic apart from Tianjin. Meat output totalled 3.2m. tons, of which 2.1m. tons were pork. Other livestock products included cows' milk (92,000 tons— goats' milk provided a further 3,000 tons), poultry eggs (331,000 tons) and honey (16,000 tons). The fishing industry is active in both seawater and freshwater, the former accounting for 53% of all aquatic production (5.9m. tons in 2000) and is less dependent on farming (47% of seawater production was artificially cul- tured, whereas 94% of the inland catch was). In 2000 the catch of fish at sea was 1.7m. tons and of shellfish 1.5m. tons. Inland the freshwater-fish catch was 2.1m. tons, giving Guangdong the second largest regional catch in China (after Hubei), as well as the leading freshwater fish-farming industry in the country. There is an extractive industry in the province, with offshore fields contributing a significant amount to the 13.9m. tons of crude petroleum produced in 2000.

Secondary activities contributed about one-half of GDP, 50.4%, in 2000. Industry alone accounted for 44.5% of the total, with construction at 5.9%. The whole secondary sector accounted for 26.2% of employed people in 2000. Guangdong has the largest number of industrial enterprises (counting all state ones and all private ones above a certain size) of any region in China, with 19,695 in 2000 (about one-eighth of the national total), with the largest total gross output value in the country at 1,248,093m. yuan, at current prices, in 2000 (almost one-seventh of the national total). Of these enterprises, 823 are large (Shandong has more large firms, although producing a smaller gross output value) and 1,228 are medium-sized. The progress of economic reform in Guangdong can be seen at a glance, in that only 17% of all these industrial enterprises are in the state sector, compared to a national average of 33%—in value terms, 25% and 47%, respectively. Moreover, while the province is not alone in receiving a great deal of foreign investment in industry, in terms of funding from Hong Kong (and, to a lesser extent, Macao and Taiwan), Guangdong is far ahead—in 2000 this type of funding benefited 6,731 industrial enterprises (or 34% of all enterprises in the province and 41% of the national total receiving such funding), with a gross output value of 474,730m. yuan. This illustrates the role of the province as the hinterland of the flourishing Hong Kong economy, which moved much of its manufacturing activities into this neighbour- ing part of the mainland from the 1980s. Light industry is rather more dominant than heavy industry, however, accounting for 62% of enterprises and 53% of gross output value. In terms of industrial products, Guangdong still has a textile industry and is a major producer of paper and paperboards (machine-made), beer, plastics, some iron and steel, cement, integrated circuits, washing machines and television sets. It is China's leading producer of microcomputers, household refrigerators and air-conditioning systems. The total output value of construction in the province, at 89.2m. yuan in 2000, was exceeded only by the totals for Jiangsu and Zhejiang.

Tertiary activities accounted for the remaining 39.3% of provincial GDP and 32.7% of salaried employment in 2000. Trade and catering services, followed closely by transport and communications (freight traffic through Guangzhou alone was exceeded only by the four great municipalities of the country in 2000), were the most important activities, while property (real estate), social services and then finance and insurance followed in importance. Transport and communications accounted for some 11% of employed workers in 2000, with large numbers employed on the rail, road, water and air networks; significantly more people than in any other region were employed in transport support services and in the post and telecommunications services. Guangdong leads the People's Republic in international tourism, aided by the strong business presence in the province and the convenience for those visitors stopping over in Hong Kong who wish to travel to the mainland. Measured in person-times, Guangdong received 119.9m. international tourists in 2000 (more than four times the number for Beijing, the next-most popular region), of whom 21.3m. were foreigners (here Beijing exceeds Guangdong). These figures reveal the number of visitors from and the importance of Guangdong's involvement with Hong Kong and, to a lesser extent, Macao. These visitors made the province the best tourist foreign-exchange earner in the country (particularly in the late 1990s and early 2000s), reaching US \$4,112m. in 2000. Tourist sites include many modern attractions, as well as the natural beauty of Qixing Yan (near Zhaoqing) or the reserve at Dinghu Shan.

In terms of foreign trade, the province is by far the leading region of the People's Republic of China, exporting commodities to the value of US \$93,427.9m. in 2000 (37.5% of the national total and more than the total of the four regions with the next largest export trades). Imports were worth \$82,059m. (36.5% of the national total). The final statement of government revenue for Guangdong in 2000 was 91,055.56m. yuan (about double the amount reaped in Shandong, the next most successful province in revenue terms) and expenditure 108,031.89m. yuan (well over one-half as much again as spent in Shandong or Shanghai, the regions with the next largest spending). The main sources of revenue were the operations tax (29.9%), income tax on enterprises (18.4%) and value added tax (14.5%), while the main destinations for government expenditure were capital construction (14.2%), education (13.4%) and government administration (9.3%). The province is the leading recipient of foreign investment in the country, with foreign direct investment totalling \$11,280.9m. in 2000 (28.0% of total regional investment) and other investment of \$1,554.0m. (such investment is mainly received at a national level, and Guangdong is the only province to receive it in substantial amounts).

Directory

Governor: LU RUIHUA; Office of the Provincial People's Government, Guangzhou (Canton).

Secretary of the Guangdong Provincial Committee of the Chinese Communist Party: LI CHANGCHUN; Office of the Secretary, CCP Secretariat, Guangzhou.

Chairwoman of the Standing Committee of the People's Congress of Guangdong: ZHANG GUOYING; Office of the Chairman, Congress Secretariat, Guangzhou.

Chairman of the Guangdong Provincial Committee of the Chinese People's Political Consultative Conference: GUO RONGCHANG; Office of the Chairman, CPPCC Secretariat, Guangzhou.

Guizhou

The Province of Guizhou (Kweichow) is located in the south-west of the People's Republic of China. The autonomous region of Guangxi Zhuang lies to the south and Yunnan to the west, stretching a little along the north-western border too, where Sichuan also reaches down. Until March 1997 most of the northern border was with Sichuan, but it is now with the separately constituted special municipality, Chongqing. To the east is Hunan. Guizhou, which means 'noble prefecture' or 'precious place', is called Qian for short. The total area of the province is some 174,000 sq km (67,160 sq miles).

The province occupies the eastern end of the Yunnan-Guizhou plateau, which thrusts out from the Tibetan highlands to separate the gentler lands of the Sichuan basin and of Guangxi Zhuang. Guizhou is, on average, over 1,000 m (3,282 feet) above sea level, but in the west many of the peaks rise to over 3,000 m. Some 87% of the province is reckoned to consist of mountains and plateaus, which long hindered its development, although it is rich in coal and the terrain, together with the ample rainfall, is very suitable for hydroelectric projects. Guizhou also contains a number of impressive waterfalls, notably China's premier cataract of Huangguoshu Dapubu (on the Bai Shui river), which is 81 m wide and has a drop of 74 m. The main rivers include the Yachi He, the Wu Jiang and, defining much of the southern border, the Nanpan Jiang. The climate is subtropical, and very humid (Guiyang is among the most humid cities in the country); it is subject to the monsoons, but otherwise there are few seasonal variations. The weather is frequently cloudy and rainy, although there are occasional spring (April–May) droughts in the west and summer (June–July) droughts in the lower land to the east. Most of the rain falls over the summer, with more precipitation in the central and south-western districts. The annual averages for the province varied between 900 mm and 1,500 mm (35–59 inches), with the total rainfall for 2000 in Guiyang, the centrally located provincial capital, at 1,441 mm. Average temperatures for January range from a minimum of 1°C to a maximum of 10°C (34°–50°F), while in July the range is 17°–28°C (63°–82°F). In 2000 the average annual temperature in Guiyang was 13.8°C (56.8°F), with the lowest monthly average being in February (3.0°C or 37.4°F) and the highest in July (22.9°C or 73.2°F).

The total population of Guizhou in November 2000 was 35.25m., giving an average population density of 203 per sq km. Ethnic groups counted for a considerable 37.9% of the total population at the time of the 2000 census. Minority nationalities represented included the Chinese-speaking Muslims, the Hui, and those widespread in the south, such as the Miao (Hmong), the Dong (also in some numbers in Hunan and Guangxi Zhuang) and some Yis and Zhuangs. There are some of the Bais usually associated with Yunnan, the Mulaos or Mulams of Guangxi Zhuang and the Tujias of the Wuling mountains (where Guizhou, Chongqing, Hunan and Hubei converge). The most prominent group mainly present in Guizhou are another Thai people, related to the Zhuang, the Buyi or Bouyei (there are 2.45m. of them, most of them in Guizhou—they favour the river valleys of the south-west); most of the 430,000 Gelos or Gelaos also live in Guizhou, as do the majority of the 340,000 Shuis. Buddhism is, traditionally, the main religion of most of these peoples.

The urban population only constituted 23.9% of the total in 2000—the only regions of China in which there were a greater proportion of rural residents was in Xizang (Tibet) and, slightly, Yunnan. The district of Guiyang, the seat of the provincial administration, had a total population of 3.3m. in November 2000, of which 1.5m. lived in the city itself. The other 12 centres classed as cities all had populations of less than 0.5m., with all but Anshun (the commercial focus for western Guizhou), Zunyi (chief city of the north) and Kaili (the main centre for the ethnic south-east), less than 200,000. These four cities are all categorized as prefectures; of the other five shire or rural prefectures three are minority nationality autonomous areas (one for the Miao and Dong of south-eastern Guizhou, the others both for the Buyi and Miao, one in southern Guizhou and one in south-western Guizhou). The province is also divided into 78 counties, with four of the nine cities at that level being autonomous areas too, as well as 42 of the rural counties.

History

Guizhou was long on the boundaries of the Empire and the Chinese world. The Han established the first imperial administration here before the beginning of the Christian era, but settlement and effective control was confined to the north and east. Even there isolation from the rest of China easily persisted, although the region generally remained within the orbit of the imperial court, with local dignitaries holding sway over the various tribal groups that inhabited the wilder districts. Chinese control was only seriously threatened in the ninth century, when the Nanzhao confederation of Yunnan expanded northwards and was engaged in a three-way struggle with Tang China and Tibet (Xizang). The consolidation of China's borders under the Yuan and Ming dynasties firmly included Guizhou into the Empire, and from the 16th century Han Chinese settlers began to displace, sometimes forcibly, the ethnic minorities from the most fertile regions in the west as well. The province remained neglected by the central administration and, indeed, the provincial authorities, which were based in Yunnan (of which Guizhou formed a part until 1911).

Guizhou rejected the Qing and declared for the republic in the first half of November 1911. The region soon fell subject to feuding warlords, however, only gaining some stability from the mid-1920s, when the Yunnan-based Tang Jiyao (Chi-yao) incorporated Guizhou into his domain. He co-operated with the republican Government and acknowledged the authority of the Guomindang in 1935-37, although any control was often tenuous. The Communists, therefore, were able to find a refuge here near the start of their 'Long March' retreat from Jiangxi, resting before beginning the trek northwards. The stop in the northern town of Zunyi is famous as the site of a Communist meeting in January 1935; the Zunyi Conference marks the beginning of the rise to supremacy within the Party of Mao Zedong (Mao Tse-tung). This interlude would have been more difficult a few years later as the development of Guizhou began during the Second World War. The Japanese invasion of 1937 forced the Guomindang to remove the capital of the Republic to Chongqing in 1938, just to the north of Guizhou, and transport links were improved and some indus-trialization introduced as the Chinese attempted to base their strength in the south-west. After the defeat of the Japanese and the Civil War, however, official neglect continued until well into the Communist era, although a sustained effort to improve the transport infrastructure and develop the mineral resources of the province then began slowly to improve the lot of this poor and isolated province.

Economy

Guizhou has the sixth-lowest regional gross domestic product (GDP) in all of China, totalling 99,353m. yuan in 2000 (current prices), despite having shown real annual growth consistently above 8% since the mid-1990s. The figure for regional GDP per head, however, at 2,662 yuan in the same year, was easily the lowest in the country and was less than of 8% of the value of the highest such figure (in Shanghai). Guizhou does now have the basis for more solid progress, with fairly good infrastructure, not least because investment in the railways has been one of the main drivers of development in the region, giving the province a relatively extensive network. The railway length in operation at the end of 2000 was about 1,642 km. The road network totalled 34,643 km in length, but although this included 258 km of expressway, there was a mere 26 km of first-class highway, and even second-class highways amounted to only a further 718 km, while more than one-quarter of villages were reported to be without road links. There were also 2,132 km of navigable waterways, and a large new airport was opened at Guiyang in 1997. Energy infrastructure was well devel-oped, initially helped by the local coal reserves, but now favouring hydroelec-tricity. The latter accounted for 45% of the relatively high electricity production of 40,470 kWh in 2000. Nevertheless, the province remains benighted by high levels of poverty (with some 8m. below the poverty line) and a population with the fourth-highest illiteracy rate in the country. Although there was a significant fall in the illiteracy rate between 1990 and 2000, from 24.3% to 13.9%, the disadvantage remains significant, particularly among the minority nationalities and in the countryside. The human geography of Guizhou is also distinguished by having a high male : female ratio—men account for 52.4% of the total population, second only to Yunnan.

The primary sector made an unusually (for a Chinese region) large contribu-tion to GDP of 27.3% in 2000. The sector also encompassed 67.3% of all employed persons. The total sown area in the province covered 4.70m. ha (46,967 sq km or about 27% of the total land area) in 2000, with foodgrains alone on 3.15m. ha—rice, corn (maize) and tubers each on over 700,000 ha, followed by wheat and, finally, soybeans. Oil-bearing crops (mainly rapeseed) and vegetables also covered a fairly extensive area. The main cash crop, however, is tobacco, which in 2000 was grown on 213,700 ha (15% of the national total and second only to Yunnan in the area covered); production amounted to 338,000 metric tons (of which 311,000 tons was flue-cured tobacco). Lower yields per hectare in Guizhou meant that this total was only just over one-half that of Yunnan's tobacco harvest, but still higher than any other region, and it accounted for 13% of the national total. In that year Guizhou also produced 4.77m. tons of rice, 3.42m. tons of maize and 1.04m. tons of wheat, as well as 1.86m. tons of vegetables, 667,000 tons of sugarcane and 662,000 tons of rapeseed. Guizhou is the leading producer of tung-oil seeds, harvesting 116,593 tons in 2000, or 26% of the national total. It also possesses medicinal herbs in profusion, particularly in its forested regions. In 2000 there were 6.6m. head of cattle and buffaloes, 700,000 horses, as well as some mules and donkeys. Of smaller animals, Guizhou counted 18.0m. pigs, 3.2m. goats and 200,000 sheep in the same year. Pork accounted for 1.05m. tons of the 1.24m. tons of meat produced in the province in that year, while other livestock products included 17,000 tons of milk (almost all cows' milk), 65,000 tons of poultry eggs and 2,000 tons of honey. All fisheries are, obviously, freshwater, and fish (rather than crustaceans or shellfish) account for the bulk of the total catch-61,700 tons of fish and 700 tons of other produce in 2000—with artificial culturing responsible for 87% of all aquatic products.

The secondary sector accounted for 39.0% of GDP in 2000 and only 9.3% of all employed persons. Among the 22 provinces, only Hainan and Qinghai have fewer industrial enterprises (these two provinces also having far fewer people), the total in Guizhou being 2,087 in 2000, together totalling a gross output value of 63,164m. yuan, at current prices. The state sector accounted for 67% of the enterprises, but 79% of the output value. Few businesses received foreign funding, or even investment from the Special Administrative Regions or Taiwan. Heavy industry accounted for 1,277 of all industrial enterprises and 42,531m. yuan out of the total gross output value. Large enterprises, 103 in 2000, generated 51% of the total gross output value of all industrial enterprises, but the 119 medium-sized firms only 11%. These patterns reflect the province's increasing dependence on its rich mineral reserves, which are now being exploited. Foremost among these resources is coal, of which 37m. metric tons were produced in 2000, making Guizhou the main producer of southern China (the province is reported to have total reserves of 241,900m. tons). Guizhou also possesses reserves of phosphorus amounting to some 44% of the national total, while despite a relatively long history of production in the province, the reserves of mercury still form 38% of the country's total. There is also bauxite, manganese, antimony and a recently developed resource of gold. Industrial activity otherwise is not particularly distinguished in the amounts or types of product, although the tobacco industry produces a large number of cigarettes locally. Construction activity (helped by the important railway-building programme) increased steadily in the 1990s, to reach a total output value of 10,905.7m. yuan in 2000, when it accounted for 7.4% of total GDP.

The tertiary sector accounted for 33.7% of GDP in 2000, but services are not a strong industry. The two main contributors to sectoral GDP were trade and catering services (7.8%—not much more than construction) and transport and communications (6.5%). The sector accounted for 23.4% of all employed persons in 2000. Tourism is becoming of growing importance, however, with attractions such as the wetlands reserve of Cao Hai and its black-necked cranes and other birds or the Huangguoshu falls. The rugged scenery and remote villages with their rich tribal cultures are also increasingly appealing to tourists. The number of international tourists visiting Guizhou experienced probably the most dramatic expansion of anywhere in China over the 1990s—a total of only 24,100 in 1990 had reached 183,900 by 2000 (of whom 71,200 were foreigners). Foreign-exchange earnings from tourism, therefore, reached US $61m. in 2000, about the same amount as in Jiangxi and about 20 times the level achieved in the region to earn the least (Ningxia Hui), but nearly 70 times less than that of the highest earner (Guangdong).

Trade is not a major activity in Guizhou and it had the fifth-lowest total trade (in value) out of all of the regions of China in 2000; exports were worth US $481.7m. and imports $374.8m. Government revenue in Guizhou during 2000 only totalled 8,523.24m. yuan, of which the only sources to raise more than 700m. yuan were the operations tax (2,033.88m. yuan, or 23.9% of the total) and value added tax (1,218.20m. yuan, 14.3%). Expenditure totalled 20,156.98m. yuan, however, an indication of the authorities' continuing resolve to counter deprivation in the region. The main destinations of government expenditure in 2000 were education (15.8%), capital construction (12.3%), government administration (12.1%), the justice system (7.2%), the subsidy of social-security programmes (5.9%) and public health (5.5%). Guizhou achieved only $25.0m. in actually used foreign direct investment in 2000, although it had gained $40.9m. in the previous year.

Directory

Governor: SHI XIUSHI; Office of the Provincial People's Government, Guiyang.

Secretary of the Guizhou Provincial Committee of the Chinese Communist Party: QIAN YUNLU; Office of the Secretary, CCP Secretariat, Guiyang.

Chairman of the Standing Committee of the People's Congress of Guizhou: LIU FANGREN; Office of the Chairman, Congress Secretariat, Guiyang.

Chairman of the Guizhou Provincial Committee of the Chinese People's Political Consultative Conference: WANG SIQI; Office of the Chairman, CPPCC Secretariat, Guiyang.

Party Committee Secretary of the Qiandongnan Miao–Dong Autonomous Prefecture: LIU GUANGLEI.

Party Committee Secretary of the Qiannan Buyi–Miao Autonomous Prefecture: HE YONGKANG.

Party Committee Secretary of the Qianxinan Buyi–Miao Autonomous Prefecture: XU ZHENGWEI.

Guizhou Government Office: North Zhonghua Road, Guiyang; tel. (851) 6825445; internet www.gzgov.gov.cn.

Hainan

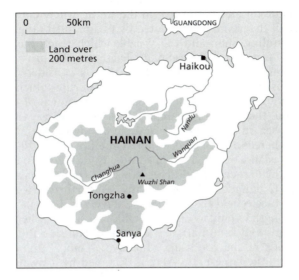

The Province of Hainan is in the South China Sea, most of its territory consisting of the island of Hainan (Hainan Dao), which lies south across the 20-km (12 miles) Qiongzhou Strait from the Leizhou peninsula of Guangdong. An old name for Hainan ('sea south') is Qiong or Qiongai. Until April 1988 it was part of Guangdong province. China's traditional claims to the islands of the South China Sea still bring it into conflict with a number of other countries, while possession is also disputed with the regime in Taiwan. Viet Nam lies along the South-East Asian coast to the west of Hainan island and the province's other constituent parts: Xisha (i.e. the West Sand Islands—otherwise known as the Paracel Islands) and Zhongsha (Middle Sand Islands—Macclesfield Bank) and the southerly and myriad Nansha (South Sand Islands—Spratly Islands). The archipelago of the Philippines lies to the east and Malaysia to the south, while in the south-western South China Sea the Chinese claims encroach on Indonesia's Natuna Islands (which are also claimed by Viet Nam). All these countries challenge Chinese sovereignty, which is concurrently claimed by Taiwan ('Republic of China'), and every country except Indonesia also maintains a physical presence in the Spratly Islands. Brunei merely disputes the maritime boundaries of its exclusive economic zone. The total area of the Province of Hainan is given as 34,380 sq km (13,270 sq miles), most of which is the island of Hainan; the largest island of Xisha, Yongxing (otherwise known as Woody Island), has an area of 2.65 sq km and is the seat of government for the South China Sea islands of the People's Republic, while the total area of Nansha is less than 8 sq km.

Hainan province extends for some 1,800 km from north to south (from the Qiongzhou Strait to Zengmu Reef in Nansha, the most southerly part of the People's Republic) and 900 km from east to west. Hainan Dao is the largest island in China, if Taiwan is excluded, and has a coastline of some 1,440 km. The coast is gentle on all sides except in the south, where cliffs rear above the sea. The centre of the island is dominated by two parallel ranges of mountains, those of the Limuling Shan and the Wuzhi, which reach their highest point, 1,867 m (6,127 feet), at Wuzhi Shan. These ranges provide the 20% of mountainous land and 15% of hilly land that is considered to occupy the territory of the island, while the rest consists of fertile tablelands and plains. The main rivers are the Nandu He, which flows for much of the length of the island to Haikou, the provincial capital on the north coast, the Wanquan He, which enters the sea on the east coast, and the Changhua He, with its mouth on the west coast. There is a large lake, Sangtao Shuiko, on the Nandu, just west of the centre of the island. About 170 km south-east of the southern tip of Hainan Dao lies Xisha, the Paracel Islands, consisting of over 30 reefs and islets divided into two groups (Xuangde and Yongle). Just a little further to the south-east is Zhongsha, the Macclesfield Bank of about 20 reefs and shoals (the most visible is known as Zhongsha Qundao), and over 400 km south of here spread the 100 islets, reefs, shoals and sand bars that constitute Nansha, the Spratly Islands. The major islands in the south are Huangyan Dao, Taiping, Zhongye and Nanwei, although the largest, Itu Aba, is occupied by Taiwan, while Swallow Reef has been developed by Malaysia. The Philippines claims some of the south-eastern islands as the Kalayaan Islands. The climate throughout the territory is tropical, with even temperatures and a monthly average that seldom falls below 20°C (68°F). At Haikou, in the very north of the province, for instance, the monthly averages for January and February of 2000 were 18.7°C (65.7°F) and 18.3°C (64.9°F), respectively, and the average temperature for each month in June–August was 28.7°C (83.7°F). However, Hainan is one of the most humid places in China, especially between March and October, and there is the annual risk of typhoons at any time between May and October. Average annual rainfall ranges from 1,600 mm (62 inches) to 2,000 mm; the total for Haikou in 2000 was 2,163 mm, most of which fell, typically, early and late in the summer.

The population grew by about one-fifth between the censuses of 1990 and 2000, to reach 7.87m. in the latter year (only Xizang—Tibet, Qinghai and Ningxia Hui had smaller populations) and to give a population density of 229 per sq km. The Han Chinese, who mainly live in the cities and on the coast, comprised 82.7% of the total population. The principal minority nationality of Hainan Dao is that of the Li, the autochthonous inhabitants, a people that numbers some 1m., most of whom live in the south and centre of the island. The Li share an autonomous area in the mountains with the Miao (Hmong), an ethnic group widespread throughout southern China and northern Indo-China, but who here number some 60,000 and live in some of the most rugged parts of Hainan Dao. There were 37 other minority nationality groups present on the island too. For example, concentrated near Xincun, in the south-east, are the Danjia (Tanha), fishermen and pearl cultivators, while just outside Sanya, near the southernmost tip of Hainan, are some 5,000 Huis, the island's only Muslims.

The urban population of Hainan province constituted 40.1% of the total in 2000. The only population centres of significance are on Hainan Dao. The two main cities are at opposite ends of the island: Haikou, the capital, had an urban population of 484,000 in 2000, and is a port city on the north coast; and Sanya is on the south coast. The other major port of Hainan is Dongfang (Basuo), on the west coast. The town of Tongzha (Tongshi) in the centre of the island, beneath the peaks of Wuzhi Shan, is the chief town of the Li and Miao Autonomous Area (constituted of six counties with that status). Haikou and Sanya are at prefectural level in the administrative hierarchy of the People's Republic, and there are seven cities at county level. There are 17 counties in all.

History

The Li first settled on Hainan island around 1000 BC, emigrating here from Fujian. The Miao (Hmong) later spread across southern China, as well as further south, and into Hainan, largely owing to Chinese emigrations from the north. This followed the subjection of the region to the Han dynasty. The Emperor Wudi (141–87 BC) first established two administrative centres on the island towards the end of the second century BC, while later dynasties added further centres and settlement by mainlanders began. This contributed to the long history of rebellion by the Li against the Empire, although the early island was not considered by the Chinese to be the desirable resort and agricultural paradise of more modern times, but rather an isolated and neglected place of exile. There is even a place of worship in Haikou called the Five Officials' Memorial Temple (Wugong Ci) commemorating five such erring bureaucrats. The island also sometimes served as a naval base for patrolling the South China Sea, while local fishermen fished off some of the islands to the south and east, with evidence for both used to bolster modern territorial claims. Certainly coastal China has a long sea-faring tradition, its naval strength reaching its height under the Tang, although the voyages cited in modern disputes began under the Han and were still being reported in the time of the Ming. There is some archaeological evidence to back documentary reports of an ancient Chinese presence on the islands of the South China Sea (although other countries, such as Viet Nam, advance their own evidence too).

Medieval China was not greatly concerned with or challenged in its claims in the southern seas, however, confining the reputation of Hainan Dao to a place of bleak exile constantly threatened by rebellious natives. Among the more famous 'political visitors' from the mainland were the Tang premier, Li Deyu, and the Song poet and statesman, Su Dongpo. Li Deyu was a ninth-century government official who served the controversial Emperor Wuzong with great distinction as prime minister between 840 and 846 (he had also served as premier under an earlier emperor), being made Duke of Wei in 844 in recognition of his success against the Uygurs and other external threats, as well as against the internal intrigues of the eunuchs in government service. However, his reputation was marred by his participation in Wuzong's great persecution of Buddhists in China, and the next emperor dismissed him from office and exiled him to Hainan, where he died. Su Dongpo (born Su Shi), who came from a distinguished scholarly and administrative family, served with great distinction during the 11th century. After gaining his academic qualifications to serve in the administration in 1057, his political career was punctuated by periods of exile (he is commemorated in the Wugong Ci), but his poetic reputation as one of the 'Eight Great Prose Masters' of the Tang and Song (along with his father, Su Xun, and brother, Su Che) is untarnished. Government service was not conducive to his critical nature (hence his exile to Hainan, and earlier reverses), but must have contributed to his substantial opus, which is noted for its substance and its spontaneity without showiness. Talented in many genres and fields of artistry, he is particularly known for his prolific output of *shi* poems and his influence in the development of *ci* poetry.

More modern figures associated with Hainan were actually from the island— the Soong (Song) siblings of Wenchang in the north-east, particularly prominent in the 1920s and 1930s. T. V. Soong was a banker who helped finance the Northern Expedition and became a finance minister in the Guomindang Government under Jiang Jieshi (Chiang Kai-shek), to whom his youngest sister, Meiling (a strict Methodist and English speaker, who was prominent in the propaganda struggle abroad during the war with Japan), was married. Another sister was married to H. H. Kong, a prominent industrialist, but the third, Song Qingling, was the widow of the founding father of the Chinese republic, Sun Yixian (Yatsen). She was prominent on the left wing of the Guomindang and urged an alliance with the Communists in 1949, remaining prominent in the political life of the People's Republicthereafter. Meanwhile, on Hainan island, which was retained for the People's Republic, the Communist regime was established and a number of Chinese settlers from Indonesia, Malaysia and, later, Viet Nam, settled here. The new regime attempted to balance this further threat to the Li minority by granting them an autonomous area. This may also have been in recognition of Li support to the Communist guerrillas against the Japanese during the Second World War (Japanese forces occupied Hainan in February 1939), despite the tradition of native resistance to the Chinese. When the Communists finally gained control of the island in January 1950, from the retreating Nationalist forces, Hainan, like the smaller islands of the South China Sea, was administered as part of Guangdong province. (Japan had claimed the South China Sea islands during the War, but then declared all occupied territories returned to China—a 1947 map asserting Chinese sovereignty throughout the Sea is the beginning of modern claims by both the People's Republic and Taiwan.)

The history of the disputed Spratly Islands, and the other South China Sea islands, assumed importance from the second half of the 20th century as China was more able to assert its claims and the newly independent nations nearby were empowered to challenge them. The tale is complicated by the involvement of two Chinese regimes (the People's Republic and the 'Republic of China' in Taiwan) advancing common claims and given added importance not only by the strategic advantage in the world's second busiest shipping lane, but also by the discovery of major hydrocarbon reserves in the region. The islands exist in four groups, the Chinese names describing their relative positions in the South China Sea. The islands nearest to the mainland are the Dongsha or East Sand Islands (the Pratas Islands), which lie some 260 km south of Shantou in Guangdong and include one of the biggest islands in the South China Sea, but are administered from Kaohsiung City on Taiwan. Some 600 km to the south-west, Xisha, the Paracel Islands, had been claimed for Viet Nam by the colonial power, France, in 1933, but in January 1974 the Chinese drove out the forces of the faltering regime of South Viet Nam and incorporated Xisha into the People's Republic.

The victorious Communists of Viet Nam, however, did not abandon national claims to the advantage of their erstwhile political allies, and by 1976 had occupied 'national territory' in the Spratly Islands hitherto held by Southern forces. The widely strewn Spratly Islands to the south, Nansha, are the most contentious piece of territory, not only owing to their wide spread, conducive to rival establishments on different islands, and the sometimes dubious definition of reefs, shoals or sand bars as land, but also to their proximity to other nations. Thus, the Philippines asserted an interest in some of the islands nearest their own shores in the 1950s, with troops occupying a few in 1968 and eight islands (Kalaayan) being formally annexed in 1971. Malaysia, meanwhile, has occupied three islets and developed Swallow Reef, including building a hotel there, while Taiwan has long occupied territory in Nansha. Most of the violence in the disputes has been between the People's Republic of China and Viet Nam (which claims all of Nansha, as well as Xisha), sometimes connected to wider conflicts over, for instance, Cambodia. Apart from the 1974 invasion of the Paracel Islands, the encounters have been in the Spratly Islands, the most serious being a naval clash near Johnson Reef in 1988, when over 70 sailors were killed. There were further incidents in 1992 and 1994, while in 1995 a Taiwanese vessel fired on a Vietnamese supply ship. Recently, however, the Philippines has been more involved in the actual military encounters, clashing with Chinese forces each year in 1995–98, and with Vietnamese forces in the last year, for instance. This indicates the difficulty of resolving the issues, as Chinese claims do not merely conflict directly with those of other countries, but also complicate separate disputes between those countries. Indonesia, with no claim on the Spratly Islands (though somewhat affected by China's exclusive economic zone—EEZ claims), has taken the lead in attempting to resolve the issues, but has met with little success, although tension has, periodically, lessened. The last country to mention in connection with the Spratly Islands is Brunei, which, using the continental-shelf principle, has an EEZ that involves it marginally in the dispute—in 1984 it declared an EEZ that included Louisa Reef. Finally, the fourth island group, Zhongsha, as indicated by its name of the Macclesfield Bank, barely has any land long enough above sea level to occupy, while its position in the centre of other claims helps to make it less immediately controversial.

Meanwhile, political developments within the People's Republic had changed the status of Hainan and the smaller South China Sea islands. A decision of May 1984 created a distinct Hainan Administrative District within Guangdong province, but in August 1987 the State Council proposed provincial status. On 13 April 1988 the Province of Hainan became the 30th region of the People's Republic of China and its largest special economic zone. The latter encouraged a flourishing of economic investment, although the island also acquired a reputation for treading the edge of lawlessness in its pursuit of progress. Hainan received an amount of international attention in early 2001, when a US military surveillance aircraft was damaged in a collision with two Chinese fighter aircraft sent to intercept it over the South China Sea, and was forced to land on Hainan, where the crew were detained for a period.

Economy

Hainan is a prosperous province, its economy dependent on tourism and agriculture, with growth strengthened since the special economic zone (SEZ) status gained with a separate provincial administration in 1988. It gained a slightly wild reputation for unregulated capitalism spiced with corruption and, although there is much visible evidence for promised investments not always coming to fruition, generally the province has prospered since separating from its large mainland neighbour, Guangdong. The regional gross domestic product (GDP) for Hainan, which had resumed real rates of growth in excess of 8% from 1998 (relatively soon after the Asian financial crisis of the previous year), had by 2000 reached a current total of 51,848m. yuan, or 6,894 yuan per head (the latter being the highest regional figure in southern and western China after Guangdong—although that is almost twice as much). Government investment has improved the infrastructure, notably expanding the ports and extending the road network. The expressway from Haikou down the east coast of Hainan Dao to Sanya has now reached as far as Dongfang (Basuo) and is eventually planned to reach right round the island. The route directly across the mountainous centre is also intended to be developed as a major highway at some point. The total length of highways at the end of 2000 was 17,401 km, of which 601 km were expressway (making Hainan, relative to its land area, the best served region of China) and 121 km first-class highway. The province also had railways of 219 km in operation and navigable inland waterways of 414 km at the same time. A new airport for Haikou opened in May 1999 and there is an airport at Sanya. The three major seaports are at Haikou, Dongfang (Basuo) and Yulin, the port of Sanya. The last remains the smallest port and, after actually going through a period of contraction in the late 1980s, failed to expand in the 1990s. Haikou is now the largest port, having gone from handling 0.7m. metric tons of freight in 1980 to 8.1m. tons in 2000. Electricity produced in the province during 2000 amounted to only 3,905 kWh, less than anywhere else in China except Tibet. The rate of illiteracy in the adult population at the time of the 2000 census was put at 7.0%.

Agriculture and fishing, as well as plantation and forest products, to a lesser extent, are fundamental to the productive economy of Hainan. The primary sector, therefore, contributed 37.9% to GDP in 2000, the highest proportion of any region in the People's Republic. In the same year 61.3% of employed persons worked in this sector, a relatively high proportion, but one here not unjustified by the size of this part of the economy. Post-Second World War changes in agriculture included the extensive plantation of rubber from 1950, the development of the now-famous Xinglong coffee by the resettling overseas Chinese from 1952 and a systematic expansion of coconut harvesting and of mangoes as the most profitable fruit crop. The total area sown with farm crops in 2000 was 906,000 ha, of which about two-fifths is normally given to rice. Vegetables and tubers are also important. At the end of 2000 there were also

141,900 ha of fruit orchards. There are no figures readily available for the amount of land currently given over to rubber plantations, but an indication might be that between 1950 and 1980 about one-half of the natural forest cover was destroyed to make way for rubber trees. Although forests now cover only some 8% of the land area (allowing the province still to produce some pine resin), Hainan is China's leading rubber producer—280,880 metric tons in 2000, or 58% of the national total. As for the rest of agricultural production (metric tons, in 2000), the most important foodgrain is rice (1.5m.), followed by tubers (398,000), while other important crop yields are of groundnuts (95,000), sugar-cane (3.4m.) and fruit (1.1m.), over one-half of the last being bananas. In the same year Hainan had a domesticated-animal population of some 3.4m. pigs and 1.4m. cattle and buffaloes, as well as 0.9m. goats. The island produced 380,000 tons of meat (227,000 tons of pork) in 2000, but minimal amounts of milk, and 29,000 tons of poultry eggs. Aquatic products are largely harvested from the sea (81.4% or 675,900 tons in 2000) and mainly consist of fish (513,300 tons). Freshwater fish, most of which are farmed, provided a catch of 133,600 tons in 2000. Perhaps the most famous marine product of Hainan, however, are the pearls of the southern coasts, many of which are cultivated.

The secondary sector is, relative to the total regional GDP, the smallest in the country, contributing only 19.8% of GDP in 2000 (the industrial product of the Autonomous Region of Xizang—Tibet is less in value, but that region has a much smaller economy overall). The industrial sector also accounted for 9.6% of employed persons. The lack of development of the secondary sector is indicated by the fact that construction provides rather more than one-third of industrial product (7.1% of total GDP). Much of the industrial activity that there is tends to be the processing of agricultural products—thus, Hainan is the fourth largest sugar producer in China, with 368,100 metric tons in 2000 (5.3% of the national total, which is considerably less than Guangxi Zhuang and rather less than Yunnan and Guangdong, but impressive given the relative size of Hainan). Industrial activity is also helped by the exploitation of mineral reserves, such as iron and salt (130,300 tons in 2000), as well as petroleum and other minerals from the South China Sea (although many claim that the potential reserves here are not as great as the Chinese authorities believe). Beyond such processing of primary products, and attendant activities such as packaging, there is a limited manufacturing industry, although a thriving construction sector (with a total output value of 3,021.4m. yuan in 2000) contributed towards the production of 3.2m. tons of cement in 2000. Hainan, therefore, has very few industrial enterprises, compared to the size of its economy—596 in 2000, with a total gross output value of only 20,287m. yuan. Most of these businesses are in the state sector and consist of light industry; only 32 are large enterprises and there are 86 medium-sized ones. About one-sixth received funding from outside the People's Republic in 2000.

In 2000 the tertiary sector provided 42.3% of GDP (and work for 29.1% of employed persons), which is very high, particularly given the size of the primary sector. That trade (wholesale and retail) and catering services account for almost one-third of this (13.3% of total GDP in 2000) indicates the importance of tourism in the local economy. This southernmost part of the country is warm even in the generally harsh Chinese winter, and there has certainly been a change from the imperial Chinese perception of Hainan as the 'gate of hell' (according to the exiled Tang premier, Li Deyu); historical records can reveal only 18 tourists in over 1,000 years under the Song, Yuan and Ming dynasties. Now, however, tourism is flourishing, being particularly well established in the domestic market, but also witnessing the number of international tourist visits increasing by over two and one-half times between 1990 and 2000, to reach 486,800 (within that total foreigners increased almost fourfold, to 93,700). This increased foreign-exchange earnings to US $109m. in 2000. Beaches and sun are the main attractions, but there is also lush tropical scenery, rich plant life and wildlife (such as the colony of Guangxi or rhesus monkeys, *Macaca mulatta*, of Nanwan Houdao, near Xincun, or other protected animals like gibbons, pangolins and civet cats), and the various ethnic cultures. Other services that make important contributions to GDP include transport and communications (9.1% of the total—notably air transport) and finance and insurance (6.5%).

Although overseas trade was not as high as it had been some years before, in 2000 exports were worth US $608.5m. and imports $485.7m. Foreign direct investment in 2000 totalled $430.8m. Total revenue raised in Hainan province, according to the final government statement for 2000, was 3,919.95m. yuan, of which 29.5% came from the operations tax and then an unusually high 11.0% from individuals' income tax. Total government expenditure at the same time was 6,411.93m. yuan, indicating the continuing pressure to develop the province, the largest destination being education (15.0%), followed by capital construction (12.3%) and government administration (10.1%).

Directory

Governor: WANG XIAOFENG; Office of the Provincial People's Government, Haikou.

Secretary of the Hainan Provincial Committee of the Chinese Communist Party: BAI KEMING; Office of the Secretary, CCP Secretariat, Haikou.

Chairman of the Standing Committee of the People's Congress of Hainan: BAI KEMING; Office of the Chairman, Congress Secretariat, Haikou.

Chairman of the Hainan Provincial Committee of the Chinese People's Political Consultative Conference: CHEN YUYI; Office of the Chairman, CPPCC Secretariat, Haikou.

Head of the Hainan Li–Miao Autonomous Area: (vacant).

Hebei

The Province of Hebei (Hopeh or Hopei) lies in northern China, abutting into the autonomous region of Nei Mongol (Inner Mongolia) from the south, with Liaoning, part of old Manchuria, to the north-east and Shandong to the south-east. There is a short border with Henan in the south and the ancient territory of Shanxi lies to the west. Traditionally the hinterland of the national capital, Hebei now encloses in the centre-north a smaller special municipality of Beijing (Peking). To the south-east, between Beijing and the coast, is another special municipality, Tianjin, part of (and the capital of) Hebei until 1967. In turn enclosed by the two urban regions is a small enclave of Hebei province, of which the chief town is Dacheng. This gives Hebei a total area of 202,700 sq km (78,242 sq miles), making it one of the larger provinces.

The old name of Hebei (Zhili or Chihli) meant 'directly administered' and referred to its administrative status under the Qing dynasty, but its name now ('north of the river') describes its geographical location on the lower reaches of the great Huang He (Yellow River). Hebei (its short name is Ji) lies on the western shore of the Bo Hai (formerly also known as the Gulf of Chihli) and edging the highlands of the southern Mongolian plateau, which reach towards the coast to separate the Manchurian lowlands from the North China Plain, on which most of the province is located. There are wide plains in the centre and the south of the province. In the west the Taihang range of mountains march from the south mid-way up the border, thence to strike north-eastwards across the province, reaching the height of Xiao (Lesser) Wutai Shan (2,870 m or 9,419 feet)

117

on the waist between Beijing and Shanxi. The north of the province generally is mountainous or hilly tableland, with ranges such as the Damaqun in the north-west, the Qilaotu in the north-east and, to the south of the latter, the Yan. The Great Wall straggles across these highlands, traversing the northern part of the province, built to defend the rich plains below where the land was still defensible. The Wall ends on the sea at Shanhaiguan (at a place called Laolongtou), where the coastal plains are at their narrowest, before widening into the Liaoning lowlands to the north of the Bo Hai. The coastline of Hebei is 487 km (302 miles) in extent, but is not itself punctured by the outlet of the Huang He (which is just to the south, in Shandong). Rather, the main river systems of the province are those of the Hai He and, in the north-east, the Luan He. The climate is a temperate monsoon one, but with seasonal and locational extremes. The province is hot and humid in summer (June–August), but very cold in winter, and is prone to flooding, dust storms and drought (for instance, five summers in a row in 1972–77). The average annual rainfall is between only 300 mm and 800 mm (12–31 inches), the 2000 total for the provincial capital of Shijiazhuang being 596 mm (more than Tianjin or Beijing to the north). In the same year the coldest month was January (with a monthly average of -4.3°C or 24.3°F) and the hottest July (28.6°C—83.5°F).

The total population of Hebei at the time of the national census in November 2000 was 67.44m., giving an average population density of 333 per sq km. Han Chinese constituted 95.7% of the total population. There were, however, 53 other ethnic groups represented in the census, mainly from among the Manchu (Man or Manzu), Mongol and Hui peoples; others included Zhuangs, Koreans, Miaos and Tujias. With the Manchu and Hui communities being the two minority nationalities to have adopted Han Chinese (the official Mandarin dialect is, in origin, local to this area) as their own language, very few other tongues are spoken at all widely in Hebei. Religious adherence, where it exists, is often heterodox so close to the cosmopolitan centres of Beijing and Tianjin, with new cults emerging next to the traditional native or imported religions.

In 2000 the urban population was put at 26.1% of the total, giving Hebei the lowest urbanization rate not only in the north and north-east of China, but also in the east, while in the south only Hunan was lower (Hebei was the sixth-most rural region in the country overall). Although there were 34 cities in Hebei, according to official definitions in 2000, only three had populations of over 1m., while 23 had less than 200,000. The provincial capital since 1967 has been Shijiazhuang (Shihkiachwang), near the western border of central south Hebei, which had an urban population of 2.14m. in 2000, although it administered a greater metropolitan area of 8.90m. Tangshan, on the still-broad coastal plains of eastern Hebei, and Handan, in the south, were the next in size. The other important cities were Cangzhou in the east of southern Hebei, Zhangjiakou (formerly Kalgan) in the north-west, on the Great Wall, Chengde (Rehe—an old imperial city and the chief town of the old province of Jehol, which was split between Hebei, Nei Mongol and Liaoning in 1955) in the north-east, and the port city of Qinhuangdao at the eastern end of the coast.

For administrative purposes, Hebei is divided, under 11 prefectural cities, into 138 counties (of which 23 are cities). There are six autonomous minority nationality areas, but they only have county status: to the north-west of

Qinhuangdao is the autonomous county for Manchus based in Qinglong; closer to the prefectural city of Chengde, but still south-east of it, is another Manchu county, that named for Kuancheng; in the far north is a joint Manchu and Mongol autonomous area based in Weichang; to the north-east of Chengde, north of Beijing, is the Fengning Manchu Autonomous County; and, finally, further south there are two Hui areas, Dacheng county in the enclave between Beijing and Tianjin (under Langfang city) and Mengcun, south-east of Cangzhou.

History

Hebei is very much part of the Chinese heartland, although its northern areas lie beyond the Great Wall. When the Zhou replaced the Shang in about the 11th century the dynasty led an expansion of the Chinese cultural area, in the east especially by close relations with the feudatory kingdom of Yan. This roughly corresponded to modern Hebei, although it soon suffered pressure from north of where the Great Wall would begin to rise. Nevertheless, it was an important bastion of the nascent 'empire' and a beacon of Chinese culture in the north-east for some 800 years. By the Warring States period (from the fifth century BC) the territory of Yan ran along the north-eastern coast of the Bo Hai, onto the defending highlands above, but it was one of the more peripheral of the 'central states' (the origin of the Chinese, which does not distinguish between singular and plural, for their own land, the 'middle kingdom'). Nevertheless, the already truncated Yan was the final conquest of Zheng of Qin, in 222 BC, and allowed him to proclaim himself Shi Huangdi, the First Emperor, in the following year. The Qin laid the foundations for the long-lasting Han dynasty and, indeed, of China itself. The ancient state of Yan came to be preserved only as an archaic name for the environs of Beijing (it was, for example, a Prince of Yan who usurped the throne as the Yongle emperor in 1402).

After the centuries of consolidating southern and western expansion, it was only at the end of the early imperial period that the Hebei region, which huddled from northern threats behind the Great Wall, began to be drawn closer to the heart of the Chinese world. Under the Sui and the Tang, designs on Korea and the consequent expansion of the canal system into the north resulted in the greater integration of Hebei into the Empire. However, it was conquests by non-Han peoples from the north and their subsequent sinicization that brought the region back into the Chinese heartland. This was particularly the case once dynastic capitals began to be established in modern Beijing or its environs (henceforth the history of Hebei very much became that of the hinterland of the court). Thus, the Khitans made it the base for the southern capital of their Liao dynasty in the 10th century. In 1121 Aguda of the Jurchens conquered the Khitan 'Supreme Capital' of Jehol and the next year proclaimed his Jin dynasty, which was to drive the Song from northern China and to site its own 'southern capital' of Yanjing in what is now Beijing. The Jurchens were, in turn, conquered by the Mongols in the 13th century. The city then became the winter (then the permanent) capital of the Mongols' Yuan dynasty, as Khanbaligh (Marco Polo's Cambulac) or Dadu. Under the twin-capital system of the Ming it became the 'northern capital', Beijing (Nanjing, now in Jiangsu, was the 'southern capital'), and, finally, the main capital, when the Yongle emperor (the former

Prince of Yan) moved the court north to counter a renewed Mongol threat in 1421. Beijing and its 'directly administered' surroundings of Zhili were still economically isolated at the time, but the completion of the Grand Canal, to deliver the grain tribute to the imperial court, laid the foundations of the modern wealth of the region (later completed by industrialization and the exploitation of local and Manchurian mineral resources). This process was mainly achieved under the Qing (who were also based in Beijing), another dynasty out of the north, and the last of imperial China.

From the late 16th century the Jurchen and other Tungusic tribes to the north-east of Hebei were united under Nurhachi and his son, Abahai. Most of Chinese Manchuria also fell under their domain, as did some of the Mongol tribes to the north of Hebei. Most of the territories beyond the Wall were held for Abahai by the 1640s, by which time he had designs on China itself. In 1636 he adopted the more propitious dynasty name of Qing (to replace the Jin revived by his father), the year after he declared that all the Jurchen tribes would henceforth be known as the Manchu people. Although Abahai died in 1643, the regents for his son, the Shunzhi emperor, carried through the ambition of conquering China. A rebel leader had seized Beijing and precipitated the suicide of the last Ming emperor in 1644. The general commanding the Great Wall at Shanhaiguan, Wu Sangui, invited the Manchus to help him retake the Chinese capital, effectively letting the Qing into their empire. Once the Manchu armies poured through the Dong Men (East Gate—more formally, the Tianxia Diyi Guan or First Pass under Heaven) they were not to leave, forming a ruling élite for the rest of the imperial period. Beijing became the Qing capital and Zhili the directly administered area subject to it (Zhili was usually controlled by a governor-general together with Henan and Shandong).

The northern areas of modern Hebei, beyond the Wall, remained more associated with Manchuria, which was administered differently to the rest of the Empire. Nevertheless, northern Hebei remained associated with imperial rule when the resort palace at Chengde (Rehe) was developed from 1703, much of its architecture increasingly reflecting Qing involvement in the tangled politics of the Mongols and the Tibetans (Xizangzu). Chengde also provided a refuge for the court when foreigners occupied Beijing in 1860. After the fall of the Qing Chengde became the seat of the province of Jehol, while Kalgan (now Zhangjiakou) to the west became the chief city of Qahar (Chahar). Zhili was renamed Hebei (in 1928), though not before it gave its name to a powerful warlord faction. This originated in the forces commanded by the Manchu governor-general of Zhili, Ronglu, at the end of the 19th century. He was loyal to the Dowager-Empress Cixi and the patron of Yuan Shikai. Ronglu's military supporters became known as the Beiyang Warlords, but after his death they quarrelled and, in 1917, split into the Anhui and Zhili factions. The Zhili clique controlled much of eastern, central and northern China; in 1922 its forces routed the armies of the main rival group, Fengtian, which retreated into Manchuria, but eventually succumbed to them later in the decade. This turmoil and the increasing Japanese threat in Manchuria meant Beijing was not the republican capital. In 1933 Jehol was annexed by the Japanese to the 'puppet' state of Manzhouguo, other parts were involved in 1935, while all of modern Hebei was occupied in 1937.

At the end of the Second World War the Nationalists and the Communists continued into a Civil War, which was gradually won by the latter. In 1949 the Communists conquered Beijing and proclaimed a People's Republic with its capital there. Although Beijing formed a separate municipality, it still meant that the Hebei region recovered a position near the centre of national affairs. The province also benefited in terms of territory during the early Communist period. In 1952 most of Qahar's vast northern territories were included in Nei Mongol, while the rest was split between Shanxi and Hebei (with Zhangjiakou in the latter). In 1955 it was decided that Jehol should be split between Hebei, Liaoning and Nei Mongol (with Chengde in Hebei). In 1958 Tianjin was reincorporated into Hebei, only for it again to become a special municipality in 1958. At that time Shijiazhuang (a small town until the railway revolution of the early 20th century) became the provincial capital. More recently the city has gained notability as the site of the largest army officer-training school in China and, through the same location, notoriety as the main centre for student induction courses after the upheavals in Beijing during 1989.

Economy

Hebei forms the 'Jing-Jin-Ji' economic zone with Beijing and Tianjin, which it surrounds, and benefits from the success of the two municipalities. In 2000 the province had the largest total gross domestic product (GDP), of 508,896m. yuan in current prices, in the north and north-east and the sixth largest in the entire People's Republic of China. In relation to its population, Hebei was the 10th-most prosperous region, with GDP of 7,663 yuan per head in the same year. Strong real growth of 12.5% during 1997 had eventually been affected by the aftermath of the Asian financial crisis of that year, but stayed fairly strong at 10.7% in 1998 and above 9.0% thereafter. Hebei is part of the transport hub centred on Beijing, although Tianjin and its own ports and networks are also important, as well as well developed. It is the best province or autonomous region after Liaoning for operational railways per sq km, with a total length of 3,632 km at the end of 2000. At the same time the total length of highways was 59,152 km (a very extensive 1,480 km were expressway and 1,458 km first-class highway). Official statistics for 2000 put the length of navigable inland waterways at only 75 km, but if this was the case it must almost entirely consist of that part of the Da Yunhe (Grand Canal) that traverses the territory. Qinhuangdao is a bustling seaport, which has long handled more freight than Tianjin, although the latter was progressing quickly towards competition in the late 1990s. Qinhuangdao was the third seaport of China in 1980, but second by 1985; it retained the latter position, after Shanghai (which handled about double the volume of freight), to 1995, but was thereafter displaced by Ningbo (Zhejiang) and Guangzhou (Guangdong), and challenged by Dalian (Liaoning), Tianjin and, even, Qingdao (Shandong). Hebei ranked fourth in the amount of electricity produced in 2000 (84,442m. kWh). Literacy was much improved during the 1990s, but the province was still compromised by rural illiteracy, to achieve an overall illiteracy rate of 6.7% in 2000 (about the same as the national average).

Although the primary sector is traditionally strong in Hebei, it only contributed 16.2% to provincial GDP in 2000. In the same year 48.8% of those in employment were engaged in the primary sector. Hebei is famous for wheat, cotton, walnuts, persimmons, tobacco, groundnuts (peanuts) and sesame. The total area sown with farm crops in 2000 was 9.02m. ha, of which 29.7% was for wheat and 27.5% for corn (maize). Relatively large areas were also planted with cotton (307,400 ha) and vegetables (866,100 ha), while, in addition, the area given to fruit orchards is the largest for any region in the country, at 1.04m. ha. The harvests in 2000 produced 12.1m. metric tons of wheat, 9.9m. tons of maize, 6.8m. tons of fruit (2.6m. tons of pears and 1.8m. tons of apples), 1.3m. tons of groundnuts (making Hebei the largest producer after Shandong and Henan), 300,000 tons of cotton and 12,000 tons of tobacco. Livestock in the province included 24.2m. pigs, 7.0m. cattle and buffaloes, 1.5m. donkeys (more than anywhere else in China), 1.1m. sheep, 1.1m. mules and horses and 1.0m. goats. Of the 4.2m. tons of meat produced in 2000, 2.4m. tons were pork. Hebei also produced 96,200 tons of milk, 84,200 tons of it from cows, making the province China's leading producer after Heilongjiang. Hebei is also the largest producer of sheep wool (27,789 tons in 2000) after Nei Mongol (Inner Mongolia) and of goat wool (5,567 tons) after Shandong. Finally, the province is, again after Shandong, the main provider of poultry eggs (3.6m. tons). Hebei's fishing industry is mainly marine; freshwater aquatic products in 2000 accounted for about 40% of total aquatic production of 809,500 tons. Seawater production is only 32% artificially cultured, while freshwater production reaches 78%. The catch of marine fish in 2000 was 187,900 tons and seawater shellfish 184,600 tons (crustaceans 80,700 tons). Of the freshwater catch, fish amounted to 306,500 tons, crustaceans 15,100 tons and shellfish 3,800 tons.

The secondary sector accounted for one-half of the economy (50.3% of GDP in 2000), a proportion equalled by one other region and exceeded by only three. Construction contributed 6.2% of the total GDP, having generated a total output value of 49,210m. yuan. About one-quarter (25.4% in 2000) of all employed persons were accounted for by the secondary sector, slightly more than the national average. Historically, coal and railways have been important to this industrial strength—rich mineral resources continue to help. Hebei has first place in China for resources of marble, potassium sand-shale and natural oilstone, second place for titanium, dolomite and vermiculite, and third for iron ore, solvent limestone, kyanite, fibrolite, iron bauxite, soda limestone and calcium carbide limestone. In 2000 the province produced 58m. metric tons of coal and 5.2m. tons of crude petroleum. The 10 key industries are rated as coal, metallurgy, building materials, textiles, chemicals, machinery, electronics, petroleum, light industry and medicine. The North China Pharmaceuticals Group in Shijiazhuang possesses the largest antibiotic production base in China, with output ranking second in the world. In 2000 Hebei was China's leading regional producer of pig iron (17.1m. tons) and cement (4.7m. tons), and second of plate glass (20.8m. weight cases). Other noteworthy individual products include machine-made paper and paperboard, salt, beer and steel. These examples indicate that heavy industry dominates the secondary sector of the Hebei economy, accounting for 55% of the 7,261 industrial enterprises in 2000, and for 66% of their total gross output value of 342,605m. yuan (current prices). There are 358 large enterprises, with a gross output value of 139,204m. yuan, and 769 medium-sized enterprises, by comparison worth only 46,447m. yuan.

The tertiary sector accounts for about one-third of GDP (33.5% in 2000) and one-quarter of employment (25.8%). The leading activities were trade and catering (9.0% of total GDP) and transport and communications (8.2%). The transport networks, for instance, employ many people, particularly on the railways, while also being useful in the encouragement of tourism. Hebei can boast the old imperial retreat of Chengde and the coastal resort of Beidaihe (popularized by Europeans in the 1890s, but now favoured by Communist grandees) among its sights. In fact, the province is reckoned to have among the highest concentration of historical relics in China, ranging from sections of the Great Wall to the sixth-century Zhaozhou bridge near Zhaoxian (the world's oldest segmental bridge, predating others by some 800 years). In 2000 Hebei earned US $142m. in foreign exchange from international tourism, when the number of tourist visits in the province reached 414,300 (359,000 foreigners).

Exports in 2000 increased appreciably to the value of US $3,278m., while imports were valued at $2,209m. Foreign direct investment in Hebei during that year totalled $679m., which was down from $1,042m. in the previous year. Government revenue from Hebei in 2000 totalled 24,876.21m. yuan, most of which came from the operations tax and value added tax, followed by the income tax on enterprises (18.6%, 17.6% and 14.3%, respectively). Expenditure in the province was significantly more than income, at 41,553.74m. yuan, with the biggest single item being education (17.7%), followed by spending on the justice system (8.0%), on the operating expenses of the tax department itself (7.6%—more than in any other region) and on capital construction (7.3%).

Directory

Governor: NIU MAOSHENG; Office of the Provincial People's Government, Shijiazhuang.

Secretary of the Hebei Provincial Committee of the Chinese Communist Party: WANG XUDONG; Office of the Secretary, CCP Secretariat, Shijiazhuang.

Chairman of the Standing Committee of the People's Congress of Hebei: CHENG WEIGAO; Office of the Chairman, Congress Secretariat, Shijiazhuang.

Chairman of the Hebei Provincial Committee of the Chinese People's Political Consultative Conference: LU CHUANZAN; Office of the Chairman, CPPCC Secretariat, Shijiazhuang.

Heilongjiang

The Province of Heilongjiang (Heilungkiang) is named for the Heilong Jiang (Black Dragon River—i.e. the River Amur), which forms much of the international border with the Russian Federation. Heilongjiang caps the north-eastern upthrust of China, and Russia lies beyond, to the north (beyond the Heilong) and to the east. To the west is one horn of the crescent of territory forming the Chinese autonomous region of Nei Mongol (Inner Mongolia), while to the south is the Province of Jilin (Kirin). Jilin, and beyond it Liaoning, together with Heilongjiang, once formed part of Manchuria, although generally under the People's Republic the area is simply described as the north-east. Heilongjiang has an area of 463,600 sq km (178,950 sq miles), making it the sixth largest unit in the People's Republic (of the 22 provinces, only Qinghai and Sichuan are larger).

Heilongjiang is a compact territory in the north-eastern corner of China, with an arm stretching north-westwards up the Heilong river to end in a fist of territory forming the country's most northerly area. The Da (Greater) Hinggan range extends Nei Mongol territory northwards and ends in the Emur and Yilehuli mountains, which border this generally hilly piece of northern Heilongjiang. The Xiao (Lesser) Hinggan Ling then extend south out of the joining arm of territory into the centre-north of Heilongjiang. Thrusting up towards them from the south, helping to bisect the province, is the heavily wooded Zhangguangcai range. Between them they divide the broad, fertile Songnen plains of the south-west (named after the Songhua and the Nen, the great rivers that dominate the centre of the province) from the Sanjiang plains of the north-east (formed from the alluvial deposits of the Heilong, Songhua and Wusuli—Ussuri rivers). There is also a small, generally marshy plain north of

124

Xingkai Hu (Lake Khanka, which is crossed from east to west by the eastern Sino–Russian border) and south of a north-eastwards extension of the Zhangguangcai Ling, the Wanda Shan. The Songnen and Sanjiang plains are connected by the great valley of the Songhua, near the western end of which (and not far from the border with Jilin) sits the provincial capital of Harbin. The yellow-silted Songhua Jiang is the third longest river to lie entirely within Chinese territory (at 2,308 km or 1,433 miles), although this is exceeded by the black-silted Heilong Jiang on the border (2,965 km). The Wusuli (most of which contributes to the definition of the eastern border and is known as the Ussuri in Russia) and the Nen are also important rivers of the province. The highest point is in the Emur Shan, at Fengshui peak, which reaches 1,398 m (4,588 feet). Parts of Heilongjiang are volcanic, which can create curious contrasts with the generally subarctic climate. The province is prone to Siberian gales, droughts in spring, flooding and short summers (in the north-west there is barely a season that could be described as summer). Annual average rainfall is only between 250 mm and 700 mm (10–27 inches), mainly falling in June–August (summer) and to the south of the Lesser Hinggans. The total for 2000 in Harbin was 488 mm, almost one-third of which fell in August alone. Average minimum and maximum temperatures throughout the province range from -32°C to 17°C (-26°–63°F) in January and from 16°C to 23°C (61°–73°F) in July. The average monthly temperatures in Harbin during 2000 were lowest in January, at -20.0°C (-4.0°F), and highest in July, at 24.9°C (76.8°F), while the annual average of 4.6°C (40.3°F) was the lowest for any regional capital in China. Mohe, in the far north-west, remains the place to record the lowest fall of temperature anywhere in China: -52.3°C (-61.1°F) in 1965.

Despite the often inclement conditions, Heilongjiang is the second-most populous of the north-eastern provinces, with 36.89m. people recorded at the 2000 census. However, the vast area means that the population density is very low, at 80 per sq km. Once the Qing allowed Han settlement in Manchuria large numbers were attracted by the natural resources and, later, the wealth brought by the railways. So, although there were 49 ethnic groups represented in Heilongjiang at the time of the census, minority nationalities accounted for only 5.0% of the population by 2000. The main group is that of the Man (Manchu or Manzu), descended from the Jurchens and other Tungusic peoples. They were all designated as Manchus by the first Qing ruler, whose dynasty went on to conquer China, making the Manchus a ruling class that had mostly lost the use of its own tongue by the 20th century. The Manchus are the second largest ethnic minority in China. There are also Mongols, Koreans, Russians and Huis (Chinese Muslims)—the latter two groups mainly in the cities—and a number of smaller groups. The Daurs, of whom there are about 120,000 in total, live mainly along the Nen Jiang. The Evenks, a Tungusic people, traditionally nomadic forest hunters, live in western Heilongjiang and the neighbouring parts of Nei Mongol (although there are only some 26,000 in China, they are also represented in an autonomous area far to the north-west in Russia). Likewise, the 6,000 or so Oroqens live mainly in north-western Heilongjiang and neighbouring Nei Mongol, and were also nomadic forest hunters of these areas—they are now generally agriculturalists and lumbermen, although some still keep reindeer. The Oroqens retain shamanist beliefs, the bear particularly being sacred and sometimes sharing the 'wind burial' used for people. The Hezhes or Hezhens, of whom there are fewer than 4,000 (less than one-half of them in China), are traditional fisherfolk around Tongjiang, in the north-east, on the Russian border. The Russian, Hui and tribal presence, therefore, diversifies the residual belief patterns usually seen in China. The province is also home to some Xibe, who practice lamaism.

Over one-half (51.5%) of the population at the 2000 census were classed as urban, more than in any other province (or autonomous region) after Guangdong and the other north-eastern state of Liaoning. The province has a number of large cities, chief among them being the seat of the provincial government, Harbin (also known as Bingcheng). Harbin is the largest provincial capital in China, and only the special municipalities had larger urban populations in 2000 (Harbin had 4.35m.). The greater metropolitan area of Harbin had a population of 9.35m., however, which was exceeded by that of Chengdu (Sichuan), although it surpassed Tianjin. Mudanjiang, in the south-east of the province, also has a population in excess of 1m., while the next largest are the cities of Daqing (Anda) and Qiqihar, to the north-west of Harbin, and Jiamusi (Kiamusze), at the other end of the Songhua valley, in north-eastern Heilongjiang. Jixi, Hegang, Yichun and Shuangyashan, all in the east, are also sizeable cities. The province is divided into 13 prefectures, of which only one is rural, and 66 counties, of which 19 are cities. Only one county is actually constituted as a minority nationality autonomous area.

History

Much of the modern province was an undeveloped frontier land for many centuries, inhabited by hunters, fishers and some traders. The more settled plains, particularly the south-western Songnen plain, shared more in the history of the other Manchurian territories to the south. These lands were desirable to whichever people dominated the region and fell successively under the Jurchens, Khitans and Mongols, as well as the Han Chinese. The dominant tribes for most of the Christian era were Tungusic, such as the Jurchen (Rezhen) peoples (the 12th-century Jin—'golden'—dynasty had a capital near Harbin). In the late 16th century these tribes were united under Nurhachi and, from 1626, his son, Abahai. It was Abahai who introduced a common name for the Jurchen tribes, that of Manchu (Manzu), and it was he that formalized his house's imperial pretensions in China, under the dynastic name of Qing. This ambition was realized for him by the regents of his son only one year after his death, when the Manchu armies were admitted into the leaderless Ming empire and occupied Beijing (which replaced the Manchurian capital of Mukden—Shenyang, now in Liaoning—as the seat of the Qing Government). Meanwhile, under Abahai, the Manchus had begun to settle the northern lands along the Heilong Jiang (River Amur), although Russian settlement was leading to some tensions. Manchu authority was firmly established south of the Heilong in the early 1640s, but Russian penetration continued, particularly once the Manchus became absorbed in the conquest of China proper.

There were minor clashes between Russians and Manchus throughout the 1650s and 1660s, particularly after the establishment of a Russian settlement at Albazin on the north bank of the Heilong, some 100 km downstream from Mohe. Encroachments continued, but it was not until the 1680s that preparations for a campaign along the Heilong could be contemplated by the Chinese authorities (Manchuria was, through conquest, now part of the Chinese Empire, although the migration of ethnic or Han Chinese to Manchuria was for long forbidden, while intermarriage between Manchus and the Han remained illegal until the early 1900s). A Qing army marched into northern Manchuria in 1683 and began clearing the territory of Russian settlements, moving up the Heilong to take and burn Albazin by 1685. The army was forced to reinvest the fort in the following year, because the Russians had again occupied it, but accepted a truce rather than its imminent surrender. Further negotiations led to the first treaty between China and a Western power, which was signed at Nerchinsk in 1689. The Russians gave up Albazin, but were acknowledged in much of the territory north of the Heilong (Amur) and gained a privileged position (for Europeans) within the Qing domains.

With the decline of Qing power by the 19th century, the tsar was as willing as any other power to exploit Chinese weakness, particularly as the wealth of Manchuria was beginning to be exploited and Russia feared the tide of Han Chinese settlement. In 1860, when the British and French forced the Conventions of Beijing on the Qing Government, Russia had offered itself as a mediator. It also managed to gain concessions, therefore, most notably acquiring all land north of the Heilong and east of the Wusuli (Ussuri—the eastern territories now constitute Russia's Maritime Krai), permitting the Russians to build a port with access to the Pacific at Vladivostok. In 1896 the Russians, who were completing their mighty Trans-Siberian and Baikal–Amur railway links, negotiated to build railways between Harbin (then a small town), the seaport of Dalian (Liaoning) and Vladivostok. By 1904 the concession was in place, but although accompanied by further Russian demands (which were to continue in one form or another until the end of the Second World War) China was spared tsarist expansionism by the Russian–Japanese War of 1904–05. This thwarted Russian ambitions (which had been permitted as protection against Japan), but they were replaced in control of the railway concession by the victorious Japanese. Thus, as China subsided into confusion after the fall of the Qing, the South Manchurian Railway Company emerged as a colonial power virtually in its own right, although a Russian influence, ironically, was reinforced by the influx of refugees from the 1917 revolution in that country.

In April 1911 a separate province was formed in northern Manchuria (including what is now north-eastern Nei Mongol), the border in the south-west roughly following the line of the Songhua and excluding Harbin (which was included in the same province as Kirin—Jilin). The whole area was dominated by the Fengtian warlord faction, initially under Zhang Zuolin, then, from 1928, under his son, the 'Young Marshall', Zhang Xueliang. It was from about 1928 that the warlords of Manchuria acknowledged the authority of the Republic under Jiang Jieshi (Chiang Kai-shek), although Japanese influence was strong. In September 1931 Japan's ambitions became explicit, with the seizure of the major cities of southern Manchuria; it had occupied most of the north in the first months of 1932, Harbin being taken in March. Japan then established a nominally independent state of Manzhouguo (Manchukuo) in north-eastern China. This was a republic, but had Puyi Aisin Gioro, the last of the Qing (emperor between 1908 and 1912 and then from 1934 until 1945), as its

Chief Executive. He was restored as the Kangde emperor on 1 March 1934, and the attempt to create a larger state dependent upon Japan was pursued when war between the Japanese and Chinese began in 1937. However, Japan was defeated in the Second World War and the forces of the USSR (the successor state of Russia) had occupied Harbin and most of modern Heilongjiang during 1945.

As the Soviet regime was more sympathetic to the Communists than to the Nationalist Government, it is no surprise to find that Manchuria had became a stronghold of the Chinese Communist Party by the time of its restoration to Chinese control in May 1946. Moreover, the USSR surrendered its share of the South Manchurian Railway in 1953. At this time the north-east was united into an administrative region that included more than the three provinces that now exist. The west and north-west of modern Heilongjiang (the south-west of the old northern Manchurian province, which was to become part of Nei Mongol, had been included with Jehol, the province based on Chengde—a city now in Hebei) consisted of Nenjiang province, the north-east of Hejiang and the southern strip of Songjiang. By 1954 the modern Heilongjiang had been formed, with Harbin (which had become a special municipality only the year before) becoming part of the united province, along with Nenjiang, Hejiang and most of Songjiang, except for the south-west around Baicheng and Taonan, which became part of Jilin province. The Communist regime encouraged the industrialization of the region and, initially, the close connection with the Russians across the border. This has resumed since the disintegration of the USSR, wealth attracting Russian trade, and the Chinese Government free of the historical fears of foreign interference in the region (helped by the presence of an ethnic Han majority and, therefore, no separatist sentiments).

Economy

Heilongjiang, despite the often extreme climate, is one of the more prosperous provinces of the People's Republic, mainly owing to its natural resources and its industry. In 2000 the total gross domestic product (GDP) of Heilongjiang, at current prices, was 325,300m. yuan, or 8,562 yuan per head. The trade with Russia has helped in recent years. The historic associations of the north-east of China with railways, as well as the province's extent, means that Heilongjiang has a greater length of railway track in operation than anywhere else in the People's Republic, at 5,013 km in 2000. The road network totalled 50,284 km (only 285 km of which was expressway and 387 km first-class highway, however) and the navigable inland waterways 5,057 km. Electricity production of 42,673m. kWh in 2000 was mainly thermally generated. An illiteracy rate of 5.8% in 2000 was better than the Chinese average, but the worst in the north-east.

The primary sector of the economy contributed only 11.0% (one of the lowest proportions in China) to regional GDP and has also shown least growth over recent years (indeed, in 2000 it contracted relative to the secondary and tertiary sectors). However, primary activity still accounted for 49.5% of employed persons in the same year. Heilongjiang is an important grain province; cereals (which covered almost one-half of the total sown area of 9.34m. ha in 2000) include maize, some rice, sorghum and various millets. Potatoes, sugar beet, soybeans (over one-third of the total sown area), sesame, sunflower seeds, flax, tussah and tobacco are also grown, while the province is noted for its ginseng, mushrooms and other edible funguses, and pine nuts. Crop production in 2000 amounted to 19.7m. metric tons of cereals, 4.9m. tons of beans, 2.5m. tons of sugar beet (the second largest producer in China, with almost one-third of the national harvest), 192,079 tons of fruit (mainly apples) and 96,000 tons of tobacco (the leading producer in northern China—81,000 tons was flue-cured). Milch cows accounted for a large proportion of the 4.6m. head of cattle numbered at the end of 2000. There were also 728,000 horses, 79,000 donkeys and 56,000 mules. The smaller domesticated beasts exceeded these totals, with 9.9m. pigs and 5.1m. sheep and goats (3.8m. sheep). Meat production (57% pork) was only 1.5m. tons in 2000, whereas a similar tonnage for milk (99% cows' milk) made Heilongjiang the biggest producer in China, providing 17% of the national total. The province also produced 13,550 tons of sheep wool, 753,000 tons of poultry eggs and 4,000 tons of honey. Other animal products are mainly taken from the wild—fur and antlers. There are some domesticated reindeer, while fur animals hunted include squirrels, alpine weasels, sables and otters. The principal economic importance of the extensive forest lands, however, is for timber. Forestry did suffer from the worst forest fire in Chinese history in 1987, in the north-west of Heilongjiang, around Mohe, when over 1m. ha of woodland were destroyed and 200 people died. It has not prevented Heilongjiang remaining the region to produce more timber than anywhere else in China—8.2m. cu m (17.4% of the national total) in 2000. Fishing, by contrast, is mostly farmed (85% in 2000), is entirely freshwater and the catch includes chum salmon, sturgeon and huso sturgeon. Fish caught in 2000 massed 380,500 tons, and there were also 1,600 tons of crustaceans.

Heilongjiang has the most industrial economy of any region of China, with the secondary sector accounting for 57.4% of GDP in 2000. Of all employed persons in the province, this sector provided work for 21.2%. Even without construction activity (which had a total output value of 22,296.2m. yuan in 2000 and alone provided 6.3% of GDP), industry consisted of over one-half of economic performance. Heilongjiang has significant mineral reserves, and much of its industry has developed from this basis. The province is the largest producer of crude petroleum in the country (530.7m. metric tons in 2000, or 32.6% of the national total), but also mines other hydrocarbons (50m. tons of coal and 2,304m. cu m of natural gas). Manufactures include heavy machinery such as generators, freight trains, building machinery, also metallurgical equipment, tools and measuring tools, as well as paper, sugar, beer and cigarettes. In 2000 there were 2,666 industrial enterprises in Heilongjiang, with a total gross output value of 126,737m. yuan in current prices. The state sector accounted for 60% of the number and 84% of the value. Heavy industry accounted for 52% and 82%, respectively, while large enterprises accounted for 10% of the enterprises and 80% of the gross output value.

The tertiary sector accounted for 31.6% of GDP and 29.3% of employed persons in 2000. Trade and catering provided almost one-third of the services product (9.8% of total GDP), transport and communications just under one-fifth (6.2%), and real estate and social services each for one-10th (3.2%). Transport is dominated by the railways, in their historic importance to economic development and, currently, in the number of people employed compared to other forms of transportation (more people are employed on the railways in

Heilongjiang than in any other region but Henan). The export of raw or semi-processed materials dominates provincial trade, which declined in 1999, but made a strong recovery in 2000. Exports totalled US $2,423.93m. in the latter year, while imports were worth $1,568.66m. International tourism is helped by the strong cross-border Russian activity, especially since the disintegration of the USSR at the end of 1991, with foreign-exchange earnings increasing from a mere $7m. in 1990 to $189m. in 2000. In the latter year there were 551,700 international tourist visits, of which 504,700 were by foreigners. Sights range from the winter Ice Lantern Festival in Harbin to the museum at the old Japanese Germ Warfare Experimental Base (731 Division—a secret camp set up in 1939, the story of which was exposed in the 1980s by a Japanese journalist). Most of the attractions are part of the province's austere natural environment, from the volcanic lakes of Wudalian Chi to the wetlands of the Zhalong Nature Reserve in the south-west, noted especially for the presence of cranes (especially the very endangered red-crowned crane, an ancient Chinese symbol of immortality). The seriously endangered tiger population is another attraction for visitors (some illegal—one tiger can greatly multiply a poacher's annual income), the local variety being known variously as the Manchurian, Amur, Siberian or North-Eastern Chinese tiger.

Government revenues in Heilongjiang during 2000 amounted to 18,533.79m. yuan. The value added tax raised the most, about one-quarter (24.9%) of the total, followed by the operations tax (18.3%) and then the tax on town maintenance and construction, enterprises' income tax, expert-project income, the agricultural tax and income tax on individuals (each raising between 8.5% and 5.3% of the total). Total expenditure by government in the province was 38,187.36m. yuan in the same year, of which 12.8% went on education and 11.6% on price subsidies (the latter is more prominent in the spending of the north-eastern provinces, with government compensating for the more extreme climatic conditions). Foreign direct investment totalled US $300.86m. in 2000, barely less than the total for the previous year.

Directory

Governor: SONG FATANG; Office of the Provincial People's Government, Harbin.

Secretary of the Heilongjiang Provincial Committee of the Chinese Communist Party: XU YOUFANG; Office of the Secretary, CCP Secretariat, Harbin.

Chairman of the Standing Committee of the People's Congress of Heilongjiang: XU YOUFANG; Office of the Chairman, Congress Secretariat, Harbin.

Chairman of the Heilongjiang Provincial Committee of the Chinese People's Political Consultative Conference: MA GUOLIANG; Office of the Chairman, CPPCC Secretariat, Harbin.

Henan

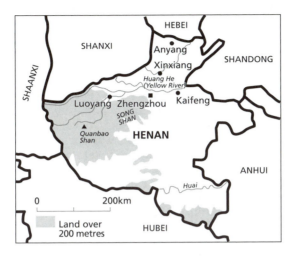

The Province of Henan (Honan) lies at the heart of China, on the Huang He (Yellow River) in the north and reaching to the drainage basin of the Chang Jiang (River Yangzi) in the south. Beyond the irregular eastern border lie the provinces of Shandong and, in the south, Anhui. Hubei lies to the south-west, Shaanxi to the west, Shanxi to the north-west and Hebei in the north. The total area of Henan is some 167,000 sq km (64,460 sq miles).

The Huang He runs from west to east across the north of Henan, most of which, as indicated by its name, lies to the 'south of the river'. There is a strip of territory on the north bank that widens downstream into a sizeable piece of territory in the north-west, in the angle of the Huang He where it turns north-westwards, into its lower reaches. Another name used for Henan (the short name for which is Yu) is Zhongzhou, 'central plain', which also describes a geographical feature of the province. Some 56% of the territory is plainland, the soft yellow loess plains of northern China. It is the loess that contributes to the heavy silting (the heaviest in the world), as well as the colour, of the Huang He, making it, historically, such a destructively flood-prone river. The loess, however, is also fertile and easily worked (encouraging the tradition of cave or ground-hewn dwellings), while the province also spans the drainage areas of the Chang Jiang, the Huai He and the Hai He, endowing Henan with generous water resources. The west is rugged and rolling, made lofty by the Funiu and other eastward extensions of the Qingling range, reaching the highest point in the province at Quanbao Shan (2,094 m or 6,873 feet). The final outthrust of these highlands is the Song Shan (the three main peaks are Shaoshi Shan, Taishi Shan and Wuru Feng), sacred to Daoists. Song Shan represents the element of earth and is the central sacred mountain, 'directly under Heaven' (the others are: Heng Shan in Shanxi, to the north, for wood; Heng Shan in Hunan, to the south, for fire; Tai Shan in

131

Shandong, to the west, for water; and Hua Shan in Shaanxi, to the east, for metal). Along the north-western border are the lower slopes of the Taihang Shan, while the Tongbai and Dabie mountains march down the south-western border. The average annual rainfall in Henan is between 500 mm and 900 mm (20–35 inches); it is higher in the southern and northern mountains. Zhengzhou (Chengchow), the provincial capital, had 637 mm in 2000. Average monthly temperatures range from -3°C to 3°C (27°–37°F) in January and 24°C to 29°C (75°–84°F) in July. In Zhengzhou the average monthly temperature overall was -1.7°C (28.9°F) in January 2000 and 27.6°C (81.7°F) in July.

Henan has the highest population of any region in the People's Republic of China, at 92.56m. in 2000. Not being a large province, it is also the third-most densely populated, with 554 per sq km. Although minority nationalities constituted only 1.2% of the population in 2000, given the large total they number over 1m. and include the Chinese-speaking Huis and Manchus (Manzus) and Mongols. In addition, Kaifeng is the first place where Jews settled in China and, although most distinctive religious beliefs and customs had died out by the 19th century, the descendants of the 'Israelites' still live there. Some claim that the Lanmao Huis, the 'Blue-capped' Muslims, are also their descendants. The city also still possesses fairly large Muslim and Christian communities. Henan is also important to Daoists, who visit the Song Shan, which also attracts visitors to the Shaolin Si, an ancient Buddhist monastery where the martial art of kung fu was developed.

The population is not very urbanized (23.2% in 2000—only Xizang, Tibet, was less so). Henan for administrative purposes is divided into 17 city-based prefectures and 110 counties (including 21 cities). Only two of these cities number over 1m. people. The total population of Zhengzhou in 2000 was 6.28m., although only 2.21m. of them lived in the city itself. Luoyang (Loyang), to the west, is the second city of Henan, while the old capital of Kaifeng, to the east, also lies on the belt of territory just to the south of the Huang He. Other major population centres are Anyang (Zhangde) in the far north and, between there and Zhengzhou but closer to the capital, Xinziang, while to the south of Zhengzhou is Pingdingshan. There are no minority nationality autonomous areas.

History

Henan consists of the major part of the Central Plains of ancient China and here, in the north, over 3,500 years ago, was the origin of Chinese civilization. The beginnings of urban settlement were presided over by the Shang dynasty, a probably indigenous development, in around 1700–1100 BC. The first capital of the Shang was at Yanshi, west of modern Zhengzhou, then in about 1383 BC the final move was from Ao to Yin or Yinxu, near modern Anyang, where archaeological evidence confirmed (in the 1920s) the existence of the previously legendary Shang. The Shang were primitive by comparison with what came later, but they lie at the root of Han civilization. The Shang had 13 kings, ending with the apocryphally tyrannical Jie. The dynasty was overthrown after the vital battle of Muye, in around 1045 BC, to be conquered by the previously vassal Zhou. Henan remained central to their realm, with

Luoyang becoming the capital of the Eastern Zhou (eighth to third centuries BC). The nominally subject state of Wei (fifth to third centuries BC) was based in Liang (modern Kaifeng—Bianzhou), but succumbed to the unifying Qin, which established the empire inherited by the Han. Under the later Hans (Eastern Hans, first to third centuries AD) Luoyang again became an imperial capital, thereafter an alternating or sister capital with Changan (Shaanxi), from where the Hans had originally relocated.

Luoyang was pre-eminent under the Wei and Western Jin (Chin) dynasties in AD 265–316. It was the capital of Wei, one of the Three Kingdoms into which the Han imperium had disintegrated (a period celebrated in Chinese literature, which has immortalized the great general, Cao Cao). Wei eventually, albeit briefly, reunited the country, initially under a dynasty with the same name (proclaimed by Wen, the regnal name of Cao Pi, the son of Cao Cao), then under the Sima clan, which usurped the throne and changed the dynasty name to Jin. This Henan-based empire was, however, weak and succumbed to Xiongnu (Hun) invasions, with Luoyang being sacked in 311 and Changan in 316. Thereafter, much of this part of China was subject to the rule of northern invaders, notably the Toba, who soon became sinicized. It was one of the first Toba dynasties, the Northern Wei, who restored Luoyang as an imperial seat, when the capital was moved here from Pingcheng (modern Datong, in Shanxi) in 494. The Northern Wei were noted for their patronage of Buddhism, for which Henan was already an important place. The first Buddhist temple in China was built here (Baima Si, near Luoyang) in the first century, after two Han envoys returned from Afghanistan with two Indian monks and a collection of scriptures and statues. In the fifth century another Indian monk, Bodidharma, preached Chan (Zen) Buddhism here and founded the famous Shaolin monastery in the Song Shan.

From the time of the Northern Wei until the 12th-century expulsion of the Song from northern China, Henan was at the political centre of the Empire. Luoyang claims to have been a capital for 13 dynasties, although for the Tang (618–907) it was secondary to Changan. The city suffered when rebels under An Lushan captured it in the 750s, before advancing on Changan and causing the imperial court to flee to Sichuan. Although the Tang were restored, it was the end of their strength, and Luoyang was to be increasingly displaced by Kaifeng as a capital. Three of the Five Dynasties in the 10th century (the Later Liang, the Later Jin—Chin and the Later Zhou) were based in northern Henan, as were the Song, and Kaifeng became a national capital when they came to power in 960. Seven of the nine Northern Song emperors are buried at Gongyi Shi (formerly Gongxian), between Luoyang and Zhengzhou, the last two (the Huizong and Qinzong emperors, father and son) having been captured by the Jurchen (Ruzhen) invaders in the 1120s, when the dynasty fled to the south of China. The Jin armies sacked Kaifeng and Luoyang at the same time, and the centres of political power moved out of Henan. The cities of the region continued to decline into the modern era, with two notable incidents of civil unrest and flooding combining to devastate the Huang He plains. In the 1640s rebels under Li Zicheng (who went on to take Beijing and cause the suicide of the last Ming emperor) destroyed the river dykes on the Huang He, overwhelming Kaifeng. This action was repeated centuries later, in April 1938, at Huayuankou, north of Zhengzhou, when Jiang Jieshi (Chiang Kai-shek) likewise ordered the destruction of the dykes, in a ruthless tactic designed to delay the Japanese advance, but which also drowned about 1m. Chinese people and rendered another 11m. homeless and exposed to starvation.

Until the fall of the Qing Henan was frequently governed with Zhili, the directly administered central region (roughly modern Hebei), so it was late to be formed as a separate province and only declared its independence from the Qing on 22 December 1911. It was only under tenuous central control, although Yuan Shikai (the last premier of the Qing, the first republican president and the declared but never crowned Hongxian emperor) is buried near Anyang, but came under Guomindang authority in 1930. Communist support in the region was no doubt aided by Jiang Jieshi's inundation tactics, which mainly harmed the peasantry (whose support Mao Zedong was cultivating) and only delayed the Japanese advance by a few weeks. By the early 1940s the Japanese controlled much of northern China as far as Kaifeng and the other Huang He cities, although it was not until 1944 that offensives through southern and eastern parts of Henan really occurred. In the civil war Kaifeng was early under Communist control, but the south of the province was not secured until 1948. The area was then the object of industrialization in the early years of the People's Republic, although the traditional agricultural base was not neglected, particularly in attempts to control the Huang He ('China's sorrow'). The most famous irrigation effort was the building of the Hongqi Hu or Red Flag Canal in Linxian county (the main town has since been renamed Linzhou Shi), which became an inspirational Maoist tale. In administrative terms, modern Henan finally took shape in 1952, when Pingyuan (Bingyuan—the eastern plains area, formerly part of Zhili, and a separate province since 1949) was split with Shandong. The capital was moved from Kaifeng to Zhengzhou in 1954.

Economy

Henan is a largely agricultural province, although under the Communists Zhengzhou and Luoyang have become major industrial centres, with Zhengzhou also developing a high-technology sector more recently. Kaifeng, the old capital, and Anyang have not developed industry to quite the same extent. In 2000 Henan had a gross domestic product (GDP) of 513,766m. yuan, after real growth of 9.4% on the previous year. Per-head GDP that year was 5,444 yuan. One of the great early works of the Communist era was extensive irrigation works, which brought some control over the Huang He, but notably the diverting of a river into the Hongqi Qu (including taking it through a mountain and down along some cliffs—in all, some 1,500 km, with hills removed, 134 tunnels delved, 150 aqueducts constructed and some 24m. cu m of earth removed). Henan is also a hub of inland communications. The province has more people than in any other territory working on the railways (129,000 at the end of 2000) and, with Shandong, working in highway transport (87,000). The total length of operational railways in Henan at the end of 2000 was 2,353 km, while the fairly dense road network was 64,453 km in extent (505 km of expressway, but only 38 km of first-class highway). The system of navigable inland waterways stretched for only 1,104 km. Henan produced 69,493m. kWh of electricity in

2000, mostly thermally generated. Illiteracy is relatively low, at 5.9% of the adult population in 2000.

The primary sector accounted for 22.6% of GDP (but is growing less well than other sectors), but 64.1% of employed persons (the only higher proportions are in three of the regions of the south-west). The province is noted for growing grain, particularly wheat, sesame, cotton and jute, and famous for Lingbao and Xinzheng dates, Zhongmu garlic, Zhengzhou watermelons and Huaiyang day lilies. Henan has the largest area sown with farm crops of any region in China (13.1m. ha), of which 69% was given over to foodgrains in 2000. Wheat took up 4.9m. ha, the largest area given to the cereal in any region and 18% of the national total (figures for 2000). The province also covered the largest area with groundnuts (1.0m. ha), the second largest area with cotton (0.8m. ha), with jute and ambary hemp (15,300 ha) and with vegetables (1.2m. ha), and the third largest area with tobacco (1.7m. ha). Yields that year amounted to the largest foodgrain (and cereal) crops in the country: 22.4m. metric tons of wheat (first in China); 10.8m. tons of corn (maize—second); 1.4m. tons of beans (second); and 2.9m. tons of tubers (first). Henan also produced the second largest crop of groundnuts (3.4m. tons), the largest crop of sesame (220,000 tons) and the best harvests of cotton (704,000 tons) and of jute and ambary hemp (33,000 tons—just over one-quarter of the national total). The 276,000 tons of tobacco (99% flue-cured) produced, although less than one-half of that in Yunnan, still exceeded the output of any other region. With the fifth largest fruit crop in China too (3.6m. tons, mainly apples), it can be seen that Henan is one of the most productive agricultural regions in the People's Republic. The main forest products are timber (1.8m. cu m in 2000), tung-oil seeds (57,054 tons in 2000) and walnuts (17,143 tons). The province has the largest number of cattle and buffaloes (with 13.4m. head in 2000) and of sheep (27.3m.), and the second largest number of pigs (35.9m.), as well as 1.1m. donkeys, horses and mules and 2.3m. goats. In recent years livestock has been increasing. Meat production of 5.0m. tons in 2000 was exceeded only in Shandong, but Henan led with pork (3.2m. tons) and beef (0.8m. tons), and was surpassed only by Xinjiang with mutton (0.3m. tons). The province also produced 202,000 tons of milk (80% cows' milk), 7,736 tons of sheep wool, 2.7m. tons of poultry eggs (only Shandong had more) and 23,000 tons of honey (making Henan the leading producer, with Sichuan). Aquatic products (321,700 tons in 2000) are entirely from fresh water and 94% artificially cultured. The fish catch amounted to only 302,300 tons (although Henan is famous for the Huang He common carp), with 6,600 tons of crustaceans and 1,100 tons of shellfish.

The secondary sector accounted for a sizeable 47.0% of GDP in 2000, and was growing strongly, but it utilized only 17.5% of employed persons. Construction, as part of this, itself accounted for 6.5% of GDP, to produce a total output value of 27,155.74m. yuan. Some of its industrial capacity is based on its mineral wealth: Henan is the leading region in China for molybdenum, blue asbestine, casting sandstone, natural alkali, pearl stone, blue spar and red mainstay. Deposits of bauxite, natural oilstone, glass-use tuff and concrete-use limestone are second in the country. Tungsten, caesium, coal (third—76m. metric tons in 2000), crude petroleum (5.6m. tons), natural gas (fourth—1,495m. cu m), nickel, gold and marble are also produced. The province, however, has a very complete industrial structure, being varied by agricultural processing, as well as coal, metallurgy, building materials and chemicals, and producing machinery and electronic components and products. Henan has about one-half the number of enterprises that Guangdong has, but only that province, Jiangsu, Zhejiang and Shandong had more. In 2000 there were 9,930 enterprises (although their total gross output value was only 349,496m. yuan, at current prices), with the largest number in China owned by collectives (4,206—but accounting for only just over one-quarter of the gross output value) and heavy industry dominant (53% of businesses and 63% of value). The 319 large enterprises accounted for 37% of the total gross output value, the 684 medium-sized ones for only 12% and the remaining 8,927 for 51%. The province produces the largest amount of plate glass (24.3m. weight cases) in China, the second largest amount of machine-made paper and paperboard (2.9m. tons in 2000) and of cigarettes (2.9m. cases), cement (fourth—37.2m. tons), textiles, iron and steel, and some chemicals.

The tertiary sector contributed 30.4% of GDP in 2000, with transport and communications providing just over one-quarter of this and trade and catering services providing just less than one-quarter. The services sector as a whole also accounted for 18.4% of employed persons in 2000 (the lowest proportion of any part of China except Yunnan). Trade is augmented by Henan's role as an important futures market—it is the main commodity-trading centre for grain and grease. Henan's own commodity exports in 2000 were steady in value at US $1,586.83m., while imports had almost doubled in value to $1,537.06m. The wealth of its history and culture provide a number of service activities, but also helps tourism in the province. Henan has the largest number of art-performance troupes (the Henan opera is one of the 10 great schools of China) and places, the most cultural centres and book stores, and the third largest number of museums and public libraries. Song Shan is a major attraction, as are the ancient imperial capitals of Luoyang and Kaifeng. Other historical sites include the oldest pagoda in China (sixth century) and the oldest surviving observatory in China (at the emperor's order, between 1276 and 1280, two astronomers charted a calendar here that differed from modern calculations by only 26 seconds). The province also contains the oldest cypress tree in China (some 4,500 years old). International tourism earned a respectable $124m. during 2000, from a relatively modest number of visitors (325,000, measured in person-times), of which foreigners accounted for 182,100.

The final statement of government revenue in Henan for 2000 put the total at 24,646m. yuan, 19.5% from the operations tax, 17.1% from value added tax and 16.1% from the income tax on enterprises. In the same year government spending in the province reached 44,552.95m. yuan, the main destination being education (17.4% of the total), followed by government administration (10.7%). Foreign direct investment was US $564.03m. in that year.

Directory

Governor: LI KEQIANG; Office of the Provincial People's Government, Zhengzhou.

Secretary of the Henan Provincial Committee of the Chinese Communist Party: CHEN KUIYUAN; Office of the Secretary, CCP Secretariat, Zhengzhou.

Chairman of the Standing Committee of the People's Congress of Henan: REN KELI; Office of the Chairman, Congress Secretariat, Zhengzhou.

Chairman of the Henan Provincial Committee of the Chinese People's Political Consultative Conference: LIN YINGHAI; Office of the Chairman, CPPCC Secretariat, Zhengzhou.

Hubei

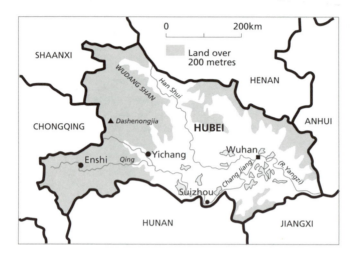

The Province of Hubei (Hupeh or Hupei) is in central China, on the Chang Jiang (River Yangzi). In the west is the special municipality of Chongqing (part of Sichuan until 1997), but otherwise Hubei is surrounded by provinces: Shaanxi in the north-west, Henan in the north-east, Anhui to the east, Jiangxi in the south-east and Hunan to the south. The total area of the province is 187,500 sq km (72,380 sq miles).

Most of Hubei is a lake-dotted plain, with often heavily forested highlands in the west. The Chang Jiang flows the length of the province, from west to east, fed by numerous tributaries, notably the Han Shui (which meets the Chang Jiang on the Jianghan plain, at Wuhan, in the east) and the Yan Shui to the north, or the Qing Jiang, which flows out of the south-west. The southern plains are also strewn with other bodies of water, giving Hubei the sobriquet of the 'land of a thousand lakes', although the province lies to the north of the great lake of Dongting (in Hunan), which is why Hubei, 'north of the lake', is called as it is (the usual short name for the province is E). The Tongbai and Dabie mountains march along the north-eastern border and the Mufu Shan lie in the south-east, along the border with Jiangxi. Western ranges include the Wuling Shan (south of Enshi, in the south-western abutment of Hubei province) and the Fangdou Shan (north of Enshi), the latter running into the Wu Shan, which span the Chang Jiang and culminate to the north in the heights of Dashennongjia (the highest peak is 3,053 m—10,020 feet), and the Wudang Shan in the north-west. Hubei has a humid, subtropical monsoon climate, with changeable weather in spring, hot summers and dry winters, and is prone to droughts and flooding. The highest temperatures are in the Three Gorges (where the Chang Jiang cuts through the western highlands) and just to the north of the south-eastern mountains. The provincial capital of Wuhan is here in the east and is known as one of the 'three furnaces' of China, with absolute maximum temperatures exceeding 40°C (104°F). Average minimum and maximum temperatures for the whole province are 1°C and 6°C (34°F and 43°F), respectively, in January and 24°C and 30°C (75°F, 86°F) in July. In Wuhan the overall monthly average for January 2000 was 2.7°C (36.9°F) and for July 31.1°C (88.0°C). Average annual rainfall in Hubei is between 750 mm and 1,500 mm (29–59 inches), while in Wuhan the total for 2000 was 1,180 mm (mainly in May–June and August–October).

The total provincial population at 1 November 2000 was 60.28m. The population density was 321 per sq km. Most of that population consisted of ethnic Han Chinese, but 4.3% consists of minority nationalities: Hui, Manchu, Mongol, Miao and Tujia. There are some 5.7m. of the last-named group in China, most of them living in the Wuling Shan (many of that number in Hubei) on the borders with Hunan, Guizhou and Chongqing. Traditional religious affiliations are not atypical for China, with noteworthy points being the ancient associations of Buddhism with Hubei and that the Wudang Shan are sacred to Daoists.

The province is fairly urbanized, at 40.2% of the total population in 2000. Wuhan is the fifth largest city in China, with an urban population of 4.4m. in 2000 (the greater Wuhan area had a population of 7.5m.). The city is actually an agglomeration of Wuchang (on the south-east bank of the Chang Jiang) and, on the other bank, divided by the Han Shui, of Hankou to the north and Hanyang to the south. The next largest cities are Suizhou, in the centre-north of the province, on the Yan Shui, and Enshi, in the south-west. Enshi is the centre for the Tujia and Miao autonomous area to which it gives its name, being the only rural prefecture and the only autonomous one. The other 12 are all city prefectures. The province is also divided into 66 counties (10 of which are autonomous), 24 being cities.

History

The eastern plains have long been settled, initially by peoples of the so-called Yangzi Culture, an early alternative to the eventually dominant Yellow River Shang civilization. Some Han Chinese settlement began around 1000 BC, and during the Zhou period the region gradually began to be drawn into the cultural sphere of the more northerly states—which were aware of the half-barbarous kingdoms around them having alien as well as familiar roots (hence they referred to themselves as the 'central states', Zhongguo, which—given that Chinese does not usually distinguish singular from plural—is the origin of the common term for China as the 'Middle Kingdom'). At this time Hubei was part of the massive state of Chu, which dominated the middle Chang Jiang (River Yangzi), and later the lower reaches of the river too, and had its capital in the west of modern Hubei, at Ying. The military pre-eminence of Chu began under Wu (740–690 BC), and it was long one of the major opponents of the western state of Qin, another semi-barbarous kingdom that commanded large resources, although it was not as well developed economically as some of the central states. Qin eventually prevailed, conquering the other states and uniting the common Chinese cultural area into an empire—an empire shortly thereafter inherited by the Han. The decline of Chu, meanwhile, had begun in 312 BC, with a major defeat by Qin, and then Ying was taken in 277, while further defeats in 226 and

224 were followed by the final conquest of the southern realm in the next year. It was in the early part of this period that Qu Yuan, a statesman and poet, complained of gullible rulers and incompetent bureaucrats weakening Chu. However, it was the south that led the reaction against the excesses of Qin rule under the First Emperor, and his successor did not long survive the revolt of various generals and princes—one, Xiang Yu, took the royal title of Chu for himself, and awarded Han to another insurgent, Liu Bang. However, it was Han that prevailed and established the next dynasty, Xiang Yu committing suicide in 202 BC. During the following four centuries the city of Wuchang was developed, becoming a regional capital in Wu, one of the Three Kingdoms that immediately followed the Han dynasty, and one of the major cities of the middle Chang Jiang.

The eastern plains of modern Hubei only became intensively settled by the Chinese from the seventh century AD (by the 11th century the province was producing a rice surplus), under the first peaceful years of the Tang. The plains were mainly administered with Hunan and Jiangxi. At the end of the Tang era, in the 10th century, a minor one of the 10 Kingdoms in the southern plains area was Southern Ping, but it, like the rest of the empire, was conquered by the Song. The Song developed Hankou as an important military stronghold, and was important in holding the line against northern invaders when the dynasty continued with a southern empire only from the 12th century. However, an empire reunited by the Mongols allowed Hankou to emerge as one of the four major commercial centres in all of China by the Ming period, and was the capital of a united province with Hunan (it was made a separate province under the early Qing— the Manchu armies conquered it in 1645). It was this commercial significance that brought the province most of its historical importance in the Qing period (although other events include the White Lotus sectarian rising at the end of the 18th century, with a centre in the far north-west, and the Taiping rebellion that controlled much of the eastern province between 1853 and 1857). By the second half of the 19th century Hankou was attracting European commercial attention and, under the 'unequal treaties' it was soon designated as an 'open port', with foreign concessions established there. However, this helped the development of the area, which became one of the first in China to industrialize, helped by the arrival of the railways in the early years of the 20th century. The third municipality of Wuhan, Hanyang, grew at this time, the first modern iron-and-steel plant being founded here in 1891 and the city generally being the leading site of heavy industry in the country (this was ruined by the 1930s' worldwide recession and then the Japanese invasion). Further upstream on the Chang Jiang, at Yichang, there was another treaty port (from 1877), and the river trade helped the exploitation of the local natural resources that were the basis of industrialization, as they had been of the early development of the Bronze Age in the region. This environment of trade, exposure to foreign ideas and early industrialization maybe contributed to the success of the revolutionary movement in Hubei.

Hubei is most famous in the 20th century as the place where the revolutionary movement against the Qing began and a republic was conceived. Trouble in Sichuan had distracted the main military forces of the Qing Government from the garrisons of eastern Hubei, leaving local units of the New Army in charge. On the evening of 10 October 1911 there was a mutiny by these units in the provincial capital of Wuchang, and on the next day they took control of the whole city. Forces based in Hankou also joined in and a new military government for the whole province was formed, declaring independence from the Qing dynasty and setting a precedent that swept China and forced the abdication of the last emperor early the next year. It took some time for a successor national regime to emerge thereafter, and Hubei was subject to warlord rule (notably for the Zhili faction in the second half of the 1920s) until the authority of the Guomindang republican Government was acknowledged in 1929. Wuhan and much of the east was then occupied by the Japanese in 1938 (other areas briefly as a result of the 1944 offensives), although a successful Communist resistance had been established in the centre-south of the province by 1945. During the Civil War, however, the Communists did not really gain control of the province until May 1949. When the People's Republic was proclaimed Hubei province did not include the special municipality of Wuhan, but the two were merged in 1954. During the 1960s Hubei was a favourite retreat of Mao Zedong, but by the end of the 20th century the province was more famous as the site of the great dam being built upstream of Yichang for the controversial Three Gorges Project.

Economy

Hubei's gross domestic product (GDP) grew strongly throughout the late 1990s and into the 21st century, and totalled 427,632m. yuan in 2000. That year GDP per head was 7,188 yuan, making Hubei one of the wealthiest inland provinces. This wealth comes from its natural resources, early industrialization and its continuing position as a vital transport hub for central China. This is particularly so in the great city of Wuhan, which is a major industrial, financial, commercial, educational and scientific-research centre, as well as a junction for road, waterway and rail routes. A long history of trade and transport was reinforced in the early Communist era by the building of a great bridge across the Chang Jiang (River Yangzi) in Wuhan—linking Wuchang and Hanyang—in 1957. There is also now a second bridge in Wuhan and, among others, one at Yichang, just downstream from the Gezhou Dam and the more famous, and more massive, Three Gorges Dam being built at Sandouping (40 km upstream from Yichang). This project, a cherished vision since early republican times, is due to be completed in 2009 and will create the world's largest water-storage reservoir, a 550-km long lake reaching up to Chongqing, but which will flood the homes of some 2m. people and scenery of famously great beauty. The project was finally sanctioned in 1992 and involves a 2-km long, 185-m high dam across the Chang Jiang, intended to generate electricity equivalent to one-fifth of China's current capacity (so as to fuel industrialization in the entire region), to improve navigability and to control flooding (there were devastating floods of the Chang Jiang, in 1931, 1935, 1954 and 1991, for instance). The project will not only cost US $20,000m., but has aroused the apprehensions and opposition of environmentalists, historians and those fearful of a disastrous dam breach upstream of so populous a part of the world. Hubei is well provided-for in more orthodox infrastructure, with good transport networks on rail (2,031 km in length in 2000), road (57,850 km—including 569 km of expressway and 611 km of first-class highway) and water (7,256 km). It also has good air-transport links with the rest of China and some of the major inland ports of the country. Hydroelectricity is beginning to make a significant contribution to overall generation, at about one-half of the 55,192m. kWh produced in 2000. Illiteracy remains relatively high, at 7.2% in 2000.

The primary sector provided 15.5% of GDP and 48.0% of employment in 2000. Foodgrains do not dominate the landscape in the same way as in many provinces, and cereals accounted for only 44% of the total area sown with farm crops in 2000 (7.6m. ha). Oil-bearing crops are relatively more important, and Hubei has the largest acreage in China growing rape (canola). Rice is the main cereal, but wheat and corn (maize) are also widely grown, as are potatoes, soybeans, vegetables, sugar cane, cotton, tobacco (much of it sun-cured) and tea. Smaller products (in volume) include silk cocoons, lotus seeds and roots, water chestnuts, peaches, oranges, chestnuts and silver fungus. Yields in 2000 amounted to: 15.0m. metric tons of rice, 2.3m. tons of wheat and 2.2m. tons of corn; 2.2m. tons of fruit (44% citrus fruits); 2.0m. tons of rapeseed (the largest harvest of any region in China) and 215,000 tons of sesame (the second largest harvest); 304,000 tons of cotton; 137,000 tons of tobacco (82,000 tons flue-cured); 63,703 tons of tea (the fourth largest harvest); and 12,195 tons of (mainly mulberry) silkworm cocoons. Forestry products include tung oil (16,030 tons of seeds in 2000), tea oil (17,343 tons of seeds), as well as the harvest from the Chinese tallow tree, and the rich medicinal-plant and other botanical resources of the Shennongjia forests, in particular, in the north-west. Hubei's livestock includes 19.0m. head of pigs, 4.3m. cattle and buffaloes and 2.2m. goats, but the province is also famous for its waterfowl. Some 2.5m. tons of meat (78% pork), 59,000 tons of milk (95% cows' milk), 1.0m. tons of poultry eggs and 9,000 tons of honey were produced in Hebei during 2000. Its inland waters also provided 2.3m. tons of produce (82% artificially cultured), of which fish (Hubei is famous for the blunt-nosed bream) accounted for 2.2m. tons, crustaceans 74,900 tons, shellfish 47,100 tons and other products (most valuably, pearls) 14,700 tons.

The secondary sector accounted for almost one-half of the economy, contributing 49.7% to GDP in 2000, but only providing 18.3% of employment. Construction alone accounted for 5.2% of GDP and had a total output value of 45,417m. yuan. Natural resources include iron ore, copper, gold (mainly in the south-east), phosphorus, gypsum, selenium (in the south-east), rock salt (2.4m. metric tons of salt were produced in 2000) and plaster stone. Such reserves, and a healthy agricultural sector, provided the original basis for industrialization in the area. Hubei is an important manufacturer of yarn (647,300 tons in 2000), cloth (1,715m. m) and silk (1,300 tons), cigarettes (2.1m. cases), as well as chemicals (Hubei was a leading producer of chemical fertilizers in 2000, with 2.2m. tons), iron and steel and other metallurgical and building products. The province also built 186,200 motor vehicles in 2000, making it the fourth largest regional producer in the country. Wuhan, in particular, is an important printing and publishing centre for inland China. There were 6,282 industrial enterprises in Hubei in 2000, with a gross output value of 306,443m. yuan. Heavy industry accounted for 3,256 of the enterprises (62% of gross output value). The 306 large enterprises provided 44% of gross output value and the 5,434 small enterprises 40%.

The tertiary sector accounted for 34.9% of GDP in 2000 and for 33.6% of employed persons. Wholesale and retail trade and catering services was by far the largest contributor, alone accounting for 10.4% of total GDP. Transport and communications contributed 6.0% and finance and insurance 4.8%. Total trade in Hubei is worth more than in most inland regions of China, with exports at US $1,899.77m. in 2000 and imports worth only slightly more at $1,992.87m. (the province last ran a trade surplus in 1998). Tourism also earned $146m. in foreign-exchange earnings in 2000. Visitors have always admired the Three Gorges river journey in the west of the province up to Chongqing, and this has proved particularly popular as the dam project has neared completion, as tourists have come to appreciate the scenery before it is flooded forever. The province remains rich in cultural and natural attractions, however, the forested regions of the western mountains being highly prized, particularly around Shennongjia (Songbai). The wild scenery hides leopards, bears, wild boars and monkeys (including the rare golden snub-nosed monkey), as well as stories of China's yeti or 'bigfoot'. Foreign visitors in any number to Hubei are relatively recent: in 1990 they accounted for about one-quarter of the 100,400 international tourist visits; and in 2000 for almost four-fifths of 450,800.

Government revenue in Hubei, according to the final statement for 2000, totalled 21,434.50m. yuan, higher than any non-coastal region in China save Henan and Sichuan. Most came from the operations tax (4,411.20m. yuan), followed by value added tax and the income tax on enterprises, then a relatively high amount as income from administrative fees (1,854.16m. yuan). Total expenditure was 36,877.01m. yuan, much of it on education (15.6%), government administration (10.0%), social-security subsidies (7.7%) and capital construction (7.6%). Foreign direct investment in 2000 was US $943.68m., and there was also other foreign investment of $92.44m. (the highest regional total for the latter after Guangdong).

Directory

Governor: ZHANG GUOGUANG; Office of the Provincial People's Government, Wuhan.

Secretary of the Hubei Provincial Committee of the Chinese Communist Party: JIANG ZHUPING; Office of the Secretary, CCP Secretariat, Wuhan.

Chairman of the Standing Committee of the People's Congress of Hubei: GUAN GUANGFU; Office of the Chairman, Congress Secretariat, Wuhan.

Chairman of the Hubei Provincial Committee of the Chinese People's Political Consultative Conference: YANG YONGLIANG; Office of the Chairman, CPPCC Secretariat, Wuhan.

Head of the Enshi Tujia–Miao Autonomous Prefecture: (vacant).

Hunan

The Province of Hunan lies at the heart of southern China. The Guangxi autonomous region is beyond the south-western borders of Hunan, while surrounding provinces include Guangdong in the south-east, Jiangxi in the east and Hubei in the north. Beyond the western border lie the special municipality of Chongqing (part of Sichuan until 1997), in the north-west, and Guizhou province. Hunan had a total area of 210,500 sq km (81,250 sq miles).

Four-fifths of Hunan is mountainous or hilly, cupping the fertile northern plains, which spread around and south from the Dongting lake into the lowlands of the centre. Hunan, 'south of the lake', is named for Dongting Hu, the second largest freshwater lake in the country (2,820 sq km—after Poyang, in neighbouring Jiangxi), but was also called Xiang, after the main river. The Xiang, the Zi, the Yuan and the Li all flow into Dongting and, thence, into the Chang Jiang (River Yangzi) near Yueyang, on the northern border. The Luoxiao Shan rise in the east of the province, the Nan Ling to the south, the Xuefeng Shan in the south-west and the Wuling Shan in the north-west. The seaward flanks of the mountains receive more precipitation, which is copious throughout the province, but it typically falls mainly in April–June, followed by droughts through the rest of the summer and into autumn. As part of a temperate subtropical climate, this makes the province one of the more humid parts of China. The average annual rainfall ranges between 1,250 mm and 1,759 mm (49–68 inches), while the total for 2000 in Changsha, the provincial capital, was 1,508 mm. Average monthly temperatures for the city that year were 3.7°C (38.7°F) in January and 30.2°C (86.4°F) in July. Temperatures in January range between a minimum average of 4°C (39°F) and a maximum of 8°C (46°F), and in July between 26°C and 30°C (79–86°F).

The total population was 64.40m., according to the 2000 national census, giving a population density of 306 per sq km. Of that total 10.2% consisted of minority nationalities, with members of the Chinese-speaking Hui and Manchu groups mainly in the cities, Miao and Tujia communities in the Wuling Shan of the north-west, and those of the Yao, Dong and Bai peoples in the south. In the far north there are even some Uygurs (Wei Wuer—Uyghurs or Uigurs), remote from their Central Asian homeland. The Heng Shan (Nanyue Shan), a mountain range in the centre-west of the province, is sacred to both Daoists and Buddhists, while the Shaoshan, the birthplace of Mao Zedong, attracts more secular pilgrims.

Only 29.8% of the population were classed as urban in 2000. Changsha, in the north-west, is the provincial capital and largest city (5.86m. people in 2000, with 1.86m. in the main urban area). Other important cities include: Zhuzhou (a major industrial centre since the 1930s and a transport hub), to the south of Changsha; Xiangtan just to the west of Zhuzhou, and Hengyang further to the south; and Yueyang in the north, on Dongting Hu, near where it joins the Chang Jiang, and Chengde, at the western end of the lake. One autonomous prefecture is in the north-west, constituted as the Western Hunan (Xiangxi) area for the Miao and Tujia minorities, and there are 15 autonomous counties. In all, there are 14 prefectures (all save Xiangxi being cities), and 88 counties.

History

Hunan has long been settled, and evolved a civilization that differed from the culture that grew up by the Huang He (Yellow River) to the north. However, the ancient kingdom of Chu was gradually drawn into the politics of the more northerly states, which were more economically developed, but lacked the raw resources of the wider realms in the south and west. The capital of Chu was in modern Hubei, but Changsha (originally called Qingyang) was already a thriving market town and urban centre. Even the northern plains of the modern province were, nevertheless, considered to be on the edge of civilization, and, most famously, Hunan served as a place of exile for the famous poet and administrator, Qu Yuan. Slandered by rivals, he was sent here by the king of Chu at the beginning of the third century BC; he wrote some of his greatest works here, before his despair at the decline of Chu contributed to his decision to commit suicide. Just over 50 years later Chu had been defeated, to be incorporated into the new empire of Qin that the Han dynasty soon gained. Changsha became the seat of a prefecture under the Qin, but then spent some time as a marquisate under the Western or Former Han, before again becoming the seat of a prefect. The boundaries of the jurisdiction varied, as, indeed, did the name, as Changsha was also called Tongzhou.

Hunan was consolidated into central China under the Tang. Between the eighth and 11th centuries AD the population increased fivefold, owing to a prosperous agricultural industry and inward migration from the north. Its wealth was not fundamentally damaged by being near the northern borders of the residual Song Empire in the south from the 12th centuries, but benefited from the restoration of a united China. The province was established as an important supplier of grain to the north under the Ming and the Qing, but became overpopulated and dominated by powerful landlords, leading to a disaffected peasantry. Hunan was, therefore, liable to welcome revolts such as the Taiping Rebellion of the mid-19th century and, later, the Communist movement of the 1920s. Moreover, Hunan also witnessed an important development in modern Chinese history owing to the Taiping upheaval. The military impotence of the Qing authorities in the face of the Taiping sectarians prompted the imperial court to commission senior Chinese officials to raise new armies in the localities. Thus, Zeng Guofan enlisted men from his home province into the Xiang or Hunan Army—loyal to the Qing, but the first precursor of the warlord bands of the early decades of the 20th century. Adding to the ferment in the countryside was the opening of Changsha to foreigners in 1904.

It was into this environment that Mao Zedong was born in December 1893 at Shaoshan, some 130 km south-west of Changsha, of a poor peasant father who had, by army service and prudent management, raised his family into the ranks of the relatively wealthy peasantry. When he was growing up he was influenced by a radical, anti-Buddhist teacher, the example of anti-landlord rebels in the hills and, perhaps most dramatically, a severe famine in Hunan and the subsequent, brutal suppression by the Manchu governor of an insurrection by starving people in Changsha. It was only when he himself went to Changsha that he met revolutionaries, however, and turned against monarchy, becoming a socialist. He was in the city, where he was to train as a teacher, at the time of the 1911 revolutions that initiated the collapse of the Qing regime. However, it was only when he went to Beijing in 1918 that he was introduced to Marxism and more comprehensive theories about what could succeed imperial China. Back in Changsha, where he finally obtained a job as a teacher, Mao organized workers' unions. Mao attended the founding of the Chinese Communist Party (CCP) in Shanghai in 1921, but was increasingly to develop orthodox Marxist theory along his own lines, adapting it to Chinese conditions and favouring the peasantry as the primary engine of revolution. From 1925 he began to organize peasant unions, but the angry landlords of Hunan forced him to flee to Guangzhou (Canton—in Guangdong). After Jiang Jieshi (Chiang Kai-shek) struck against the Communists in 1927, Mao Zedong was sent back to Hunan to rally the local CCP and organize the peasant resistance (the latter was obviously becoming more important to the success of the Chinese Communists, although Mao's view did not really prevail in the Party until the mid-1930s). Late in 1927 Mao led his worker–peasant army south from Changsha into the mountains on the Hunan–Jiangxi border, founding one of the most important Communist guerrilla bases of the struggle against both the Nationalists and the Japanese, depending on the timing. Although Mao moved the main Communist forces north on the Long March, he left active cells of Communist strength in Hunan, and these proved important in impeding the Japanese advance in the 1940s (although the north of the province suffered during the Second World War). The Communists did not gain full control of Hunan until 1949. During the Cultural Revolution of the 1960s Hunan became a major centre in the lionization of the Chairman and its favourite son, Mao Zedong, and even after the period of revisionism that followed his death in September 1976, he remains a widely revered figure.

Economy

Hunan had a gross domestic product (GDP) of 369,188m. yuan in 2000 or 5,639 yuan per head. It is an important transport node in southern China, with major railway lines, road networks and waterways (connected to the Chang Jiang—River Yangzi—through Dongting Hu, near Yueyang and its port of Chenglingji. There are fairly dense networks of roads (totalling 60,848 km in length in 2000—449 km of expressway and 239 km of first-class highway), of railways (operational length of 2,313 km) and of navigable waterways (at 10,041 km the fourth longest network in China). The amount of electricity generated in 2000 was 35,442m. kWh, of which 54% was hydroelectricity. The illiteracy rate was one of the lowest in central and southern China, at 4.65%, in 2000.

Hunan had a fairly large primary sector, which contributed 21.3% of GDP in 2000 and provided work for 60.8% of employed persons. Traditionally one of the 'breadbaskets' of medieval China, the total sown area in Hunan during 2000 was 8.0m. ha, one of the more extensive areas, and rice covered 42% of this. In 2000 86% of foodgrain crop yields consisted of rice, at 23.9m. metric tons the largest regional harvest in China. Hunan also produced 1.1m. tons of rapeseed, 158,000 tons of cotton and 70,000 tons of fibre crops, the largest such reaped outside Heilongjiang. Hunan also remained a major producer of tobacco (168,000 tons, mainly flue-cured) and of tea (57,294 tons). Overall fruit production is not particularly significant when compared regionally, but Hunan is the third largest grower of oranges (1.3m. tons in 2000). The province is China's leading producer of tea-oil seeds (337,956 tons in 2000), and also harvests tung-oil seeds, pine resin and rare medicinal plants from its forestry reserves. These woodlands also make Hunan the country's fourth largest regional timber producer (3.9m. cu m). More specialist products include silver-needle tea, lotus seeds and fragrant mushroom. Well-known livestock types from the province include Niangxiang pigs, Binhu buffaloes, the cattle and sheep of western Hunan, Wugang geese and Lingwu ducks. Most of the domesticated large animals in the province are cattle and buffalo (together numbering some 5.1m. head in 2000), but there was also a very large pig population (35.8m.) and 3.7m. goats. As a result, only Sichuan exceeded Hunan's pork production (3.7m. tons) in 2000; the province also produced a further 0.6m. tons of meat, 11,000 tons of cows' milk, 0.5m. tons of poultry eggs and 5,000 tons of honey. Aquatic produce is from inland fisheries and is mainly cultured, with fish providing 96% of the total production of 1.3m. tons in 2000.

Of total GDP, the secondary or industrial sector accounted for 39.6% in 2000 and 14.7% of employed persons. Construction accounted for 6.3% of GDP and had a total output value of 35,442.02m. yuan in 2000. Most industry is based on the processing of primary produce, be it agricultural or extractive. Thus, in 2000 Hunan was the third largest manufacturer of cigarettes (after Yunnan and Henan), at 2.3m. cases, while metallurgy and other ore processing was prominent. The province contains important reserves of minerals, notably of antimony, stibium and wolfram, but also, for example, bismuth, sepiolite, barite, manganese, arsenic, kaolin, zinc, aluminium, tin, tantalum, graphite and diamonds. Manufacturing industry is not a large sector, however, with 4,808 industrial enterprises in the province in 2000, amassing a total gross output value of only 162,794m. yuan at current prices. Almost one-half of these enterprises (49%), and a greater proportion of the output value (66%), were in the state sector, while heavy industry accounted for 59% of the enterprises and 65% of the value. Large enterprises accounted for only 5% of industrial businesses, but provided 50% of the total gross output value (medium-sized enterprises for 8% and 9%, respectively).

The tertiary sector provided 39.1% of GDP in 2000, trade and catering accounting for almost one-quarter of this, transport and communications almost one-fifth, and government and party agencies and social organizations about one-seventh. The sector also provided jobs for 24.6% of employed persons in the same year. Trade during 2000 was in surplus, and worth US $1,631.90m. in exports and $1,360.36m. in imports. Tourism earned $221m. in foreign exchange during 2000, with international tourist visits numbering 454,000 (foreigners 35%). The Wulingyuan scenic area in the north-west, with its tribal reserves, attracts many visitors, as does Shaoshan, the birthplace of Mao Zedong.

The final statement of government revenue by region in 2000 allotted 17,704.03m. yuan to Hunan, of which 3,433.57m. yuan were raised from the operations tax and 2,609.89 yuan from value added tax. Expenditure in the province totalled 34,783.24m. yuan, with education accounting for 5,088.03m. yuan, capital construction 3,808.19m. and government administration 3,277.97m. yuan, followed by spending on social-security subsidies and the expenses of the justice system and retired administrators. Foreign direct investment in Hunan in 2000 was US $678.33m.

Directory

Governor: ZHANG YUNCHUAN (acting); Office of the Provincial People's Government, Changsha.

Secretary of the Hunan Provincial Committee of the Chinese Communist Party: YANG ZHENGWU; Office of the Secretary, CCP Secretariat, Changsha.

Chairman of the Standing Committee of the People's Congress of Hunan: YANG ZHENGWU; Office of the Chairman, Congress Secretariat, Changsha.

Chairman of the Hunan Provincial Committee of the Chinese People's Political Consultative Conference: WANG KEYING; Office of the Chairman, CPPCC Secretariat, Changsha.

Head of the Xiangxi Tujia and Miao Autonomous Prefecture: WU JIHAI.

Jiangsu

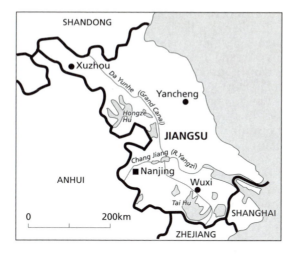

The Province of Jiangsu (Kiangsu), lies at the mouth of the Chang Jiang (River Yangzi), stretching northwards up the coastal plains along the Yellow Sea (Huang Hai). Jiangsu, 'river awakening', is named for two Qing prefectures, Jiang Ning and Su Zhou, but the province was known as Liangjiang; it is called Su for short. The special municipality of Shanghai, an area directly under the central administration of the People's Republic (like the provinces and the autonomous regions), was part of Jiangsu until 1949, but now lies to the southeast of the province, on the south bank of the Chang Jiang estuary. Zhejiang is to the south, Anhui to the west and Shandong to the north. Jiangsu has a total area of 102,600 sq km (39,600 sq miles).

Jiangsu is fertile plainsland, the north consisting mostly of the Huanghuai plain, laid down when the Huang He (Yellow River) entered the sea here. This southern part of the great North China Plain is crisscrossed by rivers, canals, irrigation ditches and lakes. The highest point in the province is also in the north, at Yuntai peak, but only reaches 625 m (2,051 feet). Most of the province is less than 50 m above sea level, as the south too consists of plains, those of the lower Chang Jiang basin. This region is dominated by the mighty Chang Jiang, more familiarly known outside China as the Yangzi, which ends its long journey to the sea in the south of the province. The Chang Jiang is the longest river in China and the third longest in the world; by the time it debouches into the East China Sea it has flowed for some 6,300 km (3,910 miles), through nine provinces, and been joined by over 700 tributaries, which together drain almost one-fifth of China's territory. The estuary is 13 km wide where it meets the sea between Shanghai and Jiangsu. The coastline of the province then stretches for some 1,000 km in a roughly north-eastward direction. The Huai He also flows into southern Jiangsu, forming the Hongze Hu (the province's second largest lake—1,960 sq km) when it crosses the central western border, then draining into the Gaoyou lake and, thence, into the Chang Jiang. The largest lake, and one of the largest freshwater lakes in China, is the island-dotted Tai Hu in the far south, which covers 2,425 sq km, but is, on average, only some 2 m deep. This profusion of natural waterways, particularly in the southern 'water country', is augmented by numerous artificial channels, notably the Da Yunhe (Grand Canal) that once linked Hangzhou (Zhejiang) to Beijing. It is the world's longest canal, at almost 1,800 km, although only about one-half of it is now practically navigable, depending on the season and the craft being used. The first 85 km were completed in 495 BC, but the main project of linking the Chang Jiang and the Huang He was undertaken under the short-lived Sui dynasty in AD 605–09. Further development took place under the Yuan and the Ming, around the 14th century, when the northern capital was finally connected to the south and its grain tributes. Jiangsu reaches into a transitional area between temperate and subtropical climates, between semi-humid and humid monsoon climates. It is generally hot and humid in summer (Nanjing—Nanking—the provincial capital in the south-west, is described as one of the 'three furnaces' of the Chang Jiang valley), but with cold, foggy winters. There is also a regular drizzle in winter, but most rain falls in the spring and summer, leaving a dry autumn. There is more rain in the south-east than in the north-west, with annual average rainfall between 800 mm and 1,200 mm (31–47 inches). Total rainfall in Nanjing during 2000 was 1,030 mm. The monthly average temperatures in the capital during 2000 were 2.3°C in January and 28.8°C in July, but extremes are experienced.

The total population of 74.38m. (2000 census figure) made Jiangsu the fifth-most populous region in the People's Republic. This population had grown by about one-10th in the decade between censuses, so the province remained more densely populated than any other province or autonomous region (or Chongqing), with a population density of 724 per sq km. The same census results revealed that, apart from Jiangxi and Shanxi, the province had the smallest proportion of minority nationalities in China (0.33% in 2000). Those that do live in the province include the mainly Chinese-speaking Huis and Manchus, reinforcing Han linguistic dominance, although the southern Wu or Shanghai dialect begins to become more influential in Jiangsu, at the expense of the nationally dominant (and official) Beijing-based Mandarin dialect (Putonghua). The presence of the Hui (mainly in the north-west) is a legacy of an old association with Islam (a 14th-century evangelist, Puhaddin, is still commemorated in the province), and there have been active Christian communities since the 17th century. The main religious traditions are Confucian and Buddhist, the latter being particularly organizationally active in Jiangsu.

The province is very urbanized, with 41.5% of the population living in towns and cities at the time of the 2000 census. Nanjing is the largest city, with 5.4m. in 2000, including 3.1m. residing in the urban area. Xuzhou (Tongshan), in the north-west, is the main city of an important coal-mining area, while Wuxi, in the south, near the Tai Hu, hosts a considerable amount of heavy industry. Other major cities include Suzhou, to the south-east of Wuxi, and Changzhou (Wujin), to the north-west, while Yancheng is the largest in the centre-east of the province. Jiangsu is divided into 13 city prefectures and 58 counties (of which 28 are cities).

History

The fossil remains of 'Nanjing Man' discovered near the provincial capital place the first human settlement in the area at about 500,000 years ago. Primitive villages began to appear some 6,000 years ago and urban civilization 3,000 years ago. Suzhou, for example, is one of the oldest towns in the Chang Jiang (River Yangzi) basin and, originally, developed as part of the Yangzi Culture, distinct from the northerly Shang. By the Warring States period much of the region of modern Jiangsu had been drawn into the mainstream of Chinese civilization, eventually as part of the large southern state of Chu. The north was a debatable area, however, as it was to continue to be in later history (over 200 wars have been fought in the area around Xuzhou, most recently three great battles between the Guomindang and the Communists), lying on the borders of northern and southern China. The main cities of the region could often become objects of rivalry (as did Nanjing—Nanking—during the time of the Warring States, only later becoming an administrative centre), but it may be that the strengths of an area of conflicting cultural influences helped towards the success of Liu Bang (who became the first Han emperor at the end of the third century BC), who was born in Xuzhou.

Towards the end of the Han era, in AD 212, a local commander built the citadel of Shitou Dushi to the west of Nanjing, marking the emergence of the city as an important economic and cultural centre for southern China. During the late fifth century the Qi (Southern Qi) dynasty encouraged Buddhism in the Jiangsu region (one of the oldest monasteries, Qixia Si, was built then and is still one of main Buddhist seminaries), and it had become established by the time Nanjing succumbed to floods, fires, peasant rebellions and military conquest in the sixth century. Thus, by the time of the Sui Nanjing had been razed, although it recovered and prospered more obscurely under the Tang, while Yangzhou become the main city. Suzhou, meanwhile, also began to prosper, as the Sui had undertaken the task of taking the Da Yunhe (Grand Canal) north from the Chang Jiang, and the city is on the junction. Suzhou soon built up a lead in the silk trade and became very successful from the 14th century, at which time Nanjing was also recovering. Both these cities were among the leaders in the commercial renaissance of the 16th century, although Nanjing owed its preeminence as much to the advent of the new dynasty.

In 1356 a peasant rebellion led by Zhu Yuanzhang against the Mongols succeeded in capturing Nanjing, although it was another 12 years before the Yuan-dynasty capital of Beijing was taken. Nanjing, the 'southern capital' as it was then named, became the main seat of Zhu Yuanzhang, the Hongwu emperor and founder of the Ming dynasty. He built a massive palace here, which was soon followed by the 1366–86 construction of the city's 33-km walls, the longest city walls in the world. Jiangsu, together with most of modern Anhui, was then constituted as Nan Zhili, the 'southern directly administered' area, corresponding to the Zhili (roughly modern Hebei) surrounding Beijing, the 'northern capital'. However, Nanjing was only the primary capital of the Ming until 1421 when the third sovereign of the dynasty, the Yongle emperor, moved the court to Beijing better to confront the Mongol threat. The Ming, however, were not to give way to another Mongol dynasty, but, much later, to a different people out of the north, the Manchus, who conquered Jiangsu in 1645, in the name of their young Qing emperor. Under the Qing the province was administered under the name of Liangjiang, from Nanjing, by a governor-general.

On 29 August 1842 Nanjing was where a peace between the Chinese Empire and the United Kingdom was signed at the conclusion of the first Opium War (which had begun in Guangdong). In this, the first of the 'unequal treaties', China paid a huge indemnity to the British, ceded Hong Kong island to them and opened a number of ports to foreign trade. Not many years later, in March 1853 Nanjing was taken by the Taiping rebels under Hong Xiuquan, who promptly renamed the city Tianjin ('heavenly capital') and made it the seat of the 'Heavenly Kingdom of Great Peace' (Taiping Tianguo). The 'Heavenly King' and his followers were sectarians greatly influenced by Christianity and by the need for social reform; they hated the Manchu 'demons' (a massacre of Manchus took place when Nanjing fell) and their Qing dynasty. However, Hong Xiuquan failed to develop links with revolts in other parts of China and his claims to be a son of the deity and the brother of the Christian messiah, Jesus Christ, tended to alienate the increasingly powerful foreign (European) presence in China. Moreover, the austerity and equality measures instituted by the 'Heavenly Kingdom' alienated most of those who traditionally held power in Chinese society, while internal struggles among the Taiping to consolidate the 'Heavenly King's' position resulted in the elimination of many of his more competent colleagues. Taiping economic policies failed, the Qing began to elicit some foreign sympathy and senior court officials began to raise the first of more modern armies in defence of the imperial regime. The Qing forces had to advance from as far away as Nanchang (Jiangxi), but gradually penetrated the Taiping territory that occupied much of central China. In 1864 Zeng Guofan of Hunan, helped by the British and by some Western mercenaries, finally recaptured Nanjing. Another slaughter ensued, with none of the 100,000 or so rebels reported to have survived, so ending what is sometimes claimed to be one of the bloodiest uprisings in world history.

Meanwhile, the small town of Shanghai, in the south-east of Liangjiang, had begun to be developed by foreign merchants, initially the British, in the early 1840s. They were joined by the French in 1847 and an International Settlement was first established in 1863, with the Japanese joining in 1895. By this time Shanghai had become the main focus of foreign interests in China, and one of the largest single investments in the world, but its territory was largely composed of enclaves immune from Chinese law. Shanghai had surpassed all other Chinese ports by 1853 and had a population of over 1m. by the end of the century. Industry, labour organization and criminal gangs all flourished in what was the busiest international port in Asia during the 1920s and 1930s. Shanghai had a huge influence on the neighbouring parts of Jiangsu (as the province was now called), of course, but the city was barely under its jurisdiction, a situation that was formalized in the People's Republic from 1949, with the creation of a separate administrative unit for the city.

Although Jiangsu did not declare its independence from the Qing until the November of the 1911 year of revolution, Nanjing was the site of the first republican assembly under Dr Sun Yixian (Yatsen—he was buried in the city after his death in 1925). At this time Jiangsu was generally held by the so-called Zhili faction of northern warlords, but it succumbed to the Northern Expedition of the Guomindang in 1927. Then, with April's Shanghai Coup against the Communists, Jiang Jieshi (Chiang Kai-shek) firmly established himself as the leader of both the Guomindang and its Government of the Republic of China, with Nanjing as the national capital from 1928. It remained the seat of the Nationalist Government until 1937, when the approach of Japanese forces required a relocation to Chongqing for the duration of the Second World War, and resumed the role between 1945 and the Communist victory in 1949. Meanwhile, the city had again experienced an extremely bloody episode, the brutal 'Rape of Nanjing', which followed the Japanese occupation of 13 December 1937. Without any official discouragement, Japanese soldiers were reported to have raped some 20,000 women and also massacred anywhere between 100,000 and 400,000 Chinese civilians within about six weeks. The incident added determination, and bitterness, to the Chinese resistance (of whatever political persuasion) and can still trouble Sino–Japanese relations when such horrifying incidents are omitted from Japanese school books.

The Chang Jiang was crossed and Nanjing taken by the Communists in April 1949, adding a South Jiangsu to the North Jiangsu province already held. Shanghai was taken in May, to become a special municipality of the imminent People's Republic. However, North Jiangsu and South Jiangsu were united in 1952, with Nanjing as the capital. The province then benefited from the liberalization of the economy in the 1980s and 1990s, and particularly from the dramatic success of Shanghai, which has once again become a focal point for foreign interests in China, and still fuels expansion in Jiangsu.

Economy

Jiangsu is rich in agriculture and ancient in its industry, and now benefits from the massive economic growth of neighbouring Shanghai. The province is rapidly developing, with real growth of 12% in 1997, 11% in 1998 and above 10% thereafter, making it among the strongest regional economies in the country and giving it the largest gross domestic product (GDP) after Guangdong: 858,273m. yuan in 2000. A high population means GDP per head, at 11,773 yuan, was not only behind that of Guangdong and the three prosperous municipalities of Shanghai, Beijing and Tianjin, but also of Zhejiang. This prosperity is supported by well-established infrastructure and links with other territories—notably the great port of Shanghai. Jiangsu itself has important seaports at Nantong (on the north bank of the Chang Jiang—River Yangzi—estuary, opposite Shanghai) and in the far north (which is less developed than the south), at Lianyungang, which is also the terminus of the revived 'Silk Road', the Eurasian Continental Land Bridge that reaches as far as Rotterdam (Netherlands) in the distant west. Nanjing and, downriver from the provincial capital, Zhenjiang (Dantu) are among the largest inland ports of China, and there are also other large river ports in Jiangsu. Many of these ports evolved along the Da Yunhe (Grand Canal) and other canal links, leaving Jiangsu with the most extensive system of waterways in China, at 23,943 km in length (in 2000) one-fifth of the national total. There has also been major infrastructural development under the Communists, notably the massive bridge over the Chang Jiang, opened in December 1968 and creating a direct rail link between Beijing and Shanghai for the first time. The railways, while not particularly long (757 km operational in 2000) are important and heavily used. The road links across Jiangsu are also good, with a total highway length of 28,198 km in 2000, but including a large extent of expressway (1,090 km) and of first-class roads (2,228 km). Jiangsu is third in the rankings of Chinese regional electricity production (90,970m. kWh in 2000), but barely any generation is hydroelectric, although the province does benefit from its own hydrocarbons reserves. Such resources have helped fuel a prosperity that has no doubt contributed to some demographic achievements in the province: only Shandong, of all the regions of China, has a better-balanced male-female ratio (for every 100 women there were only 102.58 men in Jiangsu in 2000); while the illiteracy rate improved significantly in the 1990s, falling to 6.3% by 2000.

The primary sector was the fourth largest in the country, but only accounted for 12.0% of GDP in 2000. Primary activities employed less than the national average in the sector, at 42.2% of employed persons. The province is located on some of China's most productive land and developed resource-based industry (and the associated social ills) early—thus, Suzhou was the leading silk producer by the time of the Yuan dynasty, although it was also a town prone to violence and discontent, owing to harsh working conditions. In 2000 a large amount of land was sown with farm crops (7.9m. ha—28% was under rice, 25% wheat and 13% vegetables). Crop yields in that year included the second largest rice crop in China (after Hunan), at 18.0m. metric tons, the fourth largest wheat crop, at 8.0m. tons, and the third largest cotton harvest, at 314,000 tons. Jiangsu also produced 1.8m. tons of fruit (39% of it apples), 1.4m. tons of rapeseed, 1.1m. tons of beans and 0.8m. tons of peanuts. After Zhejiang, Jiangsu collected the largest amount of silk cocoons (all mulberry), weighing 90,127 tons in total. The province has a relatively modest livestock industry, with 591,000 head of mainly dairy cattle and buffaloes (in 2000) and 126,000 donkeys (and some horses and mules), but there was a fairly large number of pigs (20.2m.) and goats (9.9m.), as well as some sheep. Animal husbandry, therefore, produced 3.3m. tons of meat in 2000, of which 2.1m. tons were pork, as well as 255,000 tons of cows' milk, 1.8m. tons of poultry eggs, 7,000 tons of honey and 1,104 tons of sheep wool (much of it fine wool, from the famous, if not numerous, Huyang sheep). Although Jiangsu is a coastal province, most aquatic production is freshwater (70.6% of 3.09m. tons in 2000) and that, in turn, is mainly cultured (86%). Fish accounted for 1.78m. tons of the freshwater catch, although there were also 315,000 tons of crustaceans, as well as other species and products. The marine catch consisted mainly of 434,300 tons of fish, 297,800 tons of shellfish and 129,200 tons of crustaceans.

The largest secondary sector in the country after Guangdong accounted for 51.7% of the provincial GDP in 2000. The sector provided 29.7% of employment. Construction accounted for 6.8% of GDP and had a total output value of 153,884.16m. yuan in 2000, the largest regional amount earned by the industry and 12% of the national total. The best-known mineral reserves, which have long provided the basis for local industry, are coal, china clay and phosphorus. The towns on the Da Yunhe that established silk production and grain storage from the 16th century have remained at the forefront of Chinese industrialization. Some processes go back even further, with Jiangsu famous for the pottery town of Dingshan since just before the Han dynasty, and for the Yixing teapots produced in the same area. Heavy industry (which accounted for 51% of industrial enterprises and 57% of gross output value in 2000) is concentrated in Nanjing and Wuxi, while other cities are stronger in light industry. Textiles generally remain a leading industry and in 2000 Jiangsu was the leading regional producer of chemical fibre (1.9m. metric tons), yarn (1.2m. tons, with 18% of national production) and cloth (3,374m. m), and the second largest producer of silk (14,200 tons—19% of the national total). Other major industrial manu-factures in 2000 included those it produced most of, such as soda ash (1.2m. tons), chemical pesticides (172,300 tons—28%), plastics (1.6m. tons) and metal-cutting machine tools (37,400 tons—21%). Jiangsu was second in the production of household washing machines (2.4m. units), cement (46.0m. tons), sulphuric acid (2.4m. tons) and caustic soda (0.9m. tons), third in colour television sets (2.9m. units) and plate glass (18.9m. weight cases) and fourth in integrated circuits (1,250m. units—21%). There is also a fair amount of machine-made paper (2.1m. tons), salt (2.9m. tons), fertilizers (1.8m. tons), motor vehicles (83,400 units), tractors (3,500) and computers (115,600 units) produced, as well as a considerable volume of steel products (14.0m. tons), which are of greater significance than are pig iron and steel in itself. Nanjing alone has the largest industrial output value of any city in the People's Republic after Tianjin, Guangzhou and Shenzhen in Guangdong, and Beijing. The province has the most industrial enterprises of any region in the People's Republic except Guangdong. These numbered 18,309 (with a total gross output value of 1,045,287m. yuan) in 2000. Although only 2,554 of these were in the state sector, they accounted for 29% of the total gross output value, though this total gave a smaller state sector than in Shandong, Shanghai or Guangdong. Economic reform has also produced the largest number of industrial enterprises organized as share-holding corporations (495, with a gross output value of 86,085m. yuan). In terms of the number of enterprises receiving foreign funding (1,644), the province was behind only Shanghai and, narrowly, Guangdong (although the value of the investments in this province was rather higher than in Jiangsu), while funding from Taiwan, Hong Kong and Macao went to more enterprises in Guangdong and Fujian than Jiangsu's 1,516. The 582 large enterprises produced 31% of gross output value, while the 1,500 medium-sized enterprises produced only 14%.

The tertiary sector of Jiangsu is, again, the largest but for Guangdong. Services contributed 36.3% to regional GDP in 2000 and accounted for 28.1% of employed persons. Trade and catering services accounted for 10.0% of total GDP, transport and communications for 6.5% and finance and insurance for 5.0%. Jiangsu had the largest trade in the country after Guangdong, with a consistently healthy surplus on the balance. Exports in 2000 totalled US $26,376.94m. and imports $22,817.43m. An indication of the importance of transport was that it employed a great many people, particularly on the roads and waterways, but also on the railways and in air transport. Tourism is attracted, for example, by the cosmopolitan former capital of Nanjing, by Suzhou for its silk and its gardens, by the Grand Canal and the 'water town' of Zhouzhuang, and by the many museums, cultural activities and artistic performances in the province. More abstrusely, Xuzhou, in the north-west, is the birthplace of Liu Bang, the first Han emperor (Gaozu or Gaodi), and near Lianyungang, in the north, is Huaguo Shan (Flowers and Fruit Mountain), one of the contenders claiming to be the inspiration for the mountain of the same name in the Ming classic tale, *Journey to the West* (popularized in the West by a 1970s television adaptation, *Monkey*), whereon can be found Shuilian Dong, the fictional home of Sun Wukong, the King of the Monkeys. The province earned $724m. in foreign exchange from international tourism during 2000, from 1.6m. international-tourist visits (1.0m. foreigners).

Nanjing had the sixth largest local-government budgetary revenue of any city in the People's Republic, after Shanghai, Beijing, Shenzhen, Guangzhou, Tianjin and Chongqing. Provincial revenue in 2000, however, totalled 44,830.97m. yuan (exceeded only by Shanghai and Shandong), with most coming from value added tax (24%), the operations tax (21%) and the income tax on enterprises (20%). The next-largest contributions ranged from 7% in individuals' income tax, through 6% on town maintenance and construction taxes, to 5% from penalties and confiscatory income (mainly from economic crimes). Government expenditure totalled 59,128.10m. yuan in 2000, and was mainly spent on education (20%), government administration (9%), innovation enterprises (9%—the highest such spending in China outside Shanghai), city maintenance (8%), capital construction (8%) and the justice system (7%). Actually used foreign direct investment amounted to US $6,425.50m. in 2000, a total exceeded only in Guangdong.

Directory

Governor: JI YUNSHI; Office of the Provincial People's Government, Nanjing.

Secretary of the Jiangsu Provincial Committee of the Chinese Communist Party: HUI LIANGYU; Office of the Secretary, CCP Secretariat, Nanjing.

Chairman of the Standing Committee of the People's Congress of Jiangsu: CHEN HUANYOU; Office of the Chairman, Congress Secretariat, Nanjing.

Chairman of the Jiangsu Provincial Committee of the Chinese People's Political Consultative Conference: CAO KEMING; Office of the Chairman, CPPCC Secretariat, Nanjing.

Jiangxi

The Province of Jiangxi (Kiangsi) lies in the interior of south-eastern China, inland from the coastal province of Fujian, which lies beyond a long border to the south-east. Guangdong lies to the south, Hunan to the west, Hubei to the north-west and Anhui to the north-east. The total area of the province is 164,800 sq km (63,610 sq miles).

Jiangxi, which literally means 'river west', is also known as Gan, for the river that drains most of its territory. At its northernmost point, the province's border runs along the Chang Jiang (River Yangzi), where the plains along the river widen into those around the great Poyang Hu (the largest freshwater lake in China, with an area of 3,583 sq km). The lowlands then taper southwards, mainly up the valley of the Gan Jiang, while surrounding highlands march along Jiangxi's western, southern and eastern borders. The Wuyi Shan range comes from the south up much of the eastern border, separating Jiangxi from Fujian. Also in the south are groups of hills such as the Jiulian Shan and the Dayu Ling. The Luoxiao Shan then dominate the west, generally lofty to the south of Jinggangshan (famous as a Communist hideaway and guerrilla base), but reaching their height (and termination) just to the east of Pingxiang, at Wugong Shan (2,301 m or 7,552 feet). North of here are parallel ranges running north-westwards, the Jiuling Shan from the border to above Poyang Hu and the Mufu Shan along the border with Hubei. Jiangxi has a subtropical humid climate. Average temperatures range between 3°C and 9°C (37°–48°F) in January and 27°C and 31°C (81°–88°F) in July. Nanchang, the provincial capital and one of the hottest cities in China, had average monthly temperatures during 2000 of 5.1°C (41.2°F) in January and 30.1°C (86.2°F) in July. Average annual rainfall in the province is 1,200–1,900 mm (47–74 inches), with rainfall highest in the north-east and during the late spring and early summer (April–June). The total rainfall in Nanchang during 2000 was 1,436 mm.

The total population of Jiangxi in 2000 was put at 41.40m., giving the province the lowest population density in eastern China, at 251 persons per sq km. Only 0.27% of the population consisted of minority nationalities, according to the same census results, the main group to have a significant presence in Jiangxi being the She, although there were also reported to be small groups of the Hui, Miao, Yao, Bai and Yi peoples. Although most of the population are, therefore, officially described as ethnically Han Chinese, this ignores some regional differences most obvious in the dialect spoken by the local people. While Mandarin, or the official version of the northern tongue, Putonghua, is widely spoken, Jiangxi is home to Gan, one of the seven other major dialect groups of Chinese.

The urban population comprised 27.7% of the total in 2000. Nanchang was by far the largest city, with a total population of 4.33m. and an urban population of 1.76m. The provincial capital is located in the northern lowlands, just to the south-west of the Poyang Hu. Traditionally the second city of Jiangxi, Jiujiang is a river port on the Chang Jiang, where the Poyang drains into the great aquatic thoroughfare of southern China. The other most populous cities are Xinyu, to the south-west of Nanchang, mid-way to the border at Pingxiang, and Jingdezhen, on the other side of the Poyang Hu, in north-eastern Jiangxi. The main city of the south is Ganzhou. For administrative purposes the province consists of 11 cities, all with prefectural status, and is further divided into 80 counties (of which 10 are cities).

History

Nanchang was a provincial centre under the Han, indicating how long Jiangxi has been a part of the Chinese world (initially as part of the pre-imperial state of Chu, which was based in Hubei). However, the Gan valley was not intensely settled by Han peasants until the eighth century AD. Hitherto, they had preferred to move from the north into Hunan, and sometimes into the plains around Poyang, but thereafter significant numbers arrived right through to the 13th century. By then a wealthy merchant class had also emerged, as silver mining and the cultivation of tea was developed. The province's role as a major route from Guangzhou by junk, however, declined as seaports took up more of the north–south trade. Nevertheless, Nanchang remained part of Chang Jiang (Yangzi) valley developments, and was at the end of the south-eastern extension of the 'water country' (between Nanjing in Jiangsu and Hangzhou in Zhejiang) heartland of wealth and manufacturing from the 16th century. Under the Tang (618–907) the Gan region had been administered with much of Hunan and with southern Anhui, but the modern province had emerged by the time of the Ming (1368–1644). In fact, Ming loyalists retained control of much of the region into the early 1650s, against the Manchu armies moving to conquer the south.

Generally, Jiangxi has been quiet in the history of China, although Nanchang did serve as the base from which Qing officials reconquered southern Jiangsu and Zhejiang from the Taiping rebels in the mid-19th century.

The city had fallen to the rebels in their first advance from the south, but the Taiping only retained the very east of Jiangxi and parts of the south after 1857. Before the final victory of the Qing over the rebels, however, Jiangxi experienced a result of a perhaps more insidious threat to the integrity of the Chinese Empire. In 1862 Jiujiang, on the Chang Jiang, become a treaty port open to foreign traders, as was happening all over China. The main local consequence, however, was the development of the famous Lu Shan resort in the highlands around Guling (Kuling), just to the south of Jiujiang. In Communist history the province features more heavily.

Jiangxi declared its independence from the Qing in October 1911, not long after the revolution started in nearby Wuhan (Hubei), but was dominated by warlords (mainly of the Zhili faction) into the 1920s. By the time of the Northern Expeditions the region was generally loyal to the idea of a united republic, although not under firm Guomindang control until 1928. The process of incorporation was interrupted by the Nanchang Rising of 1 August 1927. This was by Communist-led Guomindang troops, in reaction to the April massacre of the left in Shanghai at the orders of Jiang Jieshi (Chiang Kai-shek). Zhou Enlai and Zhu De led the 30,000 troops in seizing the city, although they were driven out by Nationalist loyalists within a few days. The failure of the Nanchang Rising helped demonstrate the unlikelihood of victory through orthodox Marxism's strategy of urban revolution, but, more importantly, it laid the foundations of a Communist army. Most of the soldiers retreated southwards to Guangdong, but some, under Zhu De, circled back into western Jiangxi to join the worker-peasant force brought together in Hunan by Mao Zedong. Together they established guerrilla bases in the mountains along the Jiangxi–Hunan border, notably near Jinggangshan, and resisted Guomindang attempts to dislodge them. Indeed, a further stronghold was established in the south-east of the province, around Ruijin (Juikin), where a Central Soviet Government was proclaimed in November 1929. This so-called Jiangxi Soviet encouraged peasant support by land reform and was, generally, the scene for experimenting with policies implemented more widely later. Here, too, the Communist forces successfully resisted the Guomindang, and the 1931–33 'Encirclement Campaigns' of Jiang Jieshi, but Mao's switch from guerrilla harassment to 'positional warfare' was not helpful, and by the second half of 1934 the Communist position had become untenable.

In October 1934 some 100,000 Communists broke through Guomindang lines and abandoned many of their southern bases. Thus began the 'Long March', during which Mao Zedong consolidated his authority, and the dominance of his peasant-based strategy, and which ended two years later when some 30,000 reached Shaanxi in the north. Guerrilla tactics, and the bases in highland Jiangxi, soon returned, in use against both the Japanese and the Guomindang, but the Communists did not gain firm control of the Nanchang and the Jiangxi lowlands until May 1949. Thereafter, Jiangxi was noted mainly as the scene of a number of important Party meetings, in the Lu Shan resort (which had also been popular with Jiang Jieshi). Perhaps the two most important meetings were in 1959 (when the Central Committee dismissed Peng Denhuai and Mao Zedong was left isolated—the start of the rise and fall of Liu Shaoqi and Deng Xiaoping) and in 1970. At the latter meeting, of the Politburo, the tale of events is obscure. However, basically, Mao, who had regained power during the Cultural Revolution, was opposed by Lin Biao, a radical who wanted to continue the Cultural Revolution. Lin Biao was dead the next year.

Economy

Jiangxi is not a particularly wealthy province, and growth has not been strong in recent years. The total gross domestic product (GDP) in 2000 was 200,307m. yuan or 4,851 yuan per head. The province possesses good transport links, with 2,153 km of operational railway in 2000, 37,138 km of roads (414 km of expressway and 248 km of first-class highway) and 5,537 km of navigable waterways. There are good domestic air links and the province also possesses two major river ports at Jiujiang and Huangshi. Electricity generated in Jiangxi during 2000 amounted to 20,335m. kWh, of which 26% was hydroelectricity. Improvements in education and a relatively low rate of rural illiteracy have contributed to the overall rate of only 5.2% in 2000.

In 2000 the primary sector accounted for 24.2% of GDP and 51.9% of employed persons. The province is, traditionally, an important grain producer, as well as being famous for specialities such as the tiny, seedless tangerines of Nanfeng. The total sown area planted with farm crops was 5.7m. ha in 2000, of which one-half was covered with rice (the largest area after Hunan). That year Jiangxi harvested the fourth largest rice crop in the country (after Hunan, Jiangsu and Hubei), at 1.5m. metric tons, as well as 1.4m. tons of sugar cane, 15,703 tons of tea and 423,403 tons of fruit (66.8% citrus). The province is the second largest producer of tea-oil seeds (after Hunan), producing 194,763 tons in 2000, while other forest products included pine resin (41,638 tons) and tung-oil seeds (13,973). Large domesticated animals are almost entirely bovine (3.7m. head in 2000), and there are a large number of pigs (17.5m.). Livestock produce in 2000 included 1.8m. tons of meat (78% pork), 56,000 tons of cows' milk, 335,000 tons of poultry eggs and 7,000 tons of honey. Poyang Hu is a major fisheries resource, and is famous for a number of varieties of carp. In 2000 82% of aquatic production, however, was artificially cultured. Total production of 1.3m. tons included 1.2m. tons of fish, 53,000 tons of shellfish and 36,700 tons of crustaceans.

The secondary sector accounted for only 35.0% of GDP in 2000, the lowest proportion except for Xizang (Tibet) in all of China. Moreover, construction contributed 8.0% to the total (although it had the lowest output value, 11,641.15m. yuan in 2000, of any regional construction industry in eastern China). Industry provided jobs for only 14.4% of employed persons in 2000, but it has been long established in the province. Thus, when the Song fled south in the 12th century, so did the imperial potters, siting themselves at Jingdezhen, in the north-east of Jiangxi, and the city has been famous for its porcelain ever since. Their choice of location was prompted by the deposits of fine Gaoling clay nearby, but Jiangxi also has other rich mineral reserves, such as copper, tungsten, coal (18m. metric tons mined in 2000), zinc and molybdenum. This provides some basis for industries such as metallurgy and ferrous metals, but the province is a major producer of few of the main product groups. In 2000 Jiangxi did produce 133,400 motor vehicles (the seventh largest producer, with 6% of the national total). There were only 3,549 industrial enterprises in Jiangxi in

2000, together accumulating a current gross output value of 93,221m. yuan. The state accounted for 71% of the enterprises and 79% of the value, and heavy industry for 52% and 66%, respectively. There were 108 large enterprises (accounting for 49% of gross output value) and 330 medium-sized ones (17%).

The tertiary sector makes an unusually large contribution to the provincial economy of Jiangxi, accounting for 40.8% of GDP in 2000 and 33.7% of jobs. Transport and communications (which employed large numbers of people) contributed 9.7% to GDP and trade and catering 9.1%. The total value of Jiangxi's trade is not high, although the province runs a healthy surplus. In 2000 total exports were worth US $1,188.37m. and imports $863.69m. Tourism earned $62m.-worth of foreign exchange in the same year, from only 163,100 international tourists (person-times), of whom a mere 55,400 were foreigners. The main tourist sights are in Nanchang, the 'porcelain capital' of Jingdezhen and the Lu Shan resort town of Guling, as well as the great Poyang Hu.

Government revenue in Jiangxi during 2000 totalled 11,155.36m. yuan, most of which came from the operations tax (24%) and value added tax (14%). Provincial expenditure was slightly more than double that, at 22,347.22m. yuan. The main spending destinations were education (17%), capital construction (12%) and government administration (9%). Actually used foreign direct investment of US $227.24m. in 2000 was only lower in some of the western regions (although Anhui had received less the year before).

Directory

Governor: HUANG ZHIQUAN; Office of the Provincial People's Government, Nanchang.

Secretary of the Jiangxi Provincial Committee of the Chinese Communist Party: MENG JIANZHU; Office of the Secretary, CCP Secretariat, Nanchang.

Chairman of the Standing Committee of the People's Congress of Jiangxi: MENG JIANZHU; Office of the Chairman, Congress Secretariat, Nanchang.

Chairman of the Jiangxi Provincial Committee of the Chinese People's Political Consultative Conference: ZHU ZHIHONG; Office of the Chairman, CPPCC Secretariat, Nanchang.

Jilin

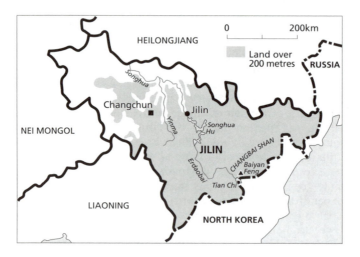

The Province of Jilin (Kirin or Chilin), 'fortunate forest', lies in north-eastern China, and has a 1,400-km international border, mainly with the Democratic People's Republic of Korea ('North Korea') to the south-east, but also with the Russian Federation to the east. The other north-eastern Chinese provinces flank Jilin, Heilongjiang beyond the north-eastern border and Liaoning beyond the southern part of the south-western border. Beyond the rest of the south-western border, and to the west, is the autonomous region of Nei Mongol (Inner Mongolia). The total area of Jilin province is 187,400 sq km (72,340 sq miles).

The province is fertile, occupying one of the three famous stretches of 'black land' in the world, with low-lying grasslands in the west, the Songliao plains in the centre and highlands in the east. The land rises to the Changbai Shan, through which the border with North Korea runs, and highest point is on that border, at Baiyan Feng (Paekdu-san), which reaches 2,750 m (9,026 feet). This lies near the source of the Songhua Jiang (which flows north into Heilongjiang) and the Tumen (which later forms part of the border with North Korea). Most of the southern part of the Korean border is along the Yalu Jiang. There is a continental monsoon climate, with distinct seasons and good rainfall, varying with altitude. The average monthly temperatures in Changchun during 2000 included -18.1°C (-0.6°F) for January and 25.2°C (77.4°F) for July. Total rainfall that year in the provincial capital, which lies on the central plains, was 416 mm (16 inches).

The total population was only 27.28m. in 2000, making Jilin the least-populous province of the north-east. The population density was 146 per sq km. At the time of the 2000 census, 9.0% of the population came from the minority nationalities. The majority Han population includes a large community of Chinese returned from abroad. There are over 40 minority ethnicities present in Jilin, the main groups being Korean (most of China's almost-2m.

ethnic Koreans live in north-eastern Jilin), native Manchu (Man or Manzu), Mongol, Muslim Hui and the lamaist Xibe. There are also other Buddhists active in the province, as well as Daoists, Muslims and Christians.

Almost one-half of the population lived in the cities and towns of the province (49.7% in 2000), the largest being the provincial capital of Changchun, which had an urban population of 2.9m. in 2000 (the greater administrative area included 7.0m. in all). The second city of the province is the eponymous Jilin, to the west of Changchun, and with a population of over 1m. Other important cities include Baicheng in the far west, Tonghua and Baishan in the far south, and Yanji in the north-east. Also in the north-east, is the 'port' city of Hunchun, near where the Chinese, Korean and Russian borders meet and where China reaches nearest to the coastline of the Sea of Japan. For administrative purposes Jilin province is divided into nine prefectures, eight of them urban, and 41 counties, 20 of them urban. The rural prefecture of Yanbian Chaoxian is the main Korean autonomous area, and occupies the north-eastern end of the province. There are 11 autonomous counties (including six cities).

History

The nomad peoples of the north-east began to establish their own dynasties in modern Manchuria and in northern China from about the 10th century. Before that the Koguryo and successor Bohai kingdoms, based in northern Korea, had held sway over much of the area. In 907 the Khitan people established the Liao dynasty, with a northern capital at Shangjing (modern Harbin, just across the border in Heilongjiang) and, eventually, a southern capital at Yanjing (Beijing). They exacted tribute from the Southern Song in the 11th century, but their Jurchen (Ruszhen) vassals revolted and in 1115 the Jurchen leader, Aguda, took the imperial name of Taizu and founded the Jin ('golden') dynasty. This empire had its capital in Beijing from 1153, but succumbed to Mongol conquest in the next century. A revival of the Jurchen peoples took place in the 16th century, when they and some of the Mongol tribes of the north-east were united under Nurhachi, who revived the Jin dynasty name. He moved beyond the Manchu homeland in what is now eastern Jilin (Kirin) and north-eastern Liaoning and established his capital at Mukden (modern Shenyang, in Liaoning) in 1625. From here his son and eventual successor, Abahai, changed his dynasty name to Qing and gave the Jurchen peoples the single name of Man or Manzu (Manchu), laying the foundations for the conquest of China from the 1640s.

Once the Qing had united Manchuria, Inner Mongolia and the rest of China into a single Empire, the development of the north-east proceeded apace and Russian incursions to the north of Jilin were repelled. The fort of Jilin was built in 1673, but Changchun not until 1800. Han settlement was at first forbidden, but the need to exploit the resources of the north-east, as well as the sinicization of the Manchus led to the abandonment of this policy (although intermarriage was forbidden until the early 1900s). By the late 19th century Russian pressure was again renewed and in 1860 the tsarist empire acquired the land north of the Heilong (Amur) and east of the Wusuli (Ussuri). In 1896 the Russians negotiated to extend their railways across Manchuria and effectively occupied much of eastern Manchuria until 1905, by which time the railway lines were very much in place. At this time Russia was forced to cede the railway concession to the

Japanese, who had established a sphere of influence throughout the south of modern Manchuria, and control over Korea, by 1918. (The west of Qing Manchuria is now largely part of Nei Mongol—Inner Mongolia.) It was the Japanese who helped the territory industrialize and who developed Changchun (Hsin-king) as the capital of the 'puppet' state of Manzhouguo (Manchukuo) in 1933–45. Before that, after the fall of the Qing, Chinese power in Manchuria had been exercised by warlords of the so-called Fengtian (then the name of Liaoning) faction. Jilin province (which had been formed in August 1908) included Harbin at this time, and the north-east of modern Heilongjiang, while Changchun was part of Fengtian. In September 1931 a minor bomb blast on the railway line near Mukden gave the Japanese a pretext to invade Manchuria, and on 6 February 1932 the state of Manzhouguo was proclaimed in Changchun. The last Qing emperor, Puyi, of the imperial Aisin Gioro clan, was made Chief Executive of this state—it was officially proclaimed a Japanese protectorate in 1933. Already having designs on the rest of China (the Japanese finally invaded in 1937), Puyi was restored to his imperial title as the Kangde emperor in Changchun on 1 March 1934. However, Manzhouguo succumbed with Japan at the end of the Second World War and in 1945 most of Manchuria, including Jilin, was occupied by the USSR (the successor state to the Russian Empire). The Soviet forces looted the already war-devastated cities of Manchuria, Changchun and Jilin among them, and eventually handed them to the soldiers of the Guomindang regime in 1946, but only after ensuring that the Chinese Communists were secure in their hold of the countryside.

In the Civil War the Guomindang forces found themselves isolated and the cities of Jilin province were taken by the Communists in 1948. Under the People's Republic the reorganization of Manchuria continued. Jilin province, which now included Changchun but excluded Hejiang in the north (which became part of modern Heilongjiang), was under the North-Eastern Administrative Council, with the rest of Manchuria until 1954. In that year the Changchun municipality formed only in the previous year was reabsorbed into Jilin and became its capital. At the same time Songjiang (Sungkiang) became part of Heilongjiang, except for the western end around Baicheng, which was absorbed into Jilin, as did much of Andong (Antung—along the Korean border), which was split with Liaoning, and Liaobei (Liaopeh), which was split with Nei Mongol. The united North-East was dissolved into provinces directly under central government, as at present.

Economy

Jilin, which has a fairly well balanced economy, is the poorest of the north-eastern provinces, but is wealthier than many of the regions of China. Total gross domestic product (GDP) in 2000 was 182,119m. yuan or 6,847 yuan per head. Infrastructure is well developed, and Jilin has good air links and access to seaports through Russia and North Korea. In 2000 the total length of operational railways, a historic engine of development in the region, was 3,474 km, while there were 35,216 km of roads (of which, 354 km were expressway and 410 km first-class highway). There were also 1,787 km of navigable inland waterways. Jilin produced less electricity than any other province of the north-east and north, and only 15% of the 31,350m. kWh generated in 2000 was hydroelectric. However, the rural population of Jilin had a lower illiteracy rate than in the other north-eastern provinces, giving it an overall rate of only 4.6% in 2000.

The primary sector accounted for 21.9% of GDP and 50.2% of employment in 2000. It is not a growth area of the local economy, although historically the north-eastern plains are important grain 'baskets' for China and prime land for cattle. The 'three treasures' of Jilin, traditionally, are ginseng (Manchurian ginseng is considered to be of the highest quality), marten fur and antlers (used in traditional medicine). Jilin is the biggest producer of both ginseng and antlers. Farm crops were sown on an area of 4.5m. ha in 2000, of which 48% was covered with corn (maize). In that year Jilin was the fourth largest producer of corn in the country, with 9.9m. metric tons. The province also produced 485,585 tons of fruit, 444,000 tons of sugar beet, 390,000 tons of oil-bearing crops, 60,000 tons of tobacco (of which, one-half was flue-cured) and 4,489 tons of walnuts. Jilin also possessed the third largest forest area in the People's Republic (7.9m. ha or 42% of the land area of the province) and was the second largest timber producer after Heilongjiang in 2000 (4.6m. cu m). Animal husbandry is important, with fewer pigs compared to cattle than is normal in much of the rest of China. In 2000 there were only 6.5m. pigs, but 4.3m. cattle, as well as 3.0. sheep, 722,000 horses, 541,000 goats, 189,000 mules and 168,000 donkeys. Jilin produced 2.2m. tons of meat (44% pork, 15% beef and 1% mutton), 150,000 tons of milk (95% cows' milk), 21,228 tons of sheep wool (90% fine wool), 0.8m. tons of poultry eggs and 5,000 tons of honey. Fishing was not a major activity of this inland province—aquatic production was 69% farmed and consisted almost entirely of fish (139,500 tons).

In 2000 the secondary or industrial sector of the regional economy contributed 43.9% to GDP. Construction accounted for a significant 7.9% of GDP in 2000, in which year the total output value of building activities was worth 23,918.4m. yuan. The whole secondary sector provided work for 19.1% of employed persons. Mineral resources, including oil-shale (the largest reserves in China), hydrocarbons (16m. metric tons of coal and 3.5m. tons of crude petroleum in 2000), iron, nickel and precious metals have been important in the development of industry. The dominant activities are engineering, petro-chemicals, pharmaceuticals, food, metallurgy and forest industries. Jilin is also noted as a long-established and leading automobile producer. Jilin still produces more motor vehicles than any other region of China (322,600 in 2000—16% of national production), although Shanghai produces more cars (about double Jilin's 125,400—21%). There are not a large number of industrial enterprises in the province (2,728 in 2000, with a gross output value of 167,991m. yuan), and most (61%) are owned by the state (accounting for 82% of the value). Heavy industry is predominant (54% of the enterprises and 78% of the value), while large enterprises number 212 (71% of the gross output value) and medium-sized ones 354 (12%).

The tertiary or services sector provided 34.2% of GDP in 2000 and 30.7% of the jobs. One-quarter of tertiary GDP was accounted for by trade and catering and a further one-fifth by transport, storage, post and communications. Trade normally runs a small deficit, with US $1,486.93m. in exports during 2000 being edged past by imports of $1,498.39m. in value. International tourism, which attracted 222,700 visits in 2000 (191,900 foreigners), earned $58m. in foreign exchange. The major attraction is the natural environment, whether for skiing, for scenery or for the wildlife. Specific sites include the spectacular Tian Chi volcanic-crater lake, where the Manchu people originated, according to legend, and which is also the deepest alpine lake in the country (at somewhere between 200 m and 350 m). Tian Chi lies on the Korean border, just to the south of Baihe, which is noted as the only place in China where the Meiren Song pine tree can be found. Perhaps more impressively, the largest nature reserve in China is found in Jilin's heavily forested Changbai Shan, where, among the rarer creatures to shelter there, can be found cranes, deer and Manchurian tigers.

The final statement of government accounts for 2000 put revenue from Jilin at 10,387.67m. yuan (operations tax 25%, value added tax 20% and income tax on enterprises 14%) and expenditure there at 26,066.94m. yuan (price subsidies 15%, education 14% and capital construction 8%). Foreign direct investment in Jilin was worth US $337.01m. in 2000.

Directory

Governor: HONG HU; Office of the Provincial People's Government, Chanchung.

Secretary of the Jilin Provincial Committee of the Chinese Communist Party: WANG YUNKUN; Office of the Secretary, CCP Secretariat, Chanchung.

Chairman of the Standing Committee of the People's Congress of Jilin: WANG YUNKUN; Office of the Chairman, Congress Secretariat, Chanchung.

Chairman of the Jilin Provincial Committee of the Chinese People's Political Consultative Conference: ZHANG YUEQI; Office of the Chairman, CPPCC Secretariat, Chanchung.

Head of the Yanbian Korean Autonomous Prefecture: NAN XIANGFU.

Liaoning

The Province of Liaoning, 'distant peace', is the heart of the old South Manchuria in north-eastern China. There is an international border with the Democratic People's Republic of Korea ('North Korea') along the Yalu Jiang in the south-east. Jilin province lies to the east, and stretches north and north-east beyond Liaoning, while the rest of the northern and the north-western borders are with Nei Mongol (Inner Mongolia) autonomous region. In the west there is a border with Hebei, running to the sea near the end of the Great Wall, the traditional separation between Beijing and the Chinese heartland to the south and any threat from the north. The total area of Liaoning is now 151,000 sq km (58,290 sq miles), making it the fourth-smallest province of the People's Republic.

Liaoning lies around Liaodong Bay, the northern part of the Bo Hai (Gulf of Bohai). The western coastal plains widen into the central alluvial plains of the province deposited by the Liao and Hun rivers. Highlands of the Inner Mongolian plateau dominate the western borders. The east is more mountainous, the highest part (around the peak of Laotuding Shan, at 1,367 m—4,486 feet) in the south-east, an extension of the Changbai Shan. The eastern highlands continue to thrust south-westwards, in the Qian (Qianlian) Shan range, which forms the backbone of the Liaodong peninsula. This peninsula helps enclose the Bo Hai and on its other side forms the north-western shore of the Korea Bay, an inlet of the Yellow Sea (Huang Hai). There is a monsoon climate throughout the province, but it varies from a subtropical, humid one on the coast to a temperate, semi-humid one in the north. Generally, there are hot, wet summers (over one-half of the annual rainfall is in June–August, and there is also more in the eastern hills) and long, cold winters. The average temperatures for Liaoning in January range between -17°C (1°F) and -5°C (23°F), and in July 21°–25°C (70°–77°F). In 2000, in Shenyang (the provincial capital—formerly Mukden), the average for January was -15.7°C (3.7°F) and for July 26.5°C (79.7°F). Annual average rainfall in the province is 400 mm–1,200 mm (16–47 inches), but, with less falling on the plains, the total in Shenyang was only 41 mm in all of 2000.

The total population of 42.38m. at the time of the 2000 census (which gave a population density of 281 per sq km) included the largest proportion (16.0%) of minority nationalities in the north-east—indeed, in all of eastern and northern China except Nei Mongol. Ethnic minorities included the Manchu (Man or Manzu), Mongol, Hui, Korean and Xibe peoples. Over 30 other groups were also represented, but most of the ethnic variation is widely dispersed. Standard Chinese is, overwhelmingly, the main language, particularly as the Manchu and Hui minorities do not possess their own languages (spoken Manchu had disappeared by the end of the 19th century, while the Hui people are distinguished by a traditional religious affiliation), but the ethnic mix does contribute to a variety of religious practice. Buddhism was probably the more dominant religion in the region in the past, but Daoists have long been present too and there are also Confucian temples. There are some small Muslim communities in the cities. Christianity is a comparatively late arrival, but has a number of adherents.

Liaoning is a very urbanized province (54.2% of the population in 2000) and has a number of large cities. The two most populous are the capital, Shenyang, with 4.3m. in 2000 (6.9m. in the whole administrative area), and Luda (the city of Dalian, together with nearby, but restricted, Lushun—formerly Port Arthur), with 2.8m. (5.5m.). Shenyang is located in the centre of the Liao plains to the north of the Bo Hai, while the great port of Dalian is on the south-western side of the tip of the Liaodong peninsula. The next largest cities are Anshan, to the south and a little west of Shenyang, Benxi, to the south-east, and Fushun, to the east. Other important centres include Dandong (formerly Andong or Antung), on the Korean border, Fuxin, in the north-west, Huludao, on the western coast, and, just inland, Jinzhou. For administrative purposes, however, the province has 14 cities of prefectural status, 17 cities of county status and a further 27 rural counties (eight of which are constituted as ethnic autonomous areas).

History

Liaoning lies where four regions meet: China, the Middle Kingdom, with its dominating culture and field for ambition; Korea, usually in rivalry with China; the north-east, the Manchuria of more recent times; and the vast territory of the Mongols. Thus, although the Liao plains were a route for Chinese armies and influence to tame the usually wilder territories beyond the Great Wall, they were also a favoured route for dynasts to enter the Empire. Contested by realms based in China and in Korea, the first sinicized dynasty from a northern people to establish its own empire in the region was that of the Liao, from the Yelu clan of the Khitans. This was in the 10th century, when many of the inhabitants of the plains were actually Mongols. It was Mongols who had established Shen (now Shenyang), a trading centre that prospered under their rule until the 12th century, when the Jurchens' Jin ('golden') dynasty displaced the Liao. In the 13th century the Mongols established their rule throughout the north-east, eventually establishing their own dynasty, the Yuan, in the Chinese Empire. The region of modern Liaoning remained under Chinese authority after the Yuan were replaced by the Ming in 1368. Shen was known as Fengtian at this time.

A Jurchen chieftain born in 1559, Nurhachi, of the Aisin Gioro clan, began to unite the neighbouring Jurchen and related Tungusic tribes. He was based in the north-east of the Liaodong peninsula and used force, diplomacy, marriage and political alliances to create the most powerful state in the north-east. A military organization of banners, with appointed, rather than hereditary, commanders solidified Jurchen rule, and Nurhachi reclaimed the name of Jin for his dynasty. At his orders a written Manchu (Man) language came into existence, although this name was not uniformly applied to the various Jurchen peoples until a decree by his son legislated it into sole use in 1635. Meanwhile, Nurhachi had moved against the Chinese domains north-east of the Great Wall and in 1625 seized Fengtian. The city was renamed Mukden (Shenqing) and became the Manchu capital. It is near here that Nurhachi is buried (he died in 1626) and it was this city that was the first imperial capital of the Qing. Nurhachi's eighth son, Abahai, gradually became the most pre-eminent banner prince as he led successful raids into Korea and against the Mongols between 1629 and 1638. Before the end of this time he was the undisputed Manchu leader and, in 1636, he adopted the more propitious dynasty name of Qing and styled himself the Huang Taiji emperor, vowing to conquer the Empire from the Ming. He established an administration that involved the Mongols and Chinese under his rule, as well as the Manchus, in a system that was a precursor of Qing government in China. However, although he raided beyond the Great Wall in 1640 and ransacked Beijing, and had extended his authority into the Mongol territories to the west and the Amur (Heilong) region of the north, Huang Taiji never displaced the Ming. The year after his death in 1643, a Ming general on the Great Wall facing Manchuria allied himself to the regents of the new Qing Shunzhi emperor and admitted the Manchu armies into China, in an effort to retrieve Beijing from rebels who had occasioned the suicide of the last Ming emperor. Before the end of the year the Qing capital had moved to Beijing and Mukden became a secondary capital.

By the 19th century, however, Qing power and its military underpinnings, the banner system, had decayed. China was also exposed to the interest of the expanding European nations, not least Russia, which had a land border with it. In 1858 (confirmed by an 1860 treaty) Russia had gained territory to the north and east of modern Manchuria, but was soon ambitious for the natural resources of the north-eastern part of the Chinese Empire for itself. However, Japan, which was already intervening in Korea and preparing to annexe it, made its move on southern Manchuria first. The Sino–Japanese War of 1894–95 ended with the humiliating defeat of the Beiyang Fleet, a product of the Self-Strengthening Movement by which Qing China had tried to modernize itself. The naval defeat took place off Lushun (which was to become more widely known as Port Arthur), near Dalian, at the southern end of the Liaodong peninsula. It was Liaodong that the Japanese claimed as the fruits of their victory, in a treaty that provoked the jealousy of the European powers, particularly of Russia. International pressure, therefore, forced the Japanese to return Liaodong to China and, in gratitude, the Qing awarded the Russian Empire a lease on Dalian (which was known in Russian as Dalny) and Port Arthur, as well as permission to build railways from Russia to the ports through

Manchuria. The area effectively became a Russian-occupied zone from 1898. However, the Russian tsar miscalculated when he provoked conflict with Japan in 1904. A pre-emptive attack on Lushun saw much of another great fleet destroyed, but this time it was a Russian one, and the ports of Liaodong were blockaded. The Japanese followed this by humiliating the Russians' Baltic fleet off Korea in May of the following year and defeating them near Mukden in the last major land battle of the war. Russia was forced to surrender Dalny (named Dairen by the Japanese) and Port Arthur (Ryojunko), as well as control of the railways in southern Manchuria. These cities became the seat of the administration of the Leased Territory of Guandong ('east of the pass'—Kwantung or, to the Japanese, Kanto) that the Qing Government was obliged to cede to Japan in southern Liaodong from 1906. With these arrangements confirmed, Japan withdrew its direct control from southern Manchuria and the Qing formed Liaoning (Fengtian) province in April 1907. Unlike the modern province, this included Changchun, and other parts of Jilin province, and extended northeastwards into a long territory reaching as far as Outer Mongolia (now Mongolia) and which is now included in the Nei Mongol (Inner Mongolia) region of China.

Although the presence of the Japanese in South Manchuria may seem to render the legalities of imperial administrative arrangements a mere technicality, much of the territory remained under Chinese control. Liaoning was not a province that declared its independence of the native Qing dynasty in 1911, and was left adrift by the abdication of the young Kangde emperor (Aisin Gioro Puyi) early in 1912. The authority of a privateer-general, Zhang Zuolin (Chang Tso-lin, later known as the 'Old Marshal'), who commanded a large private army and had dominated southern Manchuria since the Japanese withdrawal, therefore, enjoyed little formal rivalry, although he and other warlords of the so-called Fengtian faction briefly attempted a restoration of the Kangde emperor in 1917. In the 1920s his authority became more limited to Manchuria, but his regional government was widely recognized (Zhang was also the official governor between 1916 and 1922). Meanwhile, the Japanese tolerated his power, as he initially confined himself to limiting theirs, rather than moving openly against it, but as Zhang moved closer to the Guomindang they came to see him as a threat. By this time the Guandong military had acquired a command structure separate from the governor-general of the leased territory, as well as responsibility for protecting the railway interests throughout Manchuria, and was increasingly independent. In 1928 the headquarters was moved from Lushun to Mukden. In the same year, on 7 June, Japanese agents assassinated Zhang Zuolin with a bomb placed under a train. His son, the 'Young Marshal', Zhang Xueliang, inherited his power in Manchuria, but had formally acknowledged the authority of the Guomindang Government in Nanjing (Jiangsu) by December and was determined to oppose the Japanese.

The provocation sought by the Japanese Guandong Army for more direct intervention in Manchuria duly occurred on 18 September 1931. A bomb planted on the railway line near Mukden on was used as an pretext to occupy the rest of Manchuria, and a Japanese military governor, Minami Jiro, was installed. The Japanese then arranged for the proclamation, on 6 February 1932, of a new state independent of China, Manzhouguo (Manchukuo). The former Kangde emperor, Puyi, was installed as Chief Executive in Changchun. (He was formally restored to an imperial Qing throne in 1934, once Japanese ambitions had become fixed on the rest of China.) Jiro then relinquished his authority to this 'independent' state, although a Japanese protectorate was officially declared in 1933. The Fengtian forces of Zhang Xueliang had been forced out of Manchuria and were eventually located to Shaanxi and charged with the elimination of any local Communists, the priority of the Guomindang leader, Jiang Jieshi (Chiang Kai-shek). Zhang came to distrust Jiang's assurances of resistance to the Japanese and the recapture of the Manchurian homeland, while his soldiers were reluctant to fight fellow-nationals like the Communists when the Japanese were occupying parts of China (Jehol, part of which is now in Liaoning, was taken in 1934). He, therefore, made a truce with the Communists, arrested Jiang in December 1936 when he visited Xian (Shaanxi) and forced him into an anti-Japanese alliance with the Communists.

The Guomindang-Communist alliance did not long survive the Second World War. Following the surrender of Japan in August 1945 Manchuria was occupied by Soviet troops. The Soviet military governor, Aleksandr Vasiliyevskii, held power until May 1946, when his soldiers departed with much of the looted industrial infrastructure of Manchuria, leaving the cities to Guomindang garrisons (Soviet forces remained in Dalian, however, until 1954, and with a share in the South Manchurian Railway Co until 1953). However, the Communists, against Jiang's wishes, marched overland to Manchuria (and sailed from Shandong), to establish themselves while the politically sympathetic Soviet forces were still influential. With Communist support consolidated in the Manchurian countryside by land reform, the Guomindang garrisons became steadily more isolated and demoralized. The Red Army, meanwhile, swelled from the original 100,000 who had marched into the north-east to some 1.5m. combat troops. In 1948 the Communists gained control of all the main cities of Manchuria (Mukden was renamed Shenyang), and then moved on Beijing, winning three major offensives under Lin Biao between August and January 1949, in which the Guomindang lost almost 1.5m. soldiers to death, defeat or desertion. This sealed the ultimate Communist victory in China and enabled the proclamation of the People's Republic.

In the order established formally in 1949 Shenyang became the seat of the North-East Administrative Council, remaining as the capital of the restored Liaoning province in 1954. Liaoning was formed from the union of Liaodong and Liaoxi (East and West Liao) provinces (Liaobei, North Liao, was mainly split between Jilin and Nei Mongol) with southern Andong (Antung—along the Korean border and based in Dandong) and five special municipalities: Shenyang itself, Anshan, Benxi, Fushun and Luda (Dalian). In 1955 Liaoning also received some territory from the old Jehol (Rehe) province, which was largely split between Hebei and Nei Mongol (in which most of the west of old Manchuria was included).

Economy

Liaoning is one of the more prosperous provinces of China, its gross domestic product (GDP) totalling 466,906m. yuan and its GDP per head 11,226 yuan in 2000. Its natural assets are both agricultural and mineral, enhanced by the great industrial cities of the central plains. The province also boasts the 'Hong Kong of the north', the great seaport of Dalian (Luda), at the southern end of the Liaodong peninsula, which has more industrial output, revenue and traffic than the capital city of Shenyang. Dalian was the sixth largest port in the People's Republic (by volume of freight handled—90.8m. metric tons in 2000). Connecting these cities and others outside the province is a well-developed and dense infrastructure of transport links, including the greatest length of railway per square kilometre of any region (perhaps no surprise given the importance of railways in the history of southern Manchuria). The total length of operational railways was 3,556 km in 2000, while roads measured a total of 45,547 km (1,068 km of expressway and 833 km of first-class highway). There were only 813 km of navigable waterways. Liaoning also produced the fifthmost amount of electricity of any region in China, at 64,558m. kWh in 2000, although the overwhelming majority was generated thermally. Illiterates in 2000 comprised only 4.8% of the adult population.

Agriculture, forestry and fishing, the primary sector, accounts for only 10.8% of GDP (2000 figure), which is a smaller proportion of the economy than in any other province or autonomous region save Guangdong. Apart from the three eastern municipalities, however, Liaoning employs a smaller proportion than any other region in the primary sector (37.7%). Like other parts of the north-east Liaoning is known for its Manchurian ginseng and the antler trade, but also for maize, rice and apples. The total area sown with farm crops was only 3.6m. ha in 2000 (the smallest in the north-east), with cereals covering 65% of this. Fruit orchards, however, covered more hectares (392,800) than in either of the other north-eastern provinces. The cereal crop in 2000 totalled 10.3m. metric tons (54% corn—maize and 37% rice), while almost one-half of the total fruit harvest of 2.5m. tons consisted of apples. The largest groundnut (peanut) harvest in the north-east (256,000 tons) came from Liaoning, which also produced 287,000 tons of sugar beet and 39,051 tons of silkworm cocoons (very few of mulberry). Livestock numbers in the same year were put at 13m. pigs, 2.5m. cattle, 198,800 sheep, 187,300 goats, 95,300 donkeys, 37,000 horses and 34,400 mules. Animal husbandry produced 2.3m. tons of meat (1.2m. tons of pork), 219,000 tons of milk (18,900 tons of cows' milk), only 7,567 tons of sheep wool, but 356 tons of cashmere, 1.4m. tons of poultry eggs and 6,000 tons of honey. Liaoning has the biggest fishing industry in northern and north-eastern China, mainly marine, and is famous for cutlass fish, yellow croakers, shrimps, abalones and kelp. Total aquatic production was 3.38m. tons in 2000 (89% obtained from sea water). Barely over one-half of marine production was artificially cultured. Seawater shellfish together weighed 1.38m. tons, fish 766,900 tons, crustaceans 379,400 tons and algae 350,200 tons. Over 90% of the freshwater catch is farmed and 332,400 tons consisted of freshwater fish.

One-half of the economy is industrial, the sector accounting for 50.2% of GDP and a high 26.3% of employment in 2000. Construction only accounted for 4.9% of total GDP, but had a relatively large output value totalling 59,809.33m. yuan. Important mineral reserves, which have helped the development of the industrial sector, include oil-shale, manganese, magnesium and other metal ores, talcum and salt (2.8m. metric tons in 2000). Hydrocarbons are also produced: 45m. tons of coal in 2000, 14.0m. tons of crude petroleum and 1,470m. m of natural gas. The province is the second largest producer of pig iron (after Hebei—15.6m. tons), and of steel and of steel products (after

Shanghai—15.5m. tons and 14.4m. tons, respectively), and produces a large amount of cement (19.5m. tons) and plate glass (14.8m. weight cases). The textile industry produced 341,800 tons of chemical fibre, 182,900 tons of yarn, 499m. m of cloth and 2,400 tons of silk. Liaoning is the country's third largest manufacturer of colour television sets (3.7m. units) and the fourth biggest beer producer (1.5m. tons) and micro-computer manufacturer (0.8m. units—over 12% of national production). Plastics (0.9m. tons) and chemicals (including 1.2m. tons of sulphuric acid 0.9m. tons of fertilizer) are important in the northeast, as is the manufacture of metal-cutting machine tools (15,600 units). At this time, in 2000, there were 6,017 industrial enterprises in Liaoning, with a gross output value, in current prices, of 424,946m. yuan. The state held 2,454 enterprises (67% of the value), while 3,732 of them (worth 81%) were engaged in heavy industry. There were 403 large enterprises (65%) and 454 medium-sized ones (barely worth one-10th of the former).

The tertiary sector is relatively large, providing 39.0% of GDP in 2000. At the same time 36.0% of employed persons worked in the sector. Trade and catering contributes 13.5% towards total GDP, transport and communications 7.5% (employing 340,000 people) and social services 5.1%. Trade is healthily in surplus, with exports in 2000 worth US $10,589.47m. and imports $9,478.00m. The tourist industry earned a further $383m. and of the 612,200 international tourist visits, 82% were by foreigners. Visitors come for the historic sites, such as the burial places of the founders of the Qing dynasty or the bustling port city of Dalian, to view across the North Korean border or to see the hot springs and the scenery of the Qian Shan.

In 2000 government revenue in Liaoning amounted to 29,562.74m. yuan, 8,002.39m. yuan coming from the operations tax, 5,669.97m. yuan from value added tax and 3,901.81m. yuan from the income tax on enterprises. Expenditure was 51,808.41m. yuan, of which the largest single allocation was destined for the subsidy of social-security programmes (7,359.91m. yuan), followed by education (6,590.91m. yuan) and capital construction (5,294.98m. yuan). Liaoning received more foreign direct investment than any other region of the north-east or north, at US $2,044.46m., ranking the province sixth in the country in this category.

Directory

Governor: BO XILAI; Office of the Provincial People's Government, Shenyang.

Secretary of the Liaoning Provincial Committee of the Chinese Communist Party: WEN SHIZHEN; Office of the Secretary, CCP Secretariat, Shenyang.

Chairman of the Standing Committee of the People's Congress of Liaoning: WANG HUAIYUAN; Office of the Chairman, Congress Secretariat, Shenyang.

Chairman of the Liaoning Provincial Committee of the Chinese People's Political Consultative Conference: XIAO ZUOFU; Office of the Chairman, CPPCC Secretariat, Shenyang.

Qinghai

The Province of Qinghai (Tsinghai—formerly known as Kokonor) lies at the heart of the western People's Republic of China, in the north-east of the great Tibet–Qinghai plateau, the 'roof of the world'. The autonomous regions of Xizang (Tibet) and Xinjiang border the west of the province, lying to the south-west and north-west, respectively. Sichuan province lies to the south-east, while the length of Gansu curves around the rest of the border, from east to north. Qinghai is the largest province in China (three of the autonomous regions, its neighbours and Nei Mongol—Inner Mongolia—are larger), at some 721,000 sq km (278,310 sq miles).

Qinghai is named for the brackish lake in the north-east, Qinghai Hu (Qing Hai and Koko Nor both mean 'azure sea'), anciently known as the Western Sea. It lies more than 1,500 km (930 miles) from the eastern coast of China. Qinghai Hu is the country's largest inland water covering an area of 4,583 sq km. The most settled part of the province and the main areas suitable for arable farming lie in the east, on a high, grassy plateau rising between 2,500 m (8,200 feet) and 3,000 m above sea level, flanked by the Qilian Shan to the north-west of Qinghai Hu and, in the south, the Anyemaqen range. Beyond the latter range the upper reaches of the Huang He (Yellow River) cut a deep, eastward-running valley before the river loops northwards along the border, beyond the eastern end of the Anyemaqen Shan, and then back into Qinghai, before heading east again to the south of Xining, the provincial capital. The eastern part of the province is separated from the broad and lofty lands of southern Qinghai by the Bayan Har range to the south of the upper Huang He. The north-west of the province is barren, a near-desert area dotted with salt marshes and bitter lakes, enduring extreme winters. This is the Qaidam (Chaidam) basin, south-west of the northern highlands and north of the Kunlun Shan dividing it from southern Qinghai. This last area, Qingnan, is an even higher plateauland, again mainly grassland, averaging some 3,500 m in height. The highest of the many mountain ranges in Qinghai rises along the southern border with Xizang—the Tanggula Shan have peaks exceeding 6,000 m in height, while even the main pass across the south-western border is at 5,231 m (17,168 feet). Both the Chang Jiang (River Yangzi) and the Mekong have their sources in southern Qinghai, the former in the Tuotuo–Tongtian system and the latter as the Langcang Jiang. The Chang Jiang is the longest river in China and the third longest river in the world (at some 6,300 km), the Huang He the second longest river in China (almost 5,500 km) and the Mekong is the longest river of South-East Asia (flowing into the sea near the very south of Viet Nam, some 4,000 km later). The generally high altitudes mean that the climate is very cold and very dry. Average annual rainfall is less than 50 mm (2 inches) in the Qaidam basin and reaches no higher than 700 mm in the eastern river valleys (Xining received 343 mm in 2000, mainly in May–October). Most of the terrain, therefore, depends on being watered by the many streams and rivers, creating an unusual landscape of sudden contrasts between the bleak and the lush. The mildest weather conditions are in the north-east, but even in Xining the average monthly temperatures were only -7.1°C (19.2°F) in January 2000 and 19.6°C (67.3°F) in July.

The total population on 1 November 2000 was only 5.18m., giving Qinghai the smallest population of any province and making it the second least populous of any region in China. Only Xizang (Tibet) has fewer people and a smaller population density. In Qinghai the average density was seven people per sq km in 2000, although vast tracts of the land are settled far more sparsely (if at all), given that almost two-fifths of the population lives in Xining and its environs alone. In the same year 45.5% of the population consisted of minority nation-alities. Most of the majority Han Chinese and of the Hui are located in the north-east and in the urban centres. The most populous minority group is Tibetan (Xizangzu), who are spread throughout the province, but there also some Kazakhs and Mongols, mainly in the north, as well as most of the country's population of the Tu and Salar communities (some of the latter can also be found in Gansu). The Hui and Kazakh peoples contribute to a fairly large Muslim community in Qinghai (mainly in the north-east). The Hui are probably the sinicized descendents of Central Asian Muslim traders who retained their religion as they married and adapted to the Han. The Kazakhs are among the many Turkic peoples represented throughout the Chinese north-west, while the Salars, who are also Muslim, speak a Turkic tongue, but are more closely related to the Tibetans. These origins can be traced in that they, like the Tibetan Buddhists, still hold the Tian Chi to be a sacred lake. The main religion of the region is undoubtedly Buddhism, be it the lamaism of the Tibetans and Mongols or the more orthodox Mahayana Buddhism usually practised by the Han. A famous pilgrimage site near Xining is known as Kumbum to the Tibetans, the Taer Si in Huangzhong, one of the six great monasteries of the Geluk pa ('Yellow Hat' sect).

At the time of the 2000 national census 34.8% of the population of Qinghai was classed as urban. The capital, Xining (Hsining or, in Tibetan, Ziling—formerly Amdo), which is located at 2,275 m above sea level, is by far the largest city. It had an urban population of 766,100 in 2000 (1.98m. resided in the greater administrative area). South-west of Xining and just south of Qinghai Hu is Gonghe (Qabqa). In the centre of the province, below the heights guarding

Qingnan, southern Qinghai, is Golmud (at some 2,800 m), while north across the Qaidam basin is Da Qaidam Zhen. These are the only other towns of any size, the two on either side of the bleak but mineral-rich basin being on important transport routes, Golmud on the high road leading across to Xizang (Tibet) and the other on the road curving north to Dunhuang in Gansu. As most of the Han population lives in the north-east, the minority-nationality autonomous areas cover a large area. There are six autonomous prefectures for Tibetans: Haixi ('west of the sea'—Tibetan name, Tsonub), which is also for Mongols; and Haibei (Tsochang); Hainan (Tsolho); Yushu (Jyekundo); Huangnan ('south of the Huang'—Malho); and Guoluo (Golog). The Haidong ('east of the sea'—Tsohar) area is not formally constituted as an autonomous prefecture. There are only two other prefectures in the province, one of which is Xining, while there are also 39 counties, only two of which are cities. One of these urban counties is constituted as a Hui autonomous area, near Xining, and the other urban county and 33 rural counties are also minority nationality areas.

History

Most of Qinghai lies on the bleak uplands of the Tibet–Qinghai plateau and has held little interest to outside invaders. It remained largely undisturbed for centuries, therefore, except in the north-east, where the land is more hospitable and the city of Xining has long prospered on a southern path of the 'Silk Road' into Tibet (Xizang) proper. When the Tibetan kingdom (Bod to Tibetans and Tufan to the Chinese) was founded in the seventh century, balancing the political and cultural influences of China and India, it also began to incorporate the lands wandered by ethnic Tibetans (Xizangzu) in Qinghai (especially in the south). With expansionist political ambitions directed to the north and, principally, to the east, the Tibetans were soon clashing with the Tang Chinese. Xining (Amdo) and the north-east were already falling under Chinese authority, notably reinforced by the Chinese subjugation early in the seventh century of the Turkic Tuyuhun people, who had settled in northern Qinghai and were causing problems in the Gansu Corridor. Over the following centuries a powerful Tibetan kingdom also competed in the north, across Qinghai, not only with the Tang, but also with the Uygurs (Uyghurs) and other Turkic peoples, and from the eighth century with Arab peoples, mainly for control of the Central Asian trade routes. From the late eighth to the mid-ninth centuries the Tibetans held to as far north as Dunhuang in northern Gansu. In the 10th century central control in both China and Tibet declined, and the great wilderness tracts of Qinghai became less contentious.

Contact between the high plateaux and the world to the north and east resumed in the 13th century (by which time the great monastic orders held sway in the Tibetan world) with the rise of the Mongols, who converted to Tibetan Buddhism and also conquered China, establishing the Yuan dynasty. From the 14th century Xining and the north-east was usually included in Gansu province, but the fall of the house of Yuan reduced Chinese influence further afield, although suzerainty over Tibet was still claimed by the Ming. By the 16th century Xining was very much a Chinese garrison and trading city. However, it was near the city that the Geluk pa ('Yellow Hat' sect) Tibetan Buddhist order then built a major monastery (to commemorate the 1357 birth of the Yellow Hat founder, Tsong Khapa), indicating the pervasive influence of religious affiliation and the permeability of medieval borders. Political control of the wider regions beyond the Chinese garrison towns tended to be exercised by the Mongol peoples, including over Tibet. Thus, at the time of the Qing accession to power within the China after 1644, the close relations of the Mongols and the Manchus renewed Chinese contact with and prestige in Tibet. At this time the main political force based in northern Qinghai was the Khoshote (Kochot) khanate of western Mongols, who wielded considerable power in Tibet itself. This situation was later disrupted by the ambitions of another western Mongol clan, the Junggars (Dzungars), whose Dorben Oyriot khanate claimed to be the protector of the Tibetan territories between 1717 and 1720. Such an alteration to the balance of power, however, provoked the Qing, who invaded and imposed their authority in Tibet, followed by an invasion of Qinghai in 1724, thus beginning the formal incorporation of much of the area into the Chinese Empire. For the rest of the 18th century the Manchus maintained much closer scrutiny over Tibetan affairs, particularly given the religious influence over the still sometimes troublesome Mongols, but in the 19th century Qing power generally waned.

British interest in Tibet at the beginning of the 20th century provoked a reassertion of Chinese authority from 1905, but this was mainly in Tibet (Xizang) itself and was not needed in the emptier lands to the north or those heavily settled by the Han. The Chinese campaign to change suzerainty into sovereignty collapsed with the Qing in 1911, and Tibet claimed its independence in 1913. However, although Tibet claimed much of Qinghai, it did not have the strength to possess the wider territories that were much more exposed to outside forces. Chinese authority was not seriously challenged in the Qinghai region, which in 1912 had been formed into a Kokonor (Qinghai) province, ruled from Xining (which was still a part of Gansu). In 1928 the republican Government regularized the administration by including the capital within the boundaries of the province. It was held by the Guomindang until it succumbed to Communist forces in September 1949. Thereafter, the Government of the People's Republic continued a tradition of using the region as a destination for political prisoners.

Economy

With a gross domestic product (GDP) of only 26,359m. yuan or 5,087 yuan per head in 2000, Qinghai has one of the smallest economies in China, although the number of people in the province means that relative wealth is slightly enhanced. Nevertheless, most of the population lives in extreme poverty and is poorly educated (with far more men than women), despite the mineral resources of the Qaidam basin and improvements brought by the extension of the railway as far as Golmud. Operational railways extended for a total of 1,092 km in the province by 2000 and highways for 18,679 km (although there were no express-ways and first-class highways amounted to only 31 km). Other investment in infrastructure has produced China's largest artificial reservoir (at Longyang Gorge) and a number of hydroelectric projects that together generate some 80% of power (13,379m. kWh in total during 2000). With very high rural illiteracy, Qinghai still had the highest illiteracy rate in China outside Xizang (Tibet) in 2000, at 18.0%.

The primary sector accounted for only 14.6% of GDP in 2000, but for 60.9% of employment. What little arable farming there is takes place in the north-east of Qinghai, but about one-half of the province is grassland suitable for pasture, although this is not usually exploited commercially, but, particularly in the south, by semi-nomadic Tibetan herders. The province is, therefore, famous for its livestock, for its horses and yaks, and its wool-producing sheep. Traditionally, the noted primary products of Qinghai are rhubarb, caterpillar fungus, musk, Xining wool and antlers. Most of the land sown with farm crops (barely 0.6m. ha in 2000) is in the north-east, and 30% is covered with wheat. Millets, being hardier cereals, are also widely grown. However, a greater area is given to rape (canola), which covers 34% of the sown area. In 2000 Qinghai produced 439,000 metric tons of wheat, 191,000 tons of rapeseed, 149,000 tons of tubers, 66,000 tons of beans and 22,415 tons of fruit (mainly apples). The vast pasturelands fed some 13.70m. sheep (only Xinjiang and Nei Mongol had more) in 2000, 3.91m. cattle and buffaloes, 2.73m. goats, 1.04m. pigs (the fewest pigs of any region in China save Xizang, including the municipalities and Hainan), 338,000 horses and 150,000 mules and donkeys. Some 208,000 tons of meat were produced in 2000, 213,000 tons of milk, 15,558 tons of sheep wool (2% fine and 29% semi-fine), 745 tons of goat wool, 310 tons of cashmere and 13,000 tons of poultry eggs. The province, although it is known for the scaleless naked carp of Qinghai lake, had the smallest fisheries produce of any region of China (including Xizang), with only 1,200 tons of fish in 2000 (almost all of it farmed).

The secondary sector provided 43.2% of GDP and 13.4% of employed persons' work in 2000. Construction alone provided a massive 12.7% of GDP, after a total output value of 4,471.62m. yuan. Rich minerals reserves are fundamental to Qinghai's industrial sector, apart from extraction and processing, providing the basis of metallurgical industries. Qinghai, mainly in the Qaidam basin, produced 676,500 metric tons of salt, for example, 391m. cu m of natural gas and 20.0m. tons of crude petroleum, and in the north-east 1m. tons of coal (2000 figures). Modest amounts of cement, iron and steel are produced locally. Other salts and non-ferrous metals are important. Another significant natural advantage to local industry is the hydroelectric potential. Textiles and associated handicrafts, as well as carpet-making, are important industries, and the province also produces chemical fertilizers, shoe leather and sausage casings in some quantity. There were 445 industrial enterprises in Qinghai during 2000, with a total gross output value of 19,608m. yuan. The state was responsible for 362 of these (and 89% of the output value), but Qinghai is the only region with entirely no foreign funding for industrial enterprises and only six having investment from Chinese territories outside the People's Republic proper. Heavy industry accounted for 277 enterprises (91% of the value). Twenty-one of all the enterprises were large (and accounted for 70% of output value) and 302 small (25%).

The tertiary sector provided a relatively high 42.1% of GDP in 2000. A closer examination of the contributions reveals the importance of government spending: the most important services were trade and catering (8.1% to total GDP), transport and communications (mainly state run—7.3%) and government and party agencies and social organizations (7.3%). Trade earned Qinghai a mere US $133.55m. from exports in 2000, but only cost the province $92.90m. for imports. Tourism earned less in foreign exchange than in any other region except

Ningxia Hui in 2000, at $7m. International tourist visits totalled only 32,600 in 2000, including 14,600 by foreigners. People mainly pass through on the over-land trip to Xizang (Tibet), but also come to see the local cultural (such as the Taer monastery) and natural attractions (Qinghai lake, for its scenery and birdlife, or the Mengda Tian Chi nature reserve by the Huang He—Yellow River). The services sector as a whole accounted for the jobs of 25.7% of employed persons in 2000.

Revenues raised by government from Qinghai in 2000 amounted to only 1,658.43m. yuan (only Xizang earns less), 25% from the operations tax, 18% from value added tax and 13% from enterprises' income tax. Spending (6,826.14m. yuan in total) reveals the importance of government in the provin-cial economy. Most went to capital construction (16%), as part of a continuing commitment to development, social-security subsidies (12%), bureaucrats' pensions (12%), education (11%) and government administration (10%). There was no foreign investment in Qinghai during 2000, although US $459m. had been used in the previous year.

Directory

Governor: ZHAO LEJI; Office of the Provincial People's Government, Xining.

Secretary of the Qinghai Provincial Committee of the Chinese Communist Party: BAI ENPAI; Office of the Secretary, CCP Secretariat, Xining.

Chairman of the Standing Committee of the People's Congress of Qinghai: BAI ENPAI; Office of the Chairman, Congress Secretariat, Xining.

Chairman of the Qinghai Provincial Committee of the Chinese People's Political Consultative Conference: SANG GYE GYA; Office of the Chairman, CPPCC Secretariat, Xining.

Party Committee Secretary of the Guoluo Tibet Autonomous Prefecture: DENG BENTAI.

Head of the Haibei Tibet Autonomous Prefecture: n.a.

Head of the Hainan Tibet Autonomous Prefecture: GONG BAOSHANG.

Head of the Haixi Mongol, Tibetan and Kazakh Autonomous Prefecture: n.a.

Head of the Huangnan Tibet Autonomous Prefecture: n.a.

Head of the Yushu Tibet Autonomous Prefecture: n.a.

Qinghai Government Office: Xining; internet www.qh.gov.cn.

Shaanxi

The Province of Shaanxi (Shensi—'thieves' mountain west') lies west of the Huang He (Yellow River), where it loops back south out of the neighbouring Nei Mongol autonomous region, which lies to the north of the Great Wall. Here in the north, where the border follows the Wall, it is heading south-westwards, until it encounters another autonomous region, that of Ningxia Hui. The rest of the western border is with Gansu province, which abuts into central Shaanxi and draws back in the south-west. To the south the border was entirely with Sichuan, but in 1997 the municipality of Chongqing was separated from it and now lies beyond the southernmost border. To the south-east is Hubei. East of southern Shaanxi is Henan, but most of the eastern limit is defined by the Huang He, beyond which lies Shanxi. Enclosed within these boundaries is some 195,800 sq km (75,580 sq miles) of territory.

Forested mountains dominate the south of the province, the Micang and Daba Shan along the southern borders. Between them and the Qinling range to the north is the valley of the Han, a tributary of the Chang Jiang (River Yangzi). North of the Qinling watershed, which therefore marks a major boundary between southern and northern China, stretches lowland Shaanxi, dominated by the Huang He. The low central Shaanxi or Guangzhong plain is crossed, from west to east, by the Wei, which joins the Huang He where it descends the eastern border from the north, forcing it sharply eastwards. The higher, soft, loess plateau of the north (45% of the province's territory) is deeply eroded. Here in the north the monsoonal climate is a temperate semi-arid one (which has contributed to the historic desertification of the loess plains), but changes in the south to a subtropical humid one. More rain falls in the south than in the north, in the mountains than on the plains and in the summer (June–September) than in the winter. The average annual rainfall in the province, therefore, is 400–1,000 mm (16–39 inches); the 2000 total in Xian, the provincial capital on the central plains, was 539 mm. The average monthly temperatures for the city during that year were -0.5°C (31.1°F) in January and 28.1°C (82.6°F) in July.

The total population of Shaanxi in November 2000 was put at 36.05m. by the census enumerators. While population growth was not high, the male-female ratio remained poor (too many men relative to women). The average population density was 184 persons per sq km. The overwhelming majority of the population were Han Chinese and only 0.5% came from the minority nation-alities, most of them also being Chinese speakers. The main group was that of the Hui, the remnants of a much larger Muslim population reduced in number by the 19th-century rebellions and their suppression, but there were also Manchu and Mongol people. Islam remains represented in the province, but the main religion is Buddhism, which first flourished here when Changan (modern Xian) was an imperial capital. At the time, under the Tang, perhaps the greatest city in the world, at the Chinese end of the great 'Silk Road', also attracted Zoroastrian and Nestorian Christian communities, but their presence is now merely historical.

In 2000 32.3% of the population was counted as urban. Of the 13 official cities, however, only one, the capital, Xian (Sian), is of any size. Its total population in 2000 was 6.88m., of which 2.86m. lived in the urban area. The next-most populous cities are Xianyang, just to the north-west of the capital, and Weinan, downriver to the east. The other principal centres are Yanan for the north, Hanzhong for the Han valley and the south-west, and Hancheng on the Huang He. Shaanxi is divided into one rural and nine urban prefectures, and into 87 counties (four of which are cities).

History

Shaanxi is one of the longest-settled parts of China and the cradle of early civilization. There is evidence of the 'Yangshao Culture' from 6,000 years ago, but the imperial tradition starts when the region emerged into pre-eminence as the home of the Zhou, the dynasty that displaced the Shang and ruled a feudal confederation for some 800 years, though for much of the time their authority was nominal. Under the Later or Eastern Zhou the most powerful state was Qin, which had its capital in Xianyang, north of the Wei. Qin united China militarily and began the process of standardization and unification continued under the Han, who soon displaced them at the very end of the third century BC. Over 400 years later, after expanding the empire deep into west and south, the Han gave way to centuries of disunity and invasion, but left a dream of empire that was restored by the Sui towards the end of the sixth century AD. The Sui dynasty was soon displaced by the Tang, who retained the new imperial capital at Changan (built in 582—modern Xian), to the south of the Wei (and of ancient Xianyang). In the Tang period (618–907) Changan became the greatest city in Asia, with a population of some 2m. by the eighth century, and the capital of a vast empire. Shaanxi suffered as the centre of that empire from about this time, as Tang armies were defeated in Central Asia, and the north and west were plagued by Tibetan (Xizangzu) and Turkic invaders. Changan itself was sacked and with the fall of the Tang in the 10th century it ceased to be an imperial capital. After over one millennium of imperial pre-eminence, Shaanxi ceased to be at the political centre of China.

The province of Shaanxi was a fruitful field for rebellion in 1340–68 (at the end of the Yuan dynasty) and again in 1620–44 (at the end of the Ming dynasty), but did not regain the seat of Chinese government. In 1666 it was united with Shanxi across the Huang He (Yellow River), and then as part of Shenzhuan (which also included Sichuan in 1680–1731 and 1735–49). Then, until restored as a separate province in 1912, after the fall of the Qing, Shaanxi was administered with Shanxi and Gansu as Shengan. Meanwhile, the great Muslim rebellion of the mid-19th century left the province devastated and prone to severe famine in 1876–78 (5m. people died). Severe famine, killing 3m., recurred in 1915, 1921 and 1928, contributing to the sympathetic reception of the Communists in the 1930s. At the end of 1936 Mao Zedong and the army of the 'Long March' arrived in Wuqi, in northern Shaanxi. The Communist headquarters moved to Yanan in the following year and remained there until a Guomindang offensive in 1947, but by then the Communists were well on their way to victory in the Civil War (they retook Shaanxi in April 1948).

Before the resumption of Guomindang–Communist hostilities after the Second World War, however, the province was the scene of the important alliance against the Japanese invaders, centred on the so-called Xian Incident. The Dongbei (North-Eastern) Army driven from Manchuria by the Japanese and commanded by Zhang Xuelin, a warlord, had been relocated to Shaanxi by the mid-1930s. The Guomindang leader, Jiang Jieshi (Chiang Kai-shek), had ordered Zhang and his troops to impose Nationalist authority in Shaanxi and to hunt down the Communists, but they were more anxious to fight the Japanese than other Chinese. Zhang, therefore, negotiated a truce with the Communists and, in December 1936, placed Jiang under arrest when he visited Xian. With the intervention of Zhou Enlai, the Communists were able to persuade Jiang of the necessity of a national alliance, and Zhang released him to pursue the struggle against Japan (although Jiang never forgave him, and he was only released from Taiwan in 1992).

After the Communist victory Xian became a separate municipality, but was reunited with Shaanxi, of which it remains the capital, in 1954. At the same time the North-West Administrative Council (in existence since 1950 and with its headquarters in Xian) was dissolved. In the 1970s memories of the ancient past of the province were encouraged by the accidental discovery of the tomb of the Qin First Emperor (Shi Huangdi) and his 'Terracotta Army' of grave goods.

Economy

Despite its rich history and its rich mineral resources, Shaanxi is a poor province. In 2000 the gross domestic product (GDP) amounted to 166,092m. yuan or only 4,549 yuan per head. Shaanxi has a fairly dense network of roads and railways, but the intensity of its waterways has declined relative to the rest of the country since it stood at the centre of imperial China. Navigable waterways extended for 998 km in 2000, operational railways for 2,205 km and roadways for 44,006 km (expressways 349 km and first-class highways 175 km). The province only produced 27,228m. kWh of power in 2000, of which only 13% was from hydroelectric generation, despite the potential in the southern mountains. Shaanxi has the best rate of urban literacy in western China, but rural deprivation means that its overall illiteracy rate remained at 7.3% in 2000, despite significant improvement over the previous 10 years.

The primary sector contributed only 16.8% to GDP, but 55.7% of employ-ment in 2000. Traditionally, the exports of Shaanxi are dates, walnuts and tung oil, but it is also the major foodgrain producer of north-west China. The total sown area in 2000 was 4.6m. ha (3.8m. ha for foodgrains, of which 3.0m. ha was cereals) and a further 0.7m. ha gave Shaanxi the largest area of fruit orchards in western China. That year the province produced 4.9m. metric tons of fruit (79% apples), 4.2m. tons of wheat, 4.1m. tons of corn (maize), 224,000 tons of rapeseed and 15,431 tons of mainly mulberry-silkworm cocoons. The 12,935 tons of tung-oil seeds did not make Shaanxi a leading producer, but the 34,498 tons of walnuts constituted 11% of national production and put the region third in this category. Livestock in 2000 included 6.4m. pigs, 5.0m. goats, 2.6m. cattle and buffaloes and 1.4m. sheep. Pork production was the highest in north-western China, at 0.6m. tons (only 0.8m. for all meat). In the same year milk production was 0.6m. tons (only 61% cows' milk), sheep wool 3,593 tons, goats' wool 1,007 tons and cashmere 546 tons, at the same time as Shaanxi provided the north-west with the most poultry eggs (425,000 tons) and honey (3,000 tons). Inland fisheries were responsible for 60,800 tons of produce (all but 300 tons freshwater fish), 95% artificially cultured.

The secondary sector contributed 44.1% to GDP and 16.5% of the jobs in 2000. Construction is an important industrial activity, accounting for 11.0% of total GDP from a total output value of 24,230.46m. yuan (the highest in the north-west). Shaanxi also produced 9.9m. metric tons of cement in 2000. The fruits of mining and quarrying also saw 20m. tons of coal, 7.5m. tons of crude petroleum (making Shaanxi the country's sixth largest producer) and 2,110m. cu m of natural gas. Coal production was not particularly high, but reserves are reckoned to be large, as are those of other minerals, such as molybdenum, gold and other non-ferrous metals. Textiles are regionally important (156,800 tons of yarn, 71,800 metres of cloth—the largest production of both in western China— and 1,200 tons of silk in 2000), as is the manufacture of paper and paperboard (298,900 tons), cigarettes (1.0m. cases) and beer (365,500 tons). Factories produce items like refrigerators and television sets, but Shaanxi is not a major centre for such goods. There were 2,553 industrial enterprises in 2000, with a gross output value of 118,458m. yuan, of which the state accounted for 64% and 78%, respectively. Heavy industry predominated (54% and 70%), as did large enterprises (194 of them, or 8%, but accounting for 60% of the value).

The services sector accounted for 39.1% of GDP in 2000 and 27.8% of employed persons. Transport, storage and communications, and trade (whole-sale and retail) and catering services were by far the largest contributors, providing 9.4% and 6.8% of GDP, respectively. The transport sector, particu-larly the railways, employs a lot of people, while trade earned US $1,326.93m. for its exports and paid only $1,060.61m. for imports in 2000. In the same year international tourism, with more visits to Shaanxi (712,800, of which 82% were by foreigners) than anywhere else in western China but Yunnan, made $280m. in foreign-exchange earnings. Tourists visit the province for its history, notably the 'Terracotta Army' of the First Emperor and numerous imperial tombs, but also more ancient sites. Religious and Communist pilgrimage places (the sacred Hua Shan range or the old Communist headquarters of Yanan) attract some, and others simply visit the great city of Xian.

Government revenue in Shaanxi during 2000 was 11,497.11m. (operations tax 28%, value added tax 17% and enterprises' income tax 10%), while expenditure was 27,175.97m. yuan (capital construction 15%, education 14% and social-security subsidies 9%). Actually used foreign direct investment into the province was US $288.42m. in 2000, considerably more than the combined total for the other western territories.

Directory

Governor: CHENG ANDONG; Office of the Provincial People's Government, Xian.

Secretary of the Shaanxi Provincial Committee of the Chinese Communist Party: LI JIANGUO; Office of the Secretary, CCP Secretariat, Xian.

Chairman of the Standing Committee of the People's Congress of Shaanxi: LI JIANGUO; Office of the Chairman, Congress Secretariat, Xian.

Chairman of the Shaanxi Provincial Committee of the Chinese People's Political Consultative Conference: AN QIYUAN; Office of the Chairman, CPPCC Secretariat, Xian.

Shaanxi Government Office: Xincheng Square, Xian 710004; tel. (29) 7292664; internet www.shaanxi.gov.cn.

Shandong

The Province of Shandong (Shantung) is at the mouth of the Huang He (Yellow River), its territory massed around the base of the peninsula it thrusts out into the Yellow Sea (Huang Hai), bringing it to within 200 (120 miles) of Korea to the east. The Shandong peninsula is on roughly the same latitude as the border between the Democratic People's Republic of Korea—'North Korea'—and the Republic of Korea—'South Korea'. The peninsula also forms the southern shore of the Bo Hai (Gulf of Bohai), on which is Shandong's neighbour, Hebei, beyond the north-western boundaries of the province. In the south-west is the border with Henan, with Shandong pushing further down the south bank of the Huang He than on the north, almost to the point where the river begins to angle sharply north-eastwards towards the sea. Here in the south-west there is also a short southern border with Anhui, but most of the southern border is with Jiangsu. The jurisdiction of the province also includes some islands, notably the Miaodao Islands, where the Bohai and the Yellow Sea meet. Over 30 small islands straggle roughly north-eastwards from Penglai (home of the Eight Immortals, heroes of Chinese mythology), on the northern hump of the Shandong peninsula, before the main channel of the Bohai Straits intervenes between the Miaodao and the southern tip of the Liaodong peninsula (Liaoning). There are also some small islands off the south-eastern coast. Shandong province covers some 153,300 sq km (59,170 sq miles).

The province is sometimes known as Lu, for the home state of Confucius, which lay within today's southern borders. Shandong, however, means 'east of the river' and refers to the Huang He, which flows through the north-west of the province. The Huang He is the second longest river in China (according to official statistics, 5,464 km—3,393 miles) and the most silt-laden river in the world—the latter feature giving it its name and its destructiveness. By the time the Huang He reaches Jinan, the provincial capital of Shandong, evaporation and irrigation works have often reduced the flow compared to further upstream, although, as it is, the height of the river is extremely variable by season (contributing to the unsuitability for navigation). Prone to flooding, particularly along the lower reaches where it runs between high, built-up banks, the Huang He has even changed course a number of times, usually at the expense of the people of Shandong. Until the fourth century BC the river entered the Bo Hai by various channels, most of them to the north of the present course, but early irrigation works and flood defences corralled it into something like its present bed. River dykes limited the tendency of the river to change its course, although they contributed to the severity of flooding if the spate exceeded its restraints (in some 3,000 years of recorded history, the Huang He has flooded its lower reaches more than 1,500 times), but they could not prevent catastrophic change. Thus, in 1128 the river altered its direction just west of Shandong and proceeded to enter the Yellow Sea (Huang Hai) through northern Jiangsu and the lower reaches of the Huai. The great flood in 1855 receded to leave the Huang He finally back in its old course across northern Shandong, where it has steadily augmented the territory of the province in the delta ever since. (The same disaster in the 1850s rendered most of the Da Yunhe—(Grand Canal)—which traverses Shandong on route north to Tianjin and Beijing, no longer navigable.) The river cleaves its way through the fertile eastern end of the North China Plain, diverted in Shandong only by the highlands in the centre of the province. The plains dominate the west, the north and the centre-east, where they separate the central highlands from the hills on the Shandong peninsula. There is a strip of lowland along the south-eastern littoral (Shandong has about 3,000 km of coastline). The central highlands consist of the Lu, Yi, Meng and Tai hills. The Tai Shan, where Shandong reaches its highest point at Yuhuang Ding (1,524 m or 5,002 feet), is the most revered of the five Daoist sacred mountain areas (five emperors have personally offered sacrifice here, with the emperor Qianlong, 1736–96, climbing the mountains 11 times, and both Confucius and Mao Zedong making memorable pronouncements from the summit).

The climate is typical of a northerly temperate zone, but is monsoonal and tends to continental in its extremes, despite the alleviating presence of the ocean. The extremes can lead to ice in the Bo Hai, and hence the historic importance of the Shandong peninsula for ice-free ports (even on the north coast) and, earlier, the communications along the Grand Canal. The summers (June–September) are wet and more of the 560–1,170 mm (22–46 inches) of average annual rainfall falls in the south-east (which is also warmer). In Jinan total rainfall for 2000 was 721 mm. The average monthly temperatures in Jinan during 2000 were -3.3°C (26.1°F) in January and 28.5°C (83.3°F) in July.

Shandong is the most populous region in the People's Republic of China after Henan, with 90.79m. people at the time of the 2000 national census. After Jiangsu Shandong is the most densely populated province, being home to 554 people to every square kilometre, on average. However, there is a low rate of growth, despite immigration to the wealthy cities, and the province has the most equal male-female ratio in China (102.58 to 100.00 in 2000). Only 0.6% of the population is from among the minority nationalities, these mainly being Hui and Manchu. Standard Mandarin Chinese, the official Putonghua, is, therefore, the language of the entire local population. Minority religions represented in the region include Islam and Christianity. Buddhism is strong, but the area is mainly famous for the Daoist Tai Shan pilgrimage site and as the centre of the cult of Confucius (the Latinized name used in the West for 'Master Kong', Kong Fuzi, whose name was actually Kong Qiu or Kong Zhongni), which is centred in the sage's birthplace of Qufu and was presided over by the Kong family for some 2,500 years until the first-born son of the 77th generation fled to Taiwan in 1948. Confucianism, although it has temples (sacrifices were first offered in AD 37), is more an ethical code than a religion. It enjoyed some rehabilitation in the People's Republic over the latter decades of the 20th century and into the next.

Of the total population of the province, 38.0% were counted as urban in the 2000 census. The capital of the province is Jinan (Tsinan), which is located in the north-west, on the Huang He. In 2000 Jinan had an urban population of 2.3m. (greater Jinan contained 5.6m.), but it was not the largest city. The most populous city of Shandong is mid-way down the south-eastern coast, the port of Qingdao (Tsingtao), which had 2.9m. (7.1m.) people. The next largest urban centres are Dongying, in the north, on the Huang He delta, Yantai, on the north coast of the peninsula, Jining, on the Grand Canal, in the south-west, Liaocheng, west of Jinan, and Zibo, to the east of the capital. Shandong consists of 17 cities at the prefectural level, 31 cities at the county level (in total, more cities than any other region save Guangdong) and a further 61 rural counties.

History

Shandong is an ancient and illustrious part of China, but it has never formed a central political role, although it has often been at the forefront of foreign incursions. The precarious agricultural wealth of the flood-prone Huang He (Yellow River) has also formed a central part in the story of the province, not least in creating conditions in which rural discontent could lead to insurrection. However, the most ancient claim to fame of Shandong (apart from as the alleged site of the capital of Shao Hao, one of the mythical 'sage emperors') is probably as the home of Kong Qiu (or Kong Zhongni), who lived in Qufu, in the kingdom of Lu. He was known as Kong Fuzi or Kong Zi (Master Kong) to his disciples, and it is this title that has been Latinized into Confucius, which is the more familiar name outside China. Confucius, who was born in the mid-sixth century BC, was a philosopher who never held high government office, but who evolved a system of ethics and a theory of government that was to underpin the Chinese Empire for over two millennia. Venerated after his death, his main disciple and organizer of his legacy, from the end of the fourth century BC, was Meng Ke, known as Meng Zi (hence, again, the Latinized Mencius), who came from another of the small kingdoms in southern Shandong, Zou. He offered advice to, among others, the ruler of Qi, the main state of Shandong, but, like Confucius, never actually held high office. Within 60 years of Mencius' death, however, Qi had been conquered by Qin, in 226 BC, and a single, greater Chinese Empire formed for the first time since mythical times. Although the First Emperor of the Qin persecuted the Confucians, who were by now established as a major school of philosophy, they were rehabilitated under the long-reigned Han and became the undisputed theorists of empire. As time passed they took on some of the trappings of a religion. At the centre of the cult, laden with wealth and privilege, were the descendents of Confucius, the Kong family, and his direct heirs lived continuously in Qufu until the Civil War of the 1940s.

Among the other famous children of Shandong was another, if later, third-century-BC philosopher, Zou Yan, a native of Qi, who formulated the theories of the five elements (*wuxing*) and maybe linked them to those of *yin* and *yang*. Also native to the Jinan area were figures ranging from Bian Que, the founder of traditional Chinese medicine, to Zhou Yongnian, the founder of Chinese public libraries. The most famous women poet of the Song dynasty, Li Qingzhao, also lived in Jinan until forced to flee south before the invading Jurchens in the 12th century AD. At this time, since the Tang, Shandong was administered with Henan, while under the Qing the two modern provinces would generally find themselves under the jurisdiction of Zhili (now Hebei), the directly administered 'capital territory'. The calamities of northern invasion and the flight of the dynasty to become the Southern Song was, for Shandong, accompanied by the upheaval of the Huang He changing its course (to run south of the peninsula, exposing the province decisively to the influence of the north). Then, from the later part of the 16th century the Shandong coast had to endure the depredations of Japanese pirates, who moved their attentions from southern China partly in recognition of the improving wealth of the north (where political power was now based).

The Manchu armies of the Qing conquered Shandong in 1644, but they were to rule an area that became very prone to rebellion. Thus, Shandong was part of a wide area in northern China that sympathized with the anti-Qing (but, originally, much older) millenarian White Lotus Sect; an offshoot of this, the Eight Trigrams (Bagua) group, which revolted in the 1780s, enjoyed support in north-eastern Shandong, where the Huang He delta now is, while the south-west favoured the Heavenly Principle sectarian rebels in the 1810s. The latter was a similar area to that most closely affected by the Nian Rebellion, which was related to the White Lotus tradition, although without the religious perspective, and was born in the hardship caused by the shifting of the course of the Huang He between 1851 and 1855. All these cultic and insurrectionist traditions were to coalesce in the Boxer Rising of 1899–1901. The Boxers, the 'Fists of Righteousness and Harmony', were resentful of foreigners (*maozi*, 'hairy ones') and the decline of China, but were fuelled by the catastrophic flood of 1898 (particularly in Shandong, which had suffered the two previous years in drought), the bitterness of demobilized soldiers from China's 1895 defeat by Japan in Korea and of economic refugees from the south, and by successive governors of Shandong (although the first Boxer patron, Li Bingheng, was dismissed in 1897 after the murder of two German missionaries resulted in the Germans occupying territory near Qingdao).

The increasingly obvious presence of foreigners throughout China became apparent in Shandong only at the end of the 19th century, when traders, missionaries and railways all arrived. The Germans gained a formal concession on Qingdao in 1898 and extended their sphere of influence throughout much of Shandong, apart from where the British had established themselves on the north coast of the peninsula at Weihai. Although Qingdao was leased to the Germans for 99 years, the First World War intervened and, in 1914, the Japanese occupied the port, after a joint Japanese-British naval attack, and remained in possession until 1922, when it was handed over to the Guomindang, although Japanese influence remained strong throughout the 1920s. In the 1930s a local warlord gained control, until displaced by the invading Japanese again, who held most of the territory firmly only between 1941 and 1943 (Japan surrendered in 1945). By April 1946 Shandong was under Communist control and, although constituted as a separate province, spent 1950–54 under the Shanghai-based East China Administrative Council. Economic liberalization since the 1980s has allowed Shandong to capitalize on its past and its agricultural and industrial advantages to become one of the more progressive provinces of China.

Economy

Shandong is one of the wealthiest provinces in China, with the third largest regional gross domestic product (GDP—854,244m. yuan in 2000), which since the mid-1990s at least has consistently grown above 10% per year, in real terms. However, the size of its population means that GDP per head was 9,555 yuan, which puts it behind all the special municipalities except Chongqing, as well as the provinces of Guangdong, Zhejiang, Jiangsu, Fujian and Liaoning. Shandong is helped by an extremely dense transport system, with 70,686 km of highways (including the greatest length of expressways, at 2,006 km, as well as 2,599 km of first-class roads), 2,402 km of operational railways and 2,486 km of navigable inland waterways. In addition, the province possesses the major seaports of Qingdao (the seventh in ranking, by the volume of freight handled, in the People's Republic), Yantai and, since the 1990s, Rizhao (further south than Qingdao). In 2000 Shandong generated more electricity than any other region save Guangdong (100,526m. kWh), although hydroelectric capacity is minimal. The province has a surprisingly high illiteracy rate (8.5% in 2000), outside of western China exceeded only by Anhui.

The agriculture of the province is very productive, but the size of the primary sector relative to the rest of the economy (14.9% of GDP in 2000) belies this impression. The sector provided for 53.1% of the employed population in 2000. Major crops include cereals (covering 58% of the total sown area of 11.1m. ha in 2000—only Henan exceeded these figures), tubers, oil-bearing crops and tobacco, cotton, tussah and ambary hemp, and walnuts, peaches and specialities like Yantai apples, Leling dates (jujubes), Laiyang pears, Pingdu grapes and Dezhou watermelons. The province has the largest area planted with vegetables (1.8m. ha) and the fourth largest area for orchards (0.7m. ha). In 2000 Shandong grew the largest harvests of corn (maize—at 14.7m. metric tons), fruits (9.7m. tons—67% apples) and groundnuts (peanuts—3.5m. tons), and the second largest harvests of wheat (18.6m. tons), tubers (2.6m. tons) and cotton (590,000 tons), as well as of oil-bearing crops generally (mainly owing to the groundnuts) and of apples specifically. Other yields included 1.1m. tons of beans, 117,000 tons of tobacco, 54,700 tons of silkworm cocoons and 10,866 tons of walnuts. Animal husbandry, too, is important and Shandong has the largest number of poultry (figures are unavailable) in China, the second largest number of bovines (10.1m. head in 2000) and goats (21.6m.) after Henan, the fifth largest number of pigs (26.6m.) and 6.2m. sheep. Livestock produce that year included the largest amount of meat (5.6m. tons—only 2.9m. tons was pork) and poultry eggs (3.7m. tons) in all of China, the third largest amount of milk (705,000—65% from cows), 17,808 tons of sheep wool, 8,618 tons of goat wool, 1,042 tons of cashmere and 10,000 tons of honey. Shandong also had the biggest fishing industry in China, dominated by marine fishing. Less than one-half of seawater production is cultured, but over 90% of inland fisheries are farmed. The fish catch in 2000 included 2.1m. tons of marine fish and 0.9m. tons of freshwater fish, 2.8m. tons of seawater shellfish and, again from the sea, 0.5m. tons each of crustaceans and algae. Total aquatic production came to 7.0m. tons.

The secondary sector accounted for 49.7% of GDP in 2000 and 23.6% of the work-force. Construction, the total output value of which was 81,709.49m. yuan, provided 5.9% of GDP in 2000. The province has important mineral reserves, such as coal, petroleum (Shengli, near Dongying, is the country's second-biggest field), salt, iron and diamonds. In 2000 Shandong was China's leading regional producer of salt (8.3m. metric tons), the second largest in coal (80m. tons) and crude petroleum (27m. tons), and also produced 688m. cu m of natural gas. The main industrial centres are Qingdao (it has more than double the gross industrial output of Jinan), Jinan and other major cities such as Zibo (where chemical production is a growing activity). Some important manufactures produced in 2000 included: the largest amounts of paper and paperboard (4.4m. tons), beer (3.0m. tons—Tsingtao, China's premier beer company, is based in and named for Qingdao), household washing machines (3.1m. units), cement (67.5m. tons), sulphuric acid (2.5m. tons), soda ash (1.5m. tons), caustic soda (1.1m. tons) and chemical fertilizer (4.0m. tons); the second largest amounts of household refrigerators (2.8m. units), individual air-conditioning units (2.8m. units) and metal-cutting machine tools (28,200 units); and also cloth (2,760m. m), silk (5,400 tons), cigarettes (2.3m. cases), pig iron (7.3m. tons), steel (6.4m. tons), steel products (6.8m. tons), plate glass (15.6m. weight cases), plastics (0.9m. tons) and micro-computers (310,700 units). Shandong had numerous industrial enterprises, 11,679 in 2000, with a gross output value of 831,153m., at current prices. Only 24% of these enterprises (but 42% of the value) were in the state sector and a large number had foreign or 'greater China' funding. Light industry predominated in terms of number of enterprises (52% of the total), but heavy industry provided 55% of gross output value. Shandong had more large and medium-sized enterprises than any other region, with 1,087 of the former contributing 50% of the value and 1,653 of the latter only 14%.

The tertiary sector contributed 35.5% of GDP in 2000 and employed almost as many people as worked in industry (23.3% of employed persons). The most important service-industry category in that year was trade and catering (9.2% of total GDP), followed by transport and communications (6.5%—which employed 322,000 people), finance and insurance (5.3%) and property (real estate—3.6%). External trade was not as important to the economy of Shandong as the size of it might suggest, but exports in 2000 were still worth US $16,092.67m. and imports $12,157.30m. Domestic tourism is more important than international tourism (which earned a respectable $315m. in foreign exchange in 2000), although the latter still achieved 723,100 person-visits in 2000 (480,100 by foreigners). The main attractions are the Tai Shan holy mountains, Qufu, the birthplace of Confucius, and Qingdao, the brewing town and former concession port of the Germans.

In 2000 government raised more revenue only in Guangdong and Shanghai, with Shandong recording a total of 46,367.88m. yuan (value added tax 19.3%, operations tax 18.9% and the income tax on enterprises 17.7%). Shandong also spent more government money than any other region but Guangdong, at

61,307.74m. yuan (education 19.3% and government administration 10.1%). In the same year the province used US $2,971.19m. in foreign direct investment and received $56.36m. in other foreign investment.

Directory

Governor: LI CHUNTING; Office of the Provincial People's Government, Jinan.

Secretary of the Shandong Provincial Committee of the Chinese Communist Party: WU GUANZHENG; Office of the Secretary, CCP Secretariat, Jinan.

Chairman of the Standing Committee of the People's Congress of Shandong: ZHAO ZHIHAO; Office of the Chairman, Congress Secretariat, Jinan.

Chairman of the Shandong Provincial Committee of the Chinese People's Political Consultative Conference: HAN XIKAI; Office of the Chairman, CPPCC Secretariat, Jinan.

Shanxi

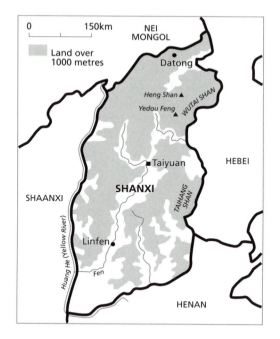

The Province of Shanxi (Shansi) stretches south from the Great Wall, from the Nei Mongol autonomous region to the north and north-west, down the left (east) bank of the Huang He, opposite Shaanxi province, to where the river angles sharply east again. Here the borders are with Henan, which lies to the south and south-east, while Hebei lies mainly on the plains beneath the mountainous eastern border. This province covers an area of 157,100 sq km (60,640 sq miles).

Shanxi lies on the eastern part of the loess plateau of northern China and, consisting of some 70% of mountains, is known as the 'land of mountains'. (Shanxi is also known as Jin, after the ancient kingdom of that name, or Sanjin ('three Jins'), after its successor states.) Shanxi's name actually means 'west of the mountains', referring to the Taihang Shan that form the eastern border. In the north are the sacred mountains of the Heng Shan (for Daoists) and the Wutai Shan (for Buddhists), the highest peak of the latter, Yedou Feng, being described as the 'roof of northern China' (3,058 m or 10,036 feet). In the south are the Zhongtiao and Taiyue mountains, while the western Luliang Shan, above the Huang He, form the watershed of the mighty Yellow River and the Fen He, which has cleft a valley of lowlands and basins down most of the centre of the province. Shanxi has a temperate, but continental, monsoon climate, which can lead to extremes of temperature. The average monthly temperature in Taiyuan, the provincial capital at the centre of the province, in January 2000 was -7.1°C (19.2°F) and in July 24.7°C (44.5°F). There is more rain in the south-east than the north-west, which is edging the barren Mongolian plateau, and the total for the year averages between 350 mm and 700 mm (14–27 inches), most of it falling in the summer. The total for 2000 in Taiyuan was 419 mm.

The total number of inhabitants at 1 November 2000 was 32.97m. and the average population density was 210 persons per sq km. Since the previous census in 1990 Shanxi had experienced a high rate of population growth (averaging 1.33% per year). The overwhelming majority of the population was Han Chinese, and the province had the least number and the smallest proportion of ethnic minorities of any region of China. What groups there were came from among the Hui, Manchu and Mongol communities. There was, therefore, a small Muslim presence in Shanxi, but the area is a traditionally Daoist or Buddhist one, rich in heritage and in some still-operating temples and monasteries.

In 2000 34.9% of the population was urban. The largest city, as well as the provincial capital, is Taiyuan (2.0m. people in 2000, or 3.1m. in the greater administrative area). Datong is, in the far north, is the second city and not far behind in population. Linfeng and Jincheng are the main cities of the south. For administrative purposes Shanxi consists of 11 prefectures, all but one being cities, and 97 counties, including 12 cities.

History

Shanxi is an early centre of Chinese civilization and features in legends of the Yellow Emperor (Huangdi) and the mythical kings, Yao, Shun and Yu, who were all meant to have had their capitals here. The area emerges from legend, however, when the northern state of Jin dominated in the angle to the north and east of the Huang He (Yellow River), from when Zhou authority had begun to decay in about the eighth century BC. Duke Wen of Jin was one of the great seventh-century hegemons, but in about 453 BC the state disintegrated, to form Zhao, Wei and Han, a date that is sometimes taken to divide the so-called Spring and Autumn era from the Warring States period, into which the Later or Eastern Zhou dynasty is divided. Zhao surrendered to Qin in 228 BC and in the empire that was then founded, and taken forward by the Han, this region became a crucial area in the defence against the nomadic barbarians beyond the newly linked Great Wall. During the struggles that followed the fall of the Han and the passing of the Three Kingdoms, some contenders for power sought the support of the northern peoples, but often found them reluctant to return beyond the Wall, and Shanxi was one of the main routes south. Thus, once the process of sincization had been completed, Shanxi was to find itself a stronghold from which the northern conquest of the Middle Kingdom could be accomplished.

The main tribal people from the north to become established south of the Great Wall in the fourth century AD were the Toba. The Toba ruling clan took the dynastic name of Wei (Northern Wei, 386–533) and from its capital at Pingcheng (modern Datong) they ruled much of the North China Plain. Buddhism was patronized by the ruling house (except for a period of persecution under Taïwu, who favoured Daoism, in the mid-fifth century). Under Xiaowen (emperor, 471–99) the Northern Wei, who were now almost completely sinicized, extended their rule over most of northern China, but also moved the capital south to Luoyang (Henan). However, in the seventh century Li Yuan and his son, Li Shimin, began a revolt in Taiyuan that led to the displacement of the reunifying Sui and the establishment of their own Tang dynasty (618–907), which maintained the original city of the rising as an alternate northern capital for some time. By the time the Song re-established a united empire later in the 10th century, however, the political centre of China had forever moved to the south or the east. Northern Shanxi again became a border region, to be ruled by another two dynasties from non-Han peoples, the Liao of the Khitans and the Jin ('golden') of the Jurchens, in the 10th–13th centuries. The Mongols then conquered the region, founding the Yuan dynasty, but they gave Shanxi sufficient security that it prospered, even in the 14th century, during the late Yuan and early Ming periods, when much of the rest of the Central Plains were devastated by war. The province then became a source of settlers for the depopulated Ming territories to the east and south. This enhanced trade and traffic through Shanxi, and it was at this time that Pingyao began the rise to financial pre-eminence that it achieved under the Qing. It was here that the first Chinese banking houses (tongs) evolved. Also under the Qing Shanxi was united administratively with Shaanxi, across the Huang He, from the late 17th century until it was re-established as a separate province after the fall of the dynasty in 1912 (until 1749 as part of Shenzhuan, which usually included Sichuan as well, thereafter as part of Shengan, which included Gansu).

After the fall of the Qing Shanxi was dominated by its military governor and warlord, Yan Xishan (Yen His-shan), who held power until 1930. It remained remote to central authority even after that, although reinforcement by the Dongbei (North-East) Army, based in Shaanxi, enforced some Nationalist control in the mid-1930s. Being so mountainous, it is a difficult territory to secure, as the Japanese found out after occupying and industrializing Shanxi during the Second World War. They held the cities, but much of the country was left to the Communist resistance. In the Civil War that followed the Communists followed similar tactics again, formally taking control of the whole province only in April 1949. The final shape of modern Shanxi then took place, in 1952, with the addition of some border territories formerly part of Qahar (Chahar) province (most of which was made part of Nei Mongol and the rest, including the chief city of Zhangjiakou—formerly Kalgan—part of Hebei). Until 1954 Shanxi was under the jurisdiction of the North-West Administrative Council, although it is now more usually classified as part of North China.

Economy

Shanxi is no longer a particularly wealthy province. In 2000 it had a gross domestic product (GDP) of only 164,381m. yuan, which was equivalent to 5,137 yuan per head, making it the poorest province of the north. Growth in 1999 and 2000 had been the slowest in China. Shanxi had a dense network of roads and railways, but the terrain meant there were few navigable waterways. The total length of operational railways in 2000 was 2,511 km. All highways together measured 55,408 km, of which 518 km were expressway and 614 km first-class highways. Electricity generation was mainly thermal, and totalled 62,031m. kWh in 2000. At 4.2% (2000) Shanxi had the second lowest illiteracy rate in the country.

The primary sector constituted the smallest proportion of total GDP of any province or autonomous region except Liaoning (10.9% in 2000). Nevertheless, it employed 46.7% of the working population. Shanxi is famous for fruits such as Jishan dates, Yuangping pears and Qingxu grapes. However, in 2000 fruit orchards only covered 0.3m. ha, whereas farm crops covered 4.0m. ha (58% cereals). Yields in the same year included 3.5m. metric tons of corn (maize), 2.2m. tons of wheat, 2.0m. tons of fruit (80% apples), 0.9m. tons of tubers, 0.6m. tons of beans, 0.5m. tons of cotton, 0.4m. tons of oil-bearing crops, 46,988 tons of walnuts (after Yunnan the largest harvest in China) and 3,754 tons of mulberry-silkworm cocoons. The numbers of head of livestock in Shanxi in 2000 were 5.8m. sheep, 4.7m. goats, 4.7m. pigs, 2.3m. cattle and buffaloes and 0.8m. donkeys, mules and horses. Production of meat totalled 637,000 tons (68% pork), of poultry eggs 403,000 tons, of milk 359,000 tons, of sheep wool 7,287 tons, of goat wool 1,659 tons and of cashmere 632 tons. Its mountainous, inland location meant that Shanxi had the least fisheries production of anywhere in China save Xizang (Tibet) and Qinghai—all but 200 tons of the 26,000 tons of fish caught were farmed.

The industrial or secondary sector accounted for 50.3% of GDP in 2000 and 24.9% of employment. Construction alone accounted for 7.4% of total GDP and had a total output value of 23,939.74m. yuan in 2000. Shanxi had huge iron and coal deposits, and had industrialized on this basis. The province produced by far the most coal in 2000, at 196m. metric tons some 20% of the national total. Consumer goods are not manufactured in large quantities, but in the same year Shanxi did produce 11.0m. tons of pig iron, 4.7m. tons of steel, 3.9m. tons of steel products and 11.9m. tons of cement. It is no surprise, therefore, to find that heavy industry accounted for 71% of the 3,275 industrial enterprises in the province and 86% of the gross output value of 121,686m. yuan. That same year of 2000 the number of large enterprises was put at 138 (49% of the value) and of medium-sized enterprises at 228 (8%).

In 2000 the tertiary sector accounted for 38.7% of GDP and 28.4% of employed persons. The main service activities were transport and communications (8.9% of total GDP), trade and catering (8.2%), finance and insurance (6.3%) and government and party agencies and social organizations (5.1%). The US $2,090.94m. earned in exports in 2000 far exceeded the $700.60m. paid for imports, although Shanxi earned less in foreign-exchange earnings than anywhere else in the north or north-east from tourism ($50m.). International tourist visits numbered 165,300 (71% by foreigners) in 2000. Attractions include the holy Heng Shan (the northernmost of the five, traditional sacred mountains of China—representing the element of wood to Daoists), the Wutai Shan (one of four Buddhist sacred mountains in China), the latter around the monastic settlement of Taihuai, the Yungang Buddhist caves near Datong or relics such as the 11th-century, 97-m pagoda that claims to be the oldest wooden building in the world (and to be constructed without any nails), as well as any number of ancient monasteries and temples or medieval walled cities.

Government revenue in Shanxi during 2000 amounted to 11,447.62m. yuan, of which 22% came from value added tax and 21% from the operations tax, and expenditure to 22,50.54m. yuan, of which 17% was spent on education and 11% on government administration. The province also used US $224.72m. in foreign direct investment in 2000.

Directory

Governor: LIU ZHENHUA; Office of the Provincial People's Government, Taiyuan.

Secretary of the Shanxi Provincial Committee of the Chinese Communist Party: TIAN CHENGPIN; Office of the Secretary, CCP Secretariat, Taiyuan.

Chairman of the Standing Committee of the People's Congress of Shanxi: LU GONGXUN; Office of the Chairman, Congress Secretariat, Taiyuan.

Chairman of the Shanxi Provincial Committee of the Chinese People's Political Consultative Conference: ZHENG SHEKUI; Office of the Chairman, CPPCC Secretariat, Taiyuan.

Sichuan

The Province of Sichuan (Szechwan) spreads east of the Jinsha Jiang, as the Chang Jiang (River Yangzi) is known on its upper reaches, to encompass the broad Sichuan basin of south-western China. The Jinsha flows out of Qinghai province, which is to the north-west and forms the rest of the length of the western border, with the Xizang (Tibet) autonomous region directly west and Yunnan to the south-west. Beyond the southern city of Panzhihua (Jinjiang or Dukou) the river turns north-eastwards, angling through the mountainous south, so Yunnan also lies to the south-east, where there is also a short border with Guizhou. The new boundary with the Chongqing municipality (part of Sichuan province until March 1997) occupies most of the eastern border. Beyond the north-eastern border lie Shaanxi and, to the north, Gansu. Sichuan spreads out over 487,000 sq km (188,470 sq miles) of varied terrain, taking up one-20th of the total area of the People's Republic and making it the largest province after Qinghai.

The vast Sichuan basin of some 165,000 sq km forms the heart of the province (except in the south-east, where it is now included in the territory of the Chongqing municipality). It is surrounded by mountains and has a mountainous, western hinterland on the edge of the Tibet–Qinghai plateau. The western elevation is some 4,000 m, while the basin is between 750 m and 200 m above sea level, sloping generally down from north to south. Chongqing isolates the territory of Sichuan from the eastern mountains, but in the north east are the Daba Shan, the ranges continuing up the north-western borders as the Micang and Min mountains. The Longmen Shan define the north-western edge of the basin country, and beyond are the mighty, southward-marching Qionglai, Daxue and Shaluli mountains. In the Daxue range is the massive bulk of

Gongga Shan, the province's highest point (7,514 m or 24,661 feet), while between the Daxue and Shaluli mountains the Yalong Jiang parallels much of the western border (joining the Jinsha in the far south) and beyond the Shaluli Shan the Jinsha (Yangzi) flows out of Qinghai. The main tributaries of the Chang Jiang joining it in the Sichuan basin (it only briefly crosses provincial territory) are the Min, the Dadu and the Tuo. Precisely which are the 'four rivers' Sichuan's name refers to can be a moot point (the province is known as Chuan for short). The climate is mild, humid and subtropical, but varies considerably with altitude and latitude. The east is more temperate, but can often be foggy, while the western highlands are cold. Chengdu, the provincial capital in the west of the basin, had an average monthly temperature in January 2000 of 5.6°C (42.1°F) and one of 26.1°C (79.0°F) that July. Average annual rainfall is about 1,000 mm in the lowlands (783 mm—31 inches—in Chengdu in 2000, but more in neighbouring Chongqing), between 500 mm and 700 mm on the western plateau and 800–1,200 mm in the southern highlands.

Sichuan had 83.29m. inhabitants in November 2000, according to the national census, making it the fourth most populous region in the People's Republic. Only 5.0% consisted of minority nationalities, of which some of the main groups were the Yi, the Tibetans (Xizangzu—largest number outside Xizang itself), the Qiang (related to the Tibetans) and the Miao, as well as the usual scattering of the Hui and Manchu peoples and some of the Tujia, the Lisu and Bai, for instance. The native Chinese tradition of Buddhism is strong in Sichuan, but is obviously augmented by the cultural influence of the Tibetans and other lamaists, and many visit the sacred Emei Shan or the Da Fo (Giant Buddha) at Leshan. The Daoists also have a sacred mountain, at Qingcheng, while some of the tribal groups have preserved or syncretized older beliefs.

In 2000 the rate of urbanization was 26.7% of the population. The capital of Sichuan is Chengdu (Chengtu), which had an urban population of 3.5m., but was home to 10.1m. in the greater administrative area (making it the largest such in China after the Chongqing special municipality). The second city is Neijiang (which has more than 0.5m. people), to the south-east of Chengdu, near Chongqing's western border. Other major urban centres include Zigong and Yibin, to the south of Neijiang, Leshan, to the west of Neijiang and the south of Chengdu, and Deyang and Mianyang, to the north-east of Chengdu, all of which lie in the basin, and, in the far, mountainous south, Panzhihua. The autonomous areas for minority nationalities consist of 50 counties (including one city) and three autonomous prefectures: the Aba (Ngawa) prefecture for Tibetans and Qiangs, in the north-west; the Ganzi (Garze) Tibetan area, in the centre-west; and the Liangshan area for the Yi, in the south, near the south-eastern border with Yunnan. The other 18 prefectures are city-based. There are 140 counties in total (including 14 cities).

History

Sichuan has been settled for many thousands of years, and came under the influence of the Huang He (Yellow River) Chinese culture early, although it had evolved its own vibrant tradition, the so-called Sanxingdui culture, of which the main political expressions were the kingdoms of Shu, in the western basin, and, to the east, Ba. The Sichuan basin was brought under the authority of a

Zhou-system state in the fourth century BC. In 316 BC Qin conquered the 'barbarian' state of Shu and subjugated its neighbour, Ba, thereby gaining control of a rich territory that must have contributed to its eventual supremacy. For development of Shu began immediately, with the foundation of Chengdu and, then, the beginning of the dam project to divert and tame the Min river—a Qin prefect, Li Bang, had constructed (in about the 270s BC) a series of weirs along the Du He, towards Chengdu, that began a system that still forms the basis for the irrigation of the Chuanxi (West Sichuan) plain. By the time the Han succeeded to the empire created by Qin, Sichuan (or Shu) was an integral part of the Chinese world, although its remoteness and its strategic advantages (a fertile basin surrounded by easily defended mountains) instituted a theme in its history of easily breaking away at times of central weakness or, indeed, of providing a refuge for beleaguered regimes.

The Han dynasty was interrupted by the revolt in AD 9–25 of Wang Mang, which gave the Sichuan basin an opportunity to seize and retain its independence until towards the end of the first century. However, Han authority was never decisively re-established and the dynasty finally collapsed in the early third century, the empire dividing into three states (the Three Kingdoms). One of these was based in Sichuan and took the name of Shu, although it is sometimes called Shu Han, as it claimed to be the legitimate successor to the Han. Despite the talents of Zhuge Liang, a military strategist made famous in the Ming classic, *Romance of the Three Kingdoms*, Shu fell to Wei in 264 and was drawn back into the brief reunification of China under the Jin (Chin) dynasty. Real reunification was only achieved in the late sixth century, when the Sui (like Qin for the Han) forged the empire anew and were succeeded by the Tang in 618. The Tang Empire was expansive and culturally energetic, and Sichuan was an important part of it, with Chengdu considered one of the great cities of China and the region a supplier of armies heading south or west. The apogee of Tang power was under Xuanzong (emperor, 712–56), although his reign ended badly with the defeat of Chinese armies in Central Asia and the revolt of An Lushan, which caused the imperial court to take refuge in Sichuan. This period and location is associated with the influential poet, Du Fu. Eventually, the Tang regained their capitals, but their authority was compromised, and local warlords steadily became more powerful and external threats more pressing. Thus, the Tibetans (Xizangzu) pressed the Chinese in the western mountains and the Yunnan-based Nanzhao confederacy (which sacked Chengdu in 829) menaced Sichuan from the south until the very end of the ninth century. Meanwhile, another rebel, Huang Chao, forced Xizong (873–88) and the Tang court again to flee to Sichuan and, although the bloodiness of that revolt contributed to its successful repression, the central Government was left without authority.

By the time the final Tang emperor was displaced in 907 a loyalist general (and a former petty criminal and imperial bodyguard), Wang Jian, had proclaimed his own kingdom in Chengdu six years before. The Shu (Former Shu) dynasty persisted after the death of the 71-year-old Wang in 918, probably presiding over the momentous export of a supposedly local invention, block printing, to Luoyang (Henan) sometime around 930, before succumbing to the Song navy, which attacked up the Chang Jiang (River Yangzi) in 965. Under the Song the province was brought back under imperial authority, although the dynasty was never particularly strong. Sichuan, however, was able to deal with the occasional

Tibetan incursions in the west and, like the rest of the Empire, enjoyed a cultural flourishing. Indeed, the province is noted as the home of Su Xun and of his two sons, Shi (or Dongpo) and Che, three noted literati of the 11th century. However, the problems of northern invaders that afflicted much of China from the 12th century (most prominently, the Song dynasty itself), was savagely visited upon it in the next century, when fierce resistance to the Mongols earned Chengdu a sacking and a massacre. It was restored as a viceregal seat under the Mongols' Yuan dynasty, and continued so under the Ming (1368–1644). In 1643 one of the two rebels who contributed to the fall of the Ming, Zhang Xianzhong (the other was Li Zicheng, who took the Central Plains and Beijing), proclaimed himself 'King of the Great West'. He had been involved in various uprisings since 1640, but had taken Changsha (Hunan) and Wuchang (Hubei) in 1641. His armies were, therefore, easily able to march into Sichuan, which he took in 1644, making the more-defensible basin his headquarters and establishing an 'imperial' capital in Chengdu, though his reign was bloody and unpopular, depending as it did on the terror and mass executions, particularly of the gentry class. The Manchu armies of the new Qing dynasty subdued the regime in 1647.

Under the Qing Sichuan was included in Shenzhuan (with Shaanxi and Shanxi) between 1680 and 1731 and from 1735—48, before being restored as a province in its own right. The 18th-century reinforcement of Chinese suzerainty in Tibet (Xizang), inherited from the Mongols, even saw the eastern Tibetan province of Kham placed under the jurisdiction of the governor-general in Chengdu and enabled the crushing of a tribal rebellion in north-western Sichuan. A further reassertion of Chinese claims in Tibet came at the very end of the Qing period, when British interest in the Himalayan territory provoked the local Chinese authorities into action. This, in turn, provoked unrest in western Sichuan and north-western Yunnan, and the Qing court sent troops under Zhao Erfeng to crush dissent in 1905. Zhao dealt severely not only with the Tibetans, but also with the peoples of western Sichuan, and earned an appointment to become the imperial resident in the Tibetan capital, Lhasa, in 1908, while his brother was made governor of Sichuan. However, the moves into Tibet were halted by the fall of the Manchu dynasty and the imperial system (Sichuan declared its independence from the Qing towards the end of November 1911), and Zhao Erfeng was murdered by revolutionaries. The territory of Sichuan was thereafter fragmented and played no clear role in the warlord struggle for China or the Guomindang–Communist strife that emerged in the 1920s. However, whichever faction was in power persisted in Chinese claims on Tibet (which had, de facto, become independent in 1913), although the new country could not press its own claims in western Sichuan or in Qinghai, and the Chinese maintained a presence on the borders that even enabled them to form a new province in eastern Tibet and western Sichuan (Xigang or Sikang) in the late 1930s. By the mid-1930s the Guomindang republican Government had successfully begun to assert its rule in Sichuan (although not enough before the region had featured briefly in the 'Long March', when the Communists had been in danger while attempting the bridge at Luding, in May 1935).

With the Japanese advancing on the republican capital of Nanjing (Jiangsu) at the end of 1937, the Guomindang Government fled eastern China and moved the national capital to Chongqing (then part of Sichuan). The area benefited from industrialization and the construction of transport links (although it also suffered from bombing by Japanese aircraft) and remained under Guomindang control when the Second World War was over. The Communists only finally seized Sichuan in November–December 1949, as the Guomindang regrouped on Taiwan. Under the new People's Republic the old province was split into four and Chongqing was made a separate municipality. However, in 1952 West, North, East and South Sichuan were merged and Chongqing lost its special status in 1954. With Chinese authority restored in Tibet since 1950, in 1955 Xigang was finally dissolved and split between Xizang (Tibet) and Sichuan. Under the Communists Sichuan was known as the birthplace of Deng Xiaoping, while its reformist credentials were earned by Zhao Ziyang, who established his reputation in the province with pioneering agricultural reforms, which have now spread throughout China. Although he rose to be General Secretary of the Party, he fell in the aftermath of the 1989 civil disturbances in Beijing's Tiananmen Square. In Sichuan itself those reforms have contributed to the rise of unemployment and some resulting unrest. In March 1997 Chongqing and a sizeable strip of territory along the south-eastern border was separated from Sichuan province and made a special municipality.

Economy

Sichuan is long settled and rich in natural advantages, with the largest economy in western China by far, but it is still industrializing and has a large population, so its per-head wealth is not so impressive. Total gross domestic product (GDP) in 2000 was 401,025m. yuan or 4,784 yuan per head. Owing to the untracked expanses of the mountainous west, the total length of roads in the province was only 90,875 km (including 1,000 km of expressway and 906 km of first-class highway), while railways operate over 2,333 km and navigable waterways spread for an extensive 5,980 km. In the Sichuan basin, at least, the infrastructure is well developed and, indeed, has in some places been established since ancient times— most remarkable is the irrigation works at Dujiangyan, which was begun in the fourth century BC. More modern developments are the hydroelectric projects for which the province is highly suited (in potential, it is second only to Xizang— Tibet). Some 63% of Sichuan's total generation was hydroelectric in 2000, the total of 50,024m. kWh making the province western China's largest producer of electricity. In a regional context again, the illiteracy rate in Sichuan (7.6% in 2000) is good compared to some of its neighbours.

The primary sector accounted for 23.6% of GDP and 59.6% of employed persons in 2000. Despite the province's vast area, much of it is mountainous and unsuitable for agriculture, although there are some 7.5m. ha of forest. The rich, red soil of the Sichuan basin, however, is eminently suitable for farming and in 2000 the province had 9.6m. ha, almost entirely in that area, sown with farm crops (Henan and Shandong have greater such areas), 54% of it for cereals. The 1.2m. ha planted with vegetables was more than any other region of China. Harvests that year reaped 16.3m. metric tons of rice, 5.5m. tons of corn (maize) and 5.3m. tons of wheat, 4.5m. tons of tubers, 2.5m. tons of fruit (53% citrus, the largest citrus-fruit producer in China), 1.9m. tons of oil-bearing crops (including 1.4m. tons of rapeseed), 1.7m. tons of sugar cane, 156,000 tons of tobacco (60% flue-cured), 87,341 tons of mulberry-silkworm cocoons, 54,513 tons of tea (making Sichuan the fifth largest regional producer in China), 46,534 tons of tung-oil seeds and 32,095 tons of walnuts. Much of the wooded terrain of the province is rugged, so timber is not a major forestry product. Animal husbandry too is a major primary activity, with Sichuan exceeded only by Henan and Shandong, again, in the numbers of cattle and buffaloes it keeps (10.0m. head in 2000), but unequalled in the number of pigs (47.8m.). There were also 9.0m. goats, 4.2m. sheep, 0.7m. horses and 0.2m. donkeys and mules. Only Shandong produced more meat than Sichuan (5.6m. tons) in 2000, but Sichuan produced the most pork (4.2m. tons). The province also produced 1.0m. tons of poultry eggs, 289,000 tons of milk (almost entirely cows' milk), 4,108 tons of sheep wool, 398 tons of goat wool and more honey than anywhere else in China at 23,000 tons (almost one-10th of national production). Inland fisheries provided 0.5m. tons of aquatic production (93% of it artificially cultured), with freshwater fish accounting for almost all of this.

The secondary sector accounted for 42.4% of GDP and only 14.5% of employed persons in 2000. Mineral reserves are rich, and Sichuan is the world-leader in titanium and third in vanadium, for example, but also has cobalt, calcium, sulphur iron, fluorite, salt (2.2m. metric tons in 2000), among other minerals. The province is China's leading producer of natural gas (8,860m. cu m.—33% of national production), but also produces coal (21m. tons) and some crude petroleum (173,200 tons). Extractive industries, as well as agriculture, have provided the basis for other industries, notable among them electronics, machinery, pharmaceuticals, food, silk, leather, chemicals, metallurgy and construction and building materials (construction in Sichuan accounted for 7.6% of total GDP in 2000 and had the third largest regional total output value, at 71,381.02m. yuan). Some examples of commodities produced during 2000 might be cement (27.7m. tons), pig iron (5.6m. tons), steel (6.0m. tons) and steel products (5.4m. tons) and plate glass (5.7m. tons), or chemicals such as sulphuric acid (1.9m. tons) and fertilizers (2.6m. tons), and beverages such as beer (0.7m. tons), in all of which Sichuan would be the leading producer in western China, but maybe not that significant in all-China terms. The large, production-line commodity manufacturers tend to be based in the east, nearer the main domestic and export markets, and, although Sichuan has a fairly large internal market, it tends to focus on more on processing. Heavy industry, therefore, is dominant, with 57% of the 4,393 industrial enterprises in Sichuan during 2000, and 58% of the gross output value in that year (207,696m. yuan, in total). The state is responsible for a good part of the sector, but there is also some foreign investment. The 293 large enterprises account for 51% of the gross output value and the 3,611 small ones for 33%.

The tertiary sector accounted for 34.0% of GDP and 25.9% of employed persons in 2000. As is generally the case, the largest two activities were trade and catering (9.5% of total GDP) and transport and communications (6.2%). Chengdu is the financial and commercial capital of the region, as well as a major transport node, but vies vainly with Chongqing for domination of the south-west of China as a whole. Trade raised US $1,433.60m. from exports in 2000, and cost $1,343.92m. in imports. From 462,000 international tourist visits (only 199,700 by foreigners) in 2000, Sichuan only raised $122m. in foreign exchange that year. Most visitors to south-west China are currently intent on the Three Gorges and Chongqing, but Sichuan might gain after the completion of the project. Meanwhile, attractions in the province itself include the Giant

Buddha (Da Fo) of Leshan and other historical monuments and pilgrimage sites, the giant pandas of the north-western hill country, the ancient city and bustling metropolis of Chengdu, and, above all, the national reserves and mountain scenery of the wilder parts of Sichuan.

The final statement of government revenue for 2000 put the total in Sichuan at 23,386.30m. Most of this came from the usual three main sources: the operations tax (24% of the total), the income tax on enterprises (15%) and value added tax (14%—on average in China, this usually raises more than the income tax). The expenditure statement gave a total of 45,200.41m. that year, the principal destinations being education (14%), government administration (11%) and capital construction (11%), the justice system (7%) and, unusually but understandably, on government agricultural, forestry, water conservancy and meteorological activities (7%). Sichuan received US $43,694m. in direct foreign investment during 2000, a significant increase on the previous year and making it still the main recipient in western China.

Directory

Governor: ZHANG ZHONGWEI; Office of the Provincial People's Government, Chengdu.

Secretary of the Sichuan Provincial Committee of the Chinese Communist Party: ZHOU YONGKANG; Office of the Secretary, CCP Secretariat, Chengdu.

Chairman of the Standing Committee of the People's Congress of Sichuan: XIE SHIJIE; Office of the Chairman, Congress Secretariat, Chengdu.

Chairman of the Sichuan Provincial Committee of the Chinese People's Political Consultative Conference: NIE RONGGUI; Office of the Chairman, CPPCC Secretariat, Chengdu.

Party Committee Secretary of the Aba (Ngawa) Tibetan–Qiang Autonomous Prefecture: HUANG XINCHU.

Party Committee Secretary of the Ganzi (Garze) Tibetan Autonomous Prefecture: JING QUANLIN.

Party Committee Secretary of the Liangshan Yi Autonomous Prefecture: LUO YUXIANG.

Sichuan Government Office: Chengdu; internet www.sichuan.gov.cn.

Yunnan

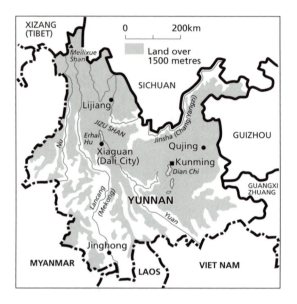

The Province of Yunnan, 'south of the clouds' (but known as Dian for short), lies in south-western China, where the great mountain ranges running down from the Tibet–Qinghai plateau descend towards the lower lands of South-East Asia. The province is on the international border with Viet Nam in the south-east (1,353 km or 840 miles), Laos in the far south (710 km) and Myanmar (Burma—1,997 km) in the south-west and west. North-western Yunnan tapers up to a short border with the Chinese autonomous region of Xizang (Tibet), while its northern border is largely along the Jinsha or Chang Jiang (River Yangzi), which heads southwards out of the high mountains towards the heart of Yunnan before angling sharply north-eastwards. Beyond the river, China's longest, is Sichuan. In the north-east, along the right bank of the Jinsha, a straggling extension of Yunnan reaches up to the border with the Chongqing special municipality (part of Sichuan until 1997). The eastern border is with Guizhou and, in the south, with the Guangxi Zhuang autonomous region. The territory of Yunnan covers 436,200 sq km (168,370 sq miles), making it only a little smaller than Heilongjiang and China's sixth largest region.

Yunnan is largely rugged mountain territory (84%, according to official statistics, with 10% hills and highlands and only 6% lowlands), generally highest in the north-west and lowest in the south-east, where the land is falling away to the plains of Guangxi. The highest point is at Kagebo peak (6,740 m or 22,121 feet) on Meilixue Shan, near Deqin. Cleft between the main ranges descending from the north are the deep valleys of some important rivers. The greatest is the Jinsha, as the Chang Jiang is known on its upper reaches, which forms much of the border with Sichuan province. It enters the territory of Yunnan in the north-west, before resuming as the line of the border just before beginning to run north again. Further east, in closely parallel valleys near the border with Myanmar are the Lancang Jiang (River Mekong—which goes on to connect five South-East Asian countries) and the Nu Jiang (a tributary of the Salween, one of the great rivers of Myanmar). Other important rivers include the Hong He and the Nanpan Jiang, as well as some of the tributaries of the Ayeyarwady (Irrawaddy—the principal river of Myanmar). The Tropic of Cancer bisects the south of the province, so the climate is generally mild, but the positioning in Asia and the huge changes in altitude contribute to the variety of climatic conditions. Yunnan is affected by both the south-east and south-west monsoons, as well as by the weather of the Tibet–Qinghai plateau, and spans three climate zones— temperate, subtropical and tropical. The average monthly temperatures for 2000 in Kunming, the provincial capital in the north-east of central Yunnan, were between 9.0°C (48.2°F) in January and 20.4°C (68.7°F) in both July and August. Average annual rainfall in the province is 600–1,200 mm (23–47 inches), with more falling in the south-east and in the summer. The 2000 total for Kunming was 886 mm.

According to the census of November 2000 the total population of Yunnan was 42.88m., which, in such a vast area, gave an average population density of only 98 persons per sq km. Many of the province's people are not Han Chinese, but from among the minority nationalities. Such groups formed 33.4% of the population in 2000, and the second largest ethnic population in China. There were the usual groups of the more widely spread peoples, such as the Hui, in significant numbers, or the Zhuang, Miao and Tibetan (Xizangzu) peoples so well represented throughout the south-west of China. Other groups are on the borders with different provinces and their populations can be represented elsewhere—such as the Bai (who can be found in Guizhou and Hunan too), the Lisu (also in Sichuan) or the Yi (Guizhou and Sichuan)—and others are separated by international borders—such as the Dai (Thai) tribes, the Tibetan-descended Hani (known as Akha in neighbouring countries), the Jingpo (known as Kachin in Myanmar) or the Jino or Jinuo (Youle). Many are, essentially, domiciled almost entirely in Yunnan: the Va, the Lahu, the Achang, the Primi or Pumi, the Bulang or Blang, the Derung or Drung, the Deang, the Wa, the Nu and the Naxi. The last two groups illustrate the mélange of cultural influences in the region: while the Nu retain their primitive, animist religion, the Tibetan-descended Naxi (who retain vestiges of a matriarchal or, at least, matrilineal society) have blended their traditional shamanist (dongpa) beliefs with elements of lamaist Buddhism, Daoism and even Islam. Generally, however, the religious of Yunnan are more orthodox, if of varied adherence. There remains a large number of Muslims, including one of the rare non-Hui (i.e. non-Han) ethnic communities that espouse Islam and some Christians, but the main religions are traditionally—as in the rest of China—Confucianism (if counted as a religion), Daoism and Buddhism. The presence of the Dai brings the South-East Asian form of Buddhism (sometimes described as Nanchuan and Xiaochen or Hinayana Buddhism) into China, where the Mahayana tradition otherwise prevails. The form of Mahayana Buddhism brought to Yunnan by the Han Chinese is known as Mijiao, while the Tibetan influence means the presence of lamaism (Tantric or Vajrayana Buddhism), including important monasteries controlled by the Karma pa ('Red Hat' sect) in the north-west.

In 2000 23.4% of the population lived in urban areas. The largest city and the provincial capital is Kunming, which had a population of 1.9m. (4.8m. in the greater administrative area) in 2000. The second biggest city is to the north-east of Kunming and is called Qujing. In the west is the old capital of Dali, which lies beyond the south end of a lake, Er Hai, and just to the north of the larger city of Xiaguan, which is confusingly called Dali Shi, as it is the chief town of Dali county, but it is not the historic city itself. Given the size of the ethnic population there are obviously numerous autonomous areas, including 78 counties (seven of which are cities), but most of the minority nationalities are grouped in eight rural prefectures: the Yi area of Chuxiong; the Bai area around Dali; Dehong's Dai and Jingpo area; the Tibetans near Deqen; the Hani area on the Hong He; the Lisu on the Nu Jiang; the Zhuang and the Miao in the Wen Shan; and the main Dai area of Xishuangbanna. There are also eight other prefectures, one-half of which are cities, and another 42 counties (four cities).

History

When the Chinese arrived in the south-west, under the Qin and Han dynasties, they prevailed against little effective opposition. Han settlements and trade posts were established amid the surrounding, and divided, aboriginal peoples. By the seventh century, however, the Bai had formed a state to the south of Dali. This confederacy of tribes evolved into a kingdom, Nanzhao, with a capital at Dali from 739, which moved from dependency on China against the threat of the Tibetans (Xizangzu) to fighting the Tang armies themselves. Later in the eighth century the Chinese outpost at Kunming fell to Nanzhao and became its secondary capital, and the kingdom became a powerful polity of the south-west, able to extend its rule into Guizhou, to threaten Sichuan (Chengdu was sacked in 829) and to disrupt Chinese influence in Annam (Annan), a tributary kingdom in northern Viet Nam. By about 875 the weakening Tang Empire had managed to restrain further expansion by Nanzhao, which was to disintegrate after a senior court official murdered the infant king and usurped the throne. The main independent successor state was based on Dali and survived until the Mongol invasions of the 13th century, which also ended the independence of the Dai (Thai) state of Xishuangbanna.

It was the Mongols who restored Yunnan as an integral part of the Chinese Empire, under their own Yuan dynasty. They also caused another feature of the province—the large number of settled Muslims, rather than the smaller communities in commercial centres—by the singular appointment of a Muslim as governor after the conquest of Yunnan in 1274. It was not that Muslim settlement hindered the incorporation of Yunnan into Yuan and then Ming China, and their loyalty was not automatically questionable (Zheng He—Cheng Ho—was a Yunnan Muslim, whose origin in a landlocked province is odder than his faith, for he became famous as the long-faring eunuch admiral and explorer of the early 15th century). Also under the Ming, Kunming (then known as Yunnanfu) was fortified and developed as the main administrative centre. Nevertheless, the region, so remote from central authority, was ever liable to seize an opportunity to follow its own course, its reputation for rebelliousness abetted by the presence of exiled dissenters (a practice continued under the Communist regime). Thus, the area held out in defiance of the Manchus and their Qing dynasty into the 1650s. Then Wu Sangui, the general who had originally invited the Manchus past the Great Wall in 1644, was ordered to crush the last Ming loyalists in Yunnan. This he did, only to make the province the base for his own revolt against the Qing. Wu Sangui died in 1678, before the Manchus moved against the 'Three Feudatories', and it was his successor who was defeated and committed suicide, leaving Kunming to the Qing in 1681. Yunnan was then united with Guizhou and a province of Yangui (still based in Kunming) lasted until the end of the dynasty in 1912.

Meanwhile, however, the situation had changed for Muslims in China, and there were a number of Muslim uprisings throughout the Empire during the 19th century, with grievances usually exacerbated by economic and social hardships. The Muslims of Yunnan rose in 1855 (many of the other ethnic-minority groups were sympathetic to them), and the following year the rebel leader, Du Xenxiu (originally known as Yang Xiu), proclaimed himself Sultan Suleiman ibn Abd ar-Rahman, the Leader of the Community of Muslims in Pingnan Guo (Pacified Southern State). His capital was in Dali, but he besieged Kunming several times between 1858 and 1868, conquering it bloodily once in 1863. He was captured and executed in 1873, and the revolt repressed, but at the cost of some 1m. lives in Yunnan alone.

Yunnan declared its independence of the Qing and in favour of a putative republic in November 1911, but was then primarily controlled by its own warlord, Tang Jiyao (Tang Chi-yao). He did participate in 1916 in a central Military Affairs Council of a number of southern provinces and Zhejiang, and was also involved in the formation of the second Republic of China in the 1920s, but above all he maintained own autonomy. By the late 1930s the local order had reached an accommodation with the Guomindang, and Yunnan necessarily became more dependent on the Nationalists during the Second World War. Moreover, a large number of people fled here from areas more exposed to the Japanese invasion, helping the industrialization of the south-west (the republican Government had moved to Chongqing), while the Western Allies supplied the resistance to the Japanese initially via the 'Burma Road' into the province. The Communists only gained control of Yunnan in 1950.

Economy

Although Yunnan is a lush agricultural province, which is also rich in minerals and hydroelectric potential, there is much poverty and the province's population has a high growth rate (1.44% per year in 1990–2000) and the worst male-female ratio in China after Guangxi, at 100.00 to 110.11 (women to men). In 2000 the gross domestic product (GDP) of Yunnan amounted to 195,509m. yuan or 4,637 yuan per head. Despite the terrain, the province has good transport infrastructure, with a greater length of roads than anywhere else in China, totalling 109,560 km in 2000 (517 km of expressway, but only 77 km of first-class highway), 1,873 km of railway and even 1,580 km of navigable waterways. Yunnan produced 29,784m. kWh of electricity in 2000, of which 66% was hydroelectrically generated. Owing to poor rural rates, the overall illiteracy rate in 2000 was still 11.4%, despite a significant improvement since 1990.

The primary sector provided 22.3% of GDP. However, the sector also supported 73.9% of employed persons in the province, the highest proportion in any region of China. Farm crops were sown on 5.8m. ha of land in 2000, with cereals on 60% of that. Tobacco covered a greater area than in any other region (3.4m. ha). That same year Yunnan grew and harvested 14.2m. metric tons of sugar cane, 5.7m. tons of rice, 4.7m. tons of corn (maize), 1.5m. tons of tubers and 0.8m. tons of fruit. Although tea plantations covered a greater area (167,400 ha in 2000) than in any other region, the harvest of 79,396 tons (12% of the national total) was easily surpassed by both Fujian and Zhejiang. Yunnan was China's leading producer of tobacco (656,000 tons—26%), most of it being flue-cured. The province is also western China's main timber producer (1.3m. cu m), and other plantation or forest products included rubber (171,650 tons, second only to Hainan), walnuts (68,788 tons, making Yunnan China's biggest producer—22% of national production), pine resin (54,360 tons) and tung-oil seeds (19,698 tons). The province is also a major source of medicinal or rare plants and new varieties of flowers to popularize for domestic use (azaleas originate in Yunnan). The well-vegetated pasturelands of the hilly province support a large population of pigs (25.9m.), cattle and buffaloes (8.5m. head in 2000), goats (7.7m.), horses (0.9m.—only Xinjiang has more) and mules (0.6m.). Livestock products include 2.0m. tons of meat (1.7m. tons of pork), 147,000 tons of milk, 106,000 tons of poultry eggs and 7,000 tons of honey. Yunnan's fish farms (accounting for 87% of total aquatic production of 166,200 tons in 2000) provided most of the 144,600 tons of fish caught.

The proportion of the provincial GDP contributed by the secondary sector in 2000 was 43.1%. The same year a mere 9.2% of workers found employment in the sector—the lowest proportion of any region except Xizang (Tibet). Construction provided 7.4% of total GDP in 2000 and earned a total output value of 30,926.45m. yuan. Industry is based on agricultural processing and the extraction and processing of minerals. Thus, Yunnan produced more cigarettes than any other region (6.1m. cases—18% of national production) and more sugar than anywhere but Guangxi (1.5m. metric tons). The many minerals in the province included zinc, lead, tin, cadmium and indium. However, there were only 2,124 industrial enterprises in Yunnan in 2000, with a gross output value of 106,336m. yuan. These were overwhelmingly in the state sector and outside investment was insignificant. Most companies were engaged in heavy industry (1,228), but light industry produced more of the gross output value (52%). There were 92 large enterprises producing 57% of the value and 295 enterprises producing 14%.

Tertiary industry accounted for 34.6% of GDP in 2000 and for 17.0% of employed persons—the smallest proportion in China. By far the largest contribution to the services product came from wholesale and retail trade and catering (10.2% of total GDP). Exports earned US $1,092.71m. in 2000 and imports cost only $791.49m. A significant $339m. in foreign exchange was added by the tourist industry, from international tourist visits numbering 1.0m. (0.7m. by foreigners) that same year. Tourism is considered a 'pillar' industry and receives considerable encouragement from the state. The province, which neighbours three other countries, has a rich variety of tribal cultures, an ancient and interesting history, a number of pilgrimage sites and a wealth of natural heritage. Mountain scenery and luxuriant foliage, be it alpine or tropical rain-forest, shelter a botanical trove and wild animals such as tigers, leopards, elephants and golden-haired monkeys.

Revenue raised by government in Yunnan totalled 18,074.50m. yuan in 2000. The operations tax raised 20.0% of this and value added tax 17.4%. Total expenditure came to 41,410.74m. yuan, of which 15.0% went on education, 14.6% on capital construction and 9.0% on government administration. Foreign direct investment in 2000, never particularly high, declined on the previous year to US $128.12m.

Directory

Governor: XU RONGKAI (acting); Office of the Provincial People's Government, Kunming.

Secretary of the Yunnan Provincial Committee of the Chinese Communist Party: LINGHU AN; Office of the Secretary, CCP Secretariat, Kunming.

Chairman of the Standing Committee of the People's Congress of Yunnan: YIN JUN; Office of the Chairman, Congress Secretariat, Kunming.

Chairman of the Yunnan Provincial Committee of the Chinese People's Political Consultative Conference: LINGHU AN; Office of the Chairman, CPPCC Secretariat, Kunming.

Party Committee Secretary of the Chuxiong Yi Autonomous Prefecture: DING SHAOXIANG.

Head of the Dali Bai Autonomous Prefecture: ZHAO LIXIONG (acting).

Party Committee Secretary of the Dehong Dai–Jingpo Autonomous Prefecture: WANG NANKUN.

Party Committee Secretary of the Deqen Tibet Autonomous Prefecture: ZHANG BAIRU.

Party Committee Secretary of the Honghe Hani Autonomous Prefecture: YANG GUANGCHENG.

Party Committee Secretary of the Nujiang Lisu Autonomous Prefecture: ZHANG YAOWU.

Party Committee Secretary of the Wenshan Zhuang–Miao Autonomous Prefecture: MA JIAN.

Head of the Xishuangbanna Dai Autonomous Prefecture: YAN ZHUANG.

Yunnan Government Office: Wuhuashan, Kunming; tel. (871) 3621773; internet www.yu.gov.cn.

Zhejiang

The Province of Zhejiang (Chekiang) is in eastern China, facing roughly south-eastwards onto the East China Sea. The northern part of the province, beyond Hangzhou bay, borders Shanghai to the north-east and Jiangsu to the north. Anhui lies inland, to the north-west, Jiangxi to the west and another coastal province, Fujian, to the south-west. The total area of Zhejiang is 101,800 sq km (39,290 sq miles). Zhejiang was the smallest province within the People's Republic of China until 1987, when Hainan was separated from Guangdong.

Zhejiang, which means the 'winding river', is a low-lying land in the north, where rivers and canals cross the flat landscape south of the Chang Jiang (River Yangzi) delta. It is here that China's eastward bulging coastline is cleft by the Hangzhou bay, and it is from the city that gives this gulf its name that the Da Yunhe (Grand Canal) began its long journey north. Some 6% of the territory of Zhejiang consists of rivers and lakes, while another 70% is hilly. Most of the highlands are in the south, reaching their height at Huangmao Jian (1,921 m or 6,305 feet). Another distinguishing feature is the heavily corrugated, 2,200-km (1,370 miles) coastline, strewn with islands. Some reports number these islands at 18,000, more than in any other region—there are certainly over 3,000 islands of 0.5 sq km or more in area. The largest, and the fourth-largest island in all China, is Zhoushan Dao (524 sq km), just off the north-eastern tip of the southern flank of Hangzhou bay. It gives its name to the Zhoushan archipelago, which strings out across the mouth of the bay, towards Shanghai, and consists of over 600 islands. There is a subtropical monsoon climate, which brings heavy 'plum rains' in June and into July, droughts for the rest of the summer, and typhoons from late August to late September. Average annual rainfall is 850–1,700 mm (33–66 inches), and is lower in the north than in the south. However, in 2000 Hangzhou, the provincial capital, in the north, had 1,198 mm, with average monthly temperatures of 4.3°C (39.7°F) in January and 29.4°C (84.9°F) in July.

Total population at the time of the 2000 census was 46.77m., giving a fairly high population density of 459 persons per sq km. Only 0.9% of the population were from ethnic minorities in 2000, and the most numerous of these, the She, only numbered some 200,000. The next largest group was the Chinese-Muslim Hui. A number of other groups were present in much smaller numbers. The Muslim presence in Zhejiang is old, dating back to the medieval period, when the cities of the province were vital ports on the international trade routes. The traditional religions of China are better represented, and the province boasts one of the four holy mountains of Chinese Buddhism, Putuo Shan, in the Zhoushan archipelago. The province is also home to the Tiantai Buddhist sect, which was heavily influenced by Daoism and is strong in Korea and Japan, and the holiest temple of the Sodo Buddhist sect (with followers in Japan), the Tiantong temple in Ningbo.

In 2000 48.7% of the population were reckoned to be urbanized. The capital, Hangzhou (Hangchow), is the largest city, with 2.3m. people in its urban area and 6.2m. in the 'greater' Hangzhou area. The next most important cities are Ningbo (Ningpo), in the north-east, but on the southern side of Hangzhou bay, and Wenzhou, on the southern coast. Jinhua is in the centre of the province, with Quzhou (Quxian) to the west and south, and Jiaxing is near the border with Shanghai. The province includes China's only autonomous county for the She minority, as well as 61 other counties (of which 24 are cities). Higher in the administrative hierarchy are the 11 urban prefectures.

History

Zhejiang is ancient in Chinese history, with archaeological remains attesting to settlement that even predates the mythological, third-millennium-BC era of King Yu, who is associated with the area in legend. A better-recorded start to the history of Zhejiang is in the eighth–third centuries BC, when the capital of the state of Yue was near Shaoxing. In 473 it defeated the neighbouring coastal state of Wu (modern Jiangsu), but itself fell to the inland power of Chu in the 330s BC. Just over one century later Chu was itself conquered, by the Qin of the First Emperor, although the Yue region was noted for its long resistance using guerrilla tactics. However, the land soon became a productive part of the Han Empire, having good farmland and good harbours conveniently located near the mouth of the Chang Jiang (River Yangzi). The province gave birth to Sun Quan, the founder of one of the Three Kingdoms, Wu, that followed the fall of the Han dynasty. Wu was conquered by Wei in AD 280. In the 10th century Qian Lu established Wu-Yue in the region, which lasted from the 907 fall of the Tang until 978 and conquest by the Song, but in the meantime it had had to contend with others of the so-called Ten Kingdoms, Wu to the north-west and Southern Tang in the south-east. It was Song rule that was to be the most glorious era in the history of Zhejiang, although the northern cities were already becoming prosperous. In 610 Hangzhou (variously called Qiantang under the

Tang, Xifu under Wu-Yue and Linan thereafter) had been linked to the Grand Canal (Da Yunhe), and the trade along this artery of commerce and culture had ensured not only its own wealth, but also the increasing importance of the other cities of northern Zhejiang (and southern Jiangsu), such as Shaoxing and Ningbo, the latter dominating the trade to Japan and the eastern islands.

In the early 12th century the Song ruler, Huizong (an indifferent emperor, but a renowned poet and patron of the arts), encouraged the Jurchens to defy the Khitans' Liao dynasty. However, he merely replaced the threat of one northern people with that of another and in the 1120s the Jin dynasty displaced the Liao. In 1125 Huizong invested his son in the purple as Qinzong, but a new emperor did not prevent the conquest of northern China by the Jin and the capture of Kaifeng (Henan), the imperial capital. The imperial family and the court fled into Jiangsu, then to head south, under the protection of Tong Guang, a general who fell victim to the jealousy of an official and was executed—Huizong and Qinzong were captured by the Jurchens and spent their last days in captivity in Manchuria. Despite this humiliating defeat, however, the dynasty survived, finding refuge on the lower Chang Jiang and eventually settling on Linan (Hangzhou) as their 'temporary halt' (Xingzai— the derivation of Quinsai, as the city was known to the Italian explorer, Marco Polo) in 1138. Hangzhou grew rapidly and flourished as the imperial capital of a thriving empire, augmented by the exiled talents and wealth of the conquered north, and enriched by an expanding sea trade from as far away as India and Arabia. The city soon became probably the biggest in the world, and probably the richest, able to afford to keep the northern border firm beyond or along the Chang Jiang.

The Mongols finally ended the Song Empire in 1279 and Hangzhou ceased to be an imperial capital, although it still benefited from the trade up the Grand Canal towards the new northern seats of power. In the 14th century the modern boundaries of Zhejiang, and the name of the province, began to emerge, although Hangzhou itself began to decline from about the 16th century (after the Ming capital had moved from nearby Nanjing, in Jiangsu). At around this time the Portuguese became established in Ningbo, dominating the trade with Japan, but making the city prosperous. The area also continued to be a cultural centre and a huge attraction to visitors, but was not a central political location. Indeed, under the early Qing (another conquering dynasty out of Manchuria), in 1656, Zhejiang was united for administrative purposes with Fujian. Ningbo, which became a treaty port open to foreigners in the 1840s, soon lost much of its attraction as it lost out to the burgeoning new rivalry of Shanghai, on the opposite side of the great bay, while Hangzhou was devastated by the Taiping Rebellion (and its suppression) in the early 1860s (over 0.5m. people died and the city was reduced to ashes). Nevertheless, the province continued to be prominent in Chinese life and is noted for being the home of the great novelist, Lu Xun, the ancestral home of Zhou Enlai (although he was actually born in Jiangsu) and the birthplace of Jiang Jieshi (Chiang Kai-shek—in Xikou). Certainly from when the Guomindang finally seized control from the warlords in 1928, Zhejiang was a bastion of Nationalist support, although it was occupied by the Japanese in November 1937. The Communists only gained control of Zhejiang in May 1949 and the province existed under the East China Administrative Council (based in Shanghai) until 1954.

Economy

Zhejiang has always been at the forefront of economic developments in China, historically as a 'grain basket' for the north, an international trading centre and the centre of industries such as silk and porcelain. The farmland remains productive, and the industry initially grown from the thriving seaports and inland waterways has matured and developed. Gross domestic product (GDP) in 2000 was 603,634m. yuan, giving the highest per-head figure (13,461 yuan) for any province. Only the bustling municipalities of Shanghai, Beijing and Tianjin were wealthier. In terms of infrastructure, Zhejiang has very dense road and waterway networks. In 2000 there were 41,605 km of highway (627 km expressway and 999 km first class), only 794 km of operational railway, but 10,408 km of navigable inland waterways. Although its major cities enjoy a long history as mighty ports, Zhejiang now only has Ningbo as a major seaport. Investment since 1980 has brought it back to rank as the second port of China (after Shanghai, just across the Hangzhou bay), in terms of freight handled (115.5m. metric tons in 2000). The province generated 62,483m. kWh of electricity in 2000, almost all of it from thermal power stations. Although Zhejiang has a good reputation for its education system, the illiteracy rate remained stubbornly above the national average, at 7.1%, in 2000.

The primary sector is not a major part of the economy, although it underpins many activities. It contributed only 11.0% to GDP in 2000, providing jobs for only 37.8% of workers. The total area sown with farm crops was 3.6m. ha in 2000 (45% with rice alone), while tea plantations occupied 128,900 ha (only slightly exceeded by neighbouring Fujian). That year Zhejiang produced 9.9m. metric tons of rice, 1.7m. tons of fruit (57% citrus) and 1.0m. tons of sugar cane, for example, and more than any other province of tea (116,352 tons—17% of national production) and silkworm cocoons (95,123 tons, almost all mulberry—17% of all cocoons and 19% of mulberry-silkworm cocoons). Zhejiang is not a major livestock area, although in 2000 it counted 10.4m. pigs, 2.3m. sheep and goats and only 0.4m. cattle and buffaloes. Production amounted to 1.2m. tons of meat (0.9m. tons of pork), 372,000 tons of poultry eggs, 112,000 tons of cows' milk, 2,132 tons of fine sheep wool and more honey than anywhere else in China at 71,000 tons (29% of national production). The province has a large fishing industry and enjoys the marine fishing grounds of the Zhoushan islands, set in shallow water at the mouth of a river. Total aquatic production was 4.7m. tons in 2000, of which the sea provided 87%. Only 17% of marine production was artificially cultured, but this rose to 87% inland. The marine catch included 2.3m. tons of fish, 0.9m. tons of crustaceans and 0.9m. tons of shellfish (and 27,200 tons of algae), while the freshwater catch was 0.5m. tons of fish and some 45,000 tons each of crustaceans and shellfish.

Secondary industry accounted for 52.7% of GDP (no other regional economy depends to a greater degree on the secondary sector) and 30.9% of jobs. Construction alone provided 5.0% of total GDP, from an industry with a total output value of 138,376.58m. yuan (a regional total exceeded only by Jiangsu). Zhejiang also produced 46.0m. metric tons of cement. Examples of other products include 47m. tons of coal, 1.5m. tons of chemical fibre, 2.8m. tons of paper and paperboard, 1.6m. tons of beer, 2.0m. washing-machine units, 7.4m. weight cases of plate glass and 293.8m. integrated-circuit units. The main industries are electronics, chemicals, pharmaceuticals and machine building.

There are also traditionally important industries such as silk production, clothes, leather, etc. Zhejiang had the largest number of industrial enterprises in the country after Guangdong and Jiangsu, 14,575 in 2000, with a gross output value of 660,365m. yuan (also exceeded by Shandong). The state played a relatively small part in the ownership and foreign investment was high. Light industry predominated, with 59% of the enterprises and 54% of the value. There were 318 large enterprises (25% of the value) and 932 medium-sized enterprises (16%).

The tertiary sector provided 36.3% of GDP in 2000 and 31.3% of employed persons' jobs. Trade and catering was, by far, the most important activity, accounting for 13.7% of total GDP, followed by transport and communications at 7.1%. Zhejiang is an important commodity-trading centre. Exports earned US $20,482.14m. in 2000, while imports only cost $11,039.56m.—not the largest trades, but one of the healthiest balances. Tourism added $514m. in foreign-exchange earnings, with international tourist visits at 1.1m. person-times (0.6m. by foreigners). Zhejiang has a very big domestic market for its tourism, with Hangzhou one of the main attractions (notably the Xi Hu), together with the pilgrimage site of Putuo Shan Dao.

Total revenue for government in Zhejiang during 2000 reached 34,277.45m. yuan, the operations tax earning 28%, value added tax 26% and the income tax on enterprises 26%. Government expenditure totalled 43,129.58m. yuan, with spending on education the most, at 18%, followed by government administration, 10%. Actually used foreign direct investment rose to US $1,612.66m. in 2000.

Directory

Governor: XI JINPING (acting); Office of the Provincial People's Government, Hangzhou.

Secretary of the Zhejiang Provincial Committee of the Chinese Communist Party: ZHANG DEJIANG; Office of the Secretary, CCP Secretariat, Hangzhou.

Chairman of the Standing Committee of the People's Congress of Zhejiang: LI ZEMIN; Office of the Chairman, Congress Secretariat, Hangzhou.

Chairman of the Zhejiang Provincial Committee of the Chinese People's Political Consultative Conference: LIU FENG; Office of the Chairman, CPPCC Secretariat, Hangzhou.

AUTONOMOUS REGIONS

Guangxi

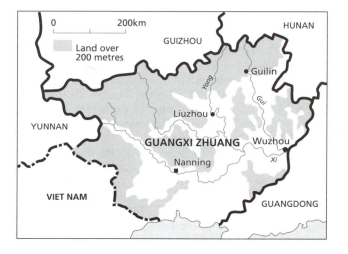

The Guangxi Zhuang (Kwangsi Chuang) Autonomous Region is located in the west of South China, against the international border with Viet Nam, which lies to the south-west, and has a relatively short coastline in the south on the Gulf of Tongking (Tonkin—Gulf of Beibu), an inlet of the South China Sea. Yunnan province is inland to the west, while Guizhou lies beyond the northern border until the most northerly end, in the east, where Hunan is wrapped around the north-eastern part of Guangxi. Guangdong lies to the south-east. The total area of Guangxi is 220,400 sq km (85,070 sq miles).

Guangxi ('wide west') is a contraction of the old name, Guangnan Xilu ('wide south, west route'), which refers to the then province's role as the main western route from the central Chinese lands to the south (Guangdong was the eastern route). It is known as Gui for short. The region consists of low hills and plains in the centre and south, surrounded by mountains, the ground highest in the north-west. More than one-half of the terrain is karst. The north falls within the drainage area of the Chang Jiang (River Yangzi), but more of the province is drained by the western part of the Zhu Jiang (Pearl River) system. The climate is subtropical, with long, hot, very humid summers (April–October), and a noticeably dry season in winter. The north is generally slightly cooler than the south, although in the height of summer the inland areas may experience some continental climatic influences. Thus, the average monthly temperatures in January 2000 ranged from 14.4°C (25.9°F) in Nanning to 8.3°C (46.9°F) in the more northerly Guilin, and from 28.7°C (83.7°F) in June–August in Nanning to 29.1°C (84.4°F) in July in Guilin. Most of the annual average of

1,200–1,800 mm (47–70 inches) in rainfall occurs in the summer (2000 totals in Nanning and Guilin were 905 mm and 2,056 mm, respectively).

The total population in 2000 was 44.89m., making Guangxi the most heavily populated of the five autonomous regions. As it is also the smallest in area apart from Ningxia, it was the most densely populated, at 204 persons per sq km. Its demography is distinguished as the region of China to have the most unequal ratio of men to women (11,268 men for every 10,000 women in 2000), but one of the lower rates of growth over the 1990s. It also had the largest population of non-Han peoples (17.2m.), although at 38.3% of the total this is not the highest percentage. The main minority nationality is the Zhuang, the largest ethnic group in China after the Han. Over 90% of them are said to live in the Zhuang autonomous area of Guangxi. The Zhuang are largely indistinguishable from the Han save for the Thai roots of their language. More obvious minorities include the Miao (Hmong), Dong, Yao, Shui, Mulam, Maonan and Yi. There are some Muslim Hui peoples, and some of the tribal groups have animist religious traditions, but what religious observance there is tends to be Daoist, Confucian or Buddhist.

According to the results of the 2000 census, 28.2% of the population lived in urban areas. The largest city and the regional capital is Nanning, in the centre-south of Guangxi (the city had a population of 1.2m. in 2000, but administered 2.9m. in all). Heading north-eastwards are the cities of Liuzhou, the second city, near the centre of the region, and Guilin, in the north-east. Qinzhou is the seaport to the south of Nanning, while the main town in the west, near the border on the main route from Yunnan, is Bose. Near the eastern border and the traditional route into Guangdong is Wuzhou. In all there are nine cities with prefectural status (and five other prefectures) and 10 with county status (and 71 other counties).

History

Chinese armies arrived in the region of modern Guangxi at the very beginning of the Empire united by the Qin. To assist the task of the conquering armies and occupying garrisons and traders, the First Emperor built what is claimed to be the first canal in China, for transport between Chang Jiang (Yangzi River) and Zhu Jiang (Pearl River) systems. With the establishment of Guilin prefecture in 214 BC, the Ling Qu was cut to link the Xiang with the south-west-flowing Tan. Guilin city was founded in 111 BC and became the main city of the region, serving as a provincial capital under the Ming. Nanning (formerly Yongzhou) was not built until the Jin (Chin) era, in the fourth century AD, and only became the provincial capital in 1914. Until that time, after the fall of the Qing, the region had been as formally dominated by the more dynamic and prosperous Guangdong as it had been for all practical purposes. Under the Qing, Guangxi was administered as part of Liangguang, from Guangzhou (Guangdong). Much earlier, in the 10th century, the two had been united in one of the Ten Kingdoms (Southern Han), and they had both shared in the unrest of the Taiping Rebellion—although the revolt originated in eastern Guangxi, where rural deprivation and ethnic tensions between the Hakka and the Bendi exacerbated the widespread unrest of the time. Piracy and banditry were common, and secret societies flourished, with the Hakka countering the strong Bendi lineage organization with quasi-religious groups. One such group evolved into the God Worshippers Society (influenced by bastardized Christian concepts), organized by Feng Yunshun. His cousin, Hong Xiuquan, was the inspiration and, as a 'brother of Jesus Christ', their messiah. Famine in 1849–51 precipitated a crisis in Guangxi and the summons of the God Worshippers to Jintian, where they fought government troops. On 11 January 1851 Hong proclaimed the Heavenly Kingdom of Great Peace and a crusade against the Manchu 'demons', and the Taiping rebels drove north to convert, or conquer, the Empire (Nanjing, in Jiangsu, was captured in 1853 and served as the Taiping capital until the revolt was crushed in 1864).

The sentiments that had provoked the Taiping Rebellion no doubt contributed to Guangxi's role as a stronghold of the early republican movement after the fall of the Qing. However, between 1920 and 1936 the province was largely autonomous under its own warlords. Accommodation with the Nationalist Government had already been reached by the time the Guomindang firmly established themselves in control in 1936, just before the Japanese invasion and the struggles of the Second World War began. Guangxi was strategically vital, on the possible route from Japanese-occupied Guangzhou to the temporary republican capital of Chongqing. As the Civil War drew to a close Guangxi was abandoned and the Communists gained control in November 1949. The new regime eventually recognized the aspirations of the Zhuang people and declared Guangxi province to be an autonomous region on 5 March 1958. By this time Guangxi was once again reverting to its role as a conduit for trade and influence from China into Viet Nam (as had been the case with the protectorate over Annam—Annan, in northern Viet Nam, which had brought the Qing into unsuccessful conflict with the French in the 19th century), but relations became estranged and even led to armed incursions in 1979 and, on occasion, thereafter. Relations have now improved.

Economy

The Zhuang autonomous region of Guangxi had a gross domestic product (GDP) of only 205,014m. yuan in 2000. The resulting per-head figure, at 4,319 yuan, was not only the lowest in southern China, but the third-lowest in the country. Guangxi has fairly dense roads (52,910 km) and waterways (5,618 km), as well as 2,012 km of operational railways (a link with Viet Nam was built in the 1950s) and five domestic airports. In 2000 28,909m. kWh of electricity were generated (58% hydroelectric). Despite the constraints on it, Guangxi had the lowest rural illiteracy rate in the country, enabling it to keep an overall rate of only 3.8% in 2000 (giving the best levels of literacy in the People's Republic).

The primary sector still accounted for 26.3% of GDP and 62% of employed persons in 2000. The total sown area that same year was 6.3m. ha, of which 37% was for growing rice and 8% for sugar cane. Fruits were grown on a further 0.8m. ha (the third largest orchard area in China). The main crop yields that year included 29.4m. metric tons of sugar cane (the country's largest regional harvest and 43% of the national total), 12.3m. tons of rice, 3.6m. tons of fruit (the sixth largest regional harvest, but including 1.1m. bananas—second only to Guangdong—and 0.9m. citrus fruits, as well as a number of other high-value tropical fruits) and 0.5m. tons of groundnuts (peanuts). The region also produced 29,542 tons of silkworm cocoons, almost all mulberry, and the biggest harvest of pine resin (216,015 tons—39% of the national total), as well as 26,268 tons of tea-oil seeds. The main forest product, however, was timber (31.5m. cu m), which is easily harvested from Guangxi's large forest area (8.6m. ha—almost two-fifths of the total area of the region). Guangxi has the third largest pig population in China, at 31.7m. in 2000, the fifth largest cattle-and-buffalo population, at 7.8m., and 2.4m. goats. Pork accounted for three-quarters of total meat production of 2.8m. tons in 2000, and the region also produced 145,000 tons of poultry eggs, 17,000 tons of cows' milk and 6,000 tons of honey. A healthy fishing industry was responsible for 2.4m. tons of aquatic production, dominated by marine fishing. That year, 2000, the catch included 0.8m. tons of seawater shellfish, 0.8m. tons of freshwater fish, 0.6m. tons of seawater fish and 0.2m. tons of seawater crustaceans.

The secondary sector only contributed 36.5% to GDP (the sector contributed less only in Hainan and Xizang—Tibet) in 2000, while employing a mere 10% of those in work. Handicrafts still important in augmenting the output of the sector. Some mineral reserves have helped the region develop its industry—for example, manganese, bauxite, coal, plaster stone, sulphur, tin, phosphorus, antimony, iron, gold, etc. Ferrous metallurgy, which is mainly based in Liuzhou and modest compared that of Guangxi's neighbours, produced 1.3m. tons of pig iron and 1.0m. tons of steel in 2000, for example. The region also produced a respectable 22.0m. tons of concrete, 3.3m. tons of sugar (47% of the national total) and a large number of motor vehicles (127,800 units). That year there were 3,155 industrial enterprises, with a gross output value of 100,324m. yuan, in current prices. Heavy industry accounted for 55% of the enterprises and 60% of the value, the 198 large enterprises for 47% of the value.

Services provided 37.2% of regional GDP and jobs for 28% of those in work. It is not a developed or balanced sector, although it is important in the local economy. Trade and catering, a powerful indicator of tourist activity, was by far the largest service sector, alone accounting for 14% of GDP, with transport and communications, at 8%, considerably ahead of the next-largest service contributors. The karst topography of Guilin has long made it the most famous beauty spot in China, and domestic tourism is strong. However, the region also received 1.2m. international tourist visits and earned US $307m. in foreign exchange from the industry. Trade earned Guangxi $1,640.48m. from exports in 2000, offset against the $644.48m. paid for imports. Government revenue totalled 14,705.39m. yuan in 2000 (19% from the operations tax, against a national average of 25%) and expenditure 25,848.66m. yuan (17% on education, as is usual in most provinces, the largest single destination of spending). In the same year foreign direct investment fell slightly to $524.66m., but the region also received $0.30m. in other foreign investment.

Directory

Chairman of the Autonomous Regional Government (Governor) of Guangxi Zhuang: LI ZHAOZHUO; Office of the Autonomous Regional People's Government, Nanning.

Secretary of the Guangxi Zhuang Autonomous Regional Committee of the Chinese Communist Party: CAO BOCHUN; Office of the Secretary, CCP Secretariat, Nanning.

Chairman of the Standing Committee of the People's Congress of Guangxi Zhuang: ZHAO FULIN; Office of the Chairman, Congress Secretariat, Nanning.

Chairman of the Guangxi Zhuang Autonomous Regional Committee of the Chinese People's Political Consultative Conference: CHEN HUIGANG; Office of the Chairman, CPPCC Secretariat, Nanning.

Guangxi Government Office: 1 Minyue Road, Kunming; tel. (771) 2807778; internet www.gxi.gov.cn.

Nei Mongol
(Inner Mongolia)

The Autonomous Region of Nei Mongol (Inner Mongolia) forms an irregular crescent in northern China, the northern, international frontier curving up to enclose Mongolia (which China once claimed as Wai Mongol—Outer Mongolia). The north-eastern horn of the crescent reaches into the northernmost tip of the People's Republic, although as this tip is mainly capped by Heilongjiang, a Chinese province, the international border with Russia is mainly to the west. Heilongjiang, therefore, lies to the north and to the east of Nei Mongol, and Jilin lies to the east. The third of the old Manchurian provinces, Liaoning, is to the south-east, followed (heading roughly south-westwards) by Hebei, Shanxi and Shaanxi. As the southern frontier begins a general curve more towards the north-west, the small Hui autonomous region of Ningxia abuts into Nei Mongol from the south. Finally, to the south-west, is the length of Gansu province. This extended territory forms the third largest region of China (after Xinjiang and Xizang—Tibet) and covers an area of over 1m. sq km or almost 0.5m. sq miles (1,177,500 sq km or 454,520 sq miles).

Nei Mongol lies along the southern and eastern rim of the great Mongolian plateau, much of its territory consisting of grasslands (Caoyuan), the traditional pastures of the Mongols and their horses. The altitude of the plateau averages around 1,000 m (3,280 feet) above sea level. The Huang He (Yellow River) flows through the centre-south of the region, flowing north out of Ningxia into central Nei Mongol and looping eastwards before heading back into the heart of China between Shaanxi and Shanxi. The plainsland caught in this loop is known as the Ordos. West of here is the edge of the Gobi Desert, a desolate region with few habitations. Most of the southern border follows the line of the Great Wall, at least between Hebei and north-western Gansu, often built where hills and mountains helped the southern Chinese defences. In the west, south of the intervening strip of the so-called Gansu Corridor, rear the heights of the Tibet–Qinghai plateau. Highlands also rise in the south-east, while in the north-east the plateau lands thrust north as the heavily forested Da Hinggan range, the land falling away on the east to the northern Manchurian plains and on the west into the basin around the great lake, Hulun Hu (Hulun Nur), which is also called Dalai Hu. Here Mongolia juts in to the south as well as lying to the west, and Russia is to the north. The climate is a temperate continental one, but tends to extremes, particularly in the west, where, in winter (December–March), snow can fall on the desert sand dunes. The weather is very sunny, however, and the short summer (June–August) is not only warm, but can even be extremely hot in the west. The north-east receives rather more rain than the central parts of Nei Mongol, and humidity levels reflect this. Each year, on average, the region has between 100 mm (4 inches) and 450 mm of rainfall (for example, 317 mm fell in Hohhot, the capital, during 2000). Most rain falls in the summer. In winter the average minimum temperatures can fall as low as -23°C (-9°F). The monthly averages for Hohhot in 2000 included -13.4°C (7.9°F) in January and 25.0°C (77.0°F) in July.

The total population of Nei Mongol was only 23.76m. on 1 November 2000, giving the region the fourth-lowest population density in China (20 per sq km). According to the census results, 20.8% of the total were from the minority nationalities in 2000. Ethnic Mongols form only about 15% of the population, and the overwhelming majority is Han. There are also Manchus (Man or Manzu—much of the east was once included in Manchuria), while in the north-east, on either side of the Heilongjiang border, are some communities from the valley-dwelling Daur and the forest-hunting Evenks (Ewenki) and Oroqen. All groups, save the Manchu and Hui, who speak standard Chinese, retain their own languages, to varying degrees, and some add in distinctive religious beliefs. The traditional faith of the Mongols in this part of the world is the Tibetan form of Buddhism (adopted from the 13th century, displacing the old, naturalist and polytheistic worship of the shamans), although orthodox Chinese Buddhism is now more prevalent, owing to Han immigration. The small, city-based Hui communities practise Islam.

The census recorded 42.7% of the population to be urban in 2000. The regional capital is Hohhot (Huhehot—formerly Guisui), in the south-east, to the north of the border with Shanxi. The urban area had a population of 2.1m. in 2000, although the municipal area itself housed only 0.9m. The second largest city is Baotou, to the west of Hohhot, on the drear north-ernmost reaches of the Huang He. There were a number of other cities and towns on the fertile strip along the Huang He or near the southern border, while in the north-east a few more are strung along the railway that runs out of Russia and through Manzhouli and Hulun (Hailar) into Heilongjiang. South of that line, near to the Heilongjiang border and to the narrow 'waist' of north-eastern Nei Mongol, is Ulanhot (the capital between 1947 and 1950), and mid-way between there and Hohhot, in the centre of the territory, is Xilinhot. In all, for official purposes, there are 20 cities, but most of these are fairly small. At the end of 2000 the Nei Mongol Autonomous Region consisted of 12 prefectures (including five cities at that level) and 84 counties (15 cities).

History

Inner Mongolia (Nei Mongol), as its name suggests, is merely part of the original, vast Mongol homeland that stretched up into Siberia. The Mongols are the latest and most long-lasting of the numerous 'barbarian' nomadic peoples of the north who traditionally threatened China and against whom the Qin and the Han connected the Great Wall. By the 11th century the area was largely inhabited by Mongol tribes. Towards the end of the 12th century Temujin began to unite the Mongol clans and his leadership of the resulting confederacy was confirmed at a great assembly in 1206, when he was acknowledged as the Great Khan (Chinggis Khan—or, the Turkic version of his name, Genghis Khan). Genghis Khan then proceeded to the conquest of most of Eurasia, starting with an assault south of the Wall in 1215—the Xi Xia state of the Tanguts (based in Ningxia) suffered, while the co-operation of a Chinese general let the Mongols into the Beijing area, then the possession of a Jurchen dynasty. China proper remained ignorant of the imminence or the magnitude of the horse-borne threat, as the main Mongol cavalries concentrated on the conquest of the West. In 1227 the death of Chinggis during a further campaign against the Xi Xia resulted in the annihilation of the Tangut kingdom and the conquest of northern China under the third son of Chinggis, Ogodei. He was elected to pre-eminence among his family when the Mongol assembly made him Great Khan in 1229, but his attention was then drawn to the subjugation of Russia. His advisers began to draw on the Chinese for the administration of the Empire in the east, but such reforms were interrupted by his death in 1241.

The conquest of China proceeded under Mangu Khan, a grandson of Chinggis, but he died from dysentery while on campaign in 1659. His brother, Khubilai (Kublai) Khan, already fighting the Song, completed the conquest of the rest of China by 1279, after dealing with challenges to his position as Great Khan from another brother and from the Golden Horde. It was Khubilai Khan, the first foreigner to rule all of China, who adopted the dynastic name of Yuan (and ruled in China as the Shizu emperor) and moved the Mongol capital from present-day Mongolia to Dadu or Beijing—the city of Khanbaligh (Cambaluc to Marco Polo, the Italian traveller) was built in 1267–92. A northern palace was built near Duolun (close to the modern border with north-eastern Hebei), called Yuanshangdu (Xanadu—now in ruins). When he died in 1294 Khubilai Khan ruled the greatest empire the world had ever seen, but he was the last Great Khan of a united Mongol realm and in China he left a weak dynasty that was finally to succumb to the Ming in 1368. By then Mongol power had disintegrated and the tribes to the north of the Great Wall had returned to their traditional lifestyles. A more lasting legacy of Khubilai Khan than was empire was the adoption of Tibetan Buddhism, which the emperor had patronized, and lamaism soon became firmly established among the eastern Mongols, the peoples of present-day Mongolia and Inner Mongolia. Moreover, the development of the region just beyond the Great Wall particularly was helped by the towns, trading posts and more settled industries that grew up around lamaseries and temples (Hohhot was founded thus in the 16th century).

The traditional lifestyle of the Mongols still included menacing northern China upon occasion, of course, and in 1449, under Esen Taiji, they not only defeated the Chinese near Beijing, but even captured Ming Yingzong, the Zhengtong emperor. This threat was only to be tamed by the Manchus, who then went on to conquer China itself and, thus, to consolidate Chinese rule over Mongolia. The Tungusic tribes of the present north-east of China (descendents of the Jurchen, and to be officially renamed as the Man or Manzu—Manchu in the 1630s) began to extend their power over the neighbouring Mongol tribes under the family that adopted the Qing dynasty name in 1636. By then Manchu pre-eminence, at least in the eastern Mongol lands, had been secured by the death of the last Great Khan, Ligdan, who died in 1634. He was the chief of the Qahars (Chahars), who had vied for supremacy with the Tumets, both of whom then succumbed to Manchu sovereignty, although they were incorporated into the empire with dignity and a status that they would later claim was that of allies. (The Qing had devised a system of administration involving the simultaneous appointments of Manchus, Mongols and Chinese even before they conquered the Chinese Empire.) Once China was conquered the Manchu armies were able to establish their supremacy in the wider Mongol world, although some clans to the west and north were merely obliged to formal submission. Under the Qing the territories north of the Great Wall enjoyed a special status as part of Manchuria (the western part of which included what is now north-eastern Nei Mongol) or Mongol territories.

Under the Qing peace the Han Chinese began to settle in the towns north of the Great Wall, particularly along the Huang He (Yellow River), but also further north after the Russians brought the Trans-Siberian railway through Chinese territory around 1900 (Manzhouli was founded as a stop in 1901, its development helped by the start of coal mining there, for instance). The nominal rule of the Qing in most Mongol areas was formalized by the Republic that succeeded them, which claimed Mongolia as an integral part of China. However, for much of the period immediately after the collapse of the imperial system Inner Mongolia was dominated by Feng Yuxiang, an autonomous warlord based in Shaanxi. He began to co-operate with the Guomindang and the new Republic from 1928, only to rebel in 1929 and be defeated in 1930. Formally, from 1928 Inner Mongolia had been organized into the Chinese province system, with Ningxia taking the western desert region and Qahar (Chahar—based in Kalgan, now Zhangliakou in Hebei) in the centre-east. (The current north-east of Nei Mongol remained the western part of northern Manchuria.) These two flanked the central part, around Hohhot (then known as Guisui) and the Huang He, which became Suiyuan. Meanwhile, Outer Mongolia (Wai Mongol or Khalkha Mongol) had effectively gained its independence, initially as a Buddhist kingdom and then with a People's Government from 1921 (a People's Republic was confirmed in 1924, after the death of the last Living Buddha god-king). This independence was recognized by the Chinese Communists when they formed their own People's Republic in 1949, although the Guomindang continued to claim Outer Mongolia as Chinese sovereign territory.

The Japanese occupation of Manchuria in 1931 was followed by their intervention in the affairs of Inner Mongolia, where they exploited separatist sentiment. In 1933 Qahar and Suiyuan were declared a protected Mongjiang (Mengkiang) or Mongol March and under De Wang an Autonomous Political Council was formed, based in Guisui. He succeeded as the head of the Inner Mongolian Federation in 1937, which was formed under Japanese occupation, but this entity disappeared with the Japanese surrender in 1945. An Inner

Mongolian People's Republic was proclaimed on 10 September, but it merged with China on 25 October. In 1946 the Communists gained control of Jehol province, which had been extended north to include much of the west of old Chinese Manchuria. The northern regions, the east of Inner Mongolia, were then taken and, on 1 May 1947, the first of the autonomous regions that now exist in the People's Republic was declared. The first capital of Nei Mongol, therefore, was at Ulanhot. In 1950 this moved to Zhangliakou (Kalgan), when Qahar was incorporated into Nei Mongol, but this territory was split in 1952, the large northern territories being retained by Nei Mongol, but Zhangliakou and the south becoming part of Hebei. The capital then moved to Guisui, now known as Suiyuan city, after the province in which it was hitherto located and which was formally incorporated into Nei Mongol in 1954. The desert western region (Shingan) was also added to Nei Mongol at this time and Hohhot received its current name. In 1955 the rest of Jehol was dismembered, most becoming part of Hebei, but the rest being split with Liaoning and Nei Mongol. Much of this expansion was reversed in 1969, however, when the western desert was split between Gansu and Ningxia, part of the south-east went to Hebei and the north-east was divided between the three Manchurian provinces, but the old borders were restored in 1979.

Economy

The gross domestic product (GDP) of Nei Mongol (Inner Mongolia) amounted to 140,101m. yuan in 2000, or 5,872 yuan per head. Transport infrastructure across such a vast territory was sparse, but linked all the main centres of population and economic activity. At the end of 2000 there were 67,346 km of highways (but no expressways and only 140 km of first-class roads), 5,011 km of railways and even 1,164 km of navigable waterways. The autonomous region is able to export some of the electricity it produces (43,922m. kWh in 2000), most of it generated from locally extracted coal. Nei Mongol has the highest illiteracy rate in northern and north-eastern China, at 9.1% of the adult population in the 2000 census year.

The primary sector contributed 25.0% of GDP and accounted for 54.5% of employed persons in the region. Arable land is limited, certainly without irrigation, but there are extensive ranges available for animal husbandry. The total sown area in 2000 amounted to only 5.9m. ha of such a vast region. That year Nei Mongol harvested 6.3m. metric tons of corn (maize), 1.8m. tons of tubers, 1.1m. tons of beans, 1.2m. tons of oil-bearing crops and 1.4m. tons of sugar beet. However, there are considerable woodland resources in the north-east (16% of the region is forested), and 32,779m. cu m of timber (7% of the national total) were produced in 2000. Some 73% of the territory is reckoned to be grasslands, so livestock rearing is an important activity. In 2000 there were 22.5m. sheep, 13.0m. goats, 8.0m. pigs, 3.5m. cattle, 1.1m. of the famous Mongolian horses (13% of all China's horses), 0.9m. donkeys, 0.6m. mules and even 0.1m. camels (37% of the national herd). Of the 1.4m. tons of meat produced in the same year, 53% was pork, and most of the 0.8m. tons of milk came from cows. Nei Mongol was, however, the country's main wool producer, leading in sheep wool and cashmere. The region produced 22% of the national total of sheep wool, at 65,051 tons (22% of the national total—57% fine and

21% semi-fine) and 35% of cashmere, at 3,815 tons, as well as 3,442 tons of goat wool. Fisheries production was limited to 72,100 tons, almost all of it fish and most of it artificially cultured.

The secondary sector accounted for 39.7% of GDP and 16.5% of employment. The development of industry is driven by the exploitation of Nei Mongol's extensive mineral reserves—it has large resources of coal, as well as, for example, deposits of salt, graphite, mica, sulphur, chromium, copper, lead and zinc. The region was the country's fourth regional coal producer in 2000, with 72m. metric tons, and also produced 1.3m. tons of salt. Other processing industries included sugar (120,400 tons), iron (4.2m. tons) and steel (3.8m. tons). The region had one of the smallest numbers of industrial enterprises in China, with 1,373 in 2000 (gross output value 74,897m. yuan). The state sector dominated, as did heavy industry (765 of the firms, but 70% of the value). There were 87 large enterprises (43% of the value) and 198 unusually strong medium-sized enterprises (30%).

The tertiary sector accounted for 35.3% of GDP in 2000, with transport, storage and communications being the leading activity (10.2% of total GDP). Services employed 29.1% of those in work. In 2000 trade earned US $1,114.00m. in exports, but imports cost $1,272.27m. Tourism earned a respectable $126m. in foreign exchange, because almost all the 391,900 international-tourist visits in 2000 were by foreigners. Attractions include the grasslands and culture of the Mongol herdsmen, the mausoleum of Chinggis (Genghis) Khan, the site of fabled Xanadu and various temple sites.

According to the final statement of government revenue for 2000 Nei Mongol raised only 9,503.20m. yuan, the largest single contributor being the operations tax (20%). Expenditure totalled considerably more, 24,726.81m. yuan, indicating the dependence on government spending by the regional economy. The largest destination is capital construction (14%). The same year the region received US $105.68m. in foreign direct investment.

Directory

Chairwoman of the Autonomous Regional Government (Governor) of Nei Mongol: ULYUNQIMG; Office of the Autonomous Regional People's Government, Hohhot.

Secretary of the Nei Mongol Autonomous Regional Committee of the Chinese Communist Party: CHU BO; Office of the Secretary, CCP Secretariat, Hohhot.

Chairman of the Standing Committee of the People's Congress of Nei Mongol: LIU MINGZU; Office of the Chairman, Congress Secretariat, Hohhot.

Chairman of the Nei Mongol Autonomous Regional Committee of the Chinese People's Political Consultative Conference: WANG ZHAN; Office of the Chairman, CPPCC Secretariat, Hohhot.

Nei Mongol Government Office: 1 Xinhua Dajie, Hohhot; tel. (471) 6944404; internet www.nmg.gov.cn.

Ningxia

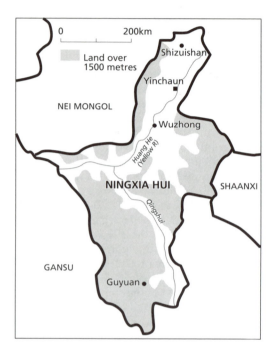

The north-west of the Ningxia (Ninghsia) Hui Autonomous Region lies on either side of the Huang He (Yellow River), where it enters the territory out of the south-west, from Gansu province, curves north and extends a strip of Ningxia deep into the Nei Mongol (Inner Mongolia) autonomous region, which, therefore, surrounds it from the north-west around to the north-east. Near the base of this extension, in the north-east of the region, Ningxia has a block of territory pushing east to meet Shaanxi province. The rest of the eastern border is with Gansu, which wraps itself around the southern part of this small region. At 66,400 sq km (25,630 sq miles), Ningxia is the smallest of the autonomous regions and smaller than every province of the People's Republic except Hainan (but still more than twice the size of either the Netherlands or the US state of Maryland).

Ningxia is situated on the north-west loess highland, on the edge of the Mongolian deserts, an irregular and knotted strip of land sheltering to the east of the mountains and defined by two rivers. In the north-west and north the Huang He flows through the Ningxia or Yinchuan plain, while the region extends into the south along the course of the Qingshui He, which joins the Huang He in the north-west, before it turns north. The east and south-east consists of loess (the fine, windblown 'yellow' soil of northern China) plateau, although the south suffers problems of water loss and soil erosion among the tangle of gullies and ravines scouring the soft earth. The Liupan Shan range shoulders into the south and continues up the south-western borders as the Quwu Shan. The curve of the north-western border is then taken by the river and the remnants of the Great Wall up to the Helan Shan, sheltering the northern extension from the desert. The highest point reaches 3,556 m (11,671 feet). The north is surrounded by desert, which compounds the extremities of the temperate continental climate. Ningxia (which means 'peaceful summer') is exposed to strong winds and can be very cold in winter. The average monthly temperature in Yinchuan in January 2000 was -8.8°C (16.2°F), although in July it was 25.7°C (78.3°F) and the maximum temperatures can get much higher over the summer. Rainfall can vary wildly from year to year, but what there is falls mainly in the summer and more rain in the south; the annual average range is 190–700 mm (7–27 inches). Yinchuan received 134 mm during 2000.

There were 5.62m. people residing in the Hui region of Ningxia at the time of the national census of November 2000 and the population density was only 85 per sq km. Growth was not limited by government policy in this autonomous area, and the population duly increased by over one-fifth between censuses (1.84% per year between 1990 and 2000). Perhaps a more noted demographic feature of the region is the longevity of the inhabitants. Although constituted as a Hui autonomy, most people in the region are Han Chinese. However, in 2000 34.5% were non-Han, most of them the predominantly assimilated (apart from their religion) and mingled Chinese-speaking Muslims, originally descended from merchant traders who had come along the 'Silk Road' and been reinforced by settlers from Central Asia during the 14th and 15th centuries. Islam is, therefore, represented in Ningxia, as well as the other religions more widespread in China—notably Daoism and Buddhism, the latter having a venerable tradition in the region.

The urbanized population was put at 32.4% of the total in 2000. Yinchuan (Yinchuen), in the north between the Huang He and the Helan Shan, is the capital and largest city of the region, although it only had a population of 564,400 in 2000 (the wider administrative area contained 1.01m.). Also in the north are Shizuishan (Dawuko), to the north of Yinchuan, and, to the south, on the river just north of the bend, Qingtongxia and the nearby Wuzhong. The only town of any size in the far south is Guyuan. The Ningxia region (until the 1940s Yinchuan was called Ningxia city) is divided into four prefectures, three of which are cities, and 85 counties (two cities).

History

Ningxia is defined by its closeness to the start of the 'Silk Road', as well as its position straddling the central area of Chinese civilization and the wild, nomadic north, as the Huang He (Yellow River) loops north beyond the Great Wall into the Nei Mongol (Inner Mongolia) desert. As the Tang succumbed to internal revolt and foreign invasion, the north-west of China particularly was exposed to incursions. During the 10th century the Tanguts, a people related to the Tibetans (Xizangzu), established a powerful state that straddled the Great Wall and that was based in Ningxia. In 1038 the Tangut ruler, Li Yuanhao, adopted the ancient Xia dynastic name, which came to be known in China as the Xi (Western) Xia. The Xia attempt to conquer the rest of China was repulsed in 1044, but the 10 successive emperors remained a power in Gansu and Shaanxi, contesting for influence with the Song of the south and the Liao of the north-east (it was not until the Mongols that Tang China was reunited). The capital of this Buddhist dynasty was near Yinchuan and called Xingchuan. In 1215 the Xi Xia bowed to the new power in the north, the recently united Mongols under Chinggis (Genghis) Khan, permitting them to pursue campaigns against the Liao and the Song. However, they were reluctant to concede their independence to the Mongols, although their long and powerful military tradition had earned the respect of Chinggis Khan, who was anxious to make them vassals or, at least, allies. He pursued six campaigns against the Xi Xia in a vain pursuit of victory. During the final campaign in 1227 Xi Xia archers insinuated themselves near the Mongol camp (near modern Guyuan, in southern Ningxia) and fatally wounded Chinggis Khan with poisoned arrows. The first Great Khan of the Mongols died, but he exacted a terrible revenge on his killers, ordering the immediate annihilation of Xi Xia. The region has not been an imperial centre since, but was brought back within a single Chinese Empire by the Mongol conquest.

Mongol (Yuan) rule saw an increase in the number of settlers from Central Asia, reinforcing the Muslim presence in the north-west of China (originating among settlements of Arab and Persian—Iranian—traders who had come down the 'Silk Road'). These Muslims adapted to the dominant Han language and culture, but preserved their religion. These Hui (Huizu or, variously throughout China, Huihui, Dungans or Panthays) only earned a reputation for dissent in the 19th century, when widespread discontent in the Qing Empire provoked a number of Muslim rebellions. The Hui revolt in the north-west, in Gansu (of which Ningxia was then a part—administered as part of Shengan, which also included Shaanxi and Shanxi) particularly, took place between 1862 and 1878. Large parts of the north-west were devastated by the uprisings as well as by the suppressions, and huge numbers of the Hui were wiped out. It was only under the Communists that the central Chinese authorities decided to recognize the distinctive Hui place in Han culture by creating an autonomous region in the north-west.

Before that a Ningxia province had been created out of Gansu (itself only restored a province upon the fall of the Qing) in 1928, when the local warlord acknowledged the authority of the Republic. It not only included the current territory, but also the deserts to the north, which now constitute the western end of Nei Mongol. This put the capital for which the province was named, Ningxia (now Yinchuan), nearer the centre of the territory than is the case now, although the northern part was a barren waste. The Communists gained complete control of the region in April 1948, with Ningxia and the other provinces placed under the authority of Administrative Councils (Ningxia and Gansu were in the North-West) between 1950 and 1954. In that year, shorn of the northern desert areas that were absorbed into Nei Mongol, Ningxia was itself incorporated into Gansu. However, on 25 October 1958 Ningxia was formed as a separate autonomous region for the Hui. In the same year the completion of the railway line between Baotou (Nei Mongol) and Lanzhou (Gansu) brought closer contact and more potential for economic development to the isolated region.

Economy

The Ningxia Hui region is not especially prosperous, although the smallness of scale sometimes obscures its achievements. The gross domestic product (GDP) was 26,557m. yuan in 2000, with only Xizang (Tibet) and, just, Qinghai, recording lower figures, although Ningxia's 4,839 yuan per head exceeded them. Considering that until the first half of the 20th century the region was very isolated, it now has fairly well developed infrastructure. The 9,649 km of highways included 83 km of expressway and 127 km of first-class road, and there were 716 km of operational railway track and 402 km of navigable waterways. The region also claimed the lowest electricity rates in China, as well as to be the only region to have connected all villages to the supply—13,661m. kWh was generated in 2000 (only 8% hydroelectric). Illiteracy, however, was high, at 13.4% in the same year.

In 2000 17.3% of GDP came from the primary sector, as did 57.8% of the jobs. With irrigation essential to any arable activity (although Ningxia has made good progress at countering desertification and even reducing the amount of unusable land) and the presence of good pastureland, livestock accounts for about three-10ths of the agricultural economy. The traditional 'five treasures' of the region include: argali wild-sheep hide and wool; facai (a moss); wolfberry (*lycium barbarum* or goji) fruit, long used in traditional medicine and to which the long local lifespans are popularly ascribed; and liquorice root (the fifth is Helan stone). In 2000 64% of the total area sown with farm crops in Ningxia (1.0m. ha) was used for cereals. Production included 0.8m. metric tons of corn (maize), 0.7m. tons of wheat, 0.6m. tons of rice, 0.2m. tons of tubers, 0.2m. tons of fruit (mainly apples) and 290 tons of mulberry-silkworm cocoons. Forestry has been encouraged, particularly as it helps in the fight against the desert. Livestock included 2.6m. sheep, 1.3m. goats, 1.2m. pigs and 0.6m. cattle and buffaloes (mainly dairy). Also in 2000 the region produced 185,000 tons of meat, 236,000 tons of cows' milk, 76,000 tons of poultry eggs and, more significantly, 4,703 tons of sheep wool, 715 tons of goat wool and 364 tons of cashmere. Aquatic production has become increasingly important, although it still amounted to only 37,000 tons in 2000, almost entirely farmed fish.

The contribution of the secondary sector to GDP was 45.2% of the total in 2000. This slightly overemphasizes the importance of industrial activity unless it is considered that construction alone provided about one-10th of total GDP. The same year the industrial sector as a whole provided jobs for 18.1% of employed persons. Considering its size, Ningxia has good mineral reserves, including coal (16m. metric tons in 2000) and crude petroleum (1.4m. tons), as well as, especially, gypsum, and, for example, calcium carbide, silicon carbide, quartz sandstone, phosphorus, copper and Helan stone (a special clay stone of the region). The main industrial activities are chemicals, metallurgy, machinery and textiles. Handicrafts are important, particularly for village industry. Some 2000 production figures are 2.8m. tons of cement, 0.5m. tons of chemical fertilizer and 0.6m. weight cases of plate glass. There were 409 industrial enterprises in the autonomous region in 2000, with a gross industrial output of 23,911m. yuan. Heavy industry accounted for 260 of the enterprises, but for 84% of the output value. The 32 large enterprises accounted for 53% of the value.

The tertiary sector comprised 37.5% of total GDP in 2000 and employed 24.1% of those in work. Trade and catering provided about 8% of total product and transport and communications 7%. Ningxia earned US $354.26m. from exports and spent an even smaller $177.85m. on imports, while foreign exchange earned from tourism amounted to only $3m., despite almost three-quarters of the international-tourist visits being by foreigners. However, the total was only 7,800, the lowest number to any region of China.

Government revenue in the Ningxia Hui Autonomous Region during 2000 was 2,082.44m. yuan, an unusually dominant 32% from the operations tax. Expenditure was 6,083.80m. yuan, the main destination being capital construction (15%), with education not far behind (13%). In the same year foreign direct investment fell to only US $17.41m., making the region the one to receive the least amount in all of China (excluding Qinghai and Xizang—Tibet—which received none), although it has done better in previous years.

Directory

Chairman of the Autonomous Regional Government (Governor) of Ningxia Hui: MA QIZHI; Office of the Autonomous Regional People's Government, Yinchuan.

Secretary of the Ningxia Hui Autonomous Regional Committee of the Chinese Communist Party: MAO RUBAI; Office of the Secretary, CCP Secretariat, Yinchuan.

Chairman of the Standing Committee of the People's Congress of Ningxia Hui: MAO RUBAI; Office of the Chairman, Congress Secretariat, Yinchuan.

Chairman of the Ningxia Hui Autonomous Regional Committee of the Chinese People's Political Consultative Conference: REN QIXING; Office of the Chairman, CPPCC Secretariat, Yinchuan.

Ningxia Government Office: 217 West Jiefang St, Yinchuan; tel. (951) 5015889.

Xinjiang

The Xinjiang Uygur (Sinkiang Uighur) Autonomous Region occupies the north-west of the People's Republic of China. This vast territory, China's largest, has borders with eight countries. Mongolia lies to the north-east, there is a short border with the Russian Federation in the north and Kazakhstan lies to the north-west. South-western Xinjiang abuts against both the Central and the South Asian states. Kyrgyzstan completes the north-western frontier, while Tajikistan and a thin, eastern extension of Afghanistan lie to the east. In the south-west are Pakistan and India. The border here is disputed with India (as is much of the Sino–Indian frontier), but complicated by the competing territorial and legal claims of Pakistan and India in the Jammu and Kashmir region. Most of the border with Pakistan has come about as a result of its occupation of much of northern Kashmir. Here, to the south of the Khunjerab pass, which the great Karakoram Highway crosses, Pakistan has conceded Chinese claims to a strip of territory that India alleges is illegally occupied (including Qogir Feng, the mountain also known as K2, the highest peak of Xinjiang, at 8,611 m or 28,261 feet). More substantially, in the very south of south-western Xinjiang, the bleak Aksai Chin plateau is administered as part of the autonomous region, although India claims it as part of Ladakh (part of Jammu and Kashmir state). India discovered the intrusion of a new road from Xinjiang into Tibet, across Aksai Chin, in 1959 and protested the *de facto* annexation. The Xizang (Tibet) autonomous region lies to the south of Xinjiang, Qinghai province to the south-east and Gansu province to the east. The total area stretches out over more than 1.6m. sq km (1,646,900 sq km or 63,570 sq miles), making Xinjiang about three times the size of France and almost as big as the largest US state, Alaska.

Xinjiang, which means 'new frontier' or 'new dominion', lies to the north of the Kunlun Shan, including the northern edge of the Tibet–Qinghai plateau and encompassing the desert country of the Tarim basin, extending east into the Turpan and Hami basins and north beyond the Tian Shan into the Junggar (Dzungar) basin. The borders lie not only along the line of the Kunlun mountains, but, notably, with Qinghai along the Altun Shan, and along the north-west and in the north by the Altai mountains. The Tian Shan thrust a divide into the region, but also continue as the border with Kyrgyzstan. In the west and south-west run the high Pamir and Karakoram ranges. The difference in altitude from the mountain peaks to the depths of the basin country is immense, with the lowest point in China (and the second lowest depression in the world, after that of the Dead Sea, between Jordan and Israel) at Aiding Hu (Lake Aydingkol), 354 m below sea level. The lake itself is a muddy morass, crusty with salt, but is officially one of the largest in China. To the south is Lop Nur, which has a hugely varying surface-water area, sometimes of some 2,500 sq km, and this probably has a better claim to be one of the largest salt lakes in the country, but it tends to be more infamous for being near the site of the Chinese nuclear-test grounds. Lop Nur is sometimes fed by the Tarim river, which flows out of the east and along the northern edge of the basin and the wide Taklamakan Desert, before it straggles to an end in the dryness. With an official length of some 2,140 km (1,330 miles) the Tarim is China's longest inland river. In the north the Ertix, which flows into Kazakhstan, is the only Chinese river, ultimately, to debouch into the Arctic Sea. The terrain and the fact that Xinjiang is located in the heart of the Asian landmass (the capital of Urumqi claims to be, in all the world, the city furthest from the sea—some 2,250 km) create a harsh climate. Even without the effect of altitude the region suffers extremes of temperature and receives little rainfall (more in the north than in the south). The oasis town of Turpan, which escapes the true desert of the Taklamakan to the south-west or the Gurbantunggur to the north, beyond the Bogda Shan, has recorded the hottest temperature in China, at 49.6°C (121.3°F). The average monthly temperatures in 2000, for example, in Urumqi, which lies on the northern flanks of the Tian Shan, were at their coldest in January, at -13.9°C (7.0°F), and their warmest in July 24.7°C (76.5°F). The annual average rainfall is only 150 mm (6 inches), but can be as little as 10 mm in the south and was 332 mm in Urumqi during 2000.

According to the national census of 2000, the total population of the Uygur Xinjiang region was 19.25m., which gave a population density of only 12 persons per sq km, the third-lowest density in China. The population is, however, growing rapidly, increasing by 27% between 1990 and 2000 (only the population of Beijing grew by slightly more), an average annual rate of 2.34%. Most of this growth is owing to immigration, particularly of the Han Chinese, which the Uygurs (Wei Wuer, Uyghurs or Uigurs) claim is officially encouraged to their disadvantage. In the 1950s the Uygurs accounted for about nine-10ths of the population, but by the end of the century their numbers had reduced to just below one-half. The Han Chinese accounted for about two-fifths of the population (most live in the north), while the next largest group, that of the Kazakhs, was about one-14th. At the 2000 census all nationality minorities together amounted to 59.4% of the total population. Smaller groups represented in the region include Manchu, Mongol and Tatar, Kyrgyz, Tajik, Uzbek, Russian and even Xibe, transplanted into the north-west from Manchuria under the Qing. The Uygurs are traditionally Muslim, and Islam replaced Buddhism as the dominant faith of the region during the medieval period, although many Mongols and the Xibe people practice lamaism, and some of the Han population adhere to the Buddhist faith.

In 2000 33.8% of the population was urban. The capital and only sizeable city is Urumqi (Urumchi or, in Uygur, Wulumuqi), which had an urban population of 1.3m. in 2000 (and only a little more in the wider area, 1.6m.). Settlement still follows the lines of the old trade routes out of Gansu, the first major city in the east being the ancient oasis city of Turpan. The road and rail routes head north-west to Urumqi, over the saddle of the mountains, and then continue to Changji and the larger city Jieshi. North-west again is Karamay and beyond that, on the Kazakhstan border, Tacheng (Qoqek), while in the far north, directly across the desert from Urumqi, is Altay (Altai). A more directly western route out of Urumqi crosses over into the Ili valley (which leads into Kazakhstan), between the Tian and the Borohoro ranges, where the city of Yining (Gulja) is situated. The southern route out of Turpan heads south-east to the edge of the Taklamakan Desert, where, near Korla, there is a choice to loop southwards around the Tarim basin (eventually passing through Hotan) or head more directly along the northern edge (via Aksu). Both routes end in the fabled city of Kashi (Kashgar), China's westernmost city, in the far south-west of Xinjiang. There are 15 prefectures (including two cities) in Xinjiang, and 85 counties (17 cities).

History

Trade was already flowing, and urban civilization spreading, when a Chinese envoy, Zhang Qian, was despatched by his emperor, Han Wudi, to seek against the Xiongnu ('Huns'), then the threat from the north. His mission failed, but he brought back information and curiosity about the 'Western Regions' of Central Asia, and it was not long before Chinese armies followed, extending the Great Wall and the Empire into what is now north-western Gansu and campaigning as far as Fergana (now in Uzbekistan), which a Han general, Li Guangli, reached in 101 BC. Suzerainty was easily gained, but a permanent presence only came in the last quarter of the first century AD, when Pan Zhao led an army of conquest into the Western Regions. There was a huge cost attached to maintaining this imperial annexe, as well as manning the Wall against whichever nomadic people was marauding from the north, and the disintegrating Han dynasty eventually could not manage even to keep itself in power, let alone to retain the territories of modern Xinjiang. Instead, the region developed a profusion of independent oasis kingdoms and hill states, inhabited not only by the Mongoloid and Turkic tribes that had menaced the Han, but also Indo-European and Altaic peoples. Here the cultural blending of the Silk Road contributed to the flourishing of powerful Buddhist cities, where Zoroastrian Manicheans and Nestorian Christians also established flourishing communities. Buddhism had certainly already reached China, but its consolidation depended on the infusion of ideas and authority down the Silk Road. Thus, Fa Xian, in around 400 and Xuan Zang in the 640s both journeyed through the region in search of Buddhist scriptures and enlightenment, the latter (immortalized in the classic tale *Journey to the West*) at the time when a resurgent Empire under the new Tang dynasty was moving against the Turkic raiders and back into Central Asia. The Chinese took Hami in around 630 and Turpan in 640, and their power extended as far as the Pamirs by the middle of the seventh century.

However, Chinese control of the Silk Road was not to be uncontested. The Turkic peoples may have been chastized, but they were far from willing to submit meekly to the Tang. Moreover, the Tibetans (Xizangzu) were also in an expansive period, and they defeated the Chinese armies in 663, occupying much of the Tarim basin and even Kashgar (modern Kashi) in 670–92. Although the Tang armies retaliated successfully during the early decades of the eighth century, the Tibetans were now a permanent threat to the communications between the bulk of the Chinese Empire and its Western Regions. Then, in 751 a new power erupted into Central Asia, when Gao Xianzhi was defeated on the River Talas by a Muslim Arab army and Tang power in the west was finally destroyed. Moreover, the Buddhist cities of Xinjiang were not only exposed to the advance of Islam along the Silk Road, but also to the depredations of the Turkic peoples (mainly the Uygurs, who probably arrived in the region in the eighth century) and the spread of desertification, partly as a result of the disruption and partly from climatic change. Thus, many of the great cities of the region are ruins, often buried in sand, though some were adopted by their new rulers, a succession of tribal kingdoms that held sway until the 13th century, the Uygurs (with their capital in Gaochang, near Turpan) until about 840 (who threatened the Chinese and the Tibetans), then their successors in the Qarakhanid and Karakitay khanates. The Uygurs initially adopted the Buddhism already prevalent in the region, and were distinguished among the Turkic peoples for becoming settled agriculturalists rather than pastoralist nomads. There were Muslims all the way down the Silk Road and into China even by ninth century, but the first Turkic ruler in Central Asia to embrace Islam was an Uygur leader, Satuk Bughra Khan, in 934. The successor of his Muslim state was to absorb a Buddhist Uyghur principality to the east in 1397 (the united realm maintaining a sometimes precarious independence until the 18th century), so that the only Uygurs to retain Buddhism into the modern era were the so-called Yellow Uygurs, who had migrated into Gansu in the ninth century and were sufficiently far east to avoid islamicization. In the early 13th century the Mongols were united under Chinggis (Genghis) Khan and they proceed to conquer to both east and west. Yili (Ili), Hotan and Kashgar were taken in 1219. Although a Mongol dynasty, the Yuan, soon sat on the Chinese throne, this did not mean the reincorporation of modern Xinjiang into the Empire. However, various Mongol tribes or the successors of a descendent of Chinggis Khan, Timur ('the lame', Tamerlane or Tamburlaine), who sacked Kashgar in the late 14th century, retained varying degrees of authority over the Uygur region.

Once the Manchus had seized the Chinese Empire and consolidated the Qing dynasty in power, they turned to subduing the rest of their Mongol allies, first of all in the regions of Nei Mongol (Inner Mongolia) and the modern-day country of Mongolia, then further to the west, where dreams of restoring the Western Regions to the Empire were reawakened. An interest in nominal Chinese suzerainty was replaced by active intervention in the 18th century, initially provoked by the rise of the Junggars (Dzungars—whose Oyriot or Oirat khanate was finally abolished in 1757), for which the north of Xinjiang is still named. In

1755 Chinese armies marched in to reclaim the Western Regions, or Eastern Turkestan, reaching as far as Kashgar, and by the 1760s military governors sat in both Yining (the chief town of Ili) and Dihua (modern Urumqi). Between then and 1863 there were reckoned to have been 42 Uygur revolts, the last resulting in the establishment of a kingdom of Kashgaria (Qashqariya) under Yaqub Beg. The independent polity, renamed Jiti Shahar in 1870, did not receive the international recognition that it sought (neither Russia, which occupied Yining in 1871–81, nor the United Kingdom, as the imperial power south of the Pamirs, favoured a new player in Central Asia) and the simultaneous occurrence of Muslim revolts throughout north-western China reinforced Qing suspicion of the Uygur uprisings. In the late 1870s the imperial armies were massed and sent into the north-west, including 'Chinese' Turkestan, to re-establish the authority of the Manchu dynasty. Kashgaria was finally extinguished, and Yaqub Beg committed suicide, in December 1877. The region acquired a new name, Xinjiang, and was formally annexed into the Empire as a province in 1884.

The region went through another period of contested authority and the eventual reassertion of central control several times after the fall of the Qing in 1911. Xinjiang initially became autonomous under local warlords who barely acknowledged the claims of republican China or even the Guomindang. Yang Zengxin held power until he was assassinated at a banquet in Urumqi in 1928, to be followed by Jin Shuren (although he had to contend with a rival warlord, Ma Chungying, who survived until 1937), whose excesses led to him being forced out of the province in 1933, only to be eventually replaced by an even more ruthless dictator, Sheng Shicai. The rule of the warlords lasted until almost the end of the Second World War, by which time the Sheng regime in Xinjiang was co-operating more with the Nationalist Government in Chongqing. During the period there were only two serious attempts to establish formal independence. In the confusion of 1933 an Islamic Republic of Turkestan (Uighuristan) was declared in Kashgar, but this had been suppressed by early 1934. Then in the aftermath of the November 1944 fall of Sheng Shicai, an ongoing rebellion of Uygurs, Mongols and Kazakhs, under Osman, a Kazakh, seized the opportunity to proclaim an East Turkestan Republic. Neither the Guomindang nor the Communists would tolerate such attempts, and the Soviet regime was not willing to antagonize its Chinese allies, but military options were limited. Eventually, the Guomindang promised real autonomy, in return for the dissolution of the new republic in Kashgaria (June 1946).

In 1948 a Muslim, Burhan, was appointed governor by the Guomindang, but it emerged that he was a supporter of the Communists, so Xinjiang fell to a new central authority. A Muslim League opposed to Chinese rule was still sufficiently strong to force negotiations on the fledgling People's Republic, but its leaders were killed in an aircraft accident on route to Beijing in August 1949, some claim in suspicious circumstances. It certainly ended effective Uygur-Muslim opposition, although Osman continued his fight from the hills until his capture and execution in 1951. Xinjiang province was by then under the authority of the North-West Administrative Council, but this was dissolved in 1954 (when Dihua was renamed Urumqi). The following year, on 1 October, the Chinese conceded an Uygur Autonomous Region in Xinjiang, although since then rising numbers of Han settlers have both consolidated central control of the region and provoked local Uygur resentment, despite the economic benefits. The region remains very sensitive, both internally and along its borders (there are disputes with India—see above—which involved armed conflict in the early 1960s, at the same time as the Chinese and the Soviet armies clashed along the Ili). Muslim unrest is severely dealt with, and the most recent troubles by those with separatist aspirations, or simply nationalist resentments, began in 1997.

Economy

The central Government has invested huge amounts of money in Xinjiang, and the development of its resources and infrastructure has made it the wealthiest region of western China. In 2000 the regional gross domestic product (GDP) was 136,436m. yuan, which was by no means a large total, but in per-head terms the measure was 7,470 yuan. The extension of the railway from Lanzhou (Gansu) to Urumqi under the Communist regime was of great benefit to the economy, and in 1999 the railway line finally reached as far as Kashi (Kashgar) in the south-west. The total length of operational railway was 2,310 km in 2000 and of roads 34,585 km (446 km of expressway and 62 km of first-class highway), but there were no navigable waterways. The illiteracy rate was the best in western China in 2000, at 5.6%.

Primary industry provided 21.1% of GDP and 57.7% of employment in 2000. The total sown area (3.4m. ha—40% for cereals), particularly given the overall extent of the territory, was not even equal to the equivalent in the municipality of Chongqing. Climatic conditions are not favourable to agriculture, although there are good stretches of pastureland, as well as desert, and the mountains can be densely forested. Generally, irrigation is essential to settlement, with the ancient system of kariz tunnels that originally maintained settlements such as Turpan now complemented by modern pumps and pipes. In 2000 the Xinjiang Uygur region harvested the largest cotton and sugar-beet crops in the country (in each case 33% of the national total), at 1.5m. metric tons and 2.7m. tons, respectively, as well as 4.0m. metric tons of wheat, 2.7m. tons of corn (maize) and 1.5m. tons of fruit (45% grapes—a famous product of the region, particularly Turpan grapes). Xinjiang also produced 11,523 tons of walnuts and 95,500 cu m of timber. Livestock numbers were dominated by sheep, of which there were more than there were people in Xinjiang and more than anywhere else in China, at 31.0m. in 2000. There were also 5.9m. goats, 3.4m. cattle and buffaloes, 1.3m. pigs, 1.3m. donkeys and 1.0m. horses, as well as 0.2m. camels. Produce included 836,000 tons of meat (45% mutton—the adherence to Islam of many of the region's inhabitants precluding the consumption of pork, the dominant meat in most of the rest of China), 782,000 tons of milk (93% from cows), 185,000 tons of poultry eggs, 66,678 tons of sheep wool (43% fine, 13% semi-fine), 3,110 tons of goat wool and 893 tons of cashmere. Fisheries product was mostly farmed and almost entirely fish, of which 59,400 tons were caught in 2000.

The secondary sector accounted for 43.0% of GDP. Construction alone provided a significant 12.1% of total GDP, mainly as a result of government development projects and the opening up of new areas of the region to contact and exploitation. The entire industrial sector only provided 13.8% of the jobs available, however. Good mineral reserves have encouraged the development of industry, but while there is some food processing and handicrafts, light industry is not very economically significant as yet. Some production figures for 2000 include 27m. tons of coal, 19m. tons of crude petroleum, 3,538m. cu m of natural gas, 397,500 tons of salt and 89,445 tons of cement, as well as 326,100 tons of sugar, 211,600 tons of beer, 717,900 tons of chemical fertilizers and 300,500 tons of plastics. There were 1,455 industrial enterprises in 2000, with a gross output value of 85,201m. yuan. The state sector was overwhelmingly dominant. Heavy industry only accounted for 48% of the enterprises, but for 81% of the output value. the 51 large enterprises accounted for 67% of value.

Tertiary industry contributed 35.9% of GDP. Transport and communications was the main contributor, followed by trade and catering, but both accounted for about 9% of GDP. Services accounted for 28.5% of employed persons. Trading volumes were large for Xinjiang in 2000 but earned a small deficit, on US $1,147.24m. in exports and $1,438.86m. in imports. Tourists are attracted by the ancient oases of the 'Silk Road', both those still bustling with the varied cultures of Xinjiang and those cities lost beneath the 'shifting sands', as well as the mountain scenery of the north or the road into Pakistan. In 2000 81% of 256,100 international-tourist visits were by foreigners, and the industry earned $95m. in foreign exchange.

Government revenue in Xinjiang during 2000 amounted to 7,907.24m. yuan, the largest contributor being the operations tax (28%). Expenditure was 19,095.29m. yuan, the main single destination being education (16%). The region only attracted and actually used US $19.11m. in foreign direct investment in the same year.

Directory

Chairman of the Autonomous Regional Government (Governor) of Xinjiang Uygur: ABULAHAT ABDURIXIT; Office of the Autonomous Regional People's Government, Urumuqi.

Secretary of the Xinjiang Uygur Autonomous Regional Committee of the Chinese Communist Party: WANG LEQUAN; Office of the Secretary, CCP Secretariat, Urumuqi.

Chairman of the Standing Committee of the People's Congress of Xinjiang Uygur: AMUDUN NIYAZ; Office of the Chairman, Congress Secretariat, Urumuqi.

Chairman of the Xinjiang Uygur Autonomous Regional Committee of the Chinese People's Political Consultative Conference: JANABIL; Office of the Chairman, CPPCC Secretariat, Urumuqi.

Head of the Bayangol Mongol Autonomous Prefecture: BA DAI.

Head of the Bortala Mongol Autonomous Prefecture: QIAO JIFU.

Head of the Changji Hui Autonomous Prefecture: LI FUYUAN.

Party Committee Secretary of the Ili Kazakh Autonomous Prefecture: LIN TIANXI.

Head of the Kizil Kergez (Kizilsu Khalkhas) Autonomous Prefecture: MAIMAITI AISHAN.

Xizang
(Tibet)

The Autonomous Region of Xizang (Tibet) lies in the south-west of the People's Republic of China, occupying the bulk of the Tibet–Qinghai plateau, except in the north-west, where Qinghai province intrudes into an inward-curving north-western frontier, and in the west, where Sichuan province occupies the highlands above the Sichuan basin. There is also a short border in the south-west with Yunnan province, which also extends into the foothills of the high plateau. At the other end of the plateau, the 'roof of the world', there is a northern border with the Xinjiang Uygur autonomous region, along the Altun Shan, which, at the western end includes a pocket of territory, Aksai Chin, that India claims is illegally occupied. In fact most of the border with India is disputed, although, in practice, it generally follows the 'McMahon Line' along the crest of the Great Himalaya suggested by the British in the 1910s (but never accepted by a Chinese Government). India lies to the west and south-west, as well as in the south-east. The rest of the international frontier between is not generally disputed. Here the kingdoms of Nepal and Bhutan lie along the line of the Himalayas, the former curving gently around from being in the south-west to the south, the latter, after another short border with India (which here incorporated its princely protectorate of Sikkim in 1975), to the south. The final part of the southern border is a short stretch with Myanmar (Burma) between India and Yunnan province. The entire region occupies 1,221,600 sq km (471,540 sq miles) of some of the bleakest territory on earth, making Xizang the second-largest unit in the People's Republic, and yet the one with fewest inhabitants.

Xizang consists of a vast, arid plateau folded into the world's highest mountain ranges and riven by deep valleys. The world's highest mountain, Qomolangma Feng (Chomo Langma in Tibetan, Sagarmatha in Nepal,

Mt Everest in English) rises to an official height of 8,848 m (29,040 feet). Xizang also includes the deepest gorge, a 370-km (230-mile) stretch, only 74–200 m wide, but 5,382 m deep, which the Yarlung Zangbo (India's River Brahmaputra) plunges through. This river, the valley of which is crucial to providing a productive area for human settlement, flows eastwards along the line of the mountains, before turning south into India in the far south-east. Apart from this south-eastern region, between the Nyainqentanglha range and the Great Himalaya to the south, the two other main geographical areas of Xizang are the crowded high mountains and deep valleys of the east and the main part of the territory, the northern plateau. The latter is bounded on the north by the Altun Shan along the Xinjiang border and the Tanggula Shan along the Qinghai border. There are numerous lakes, most of them salty, strewn across this plateauland, including one that claims to be China's second largest saline lake, Nam Co, to the north of Lhasa. In the east, where the land begins to descend, the mountain ranges begin to turn southwards from their east–west alignment. Here are the upper reaches of some of the great rivers of eastern Asia. The Chang Jiang (River Yangzi) flows out of Qinghai and forms the eastern border with Sichuan, known here as the Jinsha Jiang. Proceeding west, the Lancang Jiang becomes the great River Mekong of South-East Asia, while the Nu Jiang runs into the Salween. The average height is over 4,000 m above sea level, but altitudes vary enormously, as does the climate. Average annual rainfall for the region ranges from 60 mm to 1,000 mm (2–39 inches), with more falling in the south-east, and virtually none (certainly as rain) in the north or in the heights. Most precipitation is in the summer. the milder conditions prevalent around Lhasa can be indicated by data for 2000: annual rainfall was 530 mm; and average monthly temperatures ranged from the coldest in January (-0.5°C or 31.1°F) to the warmest in July (17.2°C or 63.0°F).

The total population on 1 November 2000 was a mere 2.62m., giving a population density of only 2 persons per sq km, the lowest density in China. However, the population had grown by 19.3% between 1990 and 2000 (an average of 1.72% per year), mainly owing to immigration. Xizang is the only region of China in which Han Chinese form a minority (5.9%, according to the results of the 2000 census). The largest group (over nine-10ths of the population) consists of the ethnic Tibetans (Xizangzu), although those living in the autonomous region comprise less than one-half of China's total Tibetan population. There are a few other small ethnic communities, such as some Chinese Muslims, the Hui, who came to Tibet under the Qing and mainly live in the cities, or equally small indigenous groups. The 7,000 or so Monbas form an ancient native group, who speak Tibetan and live in the south, while the 2,000-strong Lhoba, in the south-east, are noted for still practising a primitive, animist religion. The main religion of Xizang, however, is the lamaist version of Tantric Buddhism evolved by and adhered to by the Tibetans. There are numerous sects, the heads of which (lamas) are now sometimes based outside Xizang. Thus, the traditional head of Tibetan Buddhism is the Dalai Lama, who now lives in India, but whose office once had supreme ecclesiastical and political authority, although the Panchen Lama is considered to have superior spiritual standing.

Only 18.9% of the population was classified as urban in 2000, the lowest percentage for any region in China. The capital and largest city is Lhasa, in the south-centre of Xizang, above the central Yarlung Zangbo valley. Upriver, in the great valley, is the city of Xigaze (Shigatse), the second city of the region. Qamdo, to the north of eastern Xizang, on the Lancang, is a well known town, but there are few urban centres of any size. Most settlement is concentrated in the south-east. For administrative purposes Xizang consists of seven prefectures, one of which is a city, and 72 counties, again with only one a city. The autonomous region has fewer cities than any other region or any province of China—even the Chongqing municipality has four.

History

The Tibetans (Xizangzu) inhabited the high mountains of the great plateau and had become the dominant peoples long before the arrival of Buddhism in the third century, which they began to fuse with their native Bon religious tradition to evolve a unique form of Tantric Buddhism dominated by lamas, holy monk-leaders. The recorded history of the first major Tibetan state (Bod to the Tibetans, Tufan to the Chinese) begins in the seventh century, with the formation of a united kingdom under Songtsen Gampo (who reigned 618–41), who established a capital at Lhasa, patronized Buddhism and laid the rules for Tibetan statecraft by balancing the interests of the regional great powers through his marriage to two princesses, Wen Cheng of China and Tritsun of Nepal. However, the political interests of Tibet in this expansionary phase of its history were focused to the more accessible north and east. The armies of this hardy, mountain people raided into Yunnan and Sichuan, and seized Kashgar (Kashi, in Xinjiang) for a time at the end of the seventh century, to the consternation of the Tang armies. The Tibetans continued to contest the control of the 'Silk Road' with the Chinese and the increasingly powerful Turkic (Uygur) and Arab powers to the north, taking advantage of the defeat of the Tang by the latter in the mid-eighth century. Towards the end of that century, with Chinese power in Central Asia eliminated, the Tibetans occupied the end of the Silk Road at Dunhuang (now in north-western Gansu). Moreover, in 1763 they penetrated as far into China as the imperial capital of Changan (now Xian, Shaanxi) and sacked the city. This period came to an end only with the assassination of the king and the disintegration of the state into feuding principalities, finally confining the Tibetan armies to their own high plateau.

From the ninth century, therefore, the great monastic orders began to gain increasing influence, acquiring power and wealth to rival the secular princes. By the 13th century the land-owning orders had established their civil as well as religious authority over the Tibetans, although rivalries continued, whether between different orders, such as the Kagya and the Sakya or, later, the Geluk pa ('Yellow Hat' sect) and the Karma pa ('Red Hat' sect), or between the ancient provinces of U (based in Lhasa) and Tsang (based in Shigatse—Xigaze). Meanwhile, an important new development had taken place in the 13th century, when the Mongols were conquering all the lands to the north. A visit by a Sakya scholar to Khubilai (Kublai) Khan in 1247 resulted in the close association of Phagspa and the Great Khan of the Mongols (who adopted the Tibetan form of Buddhism), in the prototype of the 'priest–patron' relationship that was to characterize Mongol (and, to an extent, Chinese) relations with Tibet thereafter. The concept of a Mongol Buddhist theocracy certainly secured the ascendancy of the Sakya in Tibet, although physical invasion as in 1268 became less likely later, and the relationship of priestly services in exchange for force of arms became a given. However, Tibet itself descended into another period of internal strife, with the Yellow Hats acting against the Red Hats and their support for the kings based in Tsang. The Yellow Hats slowly prevailed, certainly enough to be encouraged by the Ming in the 15th century and the dominant Mongol tribe in the 16th century (when the political protector awarded the Yellow Hat leader the title of Dalai Lama—Ocean of Wisdom—in 1587). In 1642 the Great Fifth Dalai Lama, using the 'priest–patron' principle, appealed to the Khoshote (Kochot) khanate of the leading western Mongol tribe for final assistance against the Karma pa. Gusri Khan invaded and established the supremacy of the Dalai Lamas, but took a royal title for himself, as well as the role of protector of Tibet. His house held this until 1717, when a rival people disrupted the arrangement, provoked the Chinese and Qing armies invaded Tibet in 1720, establishing the suzerainty of the Manchus (who, as close allies of the Mongols, had enjoyed considerable status in Tibet since the start of the Qing adventure into imperial China). In 1723 an amban was first appointed as the Qing envoy to Lhasa and, although he enjoyed no formal authority, his influence was profound, particularly during the long regencies of a succession of junior Dalai Lamas. In 1751 the obsolete office of king was finally abolished.

Although Qing power had waned during the 19th century, it reacted forcibly to a British attempt to contact Tibet at the beginning of the 20th century. Chinese suzerainty had, hitherto, been unchallenged in the region, or certainly not by the hated European powers, and the imperial court resolved to turn its suzerainty into sovereignty. This would also resolve the ambiguity of a wider Tibetan presence in the south-west than was suitable for Chinese provincial borders. Eventually, troops under Zhao Erfeng were sent to crush Tibetan dissent in western Sichuan (which province had absorbed much of the eastern Tibetan province of Kham) and north-western Yunnan in 1905. Zhao was appointed the imperial resident in Lhasa in 1908, and his brother was made governor of Sichuan, but further attempts to consolidate Chinese authority in Tibet were ended by the fall of the Qing themselves in 1911 (Zhao was murdered by revolutionaries). Moreover, factious warlords in Sichuan meant there was no clear focus for Chinese influence on Tibet, although the Guomindang had enough authority in the south-west to force the creation of a new province, Xigang (Sikang), in western Sichuan and eastern Tibet in the late 1930s. For, by this time, Tibet had become effectively independent—a Kingdom of Tibet was proclaimed on 8 March 1913, and at the Convention of Simla (Shimla, in India) the following year the United Kingdom recognized all of Tibet, Inner and Outer (although the Tibetans themselves lacked the strength to pursue their wider territorial claims), as a state, but one over which China had suzerainty, though not sovereignty.

The victorious side in the Civil War in China, the Communists, from 1949 had the leisure to turn to outstanding 'imperial' issues. While an independent socialist state in Mongolia could be tolerated (particularly in a region otherwise dominated by another ally, the USSR), the presence of a feudal, serf-based theocracy with few democratic credentials in such a strategic location on territory long considered to be a Chinese sphere of influence, could not. On 7 October 1950 the Chinese occupied Tibet, with the formal annexation announced on 23 May 1951. In 1955 the now redundant Xigang was again split, between Sichuan and Tibet. However, resentment of the Chinese and fears for the safety of the Dalai Lama, still a nominal 'head of state', provoked unrest in Lhasa, and the ensuing trouble prompted the Dalai Lama to seek refuge in India (which, eventually, permitted him asylum), to which he fled in March 1959. India's decision to grant a home to the Dalai Lama (who is still based there) no doubt contributed to the series of border disputes and incursions by the Chinese army all along the common frontier from 1959 into the early 1960s. Meanwhile, the Panchen Lama (traditionally based at Shigatse) succeeded as the 'head of state' until the creation of the Xizang (Tibet) autonomous region on 9 September 1965. Opposition continues (although armed insurrection ended in the mid-1970s), despite the vast amount of investment (and, claim critics, Han settlers) the Chinese Government has put in to the region. A sense of oppression by many Tibetans was, no doubt, exacerbated by the extremes of the 1966–76 Cultural Revolution, which did great damage to Tibetan monuments and institutions, and offsetting any benefits of social, educational or economic reform. The increased profile in Western nations of the Dalai Lama in the latter decades of the 20th century brought greater international popular, if not governmental, attention to the Tibetan separatist cause.

Economy

The regional economy of Xizang (Tibet), like the terrain, is best described with superlatives. Although government spending ensures that, in per-head terms, gross domestic product (GDP) is far from being the lowest in China (4,559 yuan in 2000—the fifth lowest GDP per head), poverty is widespread and the total GDP, at 11,746m. yuan, is the lowest. However, many of the people continue to practise the traditional way of life, which is often at a subsistence level, and this is difficult to account for in describing the formal economy. Development has certainly proceeded rapidly since the 1950s, with one of the great early achievements, although expensive in lives, being the hewing of the great, linking highways from Lhasa to Chengdu (Sichuan) and to Xining (Qinghai), and third, from Xizang into Xinjiang (via the disputed Aksai Chin plateau). In 2000 highways totalled 22,503 km, but there were no expressways or first-class highways. There were also no railways or waterways. There is potential for hydroelectric schemes, but a limited local demand for power, and in 2000 Xizang produced only 661m. kWh (84% hydroelectrically generated). With over one-third of the rural population (the vast majority) illiterate, it is no surprise to find the highest overall illiteracy rate in China—32.5% in 2000 (down from 44.4% in 1990).

The primary sector contributed 30.9% to GDP in 2000. This was the highest proportion save in Hainan, but the overall size of the sector in Xizang is less than one-fifth of the island province's, although the proportion of those employed in the primary sector is unquestionably the highest in China, at 73.8%. The total area sown with farm crops is only 231,100 ha (83% for cereals, mainly wheat and millets), the smallest area in the country. Cereal production in 2000 was 0.9m. metric tons (0.3m. tons of wheat), and some rapeseed grown commercially came to 40,000 tons. There were also 7,418 tons of fruit (mainly apples) picked and 1,829 tons of walnuts gathered. Forestlands did produce some timber (160,000 cu m). Animal husbandry is a much more important activity than arable farming, and Xizang boasted far larger ovine (10.7m. in 2000), caprine (5.9m.) and bovine (5.3m.—including yaks) populations than human. In 2000 there were also 385,000 horses, 235,000 pigs and 125,000 donkeys. Livestock products included 149,000 tons of meat (57% beef and 38% mutton), 204,000 tons of milk, 7,947 tons of sheep wool (most of it semi-fine), 1,834 tons of goat wool and 682 tons of cashmere. Also in 2000 1,700 tons of fish were farmed and about 100 tons caught in the wild.

Industry provided 23.2% of GDP (a smaller proportion was only achieved in Hainan) in 2000. Moreover, construction accounts for almost two-thirds of this (14.5% of total GDP in 2000). Total employment in the sector is only 5.8% of the total. Cement was obviously one useful industrial product (493,200 metric tons in 2000), but most other manufactures tended to be small-scale, for local use or handicrafts. Xizang had the fewest industrial enterprises in the country, 362 in 2000, with a gross output value of only 1,643m. yuan, about one-12th the size of the next smallest in value. Heavy industry consisted of 200 enterprises (64% of the value), but there were no large enterprises and only four medium-sized ones. Small enterprises, by default, accounted for 74% of the output value.

The tertiary sector accounted for 45.9% of GDP. Government services alone provided 12.2% of total GDP and trade and catering for 12.0%. Employment in services was only for 20.4% of all those in work. Xizang exported goods to the value of US $109.02m. in 2000, but imported only $39.90m. Tourism earned $52m. in foreign exchange in 2000. In that year there had been 150,000 international-tourist visits (an exceptionally high 91% by foreigners), as people came to visit the dramatic scenery and unique culture of the Tibetans, and monuments such as the Potala Palace of the Dalai Lamas in the medieval city of Lhasa, or the temples and monasteries there, in Xigaze (Shigatse) and throughout the region.

Government raises the least revenue from any region in Xizang, at 538.48m. yuan in 2000 (36% from the operations tax, 30% from the income tax on enterprises and only 15% from value added tax—this last indicates the limited nature of the cash economy). Expenditure was more than 10 times as much, at 5,996.93m. yuan (24% capital construction and government administration 18%). There is no foreign investment in Xizang.

Directory

Chairman of the Autonomous Regional Government (Governor) of Xizang: LEGQOG; Office of the Autonomous Regional People's Government, Lhasa.

Secretary of the Xizang Autonomous Regional Committee of the Chinese Communist Party: GUO JINLONG; Office of the Secretary, CCP Secretariat, Lhasa.

Chairman of the Standing Committee of the People's Congress of Xizang: RAIDI; Office of the Chairman, Congress Secretariat, Lhasa.

Chairman of the Xizang Autonomous Regional Committee of the Chinese People's Political Consultative Conference: PAGBALHA GELEG NAMGYAI; Office of the Chairman, CPPCC Secretariat, Lhasa.

Xizang (Tibet) Government Office: Central Gyinzhu Road, Lhasa.

MUNICIPALITIES

Beijing

The Municipality of Beijing (Peking or Pekin, known as Beiping or Peiping in 1928–49) has been one of the special municipalities, a municipality under the direct authority of the central Government, since the formation of the People's Republic of China in 1949, of which it was declared the capital. The region lies in northern China, inland from the Bo Hai (Gulf of Bohai), and mainly surrounded by Hebei province. Hebei, therefore, lies to the south, the north-west and the north-east. Another special municipality, Tianjin (which was part of Hebei until 1967), lies to the south-east, between Beijing and sea. Even this border is interrupted by an enclave of Hebei, which lies between the two municipalities. The territory of Beijing covers 16,800 sq km (6,485 sq miles), which is just over one-half the size of Belgium (or a little more than the size of Connecticut, USA).

The Beijing region lies on the north-eastern edge of the North China Plain, reaching up to the Great Wall and the first heights of the Mongolian plateau. The territory has highlands the length of the north-western border and in the north-east. The city of Beijing lies at the centre of the southern part of the region. It has a temperate monsoon climate, but suffers from seasonal extremes. In 2000 the total rainfall was 371 mm (14 inches) and the average temperatures -6.4°C (20.5°F) in January and 29.6°C (85.3°F) in July.

According to the census of 2000 the Beijing region had a population of 13.82m., a total that had increased by a dramatic 27.7% since 1990, mainly owing to immigration. At the same time minority nationalities accounted for 4.3% of that population, mainly from the long-established Manchu (Man or Manzu) and Hui (Chinese Muslims) communities, who are widespread throughout China. Both these groups use standard Chinese as their language, so Putonghua (Mandarin or Northern Chinese), the official language based on the Beijing dialect, is generally used.

The census classed 77.5% of the population as urban in 2000. Beijing, the national capital, is the only city of the territory and had an urban population of 7.61m. in 2000 (making it the second largest city, after Shanghai, in China). The municipality encompasses five counties.

History

The Beijing region formed the heart of the state of Yan in the Zhou period, although after the Qin established the Empire in the third century BC the name became merely a relic from the past. It was used in the name the Liao dynasty gave to their southern capital, Yanjing ('capital of Yan'), established by the Khitans in the 10th century. The Khitans were merely one of the northern dynasties from peoples who had passed south of the Great Wall after the fall of the Tang. They were succeeded by the Jurchens in the 12th century and the Mongols in the 13th century. The latter, under Chinggis (Genghis) Khan, destroyed Yanjing utterly in 1215, but from the ashes emerged the modern city. Chinggis' son, Khubilai (Kublai) Khan, who completed the conquest of China and presided over the official start of his Yuan dynasty in 1279, established a new capital here between the Chinese heartlands and his own Mongol steppes. At what was called Dadu he ordered the construction of Khanbaligh (called Cambaluc by the Venetian traveller from Italy, Marco Polo) from 1267 and it was completed in 1292. From here the Yuan dynasty contributed to its own decline, to be displaced in 1368 by the rebel, Zhu Yuanzhang, who founded the Ming dynasty as the Hongwu emperor. He made his capital at Nanjing ('southern capital'), now in Jiangsu, and renamed the northern city, which still served as a secondary seat, Beiping ('northern peace'). However, a renewed Mongol threat prompted the Yongle emperor (whose title before he seized the throne was Prince of Yan) to move the court to what he renamed Beijing ('northern capital'—Peking) in 1421. The city was rebuilt around the imperial palace, the Forbidden City, which was then home to 24 Ming and Qing emperors. For it remained the imperial capital, being taken over by the Manchu dynasty when they removed the rebels who had caused the suicide of the last Ming emperor. The Qing went on to conquer China.

As the seat of the weakening Qing Government Beijing experienced the upheavals of the last century of imperial rule, being menaced by the Europeans during the Arrow or Second Opium War (resulting in the Beijing Conventions) and enmeshed in the Boxer Rebellion. In June 1900, at the instigation of the Qing authorities, the xenophobic Boxers laid siege to the foreign legations in the city, prompting relief by an international expeditionary force in August, which sent the imperial court fleeing to Xian (Shaanxi) until another humiliating peace was arranged. As revolution swept China in 1911 and the Qing dynasty was rejected in favour of a republic, government fell into the hands of Yuan Shikai, who supervised the abdication of the junior Xuantong emperor, Qing Puyi, early in 1912. Maintenance of his title and a pension were allowed him, but his authority was limited to the Forbidden City compound, and he outlasted Yuan Shikai and his proposal to establish himself as the Hongxian emperor. In 1917 a group of warlords briefly restored the Great Qing

Empire, during July, but in 1924 another warlord obliged Puyi to leave the Forbidden City (which became a museum). (The last gasp of the Qing dynasty involved Puyi's elevation to lead the Japanese protectorate in Manchuria, which was later raised to an empire, with Puyi as the Kangde emperor.) Meanwhile, the Guomindang's Republic under Chiang Kai-shek established its primacy over the warlords and, in 1928, when the capital was located in Nanjing, Beijing was again renamed Beiping. In July 1937 it was the site of an incident, at the Marco Polo Bridge, in the south-west of the city, that was concocted by the Japanese forces in China to precipitate an all-out invasion. The city was occupied by the Japanese until their surrender in 1945.

In January 1949, after three massive confrontations with the Guomindang forces, the Communists took Beiping and began their final assault against Nationalist positions throughout China. On 1 October Mao Zedong proclaimed the People's Republic in Tiananmen Square and Beijing had its name and its status as the national capital restored, becoming a special municipality under direct central control. More commonly known in Western countries as Peking (the Wade-Giles transliteration of the name) until the 1980s, it has remained the unchallenged centre of government ever since. Tiananmen Square remained a focal point for the expression of political dissent, however, most notably when civil unrest by reformist students led to an occupation of the square in May–June 1989, which was forcibly ended amid international protests.

Economy

Beijing is, above all, the seat of government, and, therefore, has attractions for other services, but the region has also developed a good industrial base. This has brought it considerable prosperity, which, as measured by gross domestic product (GDP), reached 247,876m. yuan in 2000, or 22,460 yuan per head (the highest figure in China after Shanghai). The city is helped by being the centre of a vast transport network, and has the highest concentration of roads in the country, as well as a lot of railway relative to its size. The total length of roads in the Beijing region in 2000 amounted to 13,597 km (267 km of expressway and 298 km of first-class highway), and there were 1,141 km of railways. There are no figures for navigable inland waterways, despite Beijing's original wealth having been aided by the extension of the Da Yunhe (Grand Canal) north to the capital in the 13th century (the northern section fell into disrepair and disuse from the mid-19th century). The region produced 14,526m. kWh of electricity in 2000 and imported the rest of its needs. Beijing is also a major educational and scientific centre, supported by good schools in the capital, and the illiteracy rate was only 4.2% of the adult population in 2000.

Although there is some agricultural land (0.5m. ha of sown land in 2000, 61% for cereals and 24% for vegetables), the primary sector is not an important contributor to the regional economy, providing only 3.6% to GDP and 11.7% of jobs in 2000. The region grew only 1.4m. metric tons of cereals (mainly wheat and maize) in 2000, as well as some fruit (0.6m. tons) and 8,816 tons of walnuts. Livestock included 2.5m. pigs, 0.7m. sheep, 0.5m. goats and 0.2m. cattle. Animal husbandry and fishing were also negligible producers compared to the scale of the demand they were meant to be feeding locally.

Industry accounted for 38.1% of GDP (construction alone for 8.0%) and 32.4% of jobs in 2000. Beijing produced, for example, 1.8m. metric tons of beer in 2000, 7.8m. tons of pig iron, 8.0m. tons of steel, 7.0m. tons of steel products, 8.3m. tons of cement, 4.3m. tons of plate glass, 137,100 motor vehicles 237m. integrated circuits and more micro-computers than anywhere else in China, at 2.6m. units. There were 4,572 industrial enterprises in Beijing in 2000, with a gross output value of 256,536m. yuan, in 2000. Most were in the state sector, but a large number also had foreign investment. Heavy industry dominated, with just 51% of the enterprises, but 76% of output value. The 242 large enterprises provided 42% of output value.

The tertiary sector accounted for 58.3% of GDP in 2000, more than anywhere else in China. Finance and insurance alone contributed 15.3% of total GDP, trade and catering 8.8%, social services 7.7% and transport and communications 7.7%. Work in the services sector accounted for 55.9% of employed persons in that year (a higher figure than anywhere else in China). The balance of trade in a consumer city was, predictably, not in surplus, with US $7,667.23m. in exports dwarfed by $16,576.55m. in imports. However, one of the 'invisibles' countering this deficit in the commodity trade was tourism, which earned $2,768m. in the same year. The region had attracted more international-tourist visits than anywhere in China but Guangdong, with 2.8m. (2.4m. by foreigners).

Government revenue was high in Beijing, 34,499.68m. yuan being raised in 2000, of which by far the most came from the operations tax (43%). The final government statement for the same year put expenditure at 44,299.69m. yuan, of which the biggest single item was education (14%), followed by capital construction (13%). Foreign direct investment totalled US $1,683.68m. in 2000.

Directory

Governor: LIU QI; Office of the Beijing Municipal People's Government, Beijing.

Secretary of the Beijing Municipal Committee of the Chinese Communist Party: JIA QINGLIN.

Chairman of the Standing Committee of the People's Congress of Beijing: YU JUNBO; Office of the Chairman of the Standing Committee, Municipal People's Congress, Beijing.

Chairman of the Beijing Municipal Committee of the Chinese People's Political Consultative Conference: CHEN GUANGWEN; Office of the Chairman, CPPCC Beijing Secretariat, Beijing.

Chongqing

The Municipality of Chongqing (Chungking) is the gateway to south-western China, lying near the centre of the country, surrounded by six provinces. It was formed (in 1997) from south-eastern Sichuan, a long strip of territory against the border, so that province still neighbours Chongqing to the north-west. In the south-west, where Sichuan continues, Chongqing is blocked by an upthrust extension of Yunnan, which forms a short border through which the Chang Jiang (Yangzi River—hitherto along its course known as the Jinsha) enters the municipality. The south-eastern border consists of three parts: southwards from Chongqing city (which is in the centre of the main southern block of the territory), is Guizhou; mid-way along the border an extension of the municipality pushes south-west (between Guizhou to the south-west and Hubei to the north-east) to meet Hunan; and Hubei is at the northern end of this long south-eastern frontier, as well as to the east. Finally, in the very north, is Shaanxi. With an area of 82,400 sq km (31,810 sq miles), Chongqing forms the largest municipal area in the world, approaching continental Portugal in its extent.

Chongqing, which means 'double celebration' (an adaptation of an original meaning, 'central capital'), is also known as Yu. It is some 470 km (290 miles) from east to west and 450 km north to south, but is generally aligned along the Chang Jiang in a south-west to north-east direction. It forms the 'pit' of the Sichuan basin, lying across the south-eastern side, where the great river of China flows up out of the mountains and then turns more eastwards into Hubei. It is here, downstream of Chongqing, that the great lake behind the dam near Yinchuan (Hubei) will flood a vast tract of the territory of the municipality, including the famously beautiful stretch of the river through the Three Gorges.

These begin in the highlands that dominate the north-east of the territory. The highlands also run the length of the south-eastern border. The main river, apart from the Chang Jiang, is the Jialing—it is at the confluence of these two waterways that Chongqing city is built. The climate makes the winters long, damp and foggy, but in summer the city is known as one of the 'three furnaces' of China (with Wuhan and Nanjing), temperatures rise towards 100°F (38°C) in July–August. In 2000 the average January temperature 7.7°C (45.9°F) and the average for July was 28.5°C (83.3°F). The total rainfall that year was 1,011 mm (39 inches).

The total population was 30.90m. in 2000, the density of it, on average, 377 persons per sq km. The municipality contains some hill territory, which shelters representatives of China's minority nationalities (6.4% of the total population in 2000), among them the Miao, the Yi and the Qiang, as well as some Hui in the cities.

Although it is constituted as a municipality, Chongqing's three counties include large rural tracts, and the urbanized population was only 33.1% of the total in 2000. The main city is Chongqing, but Wanxian, downstream to the north-east, is also sizeable. Chongqing has 6.6m. living in the city itself, but its wider area officially makes it the largest city in China (although it is more characteristic of a small province than an urban area). The municipality consists of 26 counties, including four cities.

History

Recent archaeological findings have placed hominids in this part of the Chang Jiang (River Yangzi) valley over 2m. years ago, a substantial amount of time before previously thought. This was the cradle of the Yangzi and Bayu cultures. Urban civilization began over 3,000 years ago, and the first recorded polity was the Ba kingdom. It was subjugated to the 'central state' of Qin in the fourth century BC, at the same time as its western neighbour in the Sichuan basin, Shu, was conquered by the predecessors of the First Emperor. An important town in the Sichuan region, it went by various names (Jiangzhou, Bazhou and Yuzhou) before being named Chongqing in AD 1189, when a Song prince, Zhao Dun, learned here of his accession to the imperial throne (as Guangzong).

Effectively the port of the Sichuan basin, Chongqing remained an important city throughout the imperial period, and strategic for anyone holding (or recapturing) Sichuan. Thus, the 10th-century Former Shu realm succumbed once the Song navy had control of the river. As the main centre furthest up the Chang Jiang, Chongqing was conceded as a treaty port in 1890, although not many foreigners penetrated this far into the interior. Development of a modern economy came under the Guomindang, with a desultory industrialization programme begun in 1928 being injected with urgency by the advent of the Japanese invasion (1937) and the start of the Second World War. The republican Government was obliged to flee Nanjing (Jiangsu), the capital since 1928, and it decided, like so many before, to seek refuge in Sichuan. Chongqing was settled on as the site of the temporary capital and, for the first and only time, became the seat of a national Government. The Guomindang leadership arrived at the very end of 1937 and Chongqing became the official centre of the war effort against the Japanese, with the Communist army (in an anti-Japanese alliance with the

Guomindang since 1936) represented in the city. Chongqing suffered severe bombing from Japanese aircraft throughout the War, but developed a thriving industrial base and became the centre of an improved transport network across some of the remoter parts of China, which 'rump' territories the Nationalist Government was forced to rely upon. Chongqing has continued this role at the centre of south-western industrialization and commerce ever since. When the USA joined the War Chongqing became the centre of the Allied war effort in China and the Indo-Burmese theatre to the south. The city was also the scene of the unsuccessful peace negotiations between the Guomindang and the Communists after the Second World War and, when they failed, was forced to remain as the republican capital for the duration of the Civil War that followed. Finally, early in 1949 the Guomindang realized the inevitability of defeat, gathered some 2m. soldiers and officials and their dependents together and fled Chongqing to the island refuge of Taiwan.

Under the Communists Chongqing continued to power the development of the south-west of the country. Although originally a special municipality, it was merged back into Sichuan in 1954, but its growing strength and self-confidence demanded the restoration of special status from the Government. With its importance, and population, likely to grow even more upon the completion of the controversial Three Gorges Project (scheduled for 2009), which will improve the navigation of the upper reaches of the Chang Jiang, fuel increased development with massive hydroelectric provision and site Chongqing at the head of a 550-km lake (the world's largest artificial reservoir), eventually, on 14 March 1997 Chongqing was separated from Sichuan and made a municipality directly under the authority of the central Government. (The territory's size, relative to the other special municipalities, leads some sources to refer to it, erroneously, as a province).

Economy

Chongqing is the industrial and commercial centre of south-western China, and its role is only likely to grow with the completion of the Three Gorges Project in the early years of the 21st century. In 2000 the special municipality had a gross domestic product (GDP) of 158,934m. yuan or 5,157 yuan per head. At the centre of the wider region's transport networks, Chongqing enjoyed a developed infrastructure, with 29,252 km of highway (199 km of expressway and 123 km of first-class roads), 598 km of operational railways and 2,324 km of navigable waterways. The ports of Chongqing and Fuling were among the busiest on the upper and middle reaches of the Chang Jiang (River Yangzi). The municipality also enjoys good air links with the rest of China. It produced 16,790m. kWh of electricity in 2000 (23% by hydroelectric generation). The illiteracy rate was 7.0% in 2000, the lowest figure in the south-west after Xinjiang.

The primary sector accounted for 17.8% of GDP and 56.5% of employment in 2000. the total sown area was 3.6m. ha in 2000 (one-half covered with cereals), which produced 5.3m. metric tons of rice, 2.0m. tons of corn (maize), 1.0m. tons of wheat and 2.4m. tons of root vegetables. The region also produced 0.8m. tons of fruit (mainly citrus), 39,478 tons of tung-oil seeds, 29,098 tons of mulberry-silkworm cocoons and 14,256 tons of tea. Livestock numbers in 2000 included 16.1m. pigs, 1.6m. cattle and buffaloes and

1.6m. goats, contributing to production that included 1.5m. tons of meat (86% pork), 56,000 tons of cows' milk and 279,000 tons of poultry eggs. Aquatic production, mainly from farms, amounted to some 2.0m. tons of fish.

The secondary sector contributed 41.4% to GDP (including the 8.2% of total GDP provided by construction), and employed 15.3% of those in work. Heavy industry dominates, exploiting the natural resources of the surrounding provinces, but for similar reasons food processing and beverages also figure prominently. There were 2,040 industrial enterprises in 2000, with a gross output value of 96,232m. yuan. Heavy industry accounted for 53% of the enterprises and 66% of the value. The 136 large enterprises generated 52% of the output value and the 245 medium-sized ones 18%.

The tertiary sector was strongly developed and accounted for 40.8% of GDP in 2000, the largest activity by far being transport and communications (9.7%). The whole sector employed 28.1% of those with jobs. Exports earned Chongqing US $1,060.48m. in 2000, more than offsetting the $790.59m. spent on imports. The region earned a further $138m. in foreign exchange from tourism, with many people wanting to cruise through the scenic Three Gorges on the Chang Jiang before the famous route was flooded. The 266,100 international tourists (measured in person-times) that year included 192,290 foreigners.

Government revenue in Chongqing was 8,724.42m. yuan in 2000, 28% coming from the operations tax and 17% from value added tax. Expenditure totalled 18,764.33m., the main destinations being capital construction (14%—important in a still expanding economy) and education (14%). Foreign direct investment actually used increased slightly in 2000 to US $244.36m., with an additional $1.43m. in other foreign investment.

Directory

Mayor: BAO XUDING; Office of the Chongqing Municipal People's Government, Chongqing.

Secretary of the Chongqing Municipal Committee of the Chinese Communist Party: HE GUOQIANG.

Chairman of the Standing Committee of the People's Congress of Chongqing: WANG YUNLONG; Office of the Chairman of the Standing Committee, Municipal People's Congress, Chongqing.

Chairman of the Chongqing Municipal Committee of the Chinese People's Political Consultative Conference: ZHANG WENBIN; Office of the Chairman, CPPCC Chongqing Secretariat, Chongqing.

Shanghai

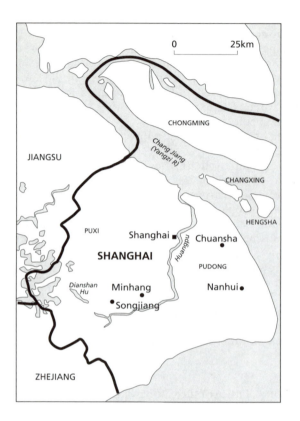

The Municipality of Shanghai lies in eastern China, on the East China Sea, at the mouth of the Chang Jiang (River Yangzi). It lies at the very south-eastern tip of Jiangsu province, from which it was formed, but there is also a short border with Zhejiang in the south-west. The region is the smallest within the People's Republic, covering only 6,200 sq km (2,390 sq miles).

The Shanghai ('on the sea') region lies on the promontory to the south of the Chang Jiang and north of the Hangzhou bay, the city itself growing up along the Huangpu Jiang, which flows into the Chang Jiang just before it joins the sea. The territory includes some islands in the mouth of China's greatest river, the largest and most northerly being Chongming Dao, which is China's largest alluvial island, at 1,083 sq km. Like the rest of the territory it is low and flat. The climate of Shanghai is subtropical and subject to the monsoons. In 2000 it received rainfall of 1,332 mm (52 inches) and had its lowest average temperature in February (4.3°C or 39.7°F), unusually, and its highest in July (29.1°C or 84.4°F).

The total population at the time of the national census in 2000 was 16.74m. In such a small area, however, the municipality achieved the greatest density of population in the People's Republic, with 2,700 persons per sq km, although this was far greater in the city area itself. The population had grown by 25.5% since 1990, its new growth attracting significant levels of immigration. It was over-whelmingly inhabited by the Han Chinese (99.4%), although linguistic variation alleviates the official ethnic uniformity—Mandarin (Putonghua) is the official language, but many of the local population speak a variety of the Wu dialect prevalent in Jiangsu and Zhejiang (it is sometimes called Shanghaiese).

In 2000 88.3% were recorded as being resident in the urban areas of Shanghai. The city of Shanghai itself had a population of 9.86m., making it the largest city in China. The region is made up of three counties.

History

Shanghai lies in the 'water lands' of southern Jiangsu and northern Zhejiang, always at the heart of China's commercial and industrial progress. The city itself, however, was, originally, the creation of the foreign powers that established themselves in the country during the 19th century. A small town of fishers and weavers at the mouth of the mighty Chang Jiang (River Yangzi) was adopted as the base for a concession by the British in 1842, at the start of the opening up of the country to foreign trade. It was in an ideal position and soon attracted the interests of others, with the French arriving in 1847, an International Settlement in 1863 and the Japanese in 1895. Most of the city was divided into patches of territory immune from Chinese law, inhabited by privileged Europeans or wealthy local magnates who controlled the local officialdom through wealth or terror, and all of them surrounded by vast hordes of the labouring and the poorly paid. The contrasting interests of the increasingly radicalized masses and those who rode the wave of exploitation and vice at the heart of Shanghai were exemplified in the 1920s, when the Guomindang leader, Jiang Jieshi (Chiang Kai-shek), employed the criminal gangs to hunt down the Communists, when he turned on his erstwhile allies in the so-called Shanghai Coup. Moreover, the settlement police of the international presence effectively co-operated in the subsequent operations to control labour organizations or worker unrest. In this formative period was born both Shanghai's appetite for wealth and its radical traditions—the Communist Party of China itself was born here in 1921.

The Second World War and Japanese occupation interrupted the success of Shanghai, but the unique style and strength of the city was only ended in 1949, with the Communist victory. The foreigners were expelled, capitalism suppressed, the slums demolished, the many thousands of opium addicts re-habilitated and labour exploitation forbidden. It was only with the economic reforms of the late 20th century (and the Chinese determination to create their own Asian financial centre) that Shanghai could resume its headlong growth, with the worst excesses of the past put behind it. Whether this will allow the flourishing of political dissent and radicalism (or, indeed, whether this will be allowed) remains to be seen. Not only was the Communist Party of China formed here, but the Cultural Revolution began here and, during that, the so-called Shanghai Commune (a short-lived attempt to govern the city with an extreme Communist ideology, based on the Paris Commune of revolutionary France) confirmed the city's reputation for radicalism. The Commune was created at the instigation of two of the members of the later 'Gang of Four' radical group, who found their principal source of support in the city (and, indeed, were known for a time as the Shanghai Gang).

Thus, Shanghai has come to represent the extremes of modern Chinese society—almost since its founding it has been a symbol for variation from the political and economic norms prevailing in the country as a whole. The power and influence of the people of the municipality (which was formed as a separate unit at the inception of the People's Republic) spreads throughout China— President Jiang Zemin was the Party chief in the region, while the premier and other ministers come from the city, as does the head of the administration in Hong Kong.

Economy

Shanghai was the richest city in Asia before the Second World War, but only really resumed its growth in the 1990s, and it is now rapidly advancing itself as the new commercial and financial capital of China, rivalling the offshore attractions of Hong Kong, although not yet surpassing it. It is certainly the richest city within the People's Republic. The gross domestic product in 2000 was 455,115m. yuan. The per-head figure was a massive 34,547 yuan, more than one-half as much again as the figure of its nearest rival (Beijing). Much of this recent success, and its sustainability, is the investment in infrastructure, not only to retain its position as China's leading port, but also to improve links both outside and within the city. This determined development of its infrastructure may enable it move beyond the structural problems that hinder so many Asian cities. In 2000 there were 4,325 km of highway (including 98 km of expressway and 390 km of first-class roads), 2,100 km of inland waterways and 257 km of railways. Shanghai remains by far the biggest port in China, handling 16% of all the freight going through every port in the country (2000). The region produced 55,309m. kWh of electricity in 2000, rather more than did two-thirds of the other regions of China. In 2000 5.4% of the population was illiterate.

Although Shanghai possesses some rich farm land (notably on Chongming), the primary sector only accounted for 1.8% of GDP (the smallest such figure in China) in 2000. Agriculture and fishing, nevertheless, provided employment for 13.1% of those in work. The total area sown with farm crops in 2000 was 0.5m. ha. That year crop yields included 1.7m. metric tons of cereals (mainly rice) and 0.2m. tons of fruit. The only animals in any number in the municipality were 2.3m. pigs and 0.5m. goats. Total aquatic production was only 0.3m. tons in 2000, rather more from freshwater fisheries (the vast majority artificially cultured) than seawater (overwhelmingly caught in the wild).

The secondary sector accounted for 47.5% of GDP and for 42.8% of employed persons. Shanghai had the largest gross industrial output, by far, of any city in China (620,452.27m. yuan in 2000) and a myriad of industry types. Examples of products in which it leads all of China range from iron (17.8m. metric tons in 2000) and steel (15.4m. tons), through motor cars (251,540 units—41% of national production), to integrated circuits (2,393m. units—41%). The municipality had 8,574 industrial enterprises contributing to its output value, many of them receiving outside funding. Heavy industry, while only occupying 46% of enterprises, accounted for 62% of the value, while 664 large concerns accounted for 58% of the value.

The tertiary sector, which is rapidly expanding, accounted for 50.6% of GDP by 2000, and finance and insurance was already the largest single contributor to the sector (15.1% of total GDP). In the same year 44.1% of employed persons worked in services. Tourism is a massive business in the city, and is encouraged by the authorities, and the reward was US $1,613m. in foreign-exchange earnings in 2000, a year in which Shanghai received 1.8m. international-tourist visits (more than anywhere but Beijing and Guangdong). Trade, meanwhile, earned US $24,639.61m. from commodity exports, although $30,063.75m. was paid for imports.

Government earned more from Shanghai than anywhere but Guangdong in 2000, raising revenues of 48,537.77m. yuan (32% from the operations tax). Expenditure was also higher than anywhere but Guangdong, at 60,856.21m. yuan, the 22% spent on capital construction dwarfing any other single item, but indicating the authorities' determination to develop Shanghai to the best of its abilities and to position it well for the future. Such expenditures were helped by US $3,160.14m. in foreign direct investment.

Directory

Mayor: XU KUANGDI; Office of the Shanghai Municipal People's Government, Shanghai.

Secretary of the Shanghai Municipal Committee of the Chinese Communist Party: HUANG JU.

Chairwoman of the Standing Committee of the People's Congress of Shanghai: CHEN TIEDI; Office of the Chairwoman of the Standing Committee, Municipal People's Congress, Shanghai.

Chairman of the Shanghai Municipal Committee of the Chinese People's Political Consultative Conference: WANG LIPING; Office of the Chairman, CPPCC Shanghai Secretariat, Shanghai.

Tianjin

The Municipality of Tianjin (Tientsin) is in northern China, on the western shore of the Bay of Bohai, part of the Bo Hai (Gulf of Bohai). The capital and part of Hebei until 1967, that province lies both to the south and west and to the north-east, as it completely surrounds Tianjin and Beijing, the latter being Tianjin's other neighbour. The territory of the capital lies to the north-east, with the border interrupted by the Dacheng enclave of Hebei. There is a short border with Beijing in the north-west, and then it swings east and north, before encountering Beijing again to the west of its northern tip. The special municipality covers 11,300 sq km (4,480 sq miles).

Tianjin's name, 'Heaven's ferry landing', aptly indicated the city's role as the entrance to the old imperial capital of Beijing, for which it was the main port. The city was built on the Hai He, at the intersection of the sea and the inland-waterway (via the Da Yunhe—Grand Canal) routes to Beijing, although silting of the river eventually led to a new port being built nearer the coast at Tanggu. The terrain is low-lying, allowing the many streams and rivers to pool easily in lakes (some expanded into reservoirs) or brackish marshes (salt fields). The region is at the eastern end of the North China Plain and only encroaches on the foothills of the highlands in the very north. The climate is temperate and subject to the monsoons, but prone to extremes. In 2000 total rainfall in Tianjin was 459 mm (18 inches), slightly higher than in Beijing owing to its proximity to the sea. The average temperature in the January of that year was -6.5°C (20.3°F) and in July 28.8°C (83.8°F).

The total population of the Tianjin in 2000 was 10.01m., making it the least populous of the special municipalities, although larger than some of the other regions. Of this total, only 2.6% consisted of non-Han nationalities, mainly

Manchus and Huis. The main language is the local and official Mandarin (Putonghua), while the usual eclectic mix of religious affiliations witnessed in any great city is present, although the largest adherence is to Buddhism.

The urbanization rate in 2000 was put at 72.0%, while the urban population of Tianjin city itself numbered 5.33m. The only other major population was at Hangu, to the north-east of the sprawl of Tianjin itself, near where the northern border with Hebei meets the Bo Hai. The municipality has jurisdiction over four counties.

History

The history of the city is dominated by that of Beijing. Tianjin grew as a grain-storage port from the 13th century, when the imperial capital had acquired a dynasty that ruled in southern China, as well as to the north, and needed to ship tribute and supplies to the seat of government. The Yuan dynasty also connected the Da Yunhe (Grand Canal) with the northern capital, and Tianjin found itself at the junction of both the maritime and the inland water routes to Beijing. By the 15th century the city was walled and garrisoned, its importance recognized. Unfortunately, the European traders of the 19th century also recognized the city's value and it was bombed in the Arrow or Second Opium War, finally forcing the Chinese to sign the Treaty of Tianjin in 1858. Among the clauses was provision for the city to be opened to foreign trade. However, the Qing court attempted to renege on this latest of the 'unequal treaties' and the British and French returned to the Bo Hai, sailing up to shell the forts that defended Tianjin harbour. The Government was forced to concede the Beijing Conventions of 1860, and the British and French established important concession posts in the city, although they became the object of suspicion and resentment to the locals. In 1870 a French-run orphanage was attacked by a rioting mob, who feared that Chinese children were being kidnapped, and some foreigners (including 10 nuns) were killed, forcing an imperial emissary into further humiliating negotiations with the now substantial foreign community in Tianjin. (During the Boxer Rebellion the international expeditionary force was to level the walls of the city.) In 1895–1900 the Japanese, the Germans, the Italians, the Belgians and even the Austro-Hungarians also set up missions in the 'Shanghai of the North', which continued to industrialize and to benefit from the trade even when the port had to move nearer the coast. This industrialization was massively expanded after the Communist victory in the Civil War (the last great battle of the campaign out of Manchuria for Beijing was fought against Guomindang forces near Tianjin). Tianjin started out in the People's Republic as one of 12 special municipalities, but, although most of them were merged back into their local regions in 1954, Tianjin survived as a separate entity. In 1958 it was restored to Hebei, as the provincial capital, but in 1967 it resumed its distinct status under the direct control of the central authorities, just like Beijing and Shanghai.

Economy

Tianjin is an industrial city and a transport hub conveniently located for the national capital, and it has benefited accordingly. Tianjin remains one of the biggest ports in China. The gross domestic product (GDP) of the region in 2000 was 163,936m. yuan, in current prices, or 17,993 yuan per head, which made it the third most prosperous of any territory in China. The special municipal area had a good intensity of road and rail networks, with roads totalling 8,946 km in 2000 (305 km of expressway and 370 km of first-class highways), operational railways 531 km and navigable inland waterways 443 km. Some 21,149m. kWh of electricity were generated in 2000. The illiteracy rate was 4.9% in 2000.

The primary sector only provided 4.5% of GDP, but employed 19.9% of those in work in 2000. Some 5.3m. ha were sown with farm crops in 2000, yielding 1.2m. metric tons of cereals, among other crops (mainly vegetables). Livestock numbers included 1.6m. pigs, 1.2m. sheep and goats and 0.2m. cattle. Fisheries product was mainly farmed inland, although there was some sea fishing, but freshwater fish accounted for 80% of the total 2000 aquatic production of 242,200 tons.

Industrial GDP was the equivalent of exactly one-half of the total in 2000, when 41.0% of employed persons worked in the sector. The gross industrial output of Tianjin was slightly greater than that of Guangzhou and Shenzhen in Guangdong and of Beijing, and exceeded only by Shanghai. The region's main mineral product, or at least its most visible, given the salt flats near the coast, is salt (2.4m. metric tons in 2000), but it also produced 7.6m. tons of crude petroleum. The city enjoys a good reputation for its brands, being associated with quality, and it manufactures a number of consumer products. It is also a major producer of electronic integrated circuits (235m. units in 2000). There were 5,430 industrial enterprises in Tianjin in 2000, with a gross output value of 260,638m. yuan. Heavy industry accounted for 49% of the enterprises and 66% of the output value, with 316 large enterprises accounting for 57% of the value.

The tertiary sector accounted for 45.5% of GDP in 2000, the largest single sector being transport, storage and communications (10.9% of total GDP). Tertiary industry accounted for 39.1% of all employed persons in the same year. Trade earned US $7,674.27m. in exports and cost $9,481.98 in imports in 2000. That year tourism earned $232m. in foreign exchange. There were 356,200 international-tourist visits.

Government revenue for 2000 was 13,360.69m. yuan, of which the operations tax earned 29%. Expenditure reached 18,705.21m. yuan, the biggest destination being education (32%). The city region received US $1,166.01m. in foreign direct investment.

Directory

Mayor: LI SHENLING; Office of the Tianjin Municipal People's Government, Tianjin.

Secretary of the Tianjin Municipal Committee of the Chinese Communist Party: ZHANG LICHANG.

Chairman of the Standing Committee of the People's Congress of Tianjin: ZHANG LICHANG; Office of the Chairman of the Standing Committee, Municipal People's Congress, Tianjin.

Chairman of the Tianjin Municipal Committee of the Chinese People's Political Consultative Conference: FANG FENGYOU; Office of the Chairman, CPPCC Tianjin Secretariat, Tianjin.

SPECIAL ADMINISTRATIVE REGIONS

Hong Kong
(Xianggang)

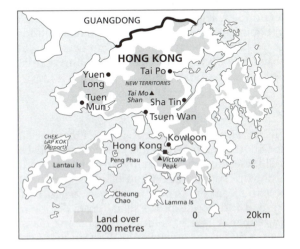

The Special Administrative Region of Hong Kong (Xianggang—in abbreviation, Gang) lies on the coast of Guangdong, in southern China, on the eastern side of the mouth of the Zhu Jiang (Pearl River). The territory, which is named for Hong Kong Island, but also includes numerous other islands and the Kowloon (Jiulong) peninsula of the mainland, covers 1,095 sq km (423 sq miles).

This part of the Chinese coast is rugged and deeply indented, with many islands off shore. The Kowloon peninsula (including the so-called New Territories) consists of highland in the north-east and the centre, where the hills rise to the highest point in the region at Tai Mo Shan (957 m or 3,141 feet). The island of Hong Kong itself lies off the southern tip of the peninsula, rising to 552 m at Victoria Peak, with the heart of the city along the north shore beneath it, facing the Kowloon part of the city across the harbour. The largest of the many other islands is Lantau Island (which rises to 934 m, in the south-west), to the west of Hong Kong Island, which is connected to the mainland by bridge, and another short bridge to the site of the Chek Lap Kok Airport just off Lantau's own north shore. The hillsides are usually covered in dense scrub, and flat land and agricultural land are scarce. The climate is subtropical and governed by the monsoons, being hot and humid in the summer (June–August), when most of the rain falls (an annual average of 2,214 mm or

87 inches), with the average monthly temperature in July being around 29°C (84°F). Severe typhoons can strike from the late summer into October. Winter is cooler (with average January temperatures of 16°C—61°F) and drier.

The total population of the Hong Kong special region was 7.21m. in 2001, giving a population density of 6,584 per sq km. The New Territories, in the north, is a less densely populated area, but pressure for space on Hong Kong Island is intense, while in parts of Kowloon (notably Mong Kok) are some of the highest population densities in the world. Over 98% of the population is Chinese, by language and place of origin, with the vast majority being of Cantonese descent, from neighbouring Guangdong. Cantonese is the predominant Chinese language spoken, therefore, but since reunification with China the official language has been Mandarin (Putonghua) and that is increasingly understood. A legacy of British control over the territory, and of its place in global commerce, English is widely spoken, and remains an official language. Most of the population are Buddhist, but Daoism is also practised and Confucianism observed, while there are over 0.5m. Christians and small communities of Muslims and other faiths.

History

The British established Hong Kong after the 1842 Treaty of Nanjing ended the Opium War. Irked by the restrictive trade practices established for foreigners dealing with the Chinese Empire and finally provoked when the Qing ordered the destruction of the opium stores held by European merchants in Guangzhou (Canton—the trade in illegal drugs put the Chinese balance of trade in deficit, while the there were also the widespread social costs of opium addiction), the British protested and then sent an expeditionary force to Guangzhou. However, the Qing had underestimated the advances in Western military technology and, indeed, the surging wealth of now established imperial powers. In November 1839 two gunboats destroyed a fleet of 29 war junks and bombarded Guangzhou, and the Qing Government ordered its local representatives to negotiate a treaty, to prevent the British blockade continuing its spread north up the Chinese coast. The draft treaty of 1841 was rejected by both sides, the emperor recalling his chief negotiator in chains, the British authorities particularly dismissive of the 'low' indemnity, the failure to dismantle the Guangzhou restriction on trade and the perceived scant benefit of a small island (Hong Kong) downriver from the main port for Chinese trade. British forces returned to the fray and by mid-1842 the emperor had conceded that he would be obliged to concede the war and, as they demanded, to treat with the foreigners on equal terms. Nanjing, therefore, became the first of the 'unequal treaties', by which the Qing paid a massive indemnity, dismantled the trading syndicate that controlled all commercial contact between foreigners and China in Guangzhou, opened a number of other ports to trade and ceded the island of Hong Kong to the United Kingdom.

The success of Hong Kong was rapid and dramatic, requiring the attention of special clauses in later 'unequal treaties' expanding the territory available to the British colony. In 1860 the Conventions of Beijing (Peking) added the immediate mainland of Kowloon (Jiulong) to the city-state, and in 1898, amid a general rush by foreign (British, French, German, Japanese and Russian) interests to exploit Qing weakness, the colony was granted a 99-year lease on the New Territories. It was this treaty that was to provide the means by which the reintegration of Hong Kong could be accomplished peacefully and legally, for, while Hong Kong Island and Kowloon had been ceded in perpetuity, the colony was unsustainable without the New Territories. This was to provide an incentive to negotiation. Meanwhile, however, the city had almost one century to make a place for itself in another Asian and international Empire, that of the British. From 1841, when the island had about 5,000 people, the colony was to receive constant immigration, with surges upon various occasions, as people were attracted by the wealth of the port or sought refuge from Qing political repression and civil unrest in mainland China. By 1941 the population had reached some 1.5m. and the city was one of the greatest financial and commercial capitals in Asia, with links all over surrounding Asian territories and in the worldwide British Empire. That year, however, Hong Kong was occupied by the Japanese, who were also invading the rest of China, and the population suffered a severe reduction, although it soon recovered after the Second World War (Japan surrendered in August 1945), when it returned to British administration. By 1949 there were 1.9m. in Hong Kong, and this number was swollen by the influx of refugees, and often their wealth, from the Civil War and, particularly, the Communist victory. These people contributed to the industrialization and economic success of the 1950s and 1960s, and the high rate of natural population growth was partly offset by the high rate of emigration to other parts of the world. The British presence remained a source of irritation to the People's Republic, however, while the prospect of the territory's eventual return to a Communist state proved unpalatable to many within the British authorities.

Progress towards a settlement of Hong Kong's future status was finally achieved in the early 1980s, after a visit by the British premier to Beijing in 1982. The final agreement of December 1984 was based on the slogan, 'one country, two systems', by which China would receive back Hong Kong, in its entirety, as a Special Administrative Region (SAR) in 1997, but its capitalist economy, legal institutions and education system, for instance, would remain unaltered for at least 50 years. Despite some reservations, mainly occasioned by the suppression of the student unrest in Beijing in 1989 or Chinese objections to the belated British introduction of some democracy (previously avoided, in case it complicated negotiations for the imperial power's withdrawal), Hong Kong was duly reincorporated into China as an SAR of the People's Republic on 1 July 1997. Despite the unfortunate coincidence of recession at about this time, Hong Kong continued to flourish and continued to maintain its separate status (although there was some anxiety about the precedent set in 1999 when the central Government in Beijing, at the request of the Hong Kong administration, for practical considerations overruled a court decision concerning residency status). The first Chief Executive, himself a refugee in 1949, was Tung Chee-hwa, who was reappointed in 2002.

Economy

Hong Kong is not only the richest part of China, but also one of the wealthiest cities in Asia. Direct comparisons with the autonomous regions, provinces and municipalities of the People's Republic is difficult, owing to the divergence of statistical measures and their application to often very different economies. Shanghai is the region that bears most similarity to Hong Kong, but the latter has experienced an expanding capitalist economy for many more decades, as well as sharing (and fuelling) the reformed expansion of the Guangdong economy since the early 1980s. According to the World Bank, Hong Kong's gross national product (GNP) in 2000, measured at average 1998–2000 prices, could be estimated at US \$176,157m., or \$25,920 per head. Infrastructure is well developed and there are good train, road and inland-waterway links with the rest of China, and copious sea and air links with the rest of the world. Moreover, Hong Kong is one of the busiest ports in the world, widely seen as the main 'gateway to China'. The amount of freight handled in the territory in 2000, for instance, amounted to 174.6m. metric tons of water-going freight, 2.2m. tons of air freight and 0.45m. tons of rail freight. The amount of electricity produced in 1997 was 28,943m. kWh. Adult illiteracy, as estimated in 2000 by UNESCO, was 6.7%, as compared with 14.8% for the People's Republic as a whole.

The two main primary activities of agriculture and fishing only contributed an estimated 0.1% to GDP in 1999, and employed 0.3% of the working population in 2000. Apart from some vegetables, fruit and nuts, the main crop on the limited land available for agriculture is flowers. Pigs and poultry are the main livestock, although crowded conditions for animals (as well as humans) meant that both populations were liable to outbreaks of disease. This also affected the fish farms (which produce about 3,000 metric tons annually)—there is also some marine fishing. In general, however, Hong Kong relies on imported food.

The secondary sector (mining, manufacturing, construction and power) provided an estimated 13.4% of GDP in 1999, while employing 20.5% of the working population in 2000. Manufacturing accounted for just over one-half of the employment and about two-fifths of the product in the industrial sector. The main manufacturing industries, by value of output, were textiles and clothing, plastic products, metal products and electrical machinery (particularly radio and television sets), but most production was moved out of the then colony into the special economic zones of the People's Republic, most notably those in neighbouring Guangdong, in the 1980s and 1990s.

Services provide the dominant sector in Hong Kong. It accounted for 86.5% of GDP in 1999 and provided 79.2% of employment in 2000. As a British colony Hong Kong became one of the major financial and commercial centres of Asia, and the Special Administrative Region (SAR) retains these advantages, as well as increasingly serving in a similar capacity for the rest of China. The city-state is not only a free port, with its own freely convertible currency (the Hong Kong dollar—HK \$) linked to the US dollar, but also imposes no restrictions on capital inflows and has an excellent telecommunications infrastructure, as well as a large number of local and international banking and commercial houses based there. Invisible exports (financial services, tourism, shipping, etc.) were reckoned to have earned the SAR between US \$35,000m. and \$40,000m. annually in the late 1990s. In 2000 Hong Kong recorded a visible trade deficit of US \$8,193m., but there was a surplus of US \$8,842m. on the current account of the balance of payments (the SAR operates a separate economy from the People's Republic, and is a separate entity within the World Trade Organization—WTO, for instance). Revenue from tourism, including spending by visitors from the rest of China, was put at some US \$7,500m. in 2000, when

13.1m. people visited (29% from the People's Republic, 18% from Taiwan and 3% from the other SAR of Macao). Many visitors enter the rest of China through Hong Kong. Likewise, large amounts of foreign investment enter China through Hong Kong, which also generates considerable capital of its own for investment.

Directory

Chief Executive: TUNG CHEE-HWA; Office of the Chief Executive, 5/F Main Wing, Central Government Offices, Lower Albert Rd, Central; tel. 28783300; fax 25090577; e-mail ceo@ceo.gov.hk.

Chairwoman of the Legislative Council: RITA FAN HSU LAI-TAI; Rm 109, Legislative Council Building, 8 Jackson Rd, Central; tel. 28699461; fax 28779600 e-mail rfan@legco.gov.hk.

Director of the Central Government Liaison Office in Hong Kong: JIANG ENZHU; Central Government Liaison Office, Lower Albert Rd, Central; tel. 28102900; fax 28457895.

Macao
(Aomen)

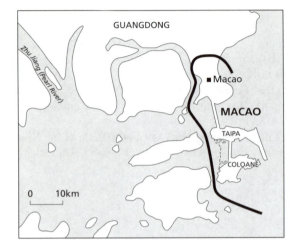

The Special Administrative Region (SAR) of Macao (Aomen, in abbreviation Ao—formerly Macau) lies on the coast of Guangdong, in southern China, on the western side of the mouth of the Zhu Jiang (Pearl River), opposite to but somewhat further south than the other SAR of the People's Republic, Hong Kong (some 60 km—37 miles—distant). The former Portuguese enclave consists of the tip of the Macao peninsula and, to the south, the islands of Taipa and then Coloane, together the special region covers an area of 23.8 sq km (9.2 sq miles—1999 figure).

Macao is derived from the Chinese for the Bay of Ah-Ma, Ah-Ma-Gau, which was named for a goddess of seafarers. This bay was on the south-east of the tip of what is now called the Macao peninsula, that tip occupied since the 16th century by the Cidade do Santo Nome de Deus de Macau (City of the Holy Name of God of Macao—the capital of the SAR). The terrain that the city was built on is hilly, the highest point being at the Guia fortress (centre-west of the city), where a lighthouse that began operations in 1865 is the first to have been set up on the Chinese coast. The peninsula ends in Barra Hill. Just to the east of here the older, 2.5-km bridge to Taipa heads south across the bay—the newer, longer bridge is further east and begins in the north-east of the peninsula. Reclaimed land and a 2.2-km causeway then link the next island to the south, Coloane (where the territory reaches its highest point at 172.4 m or 566 feet). The airport is built off the east coast of Taipa, connected by causeways and land reclamation. The climate is subtropical and monsoonal, hot, humid and wet in summer (April–October), and often afflicted by typhoons towards the end of that season. Average temperatures reach a maximum of some 28°C (82°F) in July and a minimum of 15°C (59°F) in January.

According to official estimates for the end of 1999, the total population of Macao was 437,455—making the SAR the least populous region in the sovereign territory of China, as well as the smallest in area. This small extent means the population density is very high, at an average of 18,380 persons per sq km, although given that most people live in the mainland city, the rate is even higher here (Taipa constitutes about one-fifth of the total area of the SAR and Coloane two-fifths). Just before the transfer of sovereignty in 1999, the Portuguese accounted for some 3% of the population (a proportion that has probably declined since) and the ethnic Chinese 95%. Portuguese remains an official language with Putonghua (Mandarin), although Cantonese is more generally spoken among the population, while English is also used fairly widely. The main religion is Buddhism, but Roman Catholic Christianity is strong and established. Daoism and Confucianism are also practised.

History

Macau (now Macao) was developed by the Portuguese as a base near to Guangzhou as early as the 1530s, although continuous settlement did not take place until the 1550s. Official recognition of the Portuguese outpost by the Ming authorities came in 1557, in return for some help rendered against Japanese pirates. However, the enclave was not ceded territory, Chinese officials continued to hold sway over Chinese subjects and the Portuguese paid an annual rent. Macau was an important base for the Portuguese and Jesuit links with Japan (until the 1628 'closure' of the realm to outside contact), but became increasingly unsuitable as a base for an expanding Chinese trade, although it was a popular retreat for foreigners normally restricted to Guangzhou (Guangdong). The grant of Hong Kong to the British was to be an even more serious reverse than the silting of the harbour, however, although the revelation of Chinese weakness in the 1842 Treaty of Nanjing (Nanking—in Jiangsu) encouraged the Portuguese to assert their own claims. In 1845 Macau was declared a free port and, in subsequent disputes, the Chinese officials expelled. The territory was claimed for Portugal, and this was conceded by the Qing in 1887, in return for some concessions on customs duties and the control of the opium trade.

Macau's trade was overshadowed by Hong Kong and the Portuguese colony was left with many activities that gave it a dubious reputation for smuggling, gambling and vice. The port flourished in 1938–42, after the closure of the Hong Kong–China border, but declined thereafter, owing to its isolation as the only European enclave not to be occupied by Japan during the Second World War (in which Portugal did not participate). In 1951 Macau was declared an overseas province of Portugal, which gave it representation in that country's national legislature. In 1976 it reverted to a more autonomous and separate status, the changes reflecting both political changes in Portugal and the state of relations between the colony and China. The People's Republic was prepared to tolerate the Portuguese presence, but not any move that threatened a fundamental alienation of Chinese territory. Increasing co-operation between the Portuguese and Chinese authorities can be dated, symbolically at least, from the March 1980 first 'official' visit by a governor of Macau to Beijing. With the example of the British arrangements for Hong Kong established, and the early

Portuguese concession of the principle of Chinese sovereignty, negotiations for the final return of Macau to Chinese control proceeded rapidly in 1985–87. The agreement signed in April 1987 settled for the enclave to become a Special Administrative Region (SAR), with its internal arrangements guaranteed for 50 years. Macau, officially redesignated Macao, duly became the second SAR of the People's Republic of China on 20 December 1999, with Edmundo Ho as its first Chief Executive, although it retained some vestiges of a separate identity (usually associated with its independent economic status, such as distinct membership of the World Trade Organization). Elections to the Legislative Council (10 elected directly by popular vote, 10 elected indirectly and seven appointed members) were last held in September 2001.

Economy

The Special Administrative Region (SAR) of Macao has a tradition of being a base for gambling, and the casino there remains an important part of the economy. Through the 1990s, however, the territory introduced legislation designed to deter the illegal use of financial systems and, more recently, co-operation by the Guangdong, Hong Kong and Macao authorities has increased in an attempt to counter organized criminal activities. The recovery of visitor numbers since the economic contraction occasioned by the 1997 Asian financial crisis has helped the SAR to continue to develop. According to the World Bank, Macao's gross national product (GNP) in 2000, measured at average 1998–2000 prices, could be estimated at US $6,385m., or $14,580 per head. Infrastructure is well developed and there is an ongoing land-reclamation programme (the total land area of the territory increased by about one-third during the course of the 1990s). Transport links with China and the rest of the world are good, helped by the opening of a new international airport in 1995, and internal communications were helped by the new bridge from the mainland to Taipa opened as part of the 1999 celebrations of Chinese sovereignty. Macao has long been dependent on the rest of China for much of its water and electricity supplies, but in 2000 did produce 1,526m. kWh of electrical energy. Adult illiteracy in 2000 was estimated by UNESCO at 6.2%.

Agriculture is of minimal importance in the SAR and, together with fishing (of which there is some—a total catch of some 1,500 metric tons in 1999), employed only 0.2% of the economically active population in 2000. According to estimates for 2000 the primary sector only contributed about 0.1% of gross domestic product (GDP). What crops there are tend to be rice and vegetables, but most food is imported. Some cattle, buffaloes, pigs and poultry are kept (in 2000, according to the FAO, some 1,100 metric tons of beef and veal, and an estimated 8,600 tons of pork were produced).

Industry (mainly manufacturing, construction and public utilities) employed 28.1% of the eligible population in 2000, with more than two-thirds of that total engaged in manufacturing. The secondary sector accounted for about 14.2% of GDP in 1999. There are few natural resources to provide an industrial base and the leading sectors are textiles, clothing and footwear. Textiles and clothing generally accounts for over four-fifths of commodity exports. Wine is also produced.

The tertiary sector is the dominant sector in the Macao economy, and it absorbed 71.7% of the economically active population in 2000. contributing about 85.8.% of GDP in that year. The city has never been the major financial or commercial centre that Hong Kong has been, but its separate status under the Portuguese also allowed the development of a distinct economy, this one based on gambling by the Chinese or visitors from abroad (most arriving through Hong Kong until the building of the new airport). Tourism, therefore, is the main industry in Macao. By illustration, in 1997 the gambling receipts of the licensed casinos were US $2,300m., while the tourism and gambling sector were reckoned to employ one-quarter of the work-force and to contribute more than two-fifths to gross domestic product. That year marked the start of a decline in the fortune of the industry, but by 1999 visitor numbers had recovered to over 9m. Direct taxes from gambling generally provide over one-half of government revenue in the SAR. In 2000 Macao recorded a small trade surplus of some US $287m. The SAR possesses its own currency, the pataca, which operates with a fixed link to the value of the Hong Kong dollar.

Directory

Chief Executive: EDMUNDO HO HAU WAH; Office of the Chief Executive, Government of the SAR of Macao, Palácio do Governo, Rua da Praia Grande, Macao; tel. 726886; fax 725468; internet www.macau.gov.mo.

Chairwoman of the Legislative Council: SUSANA CHOU; Alameda Dr Carlos d'Assumpcão 411–417, Edif. Dynasty Plaza, 8° andar, Macao; tel. 728377; fax 727857.

Director of the Central Government Liaison Office in Macao: (vacant); Central Government Liaison Office, Macao.

PART THREE
Indexes

Index of Alternative Names

Alphabetic List of Regions and Capital Cities
(including a gazetteer of alternative names)

Pinyin spellings are used in this book, but some of the Wade-Giles versions and the old Post Office names are listed here for reference, as well as some other names. In addition, the three autonomous regions which often have the name of the principal minority nationality attached are listed here in both forms (AR = Autonomous Region, M = Municipality, P = Province, SAR = Special Administrative Region).

	Amdo	Xining (see Qinghai)
	Amur	Heilongjiang
75	Anhui	(P)
	Anhwei	Anhui
	Aomen	Macao
244	Beijing	(M)
	Beiping	Beijing
	Canton	Guangzhou (see Guangdong)
	Changchun	*see Jilin*
	Changsha	*see Hunan*
	Chekiang	Zhejiang
	Chengchow	Zhengzhou (see Henan)
	Chengdu (Chengtu)	*see Sichuan*
248	Chongqing	(M)
	Chungking	Chongqing
	Dihua	Urumqi (see Xinjiang)
	Foochow	Fuzhou (see Fujian)
	Formosa	*see Taiwan*
82	Fujian	(P)
	Fukien	Fujian
	Fuzhou	*see Fujian*
	Eastern Turkestan	*see Xinjiang*
88	Gansu	(P)
95	Guangdong	(P)
215	Guangxi	(AR)
	Guangxi Zhuang	*see Guangxi*
	Guangzhou	*see Guangdong*
	Guisui	Hohhot (see Nei Mongol)
	Guiyang	*see Guizhou*
104	Guizhou	(P)
	Haikou	*see Hainan*
109	Hainan	(P)
	Hangchow	Hangzhou (see Zhejiang)
	Hangzhou	Zhejiang
	Harbin	*see Heilongjiang*
117	Hebei	(P)
	Hefei	Anhui
124	Heilongjiang	(P)
	Heilungkiang	Heilongjiang
131	Henan	(P)
259	Hong Kong	(SAR)

	Anhwei	. . . .	Anhui
	Hofei	. . . .	Hefei (see Anhui)
	Hokkien	. . . .	Fujian
	Honan	. . . .	Henan
	Hopeh (Hopei)	. . . .	Hebei
	Hsining	. . . .	Xining (see Qinghai)
138	Hubei	. . . .	(P)
	Huhehot	. . . .	Hohhot (see Nei Mongol)
	Hui Ningxia	. . . .	*see Ningxia*
145	Hunan	. . . .	(P)
	Hupeh (Hupei)	. . . .	Hubei
	Inner Mongolia	. . . .	Nei Mongol
149	Jiangsu	. . . .	(P)
157	Jiangxi	. . . .	(P)
162	Jilin	. . . .	(P)
	Jinan	. . . .	*see Shandong*
	Kansu	. . . .	Gansu
	Kiangsi	. . . .	Jiangxi
	Kirin	. . . .	Jilin
	Kunming	. . . .	*see Yunnan*
	Kwangsi Chuang	. . . .	Guangxi Zhuang (see Guangxi)
	Kwantung	. . . .	Guangdong
	Kweichow	. . . .	Guizhou
	Kweiyang	. . . .	Guiyang (see Guizhou)
	Kwiangsu	. . . .	Jiangsu
	Lanchow	. . . .	Lanzhou (see Gansu)
	Lanzhou	. . . .	*see Gansu*
	Lhasa	. . . .	*see Xizang*
167	Liaoning	. . . .	(P)
264	Macao	. . . .	(SAR)
	Macau	. . . .	Macao
	Manchuria	. . . .	North-East (see Areas Index)
	Mongolia, Inner	. . . .	Nei Mongol
	Mukden	. . . .	Shenyang (see Liaoning)
220	Nei Mongol	. . . .	(AR)
226	Ningxia	. . . .	(AR)
	Ningxia Hui	. . . .	*see Ningxia*
174	Qinghai	. . . .	(P)
	Nanchang	. . . .	*see Jiangxi*
	Nanjing (Nanking)	. . . .	*see Jiangsu*
	Nanning	. . . .	*see Guangxi*
	Ninghsia Hui	. . . .	Ningxia Hui (see Ningxia)
	Peking (Pekin)	. . . .	Beijing
	Peiping	. . . .	Beijing
	Republic of China	. . . .	*see Taiwan*
180	Shaanxi	. . . .	(P)
185	Shandong	. . . .	(P)
252	Shanghai	. . . .	(M)
	Shansi	. . . .	Shanxi
	Shantung	. . . .	Shandong
192	Shanxi	. . . .	(P)
	Shensi	. . . .	Shaanxi
	Shenyang	. . . .	*see Liaoning*

	Shijiazhuang (Shihkiachwang)	see Hebei
	Sian	Xian (see Shaanxi)
197	Sichuan	(P)
	Sinkiang Uighur	Xinjiang Uygur (See Xinjiang)
	Szechwan	Sichuan
	Taipei (Pinyin: Taibei)	*see Taiwan*
275	Taiwan	
	Taiyuan	*see Shanxi*
256	Tianjin	(M)
	Tibet	Xizang
	Tientsin	Tianjin
	Tsinan	Jinan (see Shandong)
	Tsinghai	Qinghai
	Urumchi	Urumqi (see Xinjiang)
	Urumqi	*see Xinjiang*
	Uygur Xinjiang	Xinjiang Uygur (see Xinjiang)
	Wuhan	*see Hubei*
	Xian	*see Shaanxi*
	Xianggang	Hong Kong
	Xining	*see Qinghai*
231	Xinjiang	(AR)
	Xinjiang Uygur	(see Xinjiang)
238	Xizang	(AR)
	Yinchuan (Yinchuen)	*see Ningxia Hui*
204	Yunnan	(P)
210	Zhejiang	(P)
	Zhengzhou	*see Henan*
	Zhuang Guangxi	Guangxi Zhuang (see Guangxi)

Index of Areas

The People's Republic uses the following macro-regional definitions for various purposes. If Hong Kong and Macao were included in the system they would be part of Centre-South (or, with Guangdong and Guangxi, in a separate South Area). Taiwan would be part of East Area. The territories are listed alphabetically within each Area.

North	East	South-West
Beijing	Anhui	Chongqing
Hebei	Fujian	Guizhou
Nei Mongol (Inner Mongolia)	Jiangsu	Sichuan
Shanxi	Jiangxi	Yunnan
Tianjin	Shandong	Xizang (Tibet)
	Shanghai	

North-East	Centre-South	North-West
Heilongjiang	Guangdong	Gansu
Jilin	Guangxi	Ningxia
Liaoning	Hainan	Qinghai
	Henan	Shaanxi
	Hubei	Xinjiang
	Hunan	

APPENDIX

Taiwan
('Republic of China')

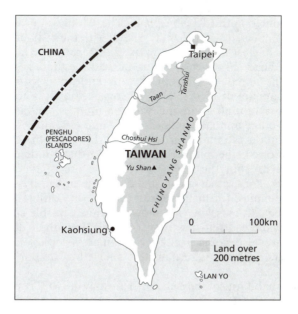

Taiwan lies off the south-east coast of China, facing Fujian (Fukien or Hokkien) province. The Government of the Republic of China, which moved its capital to the island's chief city, Taipei, in 1949, has, since then, found its authority limited to Taiwan and a number of smaller islands. Both the Republic of China and the neighbouring People's Republic on the mainland claim to be a single country, but no political resolution of Taiwan's ultimate status has been forthcoming. Both regimes persist in the pressing of wider Chinese territorial claims, and Taiwan has bases on several islands of the South China Sea, notably the Dongsha or East Sand Islands (Pratas Islands), which are nearest to the mainland (lying some 260 km—161 miles—south of Shantou, in Guangdong) and include one of the biggest islands in the South China Sea. Dongsha is administered from Kaohsiung. There is also a military presence in the hotly disputed Spratly Islands (Nansha—which the People's Republic has included in Hainan province since 1987), which involves the Republic of China in territorial disputes with the Philippines, Malaysia and Viet Nam. The territory of Taiwan province (a term used by both governments) included the island of the same name and the Penghu (Pescadores) group, but since 1949 the Republic has also administered some coastal islands of Fujian: Kinmen (Jinmen or Quemoy) and three smaller islands, off shore from Xiamen (Amoy); and Matsu (Mazu) and five smaller islands near Fuzhou. Together these territories comprise 36,006 sq km (13,902 sq miles), which is only a little bigger than the smallest province under the authority of the People's Republic, Hainan.

Taiwan, which literally means 'platform gulf', is traditionally believed to have derived from a word the natives used for foreigners (*taian*). The island was also called Formosa, the Portuguese name, Ilha Formosa, meaning 'beautiful island'. It is the largest island of all China, covering an area of some 35,788 sq km, and is 394 km (246 miles) long (north–south) and 144 wide. It is separated from the mainland by the 130-km Taiwan Strait and consists mainly of mountainous terrain, with about one-third being plain. The Chungyang Shanmo (Taiwan Shan) range dominates the centre of the island, with the peak of Yu Shan, in the centre-south, the highest point (3,958 m or 12,990 feet). The highlands descend more sharply to the sea in the east, but in the west the shore is softened by wide coastal plains. The climate is subtropical, with mild winters—average temperatures in January are about 15°C (59°F), whereas in July it is about 26°C (79°F) on average. Most rainfall is in the warmer months, making for a humid environment. Average annual rainfall is 2,580 mm (102 inches).

Official population estimates for the end of 1999 put the total at 22.03m., giving a density of 612 people per sq km. The official language is Northern Chinese (Mandarin), but the regime prefers the use of the old Wade-Giles transliteration system, rather than the Pinyin adopted by the Communist Government, so names, for instance, can appear very different to those using the Latin alphabet. In everyday use, however, most people speak one of two variants of Taiwanese, itself a variety of the Minnanhua dialect spoken in Fujian. There are also some Hakka (a Chinese people), a few remaining Japanese-speakers, and the Gaoshan, the chief ethnic minority native to the island.

The original inhabitants of the island of Taiwan were Malay peoples, who had official contacts with China from the seventh century, when the Tang Empire was at its most expansive. However, permanent Chinese settlement, and then on a small scale, did not really begin until the 14th century, but by the 17th century Han immigrants, mainly from Fujian, were arriving in considerable numbers. This helped against the depredations of Japanese, and Chinese, pirates, who favoured the island as a base for raiding the Chinese coasts. The pirates were also of concern to the Dutch, Portuguese and Spanish traders who were by now regularly visiting the island. In 1624 the Dutch settled the southern part of Taiwan, the Spanish occupying the north in 1626, only to be expelled by the Dutch in August 1642. Soon after, with rebellion sweeping the Empire, the Ming dynasty collapsed, and the Manchu Qing dynasty was invited south of the Great Wall. Many opposed the Qing advance, notably Zheng Chenggong (more familiarly known as Guoxingye—Coxinga), a member of a prominent Fujian seafaring family, but the Ming cause was hopeless. In 1661 Guoxingye took Taiwan from the Dutch, maintaining it as a base when his forces were forced to quit the mainland. He died in 1662, but his sons continued to rule a Chinese kingdom (called Tongning from 1664 and nominally loyal to the defunct Ming) on the island until it was conquered by the Qing in 1683. The conquering Kangxi emperor made Taiwan part of Fujian. Large-scale Chinese immigration continued under the Qing until 1895, when China was forced to cede Taiwan (which had been made a separate province only 10 years before) to Japan, which crushed local resistance and then began the development of the island, which was now dominated by the ethnic Chinese. China regained Taiwan in 1945 and the Nationalist Government later repressed a 1947 revolt with great brutality. Having decided that the Civil War was lost, the Kuomintang (Guomindang), the ruling party of the Republic of China, decided to consolidate its forces in an easily defensible location. In 1949 the government apparatus, along with over 2m. soldiers, officials and families, moved to the island of Taiwan, which until that point had had a population of some 6.8m. The regime has remained there ever since, although steadily losing international recognition as the legitimate Chinese Government since the 1970s. The Government of the People's Republic has generally tolerated the existence of the Taiwan anomaly, although it will not maintain diplomatic relations with anyone recognizing the 'Republic of China', but Communist forces now only resort to military manoeuvres in the Taiwan Strait if political developments on the island threaten an abandonment of the 'Government for all-China' position and, hence, a declaration of independence (increasing democratization has opened the possibility of pro-independence parties to win government and sufficient popular support to risk such a confrontation). Another restraint on the use of force by the People's Republic is, undoubtedly, the strong military support the USA gives to Taiwan.

As the only province under the authority of the Republic of China, Taiwan has, nevertheless, made rapid economic progress. It was forced to seek a wider international role when the Communist victory in mainland China effectively removed its previous market. Taiwan developed a varied and resilient industrial base, and a now-dominant services sector, and has often invested its wealth into enterprises on the mainland. By 1999 gross domestic product had reached US $287,881m. The primary sector contributed only 2.5% of this, the industrial sector 31.9% and the tertiary sector 65.7%. Much of the economic activity is located in the two main cities, Taipei, at the northern end of the island, and Kaohsiung, at the southern end. There are numerous urban settlements in between, mostly on the west of the island. At the end of 1999 the capital, Taipei, had a population of 2.64m. and Kaohsiung 1.48m.